Recommended Reference Books

for Small and Medium-sized Libraries and Media Centers

2001

Recommended Reference Books

for Small and Medium-sized Libraries and Media Centers

2001

Bohdan S. Wynar, editor

2001

Libraries Unlimited, Inc. • Englewood, Colorado

LIBRARIES UNLIMITED, INC.
P.O. Box 6633
Englewood, CO 80155-6633
1-800-237-6124
www.lu.com

Library of Congress Cataloging-in-Publication Data

Main entry under title:

Recommended reference books for small and medium-
 sized libraries and media centers.

 "Selected from the 2001 edition of American
reference books annual."
 Includes index.
 1. Reference books--Bibliography.   2. Reference
services (Libraries)--Handbooks, manuals, etc.
3. Instructional materials centers--Handbooks,
manuals, etc.   I. Wynar, Bohdan S.
II. American reference books annual.
Z1035.1.R435   011'.02   81-12394
ISBN 1-56308-889-4
ISSN 0277-5948

Contents

Introduction

Recommended Reference Books for Small and Medium-sized Libraries and Media Centers (RRB), now in its twenty-first volume, is designed to assist smaller libraries in the systematic selection of suitable reference materials for their collections. It aids in the evaluation process by choosing substantial titles in all subject areas. The increase in publication of reference books in the United States and Canada, in combination with the decrease in library budgets, makes this guide an invaluable tool.

Following the pattern established in 1981 with the first volume, *RRB* consists of book reviews chosen from the current edition of *American Reference Books Annual*. This nationally acclaimed work provides reviews of reference books and CD-ROMs published in the United States and Canada within a single year, along with English-language titles from other countries. *ARBA* has reviewed more than 50,000 titles since its inception in 1970. Because it provides comprehensive coverage of reference books, not just selected or recommended titles, many are of interest only to large academic and public libraries. Thus, *RRB* has been developed as an abridged version of *ARBA*, with selected reviews of books suitable for smaller libraries.

Titles reviewed in *RRB* include dictionaries, encyclopedias, indexes, directories, bibliographies, guides, atlases, gazetteers, and other types of ready-reference tools. General encyclopedias that are updated annually, yearbooks, almanacs, indexing and abstracting services, directories, and other annuals are included on a selective basis. These works are systematically reviewed so that all important annuals are critically examined every few years. Excluded from RRB are regional guides in the areas of biological sciences, travel guides, and reference titles in the areas of literature and fine arts that deal with individual authors or artists. All titles in this volume are coded with letters which provide worthwhile guidance for selection. These indicate that a given work is a recommended purchase for smaller college libraries (C), public libraries (P), or school media centers (S).

The current volume of *RRB* contains 480 unabridged reviews selected from the 1,561 entries in *ARBA 2001*. These have been written by more than 250 subject specialists throughout the United States and Canada. Although all titles in *RRB* are recommended acquisitions, critical comments have not been deleted, because even recommended works may be weak in one respect or another. In many cases reviews evaluate and compare a work in relation to other titles of a similar nature. All reviews provide complete ordering and bibliographic information. The subject index organization is based upon the 19th edition of the *Library of Congress Subject Headings*. References to reviews published in periodicals (see page xxi for journals cited) during the year of coverage are appended to the reviews. All reviews are signed.

The present volume contains 37 chapters. There are four major subdivisions: "General Reference Works," "Social Sciences," "Humanities," and "Science and Technology." "General Reference Works," arranged alphabetically, is subdivided by form: bibliography, biography, handbooks, and so on. The remaining three parts are subdivided into alphabetically arranged chapters. Most chapters are subdivided in a way that reflects the arrangement strategy of the entire volume: a section on general works and then a topical breakdown. The latter is further subdivided, based on the amount of material available on a given topic.

RRB has been favorably reviewed in such journals as *Booklist, School Library Media Quarterly, Journal of Academic Librarianship*, and *Reference Books Bulletin*. For example, *The Book Report* (Jan/Feb 98, p. 47) states that *RRB* is "an indispensable purchase for small and medium-sized libraries and one that most librarians rely upon for currency and reliability." The editors continue to strive to make *RRB* the most valuable acquisitions tool a small library can have.

In closing, I would like to express my gratitude to the contributors whose reviews appear in this volume. I would also like to thank the staff members who have been instrumental in the preparation of this work: Pamela J. Getchell, Shannon Graff Hysell, and Cari Ringelheim.

Contributors

Stephen H. Aby, Education Bibliographer, Bierce Library, Univ. of Akron, Ohio.

Anthony J. Adam, Reference Librarian, Prairie View A & M Univ., Coleman Library, Tex.

January Adams, Asst. Director/Head of Adult Services, Franklin Township Public Library, Somerset, N.J.

Michael Adams, Reference Librarian, City University of New York Graduate Center, New York.

Walter C. Allen, Assoc. Professor Emeritus, Graduate School of Library and Information Science, Univ. of Illinois, Urbana.

Donald Altschiller, Reference Librarian, Boston Univ.

Elizabeth L. Anderson, Part-time Instructor, Lansing Community College, Mich.

Robert T. Anderson, Professor, Religious Studies, Michigan State Univ., East Lansing.

Charles R. Andrews, Dean of Library Services, Hofstra Univ., Hempstead, N.Y.

Hermina G. B. Anghelescu, Library and Information Science Program, Wayne State Univ., Detroit.

Susan B. Ardis, Acting Head Science Libraries Division, Univ. of Texas, Austin.

David J. Argo, Associate, Bird Studies, Canada.

Christopher Baker, Professor of English, Armstrong Atlantic State Univ., Savannah, Ga.

Robert M. Ballard, Professor, School of Library and Information Science, North Carolina Central Univ., Durham.

Suzanne I. Barchers, *Weekly Reader*, Stamford, Conn.

Craig W. Beard, Reference Librarian, Mervyn H. Sterne Library, Univ. of Alabama, Birmingham.

Laura J. Bender, Science Librarian, Univ. of Arizona, Tucson.

Gail Benjafield, Librarian, St. Catharines, Ontario, Canada.

Kenneth W. Berger, Team Leader, Reference/ILL Home Team, Perkins Library, Duke Univ., Durham, N.C.

Bernice Bergup, Humanities Reference Librarian, Davis Library, Univ. of North Carolina, Chapel Hill.

Teresa U. Berry, Reference Coordinator, Univ. of Tennessee, Knoxville.

John B. Beston, Professor of English, Santa Fe, N.Mex.

Adrienne Antink Bien, Medical Group Management Association, Lakewood, Colo.

Terry D. Bilhartz, Assoc. Professor of History, Sam Houston State Univ., Huntsville, Tex.

Richard Bleiler, Reference Librarian, Univ. of Connecticut, Storrs.

Daniel K. Blewett, Reference Librarian, College of DuPage Library, College of DuPage, Glen Ellyn, Ill.

Edna M. Boardman, Library Media Specialist, Minot High School, Magic City Campus, N.D.

Michael S. Borries, Cataloger, City University of New York, New York.

Georgia Briscoe, Assoc. Director and Head of Technical Services, Law Library, Univ. of Colorado, Boulder.

Patrick J. Brunet, Library Manager, Western Wisconsin Technical College, La Crosse.

Betty Jo Buckingham, (retired) Consultant, Iowa Dept. of Education, Des Moines.

John R. Burch Jr., Director of Library Services, Cambellsville Univ., Ky.

Frederic F. Burchsted, Reference Librarian, Widener Library, Harvard Univ., Cambridge, Mass.

Robert H. Burger, Head, Slavic and East European Library, Univ. of Illinois, Urbana-Champaign.

Joanna M. Burkhardt, Head Librarian, College of Continuing Education Library, Univ. of Rhode Island, Providence.

Diane M. Calabrese, Freelance Writer and Consultant, Silver Spring, Md.

Joseph L. Carlson, Library Director, Vandenberg Air Force Base, Calif.

E. Wayne Carp, Professor of History, Pacific Lutheran Univ., Tacoma, Wash.

Bert Chapman, Government Publications Coordinator, Purdue Univ., West Lafayette, Ind.

Heting Chu, Assoc. Professor, Palmer School of Library and Information Science, Long Island Univ., N.Y.

Juleigh Muirhead Clark, Public Services Librarian, John D. Rockefeller, Jr. Library, Colonial Williamsburg Foundation, Williamsburg, Va.

Stella T. Clark, Professor, Foreign Languages, California State Univ., San Marcos.

Holly Dunn Coats, Asst. Librarian, Florida Atlantic Univ., Jupiter.

Gary R. Cocozzoli, Director of the Library, Lawrence Technological Univ., Southfield, Mich.

Barbara Conroy, Career Connections, Santa Fe, N.Mex.

Rosanne M. Cordell, Head of Reference Services, Franklin D. Schurz Library, Indiana Univ. South Bend.

Kay O. Cornelius, (formerly) Teacher and Magnet School Lead Teacher, Huntsville City Schools, Ala.

Gregory A. Crawford, Head of Public Services, Penn State Harrisburg, Middletown, Pa.

Mark J. Crawford, Consulting Exploration Geologist/Writer/Editor, Madison, Wis.

Paula Crossman, Asst. Librarian, Arizona State Univ. West Library, Tempe.

Glen W. Cutlip, Senior Policy Analyst, National Education Association, Columbia, Md.

Dominique-René de Lerma, Professor, Conservatory of Music, Lawrence Univ., Appleton, Wis.

Gail de Vos, Adjunct Assoc. Professor, School of Library and Information Studies, Univ. of Alberta, Edmonton.

Tara L. Dirst, Technology Coordinator, Abraham Lincoln Historical Digitization Project, Northern Illinois Univ., DeKalb.

Margaret F. Dominy, Head, Mathematics-Physics-Astronomy Library, Univ. of Pennsylvania, Philadelphia.

Diane Donham, Reference Librarian, Michigan State Univ., East Lansing.

John A. Drobnicki, Assoc. Professor and Head of Reference Services, City Univ. of New York—York College, Jamaica.

Bethany K. Dumas, English Department, Univ. of Tennessee at Knoxville.

David J. Duncan, Reference Librarian, Humanities, Wichita State Univ., Ablah Library, Kans.

Joe P. Dunn, Charles A. Dana Professor of History and Politics, Converse College, Spartanburg, S.C.

Bradford Lee Eden, Head of Cataloging, Univ. of Nevada at Las Vegas.

Marianne B. Eimer, Interlibrary Loan/Reference Librarian, SUNY College at Fredonia, N.Y.

Jonathon Erlen, Curator, History of Medicine, Univ. of Pittsburgh, Pa.

Patricia A. Eskoz, (retired) Catalog Librarian, Auraria Library, and Asst. Professor Emeritus, Univ. of Colorado, Denver.

G. Edward Evans, Univ. Librarian, Charles Von der Ahe Library, Loyola Marymount Univ., Los Angeles, Calif.

Elaine Ezell, Library Media Specialist, Bowling Green Jr. High School, Ohio.

Ian Fairclough, Heritage College, Toppenish, Wash.

Jerry D. Flack, Professor and President's Teaching Scholar, Univ. of Colorado, Colorado Springs.

Michael Florman, Staff, Libraries Unlimited, Inc.

Michael A. Foley, Honors Director, Marywood College, Scranton, Pa.

Lynne M. Fox, Information Services and Outreach Librarian, Denison Library, Univ. of Colorado Health Sciences Center, Denver.

David K. Frasier, Asst. Librarian, Reference Dept., Indiana Univ., Bloomington.

David O. Friedrichs, Professor, Univ. of Scranton, Pa.

Ronald H. Fritze, Assoc. Professor, Dept. of History, Lamar Univ., Beaumont, Tex.

Paula Frosch, Assoc. Museum Librarian, Thomas J. Watson Library, Metropolitan Museum of Art, New York.

Monica Fusich, Reference and Instruction Librarian, Henry Madden Library, Fresno, Calif.

Zev Garber, Professor and Chair, Jewish Studies, Los Angeles Valley College, Calif.

Pamela J. Getchell, Staff, Libraries Unlimited, Inc.

John T. Gillespie, College Professor and Writer, New York.

Lois Gilmer, Library Director, Univ. of West Florida, Fort Walton Beach.

Pamela M. Graham, Latin American and Iberian Studies Librarian, Columbia Univ., New York.

Arthur Gribben, Professor, Union Institute, Los Angeles, Calif.

Laurel Grotzinger, Professor, Univ. Libraries, Western Michigan Univ., Kalamazoo.

Ann Hartness, Asst. Head Librarian, Benson Latin American Collection, Univ. of Texas, Austin.

Ralph Hartsock, Senior Music Catalog Librarian, Univ. of North Texas, Denton.

Karen D. Harvey, Assoc. Dean for Academic Affairs, Univ. College, Univ. of Denver, Colo.

Fred J. Hay, Librarian of the W. L. Eury Appalachian Collection and Assoc. Professor, Center for Appalachian Studies, Appalachian State Univ., Boone, N.C.

Carol D. Henry, Librarian, Lyons Township High School, LaGrange, Ill.

Susan Tower Hollis, Assoc. Dean and Center Director, Central New York Center of the State Univ. of New York.

Courtney L. Holton, Asst. Instruction Librarian, Michigan State Univ., East Lansing.

Leslie R. Homzie, Reference Department, Brandeis Univ., Waltham, Mass.

Sara Anne Hook, Assoc. Dean of the Faculties, Indiana Univ., Purdue Univ., Indianapolis.

Jonathan F. Husband, Program Chair of the Library/Reader Services Librarian, Henry Whittemore Library, Framingham State College, Mass.

Shannon Graff Hysell, Staff, Libraries Unlimited, Inc.

David Isaacson, Asst. Head of Reference and Humanities Librarian, Waldo Library, Western Michigan Univ., Kalamazoo.

Dorothy Jones, Reference Librarian, Founders Memorial Library, Northern Illinois Univ., De Kalb.

Florence W. Jones, Librarian, Auraria Campus Library, Denver, Colo.

Wilma L. Jones, Deputy Chief Librarian and Head of Reference/Assoc. Professor, College of Staten Island Library/ CUNY, N.Y.

Suzanne Julian, Public Services Librarian, Southern Utah Univ. Library, Cedar City.

Elaine F. Jurries, Coordinator of Serials Services, Auraria Library, Denver, Colo.

Thomas A. Karel, Assoc. Director for Public Services, Shadek-Fackenthal Library, Franklin and Marshall College, Lancaster, Pa.

Vicki J. Killion, Asst. Professor of Library Science and Pharmacy, Nursing and Health Sciences Librarian, Purdue Univ., West Lafayette, Ind.

Christine E. King, Education Librarian, Purdue Univ., West Lafayette, Ind.

Druet Cameron Klugh, Reference Librarian, Univ. of Colorado Law Library, Boulder.

Svetlana Korolev, Science Librarian, Science and Engineering Library, Wayne State Univ., Detroit.

Lori D. Kranz, Freelance Editor; Assoc. Editor, *The Bloomsbury Review*, Denver, Colo.

Betsy J. Kraus, Librarian, Lovelace Respiratory Research Institute, National Environmental Respiratory Center, Albuquerque, N.Mex.

Marlene M. Kuhl, Library Manager, Baltimore County Public Library, Reisterstown Branch, Md.

Robert V. Labaree, Reference/Public Services Librarian, Von KleinSmid Library, Univ. of Southern California, Los Angeles.

Linda L. Lam-Easton, Assoc. Professor, Dept. of Religious Studies, California State Univ., Northridge.

Binh P. Le, Reference Librarian, Abington College, Pennsylvania State Univ., University Park.

Hwa-Wei Lee, Dean of Libraries, Ohio Univ., Athens.

Charlotte Lindgren, Professor Emerita of English, Emerson College, Boston.

Koraljka Lockhart, Publications Editor, San Francisco Opera, Calif.

Jeffrey E. Long, Interlibrary Loan/Photocopy Services Library Assistant, Lamar Soutter Library/Univ. of Massachusetts Medical Center, Worcester.

Michael Lorenzen, Library Instruction Coordinator, Michigan State Univ., East Lansing.

Sara R. Mack, Professor Emerita, Dept. of Library Science, Kutztown Univ., Pa.

Heather Martin, Arts & Humanities Librarian, Mervyn H. Sterne Library, Univ. of Alabama at Birmingham.

John Maxymuk, Reference Librarian, Paul Robeson Library, Rutgers Univ., Camden, N.J.

George Louis Mayer, (formerly) Senior Principal Librarian, New York Public Library and Part-time Librarian, Adelphi, Manhattan Center and Brooklyn College.

Dana McDougald, Lead Media Specialist, Learning Resources Center, Cedar Shoals High School, Athens, Ga.

Robert B. McKee, Professor, Mechanical Engineering, Univ. of Nevada, Reno.

Lynn M. McMain, Instructor/Reference Librarian, Newton Gresham Library, Sam Houston State Univ., Huntsville, Tex.

Lillian R. Mesner, Mesner Information Connections, Lexington, Ky.

Michael G. Messina, Assoc. Professor, Dept. of Forest Science, Texas A & M Univ., College Station.

G. Douglas Meyers, Chair, Dept. of English, Univ. of Texas, El Paso.

Elizabeth M. Mezick, Research Specialist, Center for Business Research, Long Island Univ., Brookville, N.Y.

Robert Michaelson, Head Librarian, Seeley G. Mudd Library for Science and Engineering, Northwestern Univ., Evanston, Ill.

David E. Michalski, School of Visual Arts Library, NYC, New York.

Ken Middleton, User Services Librarian, Middle Tennessee State Univ., Murfreesboro.

Paul A. Mogren, Head of Reference, Marriott Library, Univ. of Utah, Salt Lake City.

Janet Mongan, Research Officer, Cleveland State Univ. Library, Ohio.

Terry Ann Mood, Head of Collection Development, Univ. of Colorado, Denver.

Anne C. Moore, Electronic Resources Librarian, New Mexico State Univ., Alamogordo.

Diane B. Moore, Life Sciences and Agriculture Librarian, Arizona State Univ., Tempe.

Craig A. Munsart, Teacher, Jefferson County Public Schools, Golden, Colo.

Madeleine Nash, Reference Librarian, Spring Valley, N.Y.

Carol L. Noll, Volunteer Librarian, Schimelpfenig Middle School, Plano, Tex.

O. Gene Norman, Head, Reference Dept., Indiana State Univ. Libraries, Terre Haute.

Marshall E. Nunn, Professor, Dept. of History, Glendale Community College, Calif.

Herbert W. Ockerman, Professor, Ohio State Univ., Columbus.

Peggy D. Odom, Grants Resource Center Librarian, Waco-McLennan County Library, Tex.

Karen Browne Ohlrich, Retired Howard County MD Public Schools, Columbia, Md.

James W. Oliver, Chemistry Librarian, Michigan State Univ., East Lansing.

Lawrence Olszewski, Manager, OCLC Information Center, Dublin, Ohio.

Ray Olszewski, Independent Consultant, Palo Alto, Calif.

Glenn Petersen, Professor of Anthropology and International Affairs, Graduate Center and Baruch College, City Univ. of New York.

Phillip P. Powell, Asst. Reference Librarian, Robert Scott Small Library, College of Charleston, S.C.

Ann E. Prentice, Dean, College of Library and Information Services, Univ. of Maryland, College Park.

Randall Rafferty, Reference Librarian, Mississippi State Univ. Library, Mississippi State.

Jack Ray, Asst. Director, Loyola/Notre Dame Library, Baltimore, Md.

Nancy P. Reed, Information Services Manager, Paducah Public Library, Ky.

Allen Reichert, Electronic Access Librarian, Courtright Memorial Library, Otterbein College, Westerville, Ohio.

Robert B. Marks Ridinger, Head, Electronic Information Resources Management Dept., Univ. Libraries, Northern Illinois Univ., De Kalb.

Cari Ringelheim, Staff, Libraries Unlimited, Inc.

Randy Roberts, Professor of History, Purdue Univ., Ind.

John M. Robson, Institute Librarian, Rose-Hulman Institute of Technology, Terre Haute, Ind.

Deborah V. Rollins, Reference Librarian, Univ. of Maine, Orono.

Samuel Rothstein, Professor Emeritus, School of Librarianship, Univ. of British Columbia, Vancouver.

Michele Russo, Acting Director, Franklin D. Schurz Library, Indiana Univ., South Bend.

Nadine Salmons, Technical Services Librarian, Fort Carson's Grant Library, Colo.

Edmund F. SantaVicca, Librarian, Phoenix College, Ariz.

Ralph Lee Scott, Assoc. Professor, East Carolina Univ. Library, Greenville, N.C.

Robert A. Seal, Univ. Librarian, Texas Christian Univ., Fort Worth.

Karen Selden, Catalog Librarian, Univ. of Colorado Law Library, Boulder.

Earl Shumaker, Head, Government Publications Dept., Northern Illinois Univ. Libraries, DeKalb.

Leena Siegelbaum, Bibliographer of Eastern European Law, Harvard Univ., Cambridge, Mass.

Esther R. Sinofsky, Library Media Teacher, Alexander Hamilton High School, Los Angeles, Calif.

Kennith Slagle, Head of Collection Services, New Mexico State Univ., Las Cruces.

Richard Slapsys, Umass Lowell Reference Coordinator, Fine Arts Librarian, Umass Lowell, Lowell, Mass.

Mary Ellen Snodgrass, Freelance Writer, Charlotte, N.C.

Steven W. Sowards, Head of Main Reference Library, Michigan State Univ. Libraries, East Lansing.

Jan S. Squire, Reference and Instructional Services Librarian, Univ. of Northern Colorado, Greeley.

Karen Y. Stabler, Head of Information Services, New Mexico State Univ. Library, Las Cruces.

Victor L. Stater, Assoc. Professor of History, Louisiana State Univ., Baton Rouge.

Kay M. Stebbins, Coordinator Librarian, Louisiana State Univ., Shreveport.

Norman D. Stevens, Director Emeritus, Univ. of Connecticut Libraries, Storrs.

Bronwyn Stewart, Reference Librarian, Sam Houston State University, Huntsville, Tex.

Cindy Lee Stokes, Asst. Librarian, University Library, Indiana Univ., Purdue Univ., Indianapolis.

Martha E. Stone, Coordinator for Reference Services, Treadwell Library, Massachusetts General Hospital, Boston.

John W. Storey, Professor of History, Lamar Univ., Beaumont, Tex.

William C. Struning, Professor, Seton Hall Univ., South Orange, N.J.

Timothy E. Sullivan, Asst. Professor of Economics, Towson State Univ., Md.

Richard H. Swain, Reference Librarian, West Chester Univ., Pa.

Philip G. Swan, Head Librarian, Hunter College, School of Social Work Library, New York.

Nigel Tappin, (formerly) General Librarian, North York Public Library, Ont.

Paul H. Thomas, Head, Catalog Dept., Hoover Institution Library, Stanford Univ., Calif.

Mary Ann Thompson, Asst. Professor of Nursing, Saint Joseph College, West Hartford, Conn.

Linda D. Tietjen, Senior Instructor, Instruction and Reference Services, Auraria Library, Denver, Colo.

Bruce H. Tiffney, Assoc. Professor of Geology and Biological Sciences, Univ. of California, Santa Barbara.

Dean Tudor, Professor, School of Journalism, Ryerson Polytechnical Institute, Toronto.

Diane J. Turner, Science/Engineering Liaison, Auraria Library, Univ. of Colorado, Denver.

Robert L. Turner Jr., Librarian and Asst. Professor, Radford Univ., Va.

Arthur R. Upgren, Professor of Astronomy and Director, Van Vleck Observatory, Wesleyan Univ., Middletown, Conn.

Nancy L. Van Atta, Reference Librarian, Dayton and Montgomery County Public Library, Dayton, Ohio.

Mark van Lummel, Asst. Librarian, Indiana Univ. South Bend.

Graham R. Walden, Assoc. Professor, Information Services Dept., Ohio State Univ., Columbus.

J. E. Weaver, Dept. of Economics, Drake Univ., Des Moines, Iowa.

Arlene McFarlin Weismantel, Reference Librarian, Michigan State Univ., East Lansing.

Lee Weston, Assoc. Professor/Reference Librarian, James A. Michener Library, Univ. of Northern Colorado, Greeley.

Lucille Whalen, Dean of Graduate Programs, Immaculate Heart College Center, Los Angeles, Calif.

David L. White, Professor, History Dept., Appalachian State Univ., Boone, N.C.

Robert L. Wick, Asst. Professor and Fine Arts Bibliographer, Auraria Library, Univ. of Colorado, Denver.

Agnes H. Widder, Humanities Bibliographer, Michigan State Univ., East Lansing.

Albert Wilhelm, Professor of English, Tennessee Technological Univ., Cookeville.

Frances C. Wilkinson, Director, Acquisitions and Serials Dept., Univ. of New Mexico, Albuquerque.

Mark A. Wilson, Professor of Geology, College of Wooster, Ohio.

Julienne L. Wood, Head, Research Services, Noel Memorial Library, Louisiana State Univ. in Shreveport.

Neal Wyatt, Collection Management Librarian, Chesterfield County Public Library, Chesterfield, Va.

Bohdan S. Wynar, Staff, Libraries Unlimited, Inc.

Hope Yelich, Reference Librarian, Earl Gregg Swem Library, College of William and Mary, Williamsburg, Va.

A. Neil Yerkey, Assoc. Professor, School of Information and Library Studies, State Univ. of New York, Buffalo.

Arthur P. Young, Director, Northern Illinois Libraries, Northern Illinois Univ., De Kalb.

Louis G. Zelenka, Jacksonville Public Library System, Fla.

Magda Zelinská-Ferl, Professor/Faculty Advisor, Union Institute, Los Angeles, Calif.

L. Zgusta, Professor of Linguistics and the Classics and Member of the Center for Advance Study, Univ. of Illinois, Urbana.

Xiao (Shelley) Yan Zhang, Cataloger, Mississippi State Univ. Library, Mississippi State.

Anita Zutis, Adjunct Librarian, Queensborough Community College, Bayside, N.Y.

Journals Cited

FORM OF CITATION	JOURNAL TITLE
BL	*Booklist*
BR	*Book Report*
C&RL News	*College and Research Libraries News*
Choice	*Choice*
JAL	*Journal of Academic Librarianship*
LJ	*Library Journal*
RUSQ	*Reference & User Services Quarterly*
SLJ	*School Library Journal*
SLMQ	*School Library Media Quarterly*
TL	*Teacher Librarian*
VOYA	*Voice of Youth Advocates*

Part I
GENERAL
REFERENCE
WORKS

1 General Reference Works

ALMANACS

C, P

1. **Canadian Almanac & Directory 2001.** 154th ed. Toronto, Ont., Micromedia; distr., Farmington Hills, Mich., Gale, 2000. 1v. (various paging). index. $341.75. ISBN 1-895-02167-7. ISSN 0068-8193.

The 2001 edition of the *Canadian Almanac & Directory* maintains its well-deserved reputation as the definitive 1-volume reference source on Canada (see ARBA 99, entry 2, and ARBA 97, entry 3, for earlier reviews). In content, organization, and presentation it continues to be a model for country almanacs. The almanac section of the volume is followed by nine comprehensive directories, which cover key subject areas such as government, education, arts and culture, and business. New content in this edition includes the top 1,000 Canadian companies arranged by industrial sector as well as expanded education and health care sections.

The publisher has done everything possible to facilitate access to a vast quantity of information and to make it visually appealing. There is both a sectional and topical table of contents, an "Alphabetic Fastfinder" (handy for quickly locating the words to "O Canada," for example), and a 67-page index. In the middle of the volume users will find an oasis for they eyes—the flags, arms, and emblems of each province presented in vibrant color. Particularly stunning is the full page devoted to Nanavut, Canada's newest territory.

Although there is a slight discrepancy in the number of facts and figures contained in this edition—the cover says "over 50,000" while the title page says "over 47,000"—what are a few thousand facts here or there in such a remarkable resource.—**Cindy Lee Stokes**

C, P, S

2. **Chase's Calendar of Events 2000.** Chicago, Contemporary Books, 2000. 736p. illus. index. $59.95pa. ISBN 0-8092-2776-2.

Published as a day-by-day directory to special days, weeks, and months throughout the world, this is an undertaking of great magnitude, and, of course, every date of interest to every person in the world will not appear in it. The editors determine the entries that are listed, although they do encourage individuals to send in suggestions.

Events chosen to appear in the calendar fall into the categories of presidential proclamations, religious holidays and celebrations, important dates to remember, sponsored events, ethnic and international observances, sporting events, historic anniversaries, important birth anniversaries, and astronomical phenomena. Annotations for the listings include title of event, purpose and legal authority for the event, time and place of the event, and background facts that include biographical and historical data.

It is interesting to note the variety of events listed for the day on which this review is being written—among other things, England's Prince Harry and other celebrities were born; *The Lone Ranger* made its television premier; Costa Rica, El Salvador, Guatemala, Honduras, and Nicaragua celebrate their independence; the Trail of Tears Commemoration begins in Alabama; the Summer Olympics opening ceremony is held in Australia; Canada's Bracebridge Fall Fair and Horse Show begins; Greenpeace was founded; the Mountain Man Rendezvous begins in the Ozark Mountains of Missouri; Japan celebrates Old People's Day; and the Friends of Lake Forest (Illinois) Library Annual Book Sale begins.

This is not the only directory of special days available, but much information can be found in its 736 pages to enhance other directories, none of which can claim to be all-inclusive. *Chase's Calendar of Events 2000* should be available to library patrons who may be writing speeches in academic libraries or planning trips in public libraries.—**Lois Gilmer**

P, S

3. Christianson, Stephen G., comp. **The American Book of Days.** 4th ed. Bronx, N.Y., H. W. Wilson, 2000. 945p. illus. index. $105.00. ISBN 0-8242-0954-0.

In keeping with past editions, this book can be considered a useful ready-reference for all libraries. Its format consists of essays that are a day-by-day recounting of selective American historic events, including those of festivals and celebrations, written to be easily understood by all audiences. The topics of these essays vary, with the editor highlighting notable activities from military, scientific, ethnic, political, and cultural occurrences. Not limited strictly to events, essays are also devoted to individuals who played a significant role in American history. Prior to the first day of a month, the reader can find a rather extensive treatment of the meaning of the month's name, how it came to be called what it is, its place in the Gregorian calendar or Roman year, the birthstone associated with it, and significant facts associated with the stone.

The 4th edition has been updated and revised, increasing the number of articles to include events that took place after 1978 along with previously omitted events during earlier time periods. A comprehensive index and table of contents provide excellent means for finding specific topics. A concise list of days, with the events assigned to each one, can be found at the beginning of the book, facilitating those who prefer to browse. Original appendixes that provided copies of such documents as the Articles of Confederation and the Mayflower Compact were retained. Added appendixes provide copies of the Declaration of Independence and the United States Constitution and contribute to the work's value as a handy reference tool. The editor also mentions other pertinent dates at the beginning of selected articles that a researcher might find useful.

Even though the physical appearance of the text and paper is of high quality, it is distracting that the page headings do not always reflect the actual date included on each page. The 4th edition is definitely suitable for all libraries. However, please consider that it is not comprehensive in coverage, lacking entries for such events as the fall of the Berlin Wall on November 9, 1989. Nor did it include the assassination of John Lennon that took place in New York on December 3, 1980.—**Marianne B. Eimer**

C, P, S

4. *The New York Times* **Almanac 2001.** John W. Wright, ed., with the editors and reporters of *The Times*. New York, Penguin Books, 2000. 990p. maps. index. $10.95pa. ISBN 0-14-051487-2.

The New York Times Almanac has a long-standing reputation as a reputable source of current information. With access to one of the world's best news organizations, the information found in the 2001 title is timely and easy to understand and follow. An example of the timely information found within are results from both the 2000 election and the 2000 World Series. The book is arranged into six sections—"The Events of the Year," "The United States," "The World," "Science and Technology," "Awards and Prizes," and "Sports." It focuses on national and international news, including such topics as education, politics, health, sports, the economy, the environment, the Internet, and science, just to name a few. Although not as comprehensive as *The World Almanac and Book of Facts* (millennium ed.; see ARBA 2000, entry 4), it does provide more in-depth information on what it does cover. An extensive index and a 16-page color map section round out the volume. This will be a useful resource in public, school, and academic libraries.—**Shannon Graff Hysell**

C

5. **Scott's Canadian Sourcebook 2000.** 35th ed. Joe Zapotochny, ed. Don Mills, Ont., Southam, 1999. 1751p. index. $199.00. ISBN 1-55257-038-X. ISSN 1480-3038.

This is the 35th annual edition of a major compendium of facts from a well-known publisher of reference books. It would be difficult to find another source that pulls together such a wide variety of current facts and figures covering a range of subject areas from natural resources to demographics, education, banking, business, law, associations and societies, print and broadcast media, science and technology, and political information. Complete contact information for all entities as well as e-mail address and URLs are given when available. Every province, as well as the newly organized territory of Nunavut, is covered in depth.

Detailed information about ministries and legislative assemblies are provided along with some departments. For instance, a column of text is devoted to the Yukon Territory's Department of Education. It should be noted that popular culture is not covered in this reference work. New in this edition are essays entitled "The Century in Review" and "Science and Technology in Canada." There is also an index of Web addresses—an extensive list covering schools and corporations, including addresses obtained from the *Canadian Medical Directory* and the *Canadian Health Facilities Directory*. In the next edition it would be useful to have a list of both Canadian-specific Websites and Internet service providers (ISPs). This resource is highly recommended for academic libraries supporting programs in Canadian affairs as well as business, law, and large public libraries.—**Martha E. Stone**

BIBLIOGRAPHY

Bibliographic Guides

C, P, S

6.   **The Enoch Pratt Free Library Brief Guide to Reference Sources.** 10th ed. Thomas H. Patterson, John A. Damond Jr., and Rachel Kubie, eds. Baltimore, Md., Enoch Pratt Free Library, 2000. 222p. index. $12.00pa. ISBN 0-910556-31-8.

The 1st edition of this well-known, little guide was published in 1938 and listed 130 books. The 2d edition was substantially expanded and published in 1947. In 1988, the 9th edition was published with 876 entries and it was reviewed in the 1989 edition of ARBA (entry 12). The present edition contains 1,082 titles, reflecting an increased use of electronic resources in the reference process. As was true of earlier editions, this rather inexpensive reference source, prepared by the staff of the Enoch Pratt Free Library, will serve its clientele rather well. It is intended "to tame the mass of data currently available, to encourage the discovery of new resources, and serve as a user-friendly introduction to the effective and efficient use of libraries" (p. v).

There are a few technical problems, primarily with serials. For example, for *Who's Who in American Art*, the most recent year of publication is provided; while for ARBA, *Booklist*, *Literary Annual*, and so on, the concept of earliest entry is used (open entry with the first year of publication). Pro domo sua we may add that some by-products of ARBA are very useful for the public library (e.g., *Recommended Reference Books for Small and Medium Sized Libraries*, *Best Reference Books*, *Reference Books in Paperback*). All of these titles published by Libraries Unlimited have a long tradition and probably could have been included in this guide. However, this is a very handy and useful publication for public libraries and smaller institutions in this country as well as in Canada and is highly recommended.—**Bohdan S. Wynar**

C, P, S

7.   Lang, Jovian P., and Jack O'Gorman. **Recommended Reference Books in Paperback.** 3d ed. Englewood, Colo., Libraries Unlimited, 2000. 315p. index. $55.00. ISBN 1-56308-583-6.

The 3d edition of this useful book (reviews of earlier editions in ARBA 82, entry 3, and ARBA 93, entry 15) lists 1,006 paperback reference books with descriptive and evaluative annotations. The 36 alphabetically arranged chapters by 27 contributors cover academic disciplines and popular topics.

The books are well chosen with useful annotations, and the chapters are generally well balanced. But the chapter on psychology could use more scholarly titles. Books on computer-related topics are treated scantily as a subtopic of science. This literature is difficult to deal with, being multitudinous and largely ephemeral, and more thorough coverage in a separate chapter would be useful. Subject guides to Internet resources are treated under their subjects. Not every field is adequately represented in paperback. This guide is useful in adding to an established collection, but not in laying the foundations of a new one. This edition, unlike the earlier ones, cites no book reviews. The review copy is only in hardback. [R: JAL, July 2000, p. 298]—**Frederic F. Burchsted**

S

8.   **University Press Books Selected for Public and Secondary School Libraries 2000.** 10th ed. New York, Association of American University Presses, 2000. 145p. index. free by request. ISSN 1055-4173.

This is the 10th edition of a listing of university press books recommended by the Committee of Librarians from The American Association of School Libraries and The Small and Medium Sized Library Committee of the Public Library Association. There are so called "book ratings" attached to brief annotations, and bibliographic information for recommended books is complete and adequate for ordering from publishers. Obviously, criteria for selection are the responsibility of both committees but, nevertheless, it is occasionally difficult to understand why highly specialized sources are included in this bibliography. Such works as *Houser: The Life and*

Work of Catherine Bauer (p. 41) or *Recipes and Remembrances from an Eastern Mediterranean Kitchen: A Culinary Journey through Syria, Lebanon, and Jordan* (p. 59) sufficiently illustrate this point.—**Bohdan S. Wynar**

National and Trade Bibliography

United States

C
9.   **American Book Publishing Record Cumulative 1999.** New Providence, N.J., R. R. Bowker, 2000. 2v. index. $299.00/set. ISBN 0-8352-4335-4. ISSN 0002-7707.

Monthly issues, as well as annual publications, of this title have been reviewed on several occasions in previous editions of ARBA. This title is well known to all larger libraries so there is no need to repeat previous comments from ARBA reviews. It is sufficient to say that this 1999 edition covers 57,903 entries for books published or distributed in the United States. As in previous editions, the main input source is MARC II tapes. Entries that are excluded represent federal and other governmental publications, subscription books, dissertations, and journals and pamphlets under 49 pages. Additional updates of prices and distribution information are taken from the *Books in Print* database.—**Bohdan S. Wynar**

Canada

C
10.   **Canadian Books in Print 2000: Author and Title Index.** Marian Butler, ed. Toronto, University of Toronto Press, 2000. 1410p. $165.00. ISBN 0-8020-4946-X. ISSN 0702-0201.

C
11.   **Canadian Books in Print 2000: Subject Index.** Marian Butler, ed. Toronto, University of Toronto Press, 2000. 838p. $145.00. ISBN 0-8020-4947-8. ISSN 0315-1999.

The quality paper plus larger type size make these lists of 45,849 books more comfortable to use than many other similar catalogues. The one-volume hardcover *Canadian Books in Print 2000: Author and Title Index* is published annually, but a complete microfiche edition, available to customers who purchase the hardcover edition, is issued in April, July, and October. The subject index is published annually, and is in hardcover only.

The information included in *Canadian Books in Print* is gathered from lists requested and received directly from Canadian book publishers or Canadian subsidiaries of international publishing firms. The method of collecting the data is clearly described in the preface of the *Author and Title Index*. The accuracy of the information is dependent upon the publishers, and the reality of constant change may affect the status or price of a book at any time. Maps, sheet music, newspapers, periodicals, catalogues, microfiche, and annuals not thought to be of general interest are excluded. A selected group of federal and provincial government publications that are considered to be of general public interest are included. *Canadian Books in Print 2000* is primarily a list of English-language books, but does include French-language books published by predominantly English-language publishers and French-language publishers outside Quebec.

Canadian Books in Print 2000: Subject Index is a separate volume with a separate price. An alphabetic list of all subject headings that are used precedes the *Subject Index* itself. Book entries under each subject heading are complete entries so that the reader does not have to refer to the *Author and Title Index*.

Both the *Author and Title Index* volume and the *Subject Index* volume contain a publisher index and a list of publisher ISBN prefixes in numerical order. The entries in both volumes contain standard elements similar to R. R. Bowker's *Books in Print*, including author, title, publisher, and price.

The purpose of *Canadian Books in Print 2000*, as stated in the preface to the *Author and Title Index*, is to bridge the gap between R. R. Bowker's *Books in Print* and Whitaker's *British Books in Print*. It is a classic reference tool and is a necessary purchase for libraries intending to provide thorough access to the booklists of English-language publishers.—**Dorothy Jones**

BIOGRAPHY

United States

C

12.   **American National Biography.** John A. Garraty and Mark C. Carnes, eds. New York, Oxford University Press, 1999. 24v. $2,500.00/set. ISBN 0-19-520635-5.

In the interesting foreword to this landmark edition of *American National Biography* (ANB) the reader will find some background information about the much discussed replacement to the *Dictionary of American Biography* (DAB; CD-ROM version, see ARBA 99, entry 33; supplement 10, see ARBA 96, entry 36) written by Stanley N. Katz, President Emeritus of the American Council of Learned Societies (ACLS) with brief comments by John H. D'Arms, the current president of ACLS.

As is indicated in the preface, when compared to DAB, the ANB substantially broadened the criteria for inclusion of subjects, modifying the terms "American" and "significance." It now offers biographies of 17,400 men and women for all subject areas whose lives helped the nation. Garraty and Carnes serve as general editors with contributions from 2,243 authors. All subjects must have died prior to 1996 and this is probably the most important criterion that connects DAB and its supplements with ANB, along with chronological exposé of most biographies. [R: Choice, Sept 99, p. 103]—**Bohdan S. Wynar**

S

13.   Harris, Laurie Lanzen, and Cherie D. Abbey. **Biography Today: Profiles of People of Interest to Young Readers, 1999 Annual Cumulation.** Detroit, Omnigraphics, 2000. 446p. illus. index. $56.00. ISBN 0-7808-0370-1.

As with past editions of *Biography Today*, this 1999 volume features 30 people who have made news and peaked public interest in 1999. The books are designed specifically with young readers (ages nine and above) in mind and the choice of biographees reflects this audience's interests. The 1999 volume features such celebrities as Jennifer Aniston, Ben Affleck, and Sarah Michelle Gellar; sports heroes such as Mark McGwire and Venus Williams; musicians such as Shania Twain; and authors such as Sharon Draper. Obituaries of the famous are also noted here, including King Hussein, Shari Lewis, Frank Sinatra, and Gene Siskel.

Each biography is six to seven pages in length and contains at least one photograph. The entries feature the person's childhood, career, and home and personal life, along with some special anecdotes. This set from Omnigraphics will continue to be well used in school and public libraries catering to children and young adults.
—**Shannon Graff Hysell**

Canada

C

14.   **Canadian Who's Who 2000, Volume 35.** Elizabeth Lumley, ed. Toronto, University of Toronto Press, 2000. 1394p. $170.00. ISBN 0-8020-4939-7. ISSN 0068-9963.

This annual publication is the definitive source for contemporary biographical information covering the diversity of culture that is particularly Canadian. Providing a wealth of detail, from birth dates and family status to careers and honors, along with addresses (e-mail where available), it is a microcosm of the vast country it records. Within the covers of this weighty volume, readers find hockey players, merchant bankers, authors, politicians, scientists, and musicologists. More than 15,000 entries include updated "repeaters" along with over 5,000 entries for whom new biographies were compiled. The citations are not always for Canadian born figures, but include those who have become Canadian citizens and who have made a contribution to their new country and to the world as well. This is an essential work for any research, academic, or large public library.—**Paula Frosch**

DICTIONARIES AND ENCYCLOPEDIAS

C, P, S

15.   Anzovin, Steven, and Janet Podell. **Famous First Facts: A Record of First Happenings, Discoveries, and Inventions in World History.** international ed. Bronx, N.Y., H. W. Wilson, 2000. 837p. index. $95.00. ISBN 0-8242-0958-3.

Since 1933, *Kane's Famous First Facts* has been a classic in all types of libraries. The editions up to this one have been devoted to American history and topics. This 2000 edition is international in scope and meets the need for world coverage that had been requested by readers. More than 6,000 entries cover topics from agriculture to weapons. Questions about various subjects, such as the first human killed by a robot or the first military uniform designed by an artist, are readily answered here. With nearly half of the volume in indexes, searching for the entries is half the fun. A subject index, a name index, an index by years, an index by days, a personal names index, and a geographical index give plenty of access points.

There is no listing of documentation of any kind in the book, but *Famous First Facts* is the authority. For the kind of questions it serves to answer, though, it can be just that, an authority on its own. Some entries are perhaps not 100 percent accurate based on research, but H. W. Wilson has a good reputation for accuracy through the years in its array of publications.

Yet, the question does arise about the value of buying such a reference volume—(not too high at $95.00) when the Internet has a good bit of this information for free. At this point, the Web is not organized as well, leaving this volume still essential in most libraries. Given the international aspect of this edition, even if readers do not select each of the editions of *Famous First Facts*, they should probably acquire this one. [R: BL, 15 Oct 2000, pp. 482-484; Choice, Oct 2000, p. 293; BR, Nov/Dec 2000, p. 76]—**Paul A. Mogren**

P, S

16.   **Children's Illustrated Encyclopedia.** 5th ed. New York, DK Publishing, 2000. 800p. illus. maps. index. $40.00. ISBN 0-7894-6498-5.

This newly revised edition of the *Children's Illustrated Encyclopedia* has all the child-friendly attributes of DK Publishing's books—color illustrations, lively text, and easy-to-follow cross-referencing. This volume covers some 500 broad topics on everything from science and nature to art and history. The topics are further divided into 2,000 subentries, which ensures that a multitude of topics are discussed. For example, under the entry on John F. Kennedy there are subtopics for the Kennedy dynasty, the Cuban Missile Crisis, and the president's assassination, with cross-references to the Cold War, presidency, and World War II. The book is heavily illustrated with photographs, illustrations, and maps. Near the end of the volume is a 20-page fact finder that provides ready-reference information on world population, constellations, classification of living things, and U.S. statistics, to name a few.

This children's reference will be valuable in both school and public libraries. The book is presented in an easy-to-browse and easy-to-read style that will be helpful to children and adults.—**Shannon Graff Hysell**

C, P, S

17.   **The Columbia Encyclopedia.** 6th ed. Paul Lagassé, ed. New York, Columbia University Press; distr., Farmington Hills, Mich., Gale, 2000. 3156p. maps. $125.00. ISBN 0-7876-5015-3.

A mere 7 years have elapsed since the 5th edition of this work was published (see ARBA 95, entry 49). And, like its predecessors, this new edition documents the pace of time both in its content and in its 1,300 added entries. The publisher estimates that 40 percent of the existing articles have been revised. Published in July 2000, it presents information current to January of this year. With an increase of 108 pages, the newly designed encyclopedia boasts more than 50,000 articles, 40,000 bibliographic citations, 80,000 cross-references, and 700 line drawings—most of the latter retained from the previous edition.

Political changes, especially in Eastern Europe and the former Soviet Union, have necessitated revisions in the text as well as in the accompanying maps. Advances in science, medicine and health, and technology account for much of the new material. Given the ubiquity of the Internet and the explosion of information it has occasioned, it is remarkable that the 1993 edition had no entry for it—although there were entries for "computer" and "compact disc." The newer entry for the latter incorporates additional information about DVD technology. Also, in the field of biological sciences there is now an entry for the Human Genome Project that, although begun in

1990, was not included in the 5th edition. Intended for an American audience, the work's breadth, nevertheless, encompasses a full range of countries, persons, places, events, concepts, identifications, and time periods.

This is a particularly handsome edition with a newly designed cover and format. Longer articles are divided into sections making it easier to skim quickly. The type appears slightly smaller than in the 5th edition, but with the increased white space between sections reading is easier. The strengths of this large one-volume encyclopedia lie in its authority and objectivity. Libraries have relied on the encyclopedia since its inception in 1935. Given its currency and its wealth of factual information, this new edition should take its place on most library shelves next to its predecessors. [R: BR, Jan/Feb 01, pp. 78-79; BL, 1 Jan 01, pp. 994-996; Choice, Jan 01, pp. 873-874; LJ, Dec 2000, p. 106]—**Bernice Bergup**

C, P, S

18.   **Encyclopedia Americana 2000.** international ed. Danbury, Conn., Grolier, 2000. 30v. illus. maps. index. $1049.00/set. ISBN 0-7172-0133-3.

The publication of the 2000 edition of the *Encyclopedia Americana* (EA) marks its 171st year in print and its 65th consecutive annual revision. In each article, facts and interpretations are presented in a direct and orderly fashion so as to communicate clearly to a wide range of readers. Primarily designed for adult and academic research, readers can easily find the information they are looking for. For additional clarity, glossaries defining technical or difficult terms accompany some articles. EA also provides several research aids, including an index (v. 30) with more than 350,000 entries, cross-references, tables of contents at the beginning of long articles, and bibliographies at the ends of articles.

Color and black-and-white illustrations and maps are used functionally throughout the encyclopedia to clarify and supplement text. Drawings, diagrams, graphs, maps, and charts convey information that words cannot express as well. Photographs reveal the atmosphere of places and the personalities of people, show what objects look like, and make the reader a witness to important events in history. Color maps appear with articles on continents, major countries, all U.S. states and Canadian provinces, and some major cities. Black-and-white maps also accompany many articles on smaller countries, islands, and other major cities.

This new edition provides 45,000 entries, and as the preface states, "many new articles have been prepared . . . [and] . . . hundreds of articles have been revised" (p. iv). Also provided are nearly 23,000 illustrations and 1,200 maps. The ease of access and the longstanding reputation of this encyclopedia make it a worthwhile purchase for high school, academic, and public libraries looking to update their encyclopedia collections.—**Cari Ringelheim**

P, S

19.   **Merriam-Webster's Collegiate Encyclopedia.** Springfield, Mass., Merriam-Webster, 2000. 1792p. illus. maps. $34.95. ISBN 0-87779-017-5.

Two dozen academic consultants and the editorial staffs of Merriam-Webster and the Encyclopaedia Britannica have collaborated on this one-volume encyclopedia that contains about 25,000 entries on a comprehensive array of disciplines. As noted in the preface, while the average length of this resource's entry articles is 105 words, some extend to about 700 words. The subject diversity of this book's common noun entries becomes apparent at quick perusal.

Unsurprisingly, article space has been reserved for such staples as U.S. presidents and states; for such complex topics as "American Revolution," "Judaism," "Northern Ireland," "World War II"; and for some dozen subjects whose entry headwords start with "computer." However, this encyclopedia also extends uncommonly thorough treatment to such traditionally neglected or cursorily examined items as "monopoly," "sewage system," and "bacteriophage."

Unlike the vibrant renderings of birds, flowers, and nations' flags found in some rival publications, none of this compendium's 1,300 photographs and illustrations, or 350 maps and diagrams are in color. However, the graphics within this book are crisply delineated, uncluttered, and appropriately labeled; many diagrams and maps contain inset cutaway views of their subjects or locator globes. Full-page maps of North America, Canada, South America, Europe, Asia, and Africa adorn this new reference work, while the map of the United States spreads across two pages. Useful charts and lists supply information on mineral hardness, wind, metric and U.S. measurement system conversion factors, United Nations Member States, modern-day Olympic Games sites, and so forth.

A remarkable range of individual and collective biographical entries encompasses living and deceased notables from all walks of life. Years of birth and death are given as well as name changes. Entry articles typically contain a selective but generous accounting of the person's accomplishments or sources of infamy. Entries of names of world social, philosophical, scientific, legal, mathematical, musical, literary, economic, artistic, and religious geniuses and leaders (along with their respective schools, formulas, theories, movements, and doctrines) abound in this encyclopedia. Also, often neglected in other general reference works, this work includes name entries for many prominent film directors.

Although an impressive number of American folklore and popular culture figures are included, persons and events associated with passing tabloid headlines or whose fame was meteoric are usually absent. Another inconsistency is the fact that the entry for Massachusetts states that political entity is a commonwealth, while the entries for Kentucky, Pennsylvania, and Virginia do not. The publisher's declared policy of discretionary cross-referencing of entries usually stands them in good stead. However, there are some omissions.

It must be stated that the currency of entries in this encyclopedia is among its many strengths. Unlike most of its rivals, this encyclopedia contains articles for all U.S. state universities (and other institutions of higher learning), and includes a remarkable number of variant terms to entry headwords. Alternative spellings and variant Anglicized spellings are also given. Entries for many major corporations and organizations are also in plentiful supply. One significant omission, however, is that of the American Antiquarian Society. Despite a few factual and misspelling errors, and other noted shortcomings, this reference work proudly stands out as the most affordable, authoritative, and comprehensive one-volume encyclopedia available today. [R: LJ, Jan 01, p. 90]

—**Jeffrey E. Long**

P, S

20. **The New Book of Knowledge.** 2000 ed. Danbury, Conn., Grolier, 2000. 21v. illus. maps. index. $699.00/set. ISBN 0-7172-0531-2.

Compiled by an extensive staff of editors, contributors, and reviewers, *The New Book of Knowledge* continues to be an outstanding encyclopedic reference for children's and young adult library collections. Like past editions, the 21 volumes provide many illustrations, photographs, and maps to enhance the well-written text. Content for this encyclopedia is chosen by educators familiar with current curriculum standards, librarians familiar with the reading levels and research needs of children, and cultural specialists. The entries are written to be easily comprehended by young children, although those entries that are more technical in nature will most likely only be understood by the older children in the intended audience.

The volume is laid out alphabetically, with each entry containing one or more of the following to provided additional information: sidebars, diagrams, photographs, maps, chronological timelines, and *see also* references. The publisher has also made searching this encyclopedia easier with the use of word guides at the bottom of each page next to the page number and providing the index in each volume (set apart in blue paper). Many of the entries also contain "Wonder Questions," which will appeal to the natural curiosity of children. Besides the main volumes of the encyclopedia, readers also have access to a paperback supplement titled "Home and School Reading and Study Guides," which features an extensive bibliography as well as activities young users can do to become familiar with the encyclopedia.

What makes this encyclopedia so outstanding are the full-color illustrations, the well-written text, and the fact that the information provided works well with current curriculum standards. This set should be in all school library media centers and public libraries' children's reference collections. It should also be noted that Grolier provides *The New Book of Knowledge*, along with *Encyclopedia Americana* and the *Grolier Multimedia Encyclopedia*, in online versions.—**Shannon Graff Hysell**

P

21. **The Norton Dictionary of Modern Thought.** Alan Bullock and Stephen Trombley, eds. New York, W. W. Norton, 1999. 933p. $59.95. ISBN 0-393-04696-6.

The previous two editions of this eclectic dictionary were titled *The Harper Dictionary of Modern Thought* (see ARBA 88, entry 37, and ARBA 78, entry 83). This 3d edition retains the format of the earlier editions and continues to provide brief definitions for current terms found in a wide variety of disciplines.

This edition has more than 3,700 definitions from over 300 contributors. Although there have been slightly over 700 deletions from the 2d edition, the editors point to almost 1,000 new entries, especially in such fields as feminism, environmental issues, and identity politics (e.g., second wave feminism, pesticides, afrocentricity). Other new entries effectively reflect trends and events since 1988 (e.g., Rock the Vote, browser, family values). While some entries are unchanged or have received only minor changes, many entries carried over from the 2d edition do reflect the thorough revisions claimed by the editors (e.g., computing, genetics and genomics, neo-orthodoxy, affirmative action).

Among the considerable strengths of this dictionary are the variety of cross-disciplinary entries, the generally well-written and signed definitions, the excellent system of cross-references, and the frequent references to further readings. This volume is a valuable updating of the 2d edition, and in comparison with the 1st edition, an almost completely new work. [R: BL, 1 Dec 99, pp. 724-726; Choice, Mar 2000, p. 1258]—**Mark van Lummel**

P, S

22.　**The Oxford Desk Dictionary of People and Places.** Frank Abate, ed. New York, Oxford University Press, 1999. 879p. maps. $27.50. ISBN 0-19-513872-4.

This book is intended to be a reference source on two of the most popular topics encountered at reference desks—famous people and significant places. The biographical section provides information on over 7,500 individuals, from earliest recorded history up to the present. Each entry includes birth and death dates, nationality, significant achievements, and phonetic pronunciation assistance. U.S. presidents are provided special treatment and are given expanded information in boxed entries on their public careers and private lives.

The geographical section provides information on some 10,000 places. Coverage includes important regions, historical places, major or historic cities and towns, important nations of the world, capitals, and notable geographic features. Small locator maps are included in the text when appropriate to provide context and location of certain entries.

Sixteen appendixes are also provided, eight in each of the two sections. While the title indicates some objectivity in selection of the entries, the expanded coverage provided for U.S. presidents only appears rather subjective—given the importance of numerous other individuals in the history of the world. This quick-reference guide to these two popular areas is well researched and will ensure its success.—**Bradford Lee Eden**

S

23.　**Webster's New Explorer Student's Quick Reference.** Darien, Conn., Federal Street Press/Merriam-Webster, 2000. 244p. maps. $13.99. ISBN 1-892859-14-9.

This is an amalgam of various Merriam-Webster reference publications, although the lack of any introduction fails to indicate at what student level it is aimed. The 1st and major section is the dictionary, with definitions, pronunciations, variant spellings, homographs, and hyphenations. The section ends with a list of common abbreviations and a brief guide to punctuation, from apostrophe to slash. The atlas of the world is the 2d section and has 47 color maps followed by basic information concerning the countries listed. Information such as populations, capitals, and area as well as the major cities and their longitude and latitude follow each geographic citation. The 3d section on punctuation and style covers punctuation, capitalization and italics, plurals, possessives and compounds, abbreviations, numbers, and notes and bibliographies. This may be the most useful part of the entire work since it is the most clearly defined. The work ends with "Quick Homework Help"—a mix of American and Canadian historical facts, place-names and capitals; a very brief math refresher; and conversion tables for temperature, weights and measures, and metrics.

With sections on spelling, geography, history, and math, this work would seem to be the ideal desk ready-reference work, but it has a number of deficiencies. The dictionary uses typeface so small that it would only be legible to the young and eagle-eyed, and geographic information with a map locating device would be far more useful than latitude and longitude indicators. The work seems to have been thrown together using bits and pieces from a variety of sources. The low cost of the publication may make it attractive to libraries on a tight budget. However, it cannot replace any standard reference works.—**Paula Frosch**

P, S

24. **World Book Student Discovery Encyclopedia.** Chicago, World Book, 2000. 13v. illus. maps. index. $299.00/set. ISBN 0-7166-7400-9.

Created for students who are reading at the middle school grade level or below, the *World Book Student Discovery Encyclopedia* is a simpler version of *The World Book Encyclopedia* (1999 ed.; see ARBA 2000, entry 32). This general encyclopedia has thousands of color illustrations, phonetic spellings for harder words, clear cross-references, fact boxes and timelines, and hands-on activities. Articles are arranged alphabetically with prominent guide words for easy locating. An index and atlas with color maps are included in the last volume.

Every article has at least one color illustration or photograph—many have more. The article on sharks, for example, has four photographs, three color illustrations, and a chart comparing the size of different species of shark. The content of the articles is geared toward the interests of children—how many shark types there are, how they eat (ripping live fish apart), where they live, their body parts and teeth, how to be safe from shark attacks, and how people use sharks are covered. Articles could be read for pleasure or research.

The *World Book Student Discovery Encyclopedia* fills a void in the reference area. Children too young to read articles in a regular encyclopedia or off the Web will like this simply written, well-illustrated encyclopedia. Students in ESL classes and older students looking for pictures or illustrations will also find this encyclopedia useful. [R: SLJ, Aug 2000, p. 136]—**Carol D. Henry**

P, S

25. **World Book 2001.** deluxe ed. [CD-ROM]. Chicago, World Book, 2000. Minimum system requirements: Pentium IBM or compatible. Double-speed CD-ROM drive. Windows 2000, Windows 98, Windows 95, or Windows NT 4.0. 16MB RAM. 40MB hard disk space. 16-bit color. 16-bit sound card. Mouse. $66.30. ISBN 0-7166-8491-8.

Like the earlier *World Book Multimedia Encyclopedia* (see ARBA 99, entry 47), the *World Book 2001* CD-ROM is much changed from earlier print versions. It contains not only every article from the print version (some enhanced with sounds, videos, and animation) but also thousands more prepared exclusively for this format. The first of the two CD-ROMs contains the text and an atlas; the second includes the multimedia portion, but unfortunately it is not possible to run the two simultaneously. This version is family-friendly by providing links to more than 15,000 "approved" Websites. A time frame function locates information related to a specific year, decade, century, millennium, or era. Several homework wizards guide the user in creating reports, charts, timelines, and quizzes—even a rudimentary Web page. The atlas subset includes a nifty mileage guide that calculates distances between any two points in the world. The dictionary component is the latest version of World Book's own print dictionary (see entry 354).

The searching seems relatively unchanged from the previous edition, with the split screen and simple interface intact and minimal reliance on the user guide. Content has been updated through 1999 and includes Nobel Prize winners and Bill Clinton's presidency as of June 1999. Since encyclopedias are not the first choice when currency is an issue, *World Book 2001* does a valiant effort with its "What's Online" updating service in an attempt to keep the content dynamic and current.

The real purchase decision boils down to that of format and audience. For home use the CD-ROM is very attractive, especially when coupled with an additional $50 annual fee for online access. But as a stand-alone version, it is less attractive for the K-12 market at which it is targeted. School libraries may want to investigate the alternative online version that provides Web access, supports multiple users, and links to related articles from more than 260 U.S. and international magazines and newspapers.—**Lawrence Olszewski**

P, S

26. **World Book's Childcraft: The How and Why Library.** Chicago, World Book, 2000. 15v. illus. maps. index. $229.00/set. ISBN 0-7166-0197-4.

World Book's Childcraft has been specially designed to meet the educational needs of young learners. It is intended as a teaching tool for parents to provide their children with the beginning skills they will need for learning. With this in mind, *Childcraft* is geared to be fascinating and enjoyable for children. The goals of this set are to stimulate the process of learning, to develop readiness to learn to read, to encourage natural curiosity, and to create a love of books.

Each volume in the set covers a separate topic that has been selected as a result of international research conducted to identify the subjects that children are most likely to study in school. The majority of the volumes focus on various areas of science such as earth and mechanical science, biology, zoology, astronomy, and geography. The first two volumes focus on reading skills through poems, rhymes, fairy tales, and folktales. There are also volumes on art and mathematics. Two volumes introduce children to cultures around the world, including beliefs and customs along with descriptions of various celebrations in the U.S. and other countries. Multiculturalism is a theme strongly represented throughout *Childcraft*. The publisher intends to annually add new volumes to the set. Along with the 15 volumes in the set there are also 2 handbooks to introduce users to *Childcraft* and to provide suggestions for using the set with children.

This work provides a good starting point for education, but it does seem to focus more heavily on science than on reading or any other subjects. This may be in part because science topics are a large part of children's curiosity and also because science is a subject with international scope. Further, history seems to be one subject that is strongly lacking from the set. This may be because World Book has produced this work for international audiences and U.S. or European history may not appeal to readers in other parts of the world. Perhaps future volumes may at least introduce children to world history topics. Despite this shortcoming, this set is a good teaching tool for parents, teachers, and librarians.—**Cari Ringelheim**

DIRECTORIES

P

27.   **Gale's Guide to Nonprofits.** Dawn Conzett DesJardins, ed. Farmington Hills, Mich., Gale, 2000. 379p. index. (Gale Ready Reference Handbook Series). $125.00pa. ISBN 0-7876-3957-5. ISSN 1526-680X.

Indexed by geographic region and by keyword, almost 5,000 entries cover associations involved in nonprofit activities and directories that list nonprofit corporations. Contact information and a description of services offered are provided in each entry.

Compiled from a variety of reference sources, this work is divided into three chapters—organizations, publications, and databases. The organizations chapter contains information about associations involved in philanthropic activities, libraries sponsored by nonprofit organizations, publishers devoted to nonpartisan and nonprofit educational materials, and research centers that support programs and activities that enhance the role of public-interest advocacy. The publications chapter contains listings of directories that provide information on nonprofit organizations, newsletters of those organizations, and periodicals published by nonprofit organizations. Databases described in the third chapter include CD-ROMs; online databases; and databases in other formats, such as diskettes, magnetic tape, and batch access. The databases relate strictly to the missions of the sponsoring organizations.

This source should be ordered by academic, public, and special libraries. Like other Gale reference titles, it is likely to receive heavy use. [R: BL, 1 Sept 2000, pp. 178-179; BR, Sept/Oct 2000, p. 76]—**Lois Gilmer**

P

28.   **Toll-Free Phone Book USA 2000: A Directory of Toll-Free Numbers for Business Organizations Nationwide.** 4th ed. Jennifer C. Perkins, ed. Detroit, Omnigraphics, 2000. 1485p. $125.00. ISBN 0-7808-0349-3. ISSN 1092-0285.

This toll-free telephone book is a spin-off of the two-volume *Business Phone Book USA 2000* (22d ed.; see ARBA 2001, entry 116). The editor has extracted 39,000 toll-free numbers and repackaged them in this 1-volume edition. There are entries for businesses of all types, organizations, agencies, political groups, educational institutions, and government agencies. The toll-free number, other telephone numbers, fax number, and e-mail and Web addresses are given for each entry. If the toll-free prefix is not 800 the alternate one is given.

Like the parent volume, information is organized in three ways: alphabetically, geographically by state and city, and by classification type. Each entry has been assigned a classification code that designates its principal activity. The codes link all three sections of the directory. *See* and *see also* references are used in the classified section and there is also an index to the classified headings. Print is very small and the double-columns of information are single-spaced.

While Internet telephone directories abound, they are often frustrating to use and less than comprehensive. A print toll-free directory is still a necessary ready-reference tool, but if users already own the *Business Phone Book USA 2000* they do not need this one.—**Marlene M. Kuhl**

GOVERNMENT PUBLICATIONS

C, P

29.   Morehead, Joe. **Introduction to United States Government Information Sources.** 6th ed. Englewood, Colo., Libraries Unlimited, 1999. 491p. index. (Library and Information Science Text Series). $65.00/$47.50pa. ISBN 1-56308-734-0; 1-56308-735-9pa.

Morehead's latest revision of this highly useful and respected reference work does much to clarify the changing nature of the production and dissemination of government sources. Also most welcome are the addition of chapters on the impact of the Internet and on the evolving history of the GPO and its library depository program. Following this prefatory information are nine chapters that offer detailed descriptions of government publications and related materials divided into the following major categories: general finding aids and selected reference sources, the legislative branch, the presidency, administrative law, legal information, statistical sources, intellectual property, selected departments and agencies, and geographic information. Commercial sources such as the CIS indexes and Shepard's, Lexis, BNA, and West legal publications are treated, as well as a vast array of governmental sources. This edition also includes an appendix on the impeachment and trial of President Clinton, providing references to pertinent documents. The volume concludes with two indexes, one for title/series and another for subject/name.

Despite occasional lapses into somewhat baroque prose, this remains an essential tool for both the documents librarian and the novice user of U.S. government publications.—**Lee Weston**

HANDBOOKS AND YEARBOOKS

S

30.   Ash, Russell. **Factastic Millennium Facts.** New York, DK Publishing, 1999. 128p. illus. index. $12.95pa. ISBN 0-7894-4710-X; 0-7894-4948-Xpa.

Factastic Millennium Facts is a chronological book of milestone events that have shaped history in the last millennium. Each 100 years, beginning with 1000 C.E., is given a broad title (e.g., 1000–1999 is "The Age of Religion") and for each year a specific event is given. The earlier years generally have only one historical milestone listed, but as the years progress and presumably better accounts were recorded, more facts are listed. From 1600 to 1999 several milestones are listed under each year. As with all DK Publishing books there are beautiful illustrations and photographs as well as plenty of sidebars with fascinating information. Often these sidebars compare the past with the present or give century statistics. Before each century's chapter are descriptions of events that make the century memorable, such as global war in the 1900s or exploration in the 1600s.

This work and the previous volumes by Ash titled *Factastic Book of 1001 Lists* (see ARBA 2000, entry 1130) and *The Top Ten of Everything* (see ARBA 99, entry 63) are worthwhile for children's reference collections but may be of more use if they can be browsed through by children and young adults.—**Shannon Graff Hysell**

P, S

31.   McWhirter, Norris. **Norris McWhirter's Book of Millennium Records: The Story of Human Achievement in the Last 2,000 Years.** London, Virgin; distr., New York, Sterling Publishing, 2000. 256p. illus. index. $24.95. ISBN 1-85227-805-6.

McWhirter has assembled a remarkable compendium of the achievements of world civilization—north and south, east and west—that reads more like a narrative of events, places, and people. Students of world history and trivia buffs will relish the wealth of interesting information that abounds here. McWhirter's experience as the founding editor of *The Guinness Book of Records* is evident on almost every page of this volume.

The work is arranged in 10 general categories that treat achievements in the arts, science, medicine and health, politics and government, building and engineering, transport, war, communication and media, sports, and everyday life. An introductory section provides a millennium timeline, accompanied by comparative essays focused on how the world was in 1000 B.C.E., 1 B.C.E., 1000 B.C.E., and 2000 B.C.E., and how it might be in 3000 B.C.E. This chronological framework is also used as the matrix for presenting information in each of the major sections, allowing the reader to better understand how much civilization has achieved, and at what pace.

Color photographs abound, as do charts that are historical, comparative, illustrative, or thematic. A separate index of people, accompanied by a general index, allow the user to locate every bit of information presented.

Given its low cost, readability, format, and scope of content, this volume should be included in every high school, public, and academic library. The range of areas covered are the same as many reference queries, and can quickly satisfy patron demands for succinct information. This work is highly recommended. [R: VOYA, April 2000, p. 68]—**Edmund F. SantaVicca**

P, S

32.   **The 2000 World Book Year Book: The Annual Supplement to** *The World Book Encyclopedia.* Chicago, World Book, 2000. 528p. illus. maps. index. $29.00. ISBN 0-7166-0400-0. ISSN 0084-1439.

This edition continues to reflect the excellence and comprehensiveness that are expected from World Book. This edition features new World Book articles on animation, prehistoric animals, Saudi Arabia, Toronto, and the United States. Special report topics for this edition are astronomy, the telescope, baseball, Joe DiMaggio, Bosnia-Herzegovina, Serbia, Yugoslavia, the Middle East, civil rights, human rights, empires, Mongol Empire, Ottoman Empire, world literature, and William Shakespeare. The edition starts with the major news stories of the year followed by a chronological look at the year by month and date. There are 250 alphabetically arranged articles on the world's events for 1999. Many pictures, maps, and graphs are included with periodic time-capsule briefs dispersed throughout the main articles. This is an excellent summary of the year's events in an easy-to-read, one-volume source.—**Jan S. Squire**

PERIODICALS AND SERIALS

C, P

33.   Katz, Bill, and Linda Sternberg Katz. **Magazines for Libraries.** 10th ed. New Providence, N.J., R. R. Bowker, 2000. 1615p. index. $185.00. ISBN 0-8352-4267-6. ISSN 0000-0914.

This resource, which is well known in all libraries, has undergone what the editor's call a "total revision" in this 10th edition. Basically, this means that all titles from the 9th edition (see ARBA 99, entry 72) have been reevaluated and either retained or dropped after careful consideration. About 90 percent of the periodicals listed in the 9th edition can be found here but with revisions when necessary. The majority of the new periodicals added are electronic journals, which the editor states indicates the importance this media format has found in the field. The 7,850 periodicals listed and recommended here came from a pool of 170,000 journals under consideration. The headings used here remain the same as in the 9th edition, with the addition of "Fashion" and "Landscape Architecture."

Each entry includes the periodical or e-journal's title, alternative title, ISSN, date founded, frequency of publication, subscription prices, address, Website address, whether or not it is refereed, indexing, and a short annotation. A title index and subject index at the back of the volume will aid researchers in finding the periodical they are searching for or new periodicals on the topic.

This resource continues to be a reliable source of information on the most relevant and popular periodicals in libraries today. *Magazines for Libraries* is recommended for public, academic, and special libraries.
—**Shannon Graff Hysell**

C

34.   **Ulrich's International Periodicals Directory 2000.** 38th ed. New Providence, N.J., R. R. Bowker, 1999. 5v. index. $525.00/set. ISBN 0-8352-4230-7. ISSN 0000-0175.

Ulrich's International Periodicals Directory remains the standard reference for finding information on thousands of periodicals published. This latest edition contains information on some 161,000 serials throughout the world, which are classified under 974 subject headings. Some 10,000 serials are new to this edition and more than 112,000 entries have been updated since the last edition. *Ulrich's* has taken notice of the increase in electronic serials; this latest edition contains 14,757 serials that are available online (many along with print versions) and they are indicated throughout the volumes with a boldface bullet.

Information provided within this set include the serial's title, date founded, how often it is published, subscription rates, address, type of serial (e.g., trade, academic), a short description, and whether or not it is refereed. Indexes are essential in finding the information within these volumes. They are organized by ISSN, publications of organizations, title, and title change. The information is updated throughout the year by questionnaires and queries to the publishers. The publication has recently been delayed from August to November in order to provide the most up-to-date information on serial subscription prices, which often change later in the year. The print version of *Ulrich's Update*, which provided updated information, has been discontinued and replaced by an online version.—**Shannon Graff Hysell**

QUOTATION BOOKS

P

35.   **Encarta Book of Quotations.** Bill Swainson, ed. New York, St. Martin's Press, 2000. 1319p. index. $40.00. ISBN 0-312-23000-1.

It is ironic in this age of Websites and e-books that an electronic source is published in a print edition. This dictionary is a case in point. It traces its origins to the Bloomsbury Quotations database and is a component of Microsoft's *Encarta World English Dictionary*.

Some 25,000 quotations by 6,200 writers, from Hammurabi to Bill Gates, can be found in alphabetic arrangement by the author's name. Common and real names are given along with life dates, nationality, and designation. Quotes about the person are beneath their name, followed by quotes by them. Quotes are numbered and dated along with context notes and source information.

The majority of entries are attributed to an individual, but special categories such as anonymous quotes, advertising slogans, and children's verse appear as well. The quotations for arts (over 700 Shakespearean lines) and politics are the most heavily represented categories, but there are 1,000 quotations on business, money, and management. Science, technology, and popular culture are also covered. There are quotes from the likes of Steve Jobs, Bill Gates, and Nicholas Negroponte. There are also quotes (one each) by both Al Gore and George W. Bush. The next edition will certainly contain many more.

An attempt has been made to include quotations from cultures, religions, and literature that the editors feel have been underrepresented in other collections. Areas of focus are on African American, Afro-Caribbean, African, Chinese, Russian, and Asian quotations. Even so, the British bias is obvious. There are 174 Samuel Johnson quotes but only 30 by Benjamin Franklin and 40 by Thomas Jefferson.

This is a good general quotation collection that has the advantage of being the newest entry among similar titles published in the past 10 years. Its strongest competitor is the *Oxford Dictionary of Quotations* (see ARBA 98, entry 82). It is fun to browse through and easy to find specific quotations—a fine addition to the field.

—**Marlene M. Kuhl**

P

36.   Frank, Catherine, comp. **Quotations for All Occasions.** New York, Columbia University Press, 2000. 260p. index. $24.95. ISBN 0-231-11290-4.

The purpose of the book is to provide memorable comments on cultural ceremonies in public rituals and in personal lives. It is useful in offering the thoughts of famous writers, U.S. Presidents, and contemporary celebrities. The quotations are arranged in three sections: "Every Year," "Occasionally," and "Once in a Lifetime." The important festivals, religious celebrations, and customs of the different holidays throughout a calendar year are included. The diverse views on a given tradition are also represented. There are emotional thoughts shared on all days of the week, months, and seasons. The second section includes comments for a range of themes, such as taking exams, giving a speech, proposals, separation, illnesses and death, or the desire for a change (like quitting a bad habit). In the third section there are the quotations for memorable milestones, first-time events, and occasions surrounded by ceremony. There are perspectives for people to speak about and participate in the proper way.

Quotations for All Occasions is organized for ease of use. Within each section all quotations are arranged by topic. After many sentences a brief annotation is given. There is an index of sources listed alphabetically by author's last name with indication of topics and pages. The collection of quotations can be recommended for a broad audience. It is also an excellent gift for someone that likes to compose a moving statement or to spice up a speech.—**Svetlana Korolev**

P

37.   **The Oxford Dictionary of Thematic Quotations.** Susan Ratcliffe, ed. New York, Oxford University Press, 2000. 584p. $24.95. ISBN 0-19-860218-9.

This volume is another in the varied series of Oxford's dictionaries of quotations. Its smaller format makes it comfortable for browsing as well as reference. The work has a distinctly British flavor that will appeal to Anglophiles. Entries such as "Ronald Reagan," "American Civil War," and "Marilyn Monroe" are outnumbered by those on topics like "Cricket," "Wales," "Falklands War 1982," "David Lloyd George," and "Oxford" (but not Cambridge). This emphasis carries over into the selections themselves with George Bernard Shaw, William Shakespeare, Samuel Johnson, Winston Churchill, and Oscar Wilde being among the most heavily represented authors.

A strength of the volume is its inclusion of recent contemporary figures: Alan Bennett, Maeve Binchy, P. J. Rourke, and Cassie Bernal (victim of the 1999 Littleton, Colorado high school shooting). The editor has also succeeded in her attempt to reflect "a modern society with a much more varied cultural and educational experience" (p. vii). Entries on "The Internet," "AIDS," "Bisexuality," "Rock and Pop Music," "Press Photographers," and the "Twenty-First Century," to name a few, demonstrate the timeliness of the volume. Unexpected entries on subjects such as "Snow," "Masturbation," "Waiting," "Diets," and "Air Travel" offer surprising digressions. The extensive author index provides a brief phrase from each author's quotation, cross-referenced to the subject entry in which it appears. Institutional collections and home libraries alike will benefit from this work.

—**Christopher Baker**

C, P, S

38.   **Quotations for Public Speakers: A Historical, Literary, and Political Anthology.** Robert G. Torricelli, ed. Piscataway, N.J., Rutgers University Press, 2000. 302p. index. $27.00. ISBN 0-8135-2889-5.

Over the course of a political career, Torricelli has compiled an evolving list of insights and miscellaneous tidbits for various speeches. This list forms the basis for his edited work, *Quotations for Public Speakers: A Historical, Literary, and Political Anthology.*

This work has several good points. The coverage spans 26 pertinent subjects. The quotes contained in these chapters come from historical people and literary works ranging from the earliest times to the present. The index contains the authors and relevant page numbers rather than just the topics covered by the quotes. Torricelli also provides a bibliography of further readings on these areas.

However, there are a few questions that need to be asked. First, given the amount of quotation works coming out every year, is another one really needed at this time? *Bartlett's Familiar Quotations* (Little, 1992) is still the standard work, is revised frequently, and available on the Web as well as in print. In addition, Oxford and other publishers are coming out with other books similar to this one. Then, in the bibliography, Torricelli's use of Web citations, while relevant, significantly limits this work's currency.

Despite the issues, the amalgamation of knowledge should not be taken lightly. Torricelli has granted his readers a vast, interesting, and special collection of quotations. His organization (i.e., his subjects, bibliography, and index) is noteworthy. Hopefully, when the editors of *Bartlett's Familiar Quotations* and other similar works revise their texts, they will consider Torricelli's model. It is recommended for public, school, community college, and undergraduate libraries.—**David J. Duncan**

P

39.   **Random House Dictionary of America's Popular Proverbs and Sayings.** 2d ed. By Gregory Titelman. New York, Random House, 2000. 480p. $16.95pa. ISBN 0-375-70584-8.

Proverbs are an integral part of our everyday speech—a succinct means of making a point that will be understood readily by the listener. This excellent collection is an American treasury, but many of the proverbs find their origin throughout the literature of the world. This 2d edition of a well-received work includes many new entries and current citations from a variety of media. Each alphabetic entry is followed by a definition and its origin.

Variants and usage follow, along with bibliographic references. This leads into the chronological listing of the appearance.of the proverb, in differing forms and styles, with cross-references to similar or related proverbs. It is unusual to find James Joyce along with Jackie Collins and Lafayette with Oliver North, but such is the nature of this work that it reflects the language of America in the past two decades. There is an extensive bibliography and a keyword index. This work deserves a place on the shelves of both public and private libraries as a tool for improved writing and for the sheer enjoyment of browsing its pages.—**Paula Frosch**

Part II
SOCIAL SCIENCES

2 Social Sciences in General

SOCIAL SCIENCES IN GENERAL

P

40.   Li, Tze-chung. **Social Science Reference Sources: A Practical Guide.** 3d ed. Westport, Conn., Greenwood Press, 2000. 495p. index. $99.50. ISBN 0-313-30483-1.

An update of the 1990 2d edition, the 3d edition of this standard work on the reference resources of the social sciences includes not only print materials but also a variety of electronic resources, including those on the World Wide Web. The emphasis of the book is to provide a discussion of resources that will prove useful when answering reference questions in the areas covered by the social sciences. Although the work is not exhaustive, it does give both the experienced and the new reference librarian excellent direction in the use of a wide variety of English-language reference sources.

This volume is divided into two major sections: "Social Sciences in General" and "Sub-disciplines of the Social Sciences." The first section includes chapters on reference sources in an electronic age (e.g., search engines, Websites), research resources, access to sources (primarily bibliographies and indexes), sources of information (e.g., encyclopedias, dictionaries, directories, biographies), statistical sources, periodicals, and government publications. The 2d section includes 10 chapters on specific areas of the social sciences. These include cultural anthropology, business, economics, education, geography, history, law, political science, psychology, and sociology. An appendix of cited URLs, a name and title index, and a subject index conclude the work.

Although Li's book cannot compete directly with *Sources of Information in the Social Sciences: A Guide to the Literature* (3d ed.; see ARBA 87, entry 89) or *Guide to Reference Books* (11th ed.; see ARBA 97, entry 8), his work does exhibit both ease of use and currency. The inclusion of related Websites and other electronic resources, the listing of resources published primarily after 1980, and the writing style demonstrate that this is an important work and one that should be in all reference collections. Although the work is expensive, it would make a good text for social science reference courses within library schools. There is one caveat: several of the URLs listed in the book have changed since publication. [R: BL, 1 Oct 2000, pp. 380-382; Choice, Nov 2000, p. 514]

—**Gregory A. Crawford**

C, P, S

41.   **The Statesman's Yearbook Centenary Collection 1900/2000.** Barry Turner and J. Scott Keltie, eds., with I. P. A. Renwick. New York, Grove's Dictionaries, 2000. 2v. illus. maps. index. $200.00/set. ISBN 1-56159-262-5.

This 2-volume, centenary collection edition contains volume 1, which consists of the 1900 *Statesman Yearbook*, and volume 2, containing the 2000 *Statesman Yearbook*. The 2000 edition covers the politics, cultures, and economics of the world. A chronology from March 1998 to March 1999 is included. The book is broken down into the United Nations, human rights, UN systems, chemical and biological weapons proliferation, special agencies of the UN, other organs related to the UN, the North Atlantic Treaty Organization, bank and international settlements, organizations for economic cooperation and development, European organizations, American organizations, Asia-Pacific organizations, Middle East organizations, and other international organizations.

The countries are individually listed in alphabetic order. Under countries, the topics include key historical events, territory and population, social statistics, climate, constitution and government, recent elections, current administration, defense, international relations, economy, industry, international trade, communications, social institutions, culture, diplomatic representatives, and references. This is followed by a section titled "Areas Still in Search of Answers." The box set is printed on better-than-average quality paper and font size and binding are also better than average. The book will be of interest to anyone interested in world history since it gives a starting point of 1900 and also includes 2000 data for each of the countries and territories. The 2000 area brings readers up to date on each country's individual characteristics and should be in all public libraries.

—**Herbert W. Ockerman**

3 Area Studies

GENERAL WORKS

P, S

42. **Junior Worldmark Encyclopedia of Cities.** Jill Copolla and Susan Bevan Gall, eds. Farmington Hills, Mich., U*X*L/Gale, 2000. 4v. illus. maps. index. $149.00/set. ISBN 0-7876-4870-1 (v.1); 0-7876-4871-X (v.2); 0-7876-4872-8 (v.3); 0-7876-4873-6 (v.4).

This reference publication, aimed primarily at middle school students, presents a wealth of information about 50 world cities, chosen to represent the continents and cultures of the world.

Even though this reference work provides information on 50 world cities, its primary emphasis is the United States. This collection presents information on 25 cities from North America (21 from the United States), 9 from Asia, 7 from Europe, 5 from Africa, and 4 from South America. Since only 50 cities are examined, there are definite limitations to the usefulness of this work, but the content on the cities is very informative.

The examination of the cities is broken up into 22 categories of investigation, including but not limited to general demographic information, history, government, economy, environment, shopping, and sports. One of its most valuable contributions is that each city includes a section called "For Further Study," which provides the reader with many resources for further research, including Websites, government offices, tourist offices, books, and other publications.

This four-volume reference collection includes many black-and-white maps, charts, and photographs. This set would better suit its audience if it included color photographs and provided more visual stimulation, but it provides useful, informative content on its subject. It is recommended for school and public libraries.
—**Tara L. Dirst**

S

43. Lye, Keith. **Philip's World Factbook.** 3d ed. New York, Sterling Publishing, 2000. 352p. illus. maps. index. $17.95pa. ISBN 0-540-07823-9.

This work attempts to give the basic facts about every country in the world in one volume. Overall, the attempt is fairly successful. Basic facts about the climate, history, politics, vegetation, economy, and population are provided for most countries.

The organization is mainly alphabetical but some smaller countries are treated in articles next to their larger neighbors (i.e., the article on Monaco comes after that on France). Also, most island countries of the Atlantic, Caribbean, Indian, and Pacific Oceans are grouped together by ocean, each country receiving an extremely brief notice. (Cuba, however, is treated separately.) There are no cross-references in the text for these exceptions, making the index indispensable in locating smaller countries.

It can only be expected that the information given will be brief and somewhat uneven. It is admirable that in most cases the history of countries in Africa and the Americas before the arrival of the Europeans is mentioned. It was noted, however, that Belgium fares better than the Netherlands in historical treatment, even though they both share much of the same history. Two errors of fact were noted. Luxembourg did not become an "independent state" in 936, but only a separate territory within the Holy Roman Empire, and the history of Poland-Lithuania is reversed (Poland-Lithuania was divided between Austria, Prussia, and Russian in the eighteenth century, then much of Poland was made independent by Napoleon as the Grand Duchy of Warsaw, most of which was annexed by Russia after the fall of Napoleon, the rest going again to Austria and Prussia).

In short, this book can be useful for answers to simple, basic questions about individual countries. For more than that, however, other sources must be used.—**Michael S. Borries**

P, S

44. **World Facts & Maps 2000.** Skokie, Ill., Rand McNally, 2000. 224p. maps. $10.95pa. ISBN 0-528-84176-9. ISSN 1057-9834.

As a compact paperback this volume provides a quick source for basic information, such as population, political parties, and land use, along with brief paragraphs on the people, economy, and history of each country. The format is closest to a much-condensed *Countries of the World and Their Leaders Yearbook* (1999 ed.; see ARBA 99, entry 658). Each provides maps and basic facts. Obviously *Countries of the World*, with two much larger volumes, incorporates a level of depth not found with the Rand McNally publication. *World Facts & Maps* seems to have been produced for a wide market, including home and business use, but not necessarily for larger college library collections. Larger reference collections would already house multiple volumes that would address each of the areas covered, and to a significantly greater degree.

In at least one instance there is a discrepancy between population data provided in one country profile (Pitcairn, p. 179), and another chart that lists the places and possessions of the United Kingdom (p. 215). In one case it could simply be a typographical error, but in the other case the numbers are quite different. This sort of oversight is unfortunate in a volume whose sole purpose is to provide reliable and accurate data. Although the frequency of requests for Pitcairn population figures is admittedly going to be few and far between, the lack of careful proofreading in this case is disconcerting, especially since it required only a check from one table to another.

Roughly one-third of the book presents small essays on "Hot Spots," divided by major geographic regions such as Europe, North America, and South Asia. Within each section specific countries are included for discussion, such as Yugoslavia and the War in the Balkans. Some 36 mini presentations are supplied covering all of the world's regions and countries in turmoil.

Overall, this contribution would be best for small libraries that might not be in a position to collect some of the more expensive standard reference tools. For large college libraries the only value would be as a supplement for times when the standard resources are in use.—**Graham R. Walden**

P, S

45. **Worldmark Yearbook 2000.** Mary Rose Bonk, ed. Farmington Hills, Mich., Gale, 2000. 3v. maps. index. $295.00/set. ISBN 0-7876-4931-7. ISSN 1527-6503.

Most libraries will find value in placing this work in a ready-reference collection, as it provides more information than is typically found in an almanac. The major portion of the text is arranged alphabetically by country, with profiles ranging from 10 to 20 pages. Entries for each country are in two sections. The first provides an overview in prose with summaries of recent history, government, economics, social welfare, and education. There is also a bulleted list of key events for 1999 (through December) with an analysis of those events and directory information on key government offices and officials, political organizations, and diplomatic representation abroad. A list of further reading materials, articles and books, regarding the culture and recent developments of the country is also provided. The second part presents statistical data relating to geography, demographics and vital statistics, religion, education, government, labor, energy production, finance, manufacturing, economics, and trade (imports and exports). Complementing the main text is a 400-page directory of international organizations, providing 10 to 30-line profiles for each organization, as well as contact information.

An identification of source materials and an overview of global developments open the set, and a full analytic index supplements the whole. Each volume contains a full set of color flags, seals, and regional maps. Purchase of this set provides free access to *Worldmark Yearbook* online, an electronic resource that allows full searching capability of this print version, as well as providing updates of events that have transpired since publication. High school, public, and academic libraries will benefit tremendously by having this set at the reference desk. [R: BL, 1 Oct 2000, p. 382; SLJ, Nov 2000, p. 88; BR, Jan/Feb 01, p. 71; Choice, Dec 2000, p. 692; LJ, Dec 2000, p. 112]—**Edmund F. SantaVicca**

UNITED STATES

C, P

46.   Duchak, Alicia. **A-Z of Modern America.** New York, Routledge, 1999. 405p. index. $24.99pa. ISBN 0-415-18756-7.

This interesting dictionary provides more than 3,000 terms that are part of the language that culturally defines modern America. The entries provide information on key people (e.g., presidents, select celebrities), customs, clothing, education, religions, government, minorities, and civil rights, among others. A "Nickname Abbreviations" list begins the volume—basically, a list of acronyms of associations and organizations. The definitions provide an indication of which area or field the term is used (e.g., daily life, legal system, geography), various spellings of the term, the terms abbreviation (if any), a thorough description, and cross-references. Nine appendixes conclude the volume: a list of states (with population, nickname, and region), a list of presidents (with party affiliation, vice president, years in office, and platform), professional sports teams, education levels (from nursery school to Ph.D. programs), grading systems, college football bowl games, military ranks and ensignia, a diagram of a baseball diamond, and a diagram of a football field. How these particular subjects were chosen is unclear and leaves the reader wondering.

This volume is interesting to peruse and presents good definitions of many things uniquely American. In a work of this nature there are bound to be some topics forgotten or omitted, but what is included here is worthwhile. *A-Z of Modern America* will find use in public and undergraduate academic libraries.

—**Shannon Graff Hysell**

C, P, S

47.   **The 50 States.** R. Kent Rasmussen, ed. Hackensack, N.J., Salem Press, 2000. 992p. illus. maps. index. $115.00. ISBN 0-89356-999-2.

The purpose of this publication is to provide basic information and statistics about the individual states within the United States to a general public and student audience. The information contained in this book is available in many other places, but this book offers a unique contribution with its compilation.

The book is organized into state chapters. Each chapter includes general state trivia and a concise history, which provides an excellent resource for the general reader. The majority of each chapter consists of statistical tables that provide general information on common interests, such as the economy, politics, health care, housing, education, and crime. The table of contents and the subject index easily inform the user as to the kind of information available.

One of the problems with providing statistical information in print format is the tendency for the information to date itself. Much of the statistical information is given in a range of years that will keep it useful even after more current statistical information is available. However, the Web resources section of each chapter's "Notes for Further Study" would have been an excellent place to include Web links to current statistical information so that users could find more recent information.

This book is well organized, provides a great deal of information about individual states in one compendium, and makes an excellent resource for the general audience. Public and school libraries will find this book useful for students and the public at large, as will larger undergraduate libraries.—**Tara L. Dirst**

S

48.   Ricciuti, Edward, Jenny Tesar, and Tanya Lee Stone. **America's Top 100: Our Nation's Most Awe-Inspiring Natural Features and Landmarks.** Woodbridge, Conn., Blackbirch Press, 2000. 240p. illus. index. $39.95. ISBN 1-56711-151-3.

This guide pulls together information from the America's Top 100 series into one source. The 10 sections cover bridges, cities, construction wonders, curiosities, mountains, national monuments, national parks, natural wonders, rivers, and skyscrapers. Full-page, color photographs are provided for each site along with a brief one-page description and history of the site. Sidebars point out interesting and significant facts.

Since the main audience for this work is young adults the descriptions are very simplistic and easy to read. A glossary is included to define terms that may be unfamiliar to young readers. There is also a list of additional references, including books and Websites, for further research. Each entry has a small map pinpointing the sites and there is also a full map of the United States denoting all of the sites mentioned in the guide. An index is included for additional ease of use.

This is a good reference work for young readers interested in learning about different features in the United States. Since the information provided in this guide is very basic, students who are interested in a specific site will need a more detailed reference to gain a more detailed knowledge of the site. *America's Top 100* is recommended for juvenile reference collections in public and school libraries.—**Cari Ringelheim**

AFRICA

C, P

49.   Skreslet, Paula Youngman. **Northern Africa: A Guide to Reference and Information Sources.** Englewood, Colo., Libraries Unlimited, 2000. 405p. index. (Reference Sources in the Social Sciences Series). $85.00. ISBN 1-56308-684-0.

This is an annotated bibliography of Northern Africa. It includes materials in English, French, German, and transliterated Arabic. The entry titles are given in the language of publication. Although some indicate that the language of the work is French or German, for others whose titles are not in English it is unclear whether the works are written with English translations. The first part consists of general reference works such as handbooks, dictionaries, statistical sources, travel information, and general journals. The second part provides references by subject; history and antiquities; social sciences; government, politics, and law; economics-commerce; industry and aid; arts and learning; and religion. Under the Mahgreb-Arabic speaking countries of North Africa are Algeria, Egypt, Libya, Morocco, and Tunisia. Chad, Mali, Mauritania, Niger, Sudan, and Western Sahara are included in the Sahel Region–Sahara. The Horn of Africa section of countries covers Djibouti, Eritrea, Ethiopia, and Somalia. Every citation includes all bibliographic data available except the price. In addition to more than 1,000 printed sources, about 400 electronic references are given—both proprietary databases and services and public Internet Websites. Their selection was based on authority, currency, scope, and uniqueness. Since not all of the works are as helpful as their titles suggest, some inadequate works are included with their drawbacks mentioned. An entry may be repeated if it is relevant to more than one subject area. There are name, title, and subject indexes.

—**J. E. Weaver**

ASIA

China

C, P

50.   **Encyclopedia of the Chinese Overseas.** Lynn Pan, ed. Cambridge, Mass., Harvard University Press, 1998. 399p. illus. maps. index. $59.95. ISBN 0-674-25210-1.

Even though it is an encyclopedia and its contents are written by some 50 scholars or specialists, this important work on overseas Chinese is very readable in its entirety—infused with photographs, illustrations, maps, tables, figures, and boxed features, and filled with interesting anecdotes and vivid details. The 399-page encyclopedia provides a panoramic view across past and present overseas Chinese communities in every part of the world. The editor, Lynn Pan, a noted author, journalist, and book editor, has done an outstanding service to the growing worldwide interest in the study and understanding of overseas Chinese by producing this timely publication.

The main body of this encyclopedia is divided into five parts. The first four parts, consisting of about one-third of the entire volume, are devoted to thematic descriptions of the origins of overseas Chinese, their migration, institutions, and relations with local non-Chinese and with China. The first part takes up about two-thirds of the volume and consists of country-by-country profiles of Chinese communities grouped under Southeast Asia, the Americas, Australasia and Oceania, Europe, East Asia, and Indian Ocean and Africa.

Other useful features following the text are a table of timelines on relevant historical events; a Chinese character list of proper names and terms; an extensive bibliography of Chinese, English, French, Spanish, and Russian sources; and an index.

The encyclopedia is scholarly and authoritative enough for academic specialists, but is also suitable for general readers who are interested in information on overseas Chinese. This work is highly recommended for all libraries as a standard reference book. [R: Choice, Oct 99, p. 312]—**Hwa-Wei Lee**

Korea

P, S

51. Clark, Donald N. **Culture and Customs of Korea.** Westport, Conn., Greenwood Press, 2000. 204p. illus. maps. index. (Culture and Customs of Asia). $45.00. ISBN 0-313-30456-4.

The United States had already fought three major wars, one of which was the Korean War, in Asia in the twentieth century. Today, Asia is not only one of America's leading trading partners, but also the ancestral home-lands of one of America's fastest growing minorities. But for some reason, as the editor of the series has noted, Asia remains for most of us a relatively unfamiliar, if not stereotypical or even mysterious, "Oriental" land.

The work under review, *Culture and Customs of Korea*, should serve as an excellent introduction in help-ing Americans get a better understanding of one of Asia's major civilizations. It is organized into nine chapters, covering every aspect of Korea's culture and customs, such as thought and religion; arts and literature; perform-ing arts; life in urban Korea; and gender, marriage, and the lives of Korean women. Although the information provided is rather brief, users should be able to learn virtually every essential characteristic of Korean culture and customs (rituals of courtship, traditional Korean marriage ceremony, traditional Korean costumes, funeral customs, and so on). The coverage of modern life in North Korea, however, is rather limited. Also included in the text are a chronology (2333 B.C.E.–2000 C.E.), a glossary, and a subject index.

High school and college students, business people, and tourists should find this work useful. School, public and academic libraries ought to purchase this publication in order that it may be used as a reference source or as an introductory textbook.—**Binh P. Le**

CANADA

C, P

52. **Encyclopedia of British Columbia.** Daniel Francis, ed. Madeira Park, Harbour, 2000. 806p. illus. maps. index. $99.00. ISBN 1-55017-200-X.

The *Encyclopedia of British Columbia* is a single-volume, 800-page, 4,000-article, spectacularly illus-trated resource that will be treasured by public, high school, and college librarians who wish to provide informa-tion access to this unique corner of North America. The editor, a seasoned social studies textbook author, edited both the Hurtig *Junior Encyclopedia of Canada* and the Hurtig *Canadian Encyclopedia*. The publisher has published several books on British Columbia. Together they have produced a resource that mimics the style and format of *World Book Encyclopedia*

The articles, which range from about 350 words to several pages, depict their subjects authoritatively in a clear objective prose. Each article contains cross-references to related articles and a few contain bibliographic citations for further reading. Additional access points are provided in a combined subject and name index in the back of the book. This index, however, does not duplicate or cross-reference the entry titles, which may cause some confusion. For instance, a searcher looking for information on the 1915 Stanley Cup champion hockey team from British Columbia will have to know to look up the team as the Vancouver Millionaires, for neither the index nor the encyclopedia text contains a cross-reference for Millionaires. The scope of the volume is wide, extending to all disciplines of the sciences and humanities. There is, however, a remarkable emphasis on popular culture, historical events, and biographical information lending the volume vivaciousness. The coverage is also up-to-date, providing a complete picture of British Columbia in the twentieth century. The most notable aspect of the volume are the neatly captioned color photographs that accompany the articles and grace nearly every page. There are also a variety of high-impact charts, figures, and maps. The edition also is available as a CD-ROM, which encompasses the print edition and adds both audio and video clips. The print version, however, will be suitable for most libraries that can afford the shelf space for this unique and fascinating pictorial encyclopedia.—**David E. Michalski**

S
53.   **Junior Worldmark Encyclopedia of the Canadian Provinces.** 2d ed. Timothy L. Gall and Susan Bevan Gall, eds. Farmington Hills, Mich., U*X*L/Gale, 1999. 254p. illus. maps. index. $45.00. ISBN 0-7876-3811-0.

The 2d edition of the *Junior Worldmark Encyclopedia of the Canadian Provinces* (see ARBA 98, entry 119, for a review of the 1st edition) describes in detail the 10 provinces and 3 territories that make up Canada. Each province or territory is listed alphabetically in the book and is described in about 15 pages, including maps and photographs. There are data provided on 40 categories of interest, including location and size, topography, climate, plants and animals, population, languages, history, local government, industry, agriculture, commerce, housing, education, libraries and museums, and a bibliography listing books and Websites. Introductory information provided for each territory or province includes its name; nickname; capital; date it entered the confederation; time zone; and state motto, coat of arms, flag, floral emblem, tartan, mammal, provincial bird, tree, and stone. A glossary, list of abbreviations, and index conclude the volume. This work is designed mainly for middle and high school students.—**Shannon Graff Hysell**

EUROPE

General Works

C, P
54.   Leach, Rodney. **Europe: A Concise Encyclopedia of the European Union from Aachen to Zollverein.** 3d ed. Chicago, Fitzroy Dearborn, 2000. 273p. $45.00. ISBN 1-57958-279-6.

Scanning the entries in this title may make one feel as though they have fallen into a bowl of alphabet soup that is heavy on the E's. Don't be alarmed. The multiple acronyms are among the entries related to the founding, development, and operation of the European Union (EU). Some entries attempt to clarify the role of the many different organizations with similar names. Others deal with individuals and their significance in relation to the EU. Each EU member country is discussed in terms of its relation to the union. In addition, relevant terms (e.g., *Euro, convergence*), concepts, and treaties are defined and explained.

The author, a London financial strategist, acknowledges that even experts are confused by the "similarity of different institution's names, the plethora of acronyms and initials and the changing titles and numbering of the treaties." His goal is to provide clarification on the many aspects of the EU. The criterion for inclusion are whether or not a particular term is likely to turn up in an "informed discussion of the European Union." Right away one realizes that this is not a source for the novice.

This is the 3d edition of the encyclopedia and the first U.S. edition. The clearly stated objective of the first two volumes was to provide an alternative source of EU information since, in Leach's opinion, most other sources originate from the Union itself. That said, readers will quickly spot an anti-EU bias in the book almost bordering on paranoia. The introductory essay draws the line in the sand between the integrationists and the nationalists. Strange entries reinforce this stand. *Constructive ambiguity* is defined as the "deliberately equivocal language used to obscure integrationist's intentions." The entry for *propaganda* states that enormous amounts of money are spent by the EU on presenting positive information and regulating the right of public access to relevant documents. The Ryder Cup merits its own entry as the only example of a European consciousness which "is entirely free from community involvement." The Republic of Ireland receives a mean-spirited tirade, which describes the country as "Catholic, neutral in World War II, with a leaning to the German side."

In spite of the narrowly subjective approach, the encyclopedia does contain good information. There are lengthy, informative essays on the European Parliament and the European Monetary Fund, which present pros and cons. For the neophyte attempting to make sense of the EU the articles on the three pillars do a good job of delineating the organizations complex structure. Several appendixes cover the EU's chronology, the composition of the Parliament, and national voting strength.

While Leach would most likely dismiss the value of Desmond Dinan's *Encyclopedia of the European Union* (2d ed.; see ARBA 99, entry 691) since it was commissioned by an EU press information officer, it does present a less radical and more scholarly approach to the study of the EU. Its 700 articles, most signed by academic authors, covers the same ground as the review title. Its entry on the Treaty on the European Union runs four pages and contains an analysis, origins, contents, and a discussion of the treaty's strengths and weaknesses. Leach gives the treaty one paragraph. Another example is the entry for integrationist theory. Leach again provides a short paragraph in which he dismisses the "turgid academic industry of integration theories." Dinan's entry covers the "turgid" theories in a well-organized 10-page presentation. Each volume has its own perspective and looking at both together raises more questions as to which view is accurate. Perhaps the definitive work on the EU has yet to be written. In the meantime both provide food for thought. In some strange way, Leach's strident position makes for interesting reading and since it is so obviously biased it will peak one's interest to examine other titles on the subject.—**Marlene M. Kuhl**

Czech Republic

C, P

55.   **Czech Republic.** rev. ed. Vlad'ka Edmondson and David Short, comps. Santa Barbara, Calif., Clio Press/ABC-CLIO, 1999. 430p. maps. index. (World Bibliographical Series, v.219). $110.00. ISBN 1-85109-304-4.

This comprehensive annotated bibliography of books and journal articles about the Czech Republic updates David Short's 1968 bibliography on Czechoslovakia in the same series. Sources for the bibliography were the collections of the British Library, the School of Slavonic and East European Studies at the University of London, and other collections in England and abroad. Although the majority of the entries are English language ones, there are also entries for German, French, and Czech works. There is some minor overlap of material with Susie Lunt's bibliography on Prague (volume 195 in the same series).

The 1,166 annotated entries are arranged in several topical chapters including geography and geology, tourism and travel guides, flora and fauna, history, nationalities and minorities, folklore, religion, social conditions, education, philosophy, politics and law, economics, industry and trade, science and technology, sport and recreation, language, literature, the arts, music, newspapers and periodicals, and others. Within each chapter and subsection, the entries are arranged in an idiosyncratic scheme devised by the authors. The authors have also provided separate indexes for authors, titles, and subjects. The annotations provided are both descriptive and evaluative. An introduction to the bibliography by David Short provides a brief history of the Czech Republic.

The bibliography is comprehensive and serves as an excellent introduction to the literature in many areas. The annotations are of sufficient detail to provide a good understanding of the scope and depth of the subject's treatment by the cited author. [R: Choice, Sept 2000, p. 104]—**Robert H. Burger**

Ireland

C, P

56.   **Encyclopedia of Ireland: An A–Z Guide to Its People, Places, History, and Culture.** Ciaran Brady, ed. New York, Oxford University Press, 2000. 389p. illus. maps. $39.95. ISBN 0-19-521685-7.

A simplified definition of "encyclopedia" is "a book giving a great deal of information about many things; encyclopedias often contain a large number of articles about various subjects." In this reviewers opinion, *The Encyclopedia of Ireland* lives up to this definition.

The information provided is concise, extensive, and visually appealing. Unlike typical encyclopedias, this book has in-depth essays on important themes of Ireland, such as "Troubles," tracing Irish ancestors, and the meaning of Irish symbols. There are more than 300 biographies (yes, Michael Flatley of *Riverdance* and *Lord of the Dance* fame is included), 500 historical and cultural entries, 400 geographical entries (including key sightseeing attractions), and 200 quotations on Ireland (which are set apart in a pleasing typeface). Black-and-white photographs and line drawings are plentiful and there is the added delight of 73 beautiful color photographs, presented in an artistic manner, grouped in two sections. *The Encyclopedia of Ireland: An A–Z Guide to Its People, Places, History, and Culture* will make an excellent addition to any library. [R: LJ, Jan 01, p. 88]—**Pamela J. Getchell**

C, P

57. **Local Ireland Almanac and Yearbook of Facts 2000.** millennium ed. Helen Curley, ed. Chester Springs, Pa., Dufour, 2000. 493p. index. $17.95pa. ISBN 0-9536537-0-6.

First published in 1997 under the title *Irish Almanac and Yearbook of Facts* (see ARBA 98, entry 133), this millennium edition with its new title of *Local Ireland Almanac and Yearbook of Facts* is accompanied by a Website located at http://www.localalmanac.ie. Together, the new book and its sister site offer a truly impressive collection of facts and figures about Ireland, both the north and south. Anyone with a need to know detailed statistical information accurately reflecting the essence of contemporary Ireland should have this book. It depicts an Ireland fully engaged with business, the arts, culture, sports, and education—a powerhouse of thought and action.

With the millennium in mind, *Local Ireland Almanac* includes a new chapter on the history of Ireland during the past 1,000 years. It offers a detailed chronology of Ireland over the period, ass well as a synopsis of the main events that defined each of the past centuries. Other new features have been introduced to make the book more user friendly. For instance, the "At a Glance" statistics table at the beginning of each chapter provides a handy summary of the detailed facts and figures from each field of life, from the arts to education.

As before, the *Almanac* chronicles the year leading up to publication, in this case October 1998 to September 1999. It also includes the most important news stories from the 12-month period. Not surprisingly, the Peace Process is at the forefront, although other salient stories of the year, savory and unsavory (e.g., the findings of the Moriarty Tribunal on scandal and corruption in Irish government), are also covered.

In-depth articles from experts on Irish life, who may or may not tell one what one wants to hear, provide food for thought about the "Celtic Tiger" that has emerged at the turn of the millennium. Articles include the text of John Hume's lecture delivered to the Nobel Foundation on the occasion of his Nobel Prize for peace. Others deal with Ireland and the world of e-commerce, Irish industry, the prison system, the state of religion in Ireland, and even the plight of postgraduate doctors in training in Ireland.

Other excellent features of *Local Ireland Almanac* are the detailed sections on politics and the political parties; listings of the various offices for public administration, both national and local; listings for the major business interests and their subsidiaries; the main religious denominations and where to find them; and arts, culture, entertainment, tourism, and sports. Rounding out the book is the index, a truly useful feature in a remarkable smorgasbord of facts and figures. *Local Ireland Almanac of Facts and Figures* is a must on the desk of anyone from academia to business to religion and politics or anyone with an interest in Ireland.—**Arthur Gribben**

Ukraine

C, P

58. Wynar, Bohdan S. **Independent Ukraine: A Bibliographic Guide to English-Language Publications, 1989–1999.** Englewood, Colo., Ukrainian Academic Press/Libraries Unlimited, 2000. 552p. index. $85.00. ISBN 1-56308-670-0.

This bibliography is primarily a supplement to Wynar's earlier *Ukraine: A Bibliographic Guide to English-Language Publications* (see ARBA 91, entry 115) and reflects a decade in which there has been an almost "unprecedented increase of information on all aspects of Ukrainian culture, history, and the present conditions" (p. xiii). Hence, there are more than 1,700 entries in this volume, with "several thousand" more items mentioned in the annotations, compared to 1,084 in the earlier compilation, which covered material published prior to 1990. Although Wynar acknowledges the difficulty of tracking all of the pertinent recent publications, he achieves a notable success with this bibliography.

The book is organized around the same basic framework as the 1990 volume: 12 broad sections (rather than 13), although most of the sections are expanded and some of the section titles have been modified. For example, "Art and Architecture" is now called "Art, Folklore, and Ethnography," and "Geography and Travel" is now "Geography, Environment, and Demography." There is now a separate section for "Law," although the former category of "Philosophy, Sociology, and Demography and Statistics" has been dissected and distributed into other new groupings. The arrangement of section 7, "History and Political Science," has been significantly revised to reflect Ukraine's independence. There is now a clear distinction between "Soviet Ukraine" and simply "Ukraine."

Wynar begins each section of the bibliography with an introductory page that highlights several of the most important recent publications and explains the arrangement and selection of the material. Each entry is liberally annotated and most contain references to additional publications. Books, book chapters, journal articles, dissertations, encyclopedia entries, conference proceedings, and some official documents are covered. For many of the books listed, references to reviews are included in the annotation. This is a truly comprehensive survey of contemporary Ukrainian culture, history and politics, and belongs in all academic libraries. Given the current publication rate in this area, we can expect another supplement to Wynar's ongoing bibliography within a few short years. [R: Choice, Jan 01, p. 888]—**Thomas A. Karel**

LATIN AMERICA AND THE CARIBBEAN

P

59. Levine, Robert M. **The History of Brazil.** Westport, Conn., Greenwood Press, 1999. 208p. maps. index. (The Greenwood Histories of the Modern Nations Series). $35.00. ISBN 0-313-30390-8.

According to the preface of this volume, this contribution to The Greenwood Histories of the Modern Nations Series, based on recent scholarship in the field, aims to "introduce Brazil to readers who neither are specialists nor are seeking exhaustive detail." Brazilian history is summarized in chapters arranged in chronological order, from its discovery in 1500 by a Portuguese sea captain to 1998, followed by two chapters on its contemporary political culture and its social and economic realities. A biographical essay complements the bibliographic notes listed at the end of each chapter.

Other features are a chronology of Brazilian history; a glossary of selected terms associated with Brazilian Portuguese; and biographical notes in a five-page chapter entitled "Notable People in the History of Brazil" that includes a potpourri of figures from the world of art, anthropology, politics, journalism, literature, and other fields. The latter is limited in its usefulness because of its brevity. A good index provides access to the text.

This work provides a well-written account of Brazilian political, social, and cultural history for the general reader. It would be a good addition to any library developing a collection that includes the Latin American countries, or the world's larger countries in demographic, geographic, and economic terms.—**Ann Hartness**

MIDDLE EAST

C, P

60. Goldschmidt, Arthur, Jr. **Biographical Dictionary of Modern Egypt.** Boulder, Colo., Lynne Rienner Publishers, Inc., 2000. 299p. index. $65.00. ISBN 1-55587-229-8.

We know a great deal about the history and society of modern Egypt—here defined as the region or country ruled from Cairo (excluding Sudan) from the reigns of the Mamluks 'ali Bey and Muhammad Bey Adu al-Dhahab in the late eighteenth century to the present President [Muhammad] Husni Mubarak—but accessible biographical information in English on the movers and shakers of the country's national life is sorely lacking. Goldschmidt helps fill that lacuna in this up-to-date, one-volume biographical dictionary. Intended as a research tool for scholars and writers, this volume provides source material for approximately 400 important men and women (mainly Egyptian nationals), who have influenced greatly Egypt's national identity and destiny. Annotated entries encapsulate the accomplishments of artists, leaders, educators, entertainers, entrepreneurs, literati, politicians, revolutionaries, and religious leaders. The book concludes with an extensive 55-page index of articles and books on events and trends that speak about and to the persona of the text. For some, Goldschmidt's selection of who shaped Egypt's direction and durability in the past 200 years is disputable (e.g., ordinary citizens and new pioneers of the arts and sciences are barely noticeable), but this does not detract from the scope of his project. This is a definitive reference work. [R: Choice, Nov 2000, p. 512]—**Zev Garber**

4 Economics and Business

GENERAL WORKS

Dictionaries and Encyclopedias

C, P, S

61. **Gale Encyclopedia of U.S. Economic History.** Thomas Carson and Mary Bonk, eds. Farmington Hills, Mich., Gale, 2000. 2v. illus. maps. index. $195.00/set. ISBN 0-7876-3888-9.

The *Gale Encyclopedia of U.S. Economic History* is a beautifully produced and carefully researched two-volume set that would be appropriate for high school and public libraries as well as for academic libraries that serve an undergraduate population. Intended for juniors and seniors in high school and first- and second-year college students, the encyclopedia provides comprehensive coverage of U.S. economic history from the Paleolithic Age to the present, although the emphasis is on the nineteenth and twentieth centuries. Articles for the encyclopedia were selected by a nine-member editorial board of university and high school teachers and librarians. In addition, Charles K. Hyde, professor of history at Wayne State University, was responsible for reviewing all articles to ensure content of the highest quality.

Articles for the *Gale Encyclopedia of U.S. Economic History* have been crafted with specific purposes in mind and can be characterized as era overviews, issues in economic history, geographical profiles, key events and movements, geographies, historic business and industry profiles, and economic concepts and terms. Articles range from a paragraph or two to several pages. Most articles include suggestions for further reading and there are many cross-references to other articles. For example, the article on Harley-Davidson, Inc., is nearly 3 pages in length, includes an illustration of a 1927 motorcycle typical of Harley-Davidson products, and has 7 citations for additional reading. The article on Indiana is just under two pages of text but includes a full-page map showing major cities, points of interest, and highway routes. An article on George Washington Carver, complete with photograph and suggested readings, covers not only his inventions, but also his work with the Tuskegee Institute and his many honors and awards. Articles are easy to read and offer a good balance between fact and analysis.

There are several additional features of the *Gale Encyclopedia of U.S. Economic History* that make it a particularly good reference source. It has an index of more than 100 pages, so students should be able to find information without difficulty. In addition, a detailed 33-page chronology covering approximately 50,000 years provides a quick way to verify dates and will help students to place an event within its historical context. There is also a list of "contents by era" divided into 10 eras. A research scholar has prepared an overview for each of these eras. In the front of the set these "eras" and their corresponding articles are listed. The encyclopedia has more than 200 finely reproduced photographs and illustrations that make it a treat to look at. There are detailed maps for states and regions, which should be particularly useful to students.

The *Gale Encyclopedia of U.S. Economic History* is attractively produced with clear, easy-to-read type and an engaging cover design and is reasonably priced. It will be an excellent addition to the reference collections of high school, public, and academic libraries. [R: Choice, Sept 2000, p. 104; BR, Sept/Oct 2000, p. 79]

—**Sara Anne Hook**

Handbooks and Yearbooks

P
62.   **Business Statistics of the United States 1999.** 5th ed. Courtenay M. Slater, Cornelia J. Strawser, and James B. Rice, eds. Lanham, Md., Bernan Associates, 1999. 479p. index. $74.00pa. ISBN 0-89059-213-6. ISSN 1086-8488.

   Business managers, students, economic analysts, government officials, and concerned citizens all find it necessary to understand current trends in U.S. business and the economy in which it operates. The most common approach used to describe and analyze the status of business and the economy is to order relevant data by time. *Business Statistics of the United States 1999* provides ready access to the most widely used business and economic time series. The book contains about 2,000 time series, selected largely from the vast flow of data from the federal government. To assist the reader in understanding, a section by Slater overviews and relates the various individual series, while Strawser provides a discussion of current issues and problems involved in measuring economic variables. In addition, extensive notes are included to identify specific sources and to offer further description of each time series. The time series, in tabular format, has been arranged in four categories: the overall U.S. economy, broad industry profiles, historical series that provide annual data back to 1961 (most of the series start with 1970), and state/regional tables. Many sections are preceded by an analysis of trends and their meaning to the current situation. The 1999 edition is the 5th in a series that began in 1995. The publisher revived and expanded an earlier series of publications, *Business Statistics*, that had been made available by the Bureau of Economic Analysis of the U.S. Department of Commerce, but which was discontinued in 1992 after 27 periodic editions. *Business Statistics of the United States* offers a vast array of statistical data in a single volume with source notes to facilitate further investigation and represents an essential reference on recent and historical data on the U.S. economy.—**William C. Struning**

P
63.   Frumkin, Norman. **Guide to Economic Indicators.** 3d ed. Armonk, N.Y., M. E. Sharpe, 2000. 328p. index. $64.95; $24.95pa. ISBN 0-7656-0436-1; 0-7656-0437-Xpa.

   This is an efficient and practical handbook that outlines more than 70 commonly used concepts and statistical measures of economic activity. It outlines the relative significance and application of various economic statistics and terminology used in forecasting macroeconomic activity. An appealing feature of this handy reference work is that, when appropriate, explanations are provided not only in the context of the U.S. economy but also in an international context. As a reference work it is intended for a general audience, including students, investors, journalists, and other interested laypersons, although it also provides a quick and straightforward handbook for economists and other social scientists.

   The alphabetically arranged economic indicators are organized under 551 general categories. Even though some indicators are necessarily cross-referenced, indicators are also organized into 13 broad categories, which is an effective method to demonstrate the interrelationships and correlations between measurements and concepts. The broad categories are economic growth, household income and expenditure, business profits and investment, labor, inflation, production, housing, finance, government, international, cyclical indicators and forecasting, economic well-being, and psychology. Entries initially provide a concise description of the indicator or statistical measure and then go on to provide practical and useful information about the application and relevancy of the indicator or measurement. Knowing where and when the statistics are available, the content of the material released, the methodology used to generate the information, and the accuracy and relevance of the information as well as seeing recent trends in the information and having references from primary data sources helps to make this handbook functional and useful.—**Timothy E. Sullivan**

ACCOUNTING

P

64.   Siegel, Joel G., and Jae K. Shim. **Dictionary of Accounting Terms.** 3d ed. Hauppauge, N.Y., Barron's Educational Series, 2000. 488p. $12.95pa. ISBN 0-7841-1259-7.

The authors' intention in writing this dictionary is to provide business executives, accountants, or business students with the most up-to-date accounting and financial terms and their definitions. The vocabulary of accounting is constantly changing, with new words and phrases being developed as business and tax laws evolve. Business executives, accountants, or students have to be cognizant of these new terms to be successful in the accounting field.

The standard and the new accounting terms have been gathered from all areas of finance and accounting. Approximately 2,500 terms have been defined concisely and if examples are required for understanding, they are provided.

The entries are alphabetized by letter not by the word. A list of abbreviations and acronyms are provided in the appendix. Cross-references help clarify related or contrasting terms. Special organizations that have played key roles in the field of accounting have been included as entries, such as "American Accounting Association."

The appendix has a table covering compounded values of the dollar and annuities. This little dictionary is a must purchase for academic and public libraries to help provide quick reference for accounting terms. Undergraduate accounting students will find this dictionary a handy reference for their personal research.—**Kay M. Stebbins**

BUSINESS SERVICES AND INVESTMENT GUIDES

P

65.   **Bond's Minority Franchise Guide.** 2000 ed. Robert E. Bond and Nicole Thompson, eds. Oakland, Calif., Source Book Publications, 2000. 268p. index. $19.95pa. ISBN 1-887137-16-5.

Bond's Minority Franchise Guide is intended to expose minorities to business opportunities in the area of franchising. This book features some 400 franchises that actively support recruiting minorities into their business. The book is divided into 39 business categories, which include everything from automotive services and financial services to food services and retail. The information gathered for this book was acquired from a questionnaire issued to franchises throughout the United States. The book provides the company name, address, and telephone and fax numbers; a description of the business; the background of the business (e.g., date established, a breakdown of what percentage of the franchises are owned by which minorities); a brief financial record and terms of the franchise contract; a description of the support and training provided; and any future plans for the franchise to expand. Each franchise receives only about one-third of a page for explanation, which will require an interested party to do further research. Along with the descriptions of the franchise opportunities, this book also offers advice on how to most effectively use the data, recommended readings for those interested in pursuing this career path, advice from the seven corporate sponsors, resources for minority investors, and a sample of the questionnaire.

This directory will be well received in public libraries that serve minority clientele. The book is easy to understand and will answer many preliminary questions that patrons pursuing this type of career will need to know.
—**Shannon Graff Hysell**

CONSUMER GUIDES

P

66.   **Directory of MasterCard & Visa Credit Card Sources.** 3d ed. Barry Klein, ed. West Nyack, N.Y., Todd Publications, 1999. 71p. $50.00pa. ISBN 0-915344-78-5.

For those unfamiliar with how credit cards work and how they make their money this resource will offer a wealth of information on finding the right card with a low interest rate and how to go about getting approved. The introduction explains the difference between secured and nonsecured cards; offers tips on locating a card with a better interest rate; describes the terms often associated with credit cards (e.g., grace period, annual percentage rate, tiered interest rate); provides names and telephone numbers of secured and nonsecured credit card companies; and provides information on credit card companies that offer low interest rates, no annual fees, and good introductory rates. It also presents companies that offer corporate cards, frequent-flyer cards, and cards for those in national organizations (e.g., AAA cards, Wall Street Club).

The bulk of the directory alphabetically lists directory information of companies issuing credit cards. The information provides the company's name; where their cards are offered; telephone number and address; the annual membership fee, annual interest rate, minimum income required, and credit line range for both regular cards and gold cards; and the grace period, any additional charges, and extra benefits. This volume, along with forthcoming editions, will be valuable additions to the business or finance collections of public libraries. Because so many Americans are using credit cards and trying to find the best deals, this work can answer a lot of questions at the reference desk.—**Shannon Graff Hysell**

P

67.   Krantz, Les, and Sharon Ludman-Exley. **The Best of Everything for Your Baby.** Paramus, N.J., Prentice Hall, 2000. 334p. illus. index. $15.00pa. ISBN 0-7352-0032-7.

The Best of Everything for Your Baby is more than just a buying guide for infant and toddler necessities; it also provides tips and advice for novice parents. The guide covers essential purchases that babies and toddlers need as well as a few convenient and playful items. The authors have drawn on their own experiences, along with opinions from other parents, to provide sound advice for new parents no matter what their budget is.

The first section of the guide directs readers in purchasing items that are necessary before the baby arrives. Tips are given about what features to look for on items such as cribs, monitors, changing tables, and playpens. This section also lists accessories that are not necessary, but they are recommended. The second section covers items that parents will need after the baby arrives, such as nursing and bottle feeding items, highchairs, toiletries, and bath gear. The third section lists educational and stimulating toys for infants and toddlers as well as videos, music, software, and books. The last section features items for traveling, such as car seats, carriers, and strollers. This section also provides safety tips for staying at hotels, shopping, and air travel. The appendixes list toll-free numbers for consumer relations departments at a number of manufacturers and Websites for shopping and information.

Overall, this guide offers more advice on what to buy and what to look for than actual reviews of products. Safety is a key issue that is continuously stressed throughout the work. This is a highly recommended guide for novice parents. It gives good advice about a number of basic concerns for new parents. [R: LJ, 1 Oct 99, p. 82]
—**Cari Ringelheim**

INDUSTRY AND MANUFACTURING

C, P

68.   **Encyclopedia of Tourism.** Jafar Jafari, ed. New York, Routledge, 2000. 683p. index. $140.00. ISBN 0-415-15405-7.

This timely reference work is the joint effort of an extensive editorial team and a long list of contributors and was five years in the making. Because this field of study is relatively new when compared to others there are few scholarly reference books on the subject, making this work especially valuable. There are more than 1,200 alphabetically arranged entries listed here, all of which are signed by the contributor. The entries range from a full page for often-used words (e.g., marketing, destination, recreation) to a few sentences (e.g., manpower development, collaborative education). Words appearing in the entries that have their own entry elsewhere in the volume are set apart in bold typeface. Many of the entries also contain *see also* references and a list for further reading. The editor points out in the introduction of this work that there are a few problems within the volume. Namely, because entries were written by many different contributors there tends to be an overlap of information in many of the entries. Also, subject areas tend to be unevenly represented, with some less-important entries receiving a more detailed description than the more important entries. Another drawback for American researchers is that British spellings are used instead of American English.

In spite of these few problems, this work will fill a niche in the field of tourism and travel. It is highly recommended for academic libraries offering classes in the field of tourism and the hospitality industries. [R: LJ, Jan 01, p. 88]—**Shannon Graff Hysell**

INTERNATIONAL BUSINESS

General Works

Handbooks and Yearbooks

C, P

69.   **World Economic and Social Survey 1999: Trends and Policies in the World Economy.** By the Department of Economic and Social Affairs. New York, United Nations, 1999. 197p. $55.00pa. ISBN 92-1-109135-7. S/N E.99.II.C.1.

This scholarly annual is divided into two parts. The first three chapters provide a state of the world economy with a summary for 1999 that focuses on macroeconomic changes in the global economy. The remaining six chapters in part 2 focus on the microeconomic scale, that is, how to bring capital to traditionally capital-deprived groups in developing (i.e., Third World) or transitioning (i.e., formerly controlled or socialist) economies. The United Nations clearly values stable growth. This is more a political and economic appraisal than a "social" review. The "social" of the title reflects how the national and global economies affect the societies in individual countries and regions. In fact, the subtitle is more accurate than the title.

More than 40 tables or sidebars are interspersed within the scholarly text. An annex provides an additional 40 pages of tables. Like so many UN documents, there is no index but there is a long and detailed table of contents that does include all tables and sidebars. There is no CIP. The writing is professional and is aimed at economists, bureaucrats, and graduate students. While titles like the *Europa World Yearbook* (39th ed.; see ARBA 99, entry 66) duplicate some data, in reality, the title is unique. This work is recommended for libraries serving international business, economic, and finance students and libraries serving the banking and multinational business community.

—**Patrick J. Brunet**

P

70.   **World Labour Report 2000: Income Security and Social Protection in a Changing World.** Washington, D.C., International Labour Office, 2000. 321p. $34.95pa. ISBN 92-2-110831-7.

Published by the International Labour Organization, whose purpose is to promote social justice, and prepared by the Social Security Department, this report indicates where nations stand globally on income security and social protection. It also discusses the instruments that have been used for successes and failures. It looks at the challenges for the future and has demographics on social patterns that are changing the needs for social security. This volume examines trends in social security expenditures and looks at specific problems such as pensions, health care, disability, unemployment, and other benefits. It also discusses how protection might be extended to reach the population as a whole and describes restructuring to meet new needs. Gender equality is also discussed. The chapters include information on income security and social protection; demographics within family and labor markets structures; social security expenditures in the economy; existing mechanisms for social protection, such as health care, social protection during incapacity, old, age, and survivors' pension; social protection against unemployment; social benefits for parents and children; and social assistance. Future needs and prospects, including extending personal coverage, restructuring social protection systems, and the main policy conclusions, are examined. Statistical indexes include tables looking at dependency ratio, aging, fertility, child and mental immortality, life expectancy at birth, economically active population, economic development, unemployment rates, informal sector employment, poverty, income distribution, access to health services, social protection coverage, coverage of pension schemes, benefit levels, pensions, and public social security expenditure.

The volume is scattered with graphs and tables to illustrate the various points, and the reference area is adequate. This increasing globalization and trade liberalization have created greater insecurities for many individuals. This book should be of interest to people who have administrative responsibilities for these areas and also for the general public who has to live under their decisions. The report should be in all general-purpose libraries and also libraries that concentrate on labor and social security problems.—**Herbert W. Ockerman**

Asia

C

71.   **Economic and Social Survey of Asia and the Pacific 2000: Economic and Financial Monitoring and Surveillance.** New York, United Nations, 2000. 248p. $55.00pa. ISBN 92-1-119955-7. ISSN 0252-5704. S/N E.00.II.F.19.

Many of the countries of Asia and the Pacific (ESCAP region) have shown recovery from the Asian financial crisis of 1997–1998. Analysis of the recovery, together with prospects for future economic growth, comprises the central theme of *Economic and Social Survey of Asia and the Pacific 2000*, published by the United Nations. The book opens with a concise, but comprehensive, review of world economic developments, primarily for the period of 1999 and early 2000. A global perspective is a necessary background since the ESCAP region is strongly affected by outside influences. Of special importance to ESCAP are economic developments in the United States. Although the outlook for that country for 2000 is considered to be generally positive, the potential for stock market prices is mentioned as a potential negative.

The economies of countries in other regions of the world, external to ESCAP, are also considered in brief. A précis of recent economic developments in each of the ESCAP regions and in individual countries is provided. Tables containing macroeconomic data for these countries will be of value to those seeking such information and is conveniently gathered in one source. Roughly two-fifths of the text is devoted to monitoring and surveillance techniques and systems for spotting incipient problems in the ESCAP economies. However, that review would be of interest to those interested in applying similar mechanisms to other areas of the world, particularly other developing regions. By prompt and proper identification of economic problems, it is hoped that solutions will be more effective.

Among the situations discussed are reducing the hardships associated with unemployment, income for those in older age groups, and providing health care for employees. The current status of those situations in ESCAP countries is presented as well as recommendations for future improvements. An excellent bibliography of recent publications in monitoring and surveillance is also included, along with a list of previous studies in the ESCAP region from about 1957. A table of contents and a list of tables and figures are of assistance in locating materials of specific interest.—**William C. Struning**

LABOR

Career Guides

P

72.   Brommer, Gerald F., and Joseph A. Gatto. **Careers in Art: An Illustrated Guide.** 2d ed. Worcester, Mass., Davis Publications; distr., New York, Sterling Publishing, 1999. 256p. illus. index. $29.95. ISBN 0-87192-377-7.

The authors indicate that this guide is for anyone who is interested in an art career—students, teachers, curriculum specialists, guidance counselors, and parents. The introduction discusses the general career area, typical jobs, qualities needed for success in those jobs, alternate careers, college programs, and portfolios and résumés. Each of the first six chapters covers a specialized job area: environmental design, designing for communication, product and fashion design, entertainment, cultural growth and enrichment, and art services. Major job categories are discussed within those chapters.

Notable people from each field are profiled in each chapter, along with some noteworthy projects in that field. For example, chapter 1 covers environmental design and begins with a profile of Michelle Rickman, a designer for an architectural firm. This profile is followed by a definition and description of the field of architecture and an explanation of what architects do. A brief summary of the Denver Public Library project is presented next and a profile of architect Frank O. Gehry concludes the section. Sections on urban design, landscape architecture, and other careers in architecture round out the chapter.

The final chapter is called "Resources." It includes a bibliography of books, videos, and art magazines, along with a list of professional societies and organizations, Websites, and colleges and art schools. A chart profiles many U.S. and Canadian college art programs, indicating the art areas in which they excel. The book also includes an index. This work will be useful for general career collections and would probably be most useful in public and high school libraries. [R: LJ, 15 June 99, p. 68]—**Joanna M. Burkhardt**

C, P

73.　Echaore-McDavid, Susan. **Career Opportunities in Law Enforcement, Security, and Protective Services.** New York, Checkmark Books/Facts on File, 2000. 239p. index. (Career Opportunities). $35.00. ISBN 0-8160-3955-0.

This vocational guidance aid covering occupations in law enforcement and related fields will make a useful addition to career-planning collections. The main body of the work is divided into 12 sections ranging from police work, forensic investigation, private investigations, and computer security to construction inspectors and aviation security. The 70 jobs profiled range from the obvious, such as police officer or sheriff's deputy, to the more unexpected (e.g., locksmith, food inspector, plumbing inspector, lifeguard).

Individual entries provide duties, salary range, prospects, advancement, career ladder, education and training, skills, entry tips, and unions or associations. Each entry is about two 11-by-8 $\frac{1}{2}$-pages in length, with 1 or 2 slightly longer (e.g., fire fighter, security guard). All entries start with a brief summary, with more detailed text of expanded information below. The entries give a good description and idea of what occupations are about.

The clear introductory materials outline how to use the book, give sources, and make suggestions for following up interesting prospects. In addition to contents and index, there are 10 appendixes providing a variety of useful information, including Internet resources, state and federal employers and certification agencies, occupational groups, colleges and universities, a bibliography, and a glossary. The educational institutions, however, only cover those offering programs related to fields where formal training is not widely available. This book is a thorough and useful career guide that is well worth considering for employment collections. [R: LJ, 15 Mar 2000, p. 70; RUSQ, Sept 2000, p. 402]—**Nigel Tappin**

P

74.　Field, Shelly. **Career Opportunities in the Music Industry.** 4th ed. New York, Checkmark Books/Facts on File, 2000. 280p. index. (Career Opportunities Series). $45.00; $18.95pa. ISBN 0-8160-4083-4; 0-8160-4084-2pa.

The 4th edition of *Career Opportunities in the Music Industry* gives information about 86 jobs in all aspects of the music industry, including such diverse positions as artist relations and development representative, sound technician, piano tuner, opera singer, or nightclub manager. Each entry gives alternative titles, a career ladder that illustrates a normal job progression, a position description, salary ranges, employment and advancement prospects, and minimum education and training required. Entries also contain helpful advice on desired experience, skills, and personality traits; the best geographic location to find a job; valuable unions and associations; and tips for entry. These tips include suggestions on where to look for jobs (i.e., classified ads), if internships are available, and how and where to market businesses. These are particularly helpful, especially when considering that over 80 percent of the jobs described are listed as having either poor or fair job entry prospects.

There are 11 appendixes that include information such as the names and addresses of colleges and universities that offer degrees in related fields, relevant unions and associations, record companies and distributors, booking agencies, music publishers, and entertainment industry attorneys and law firms. There is also a bibliography that includes publications as recent as 1999. The major omission from this work is information regarding the use of the Internet for job searching. Although the appendix that lists unions and associations includes e-mail and homepage addresses, there could be more information throughout the book on how to take advantage of this medium. Overall, however, the book is informative and should be helpful for anyone exploring a career in the music industry. [R: LJ, 1 Sept 2000, pp. 192-194]—**Michele Russo**

C, P

75.　Fogg, Neeta P., Paul E. Harrington, and Thomas F. Harrington. **The College Majors Handbook: The Actual Jobs, Earnings, and Trends for Graduates of 60 College Majors.** Indianapolis, Ind., JIST Works, 1999. 619p. $24.95pa. ISBN 1-56370-518-4.

This volume assists individuals in making a college investment decision and choosing an undergraduate major. Several occupational degrees are described, with a comprehensive description of the nature of the field and its workplaces and workers, activities, positions, and salaries along with employment outlook projections through 2000. Much of the data are based on the *National Survey of College Graduates* (National Science Foundation, 1993) which sampled 148,000 U.S. respondents. Employment projections and analyses are from the 1998 *U.S. Bureau of Labor Statistics* and other Department of Labor publications.

An initial section on "The Importance of Career Choice" establishes a base in the psychology of career choice and its basis on assessing abilities, interests, and values. It also provides useful tools for the user to clarify these aspects personally. A second section on the economics of career choice provides a revealing look at the educational and labor market experiences of college graduates, along with employment experience and earnings data. This is the most uniquely useful section of the book in that it gives a strong reality framework for choosing an education investment. Both employability and earnings data offer a perspective to bring to this key choice for early- or mid-life career seekers.

This guide is valuable for career counselors, academic advisors, and librarians since it brings together information from several sources in a well-researched and clearly written volume. It, unfortunately, does not have an index, but the definitive organization and comprehensive table of contents will assist users.—**Barbara Conroy**

P

76. Guiley, Rosemary Ellen, and Janet Frick. **Career Opportunities for Writers.** 4th ed. New York, Facts on File, 2000. 244p. index. (Career Opportunities Series). $45.00. ISBN 0-8160-4143-1.

The 4th edition of *Career Opportunities for Writers* continues the Facts on File series designed to provide the best single source of information about jobs for all kinds of writers. Students considering a writing career will find information about entry-level jobs, while experienced writers desiring a career change can get specific information on possible employers. The book begins with an introductory essay on the outlook for employment for writers and other communicators. Individual chapters cover the mass media: newspapers and news services, magazines, television, and radio. Other chapters discuss book publishing; arts and entertainment; business communications and public relations; advertising; federal government; scholastic, academic, and nonprofit institutions and freelance services; and self-publishing. Each job listing has a quick-look heading listing the job's duties, salary range, employment prospects, and prerequisites, followed by complete information garnered from many sources, including interviews with present holders of similar positions.

The job descriptions are followed by four appendixes that list educational institutions offering undergraduate degrees in journalism and communication; useful Websites for writers; professional, industry, and trade associations and unions; and major trade periodicals. Also provided are a bibliography and an index.

Volumes like *Career Opportunities for Writers* will be most valuable to high school students and others in search of a career or seeking to make a career change. The volume is clearly written and easy to use. As with all such books, part of the material will soon be outdated, but for the foreseeable future, this volume contains much to recommend it as part of a collection of career guidance materials.—**Kay O. Cornelius**

C, P

77. Maxwell, Bruce. **Insider's Guide to Finding a Job in Washington: Contacts and Strategies to Build Your Career in Public Policy.** Washington, D.C., Congressional Quarterly, 2000. 256p. index. $29.50. ISBN 1-56802-473-8.

This career guide to job hunting in Washington, D.C., is published by a well-respected publisher of political materials. The author clearly explains the kinds of careers available in Washington as well as the process of hiring that many of the offices use. The book is divided into eight chapters, which are further divided into shorter sections. The book begins by giving tips on how to research jobs in Washington, D.C., both before one arrives and after one is in the city. It then goes on to cover how to get a Washington, D.C., internship, a congressional job, a job with a federal agency or department, a position with an interest group, a job with a trade association or labor union, or a job working with the Washington media. The chapters cover such topics as what qualities those hiring are looking for, what kind of work will be required, and the pluses and minuses of the positions. Each chapter concludes with a directory of organizations job seekers can contact. The five appendixes provide sample résumés and cover letters, a list of what college majors are appropriate for what federal job, examples of federal government vacancy announcements, a government job application, and Internet sites for government job hunting. The book concludes with a bibliography, a subject index, and a contact index.

This book will be very useful in academic libraries with strong political science departments. It will also be well received in larger public libraries.—**Shannon Graff Hysell**

P

78. Wischnitzer, Saul, and Edith Wischnitzer. **Health-Care Careers for the 21st Century.** Indianapolis, Ind., JIST Works, 2000. 436p. $24.95pa. ISBN 1-56370-667-9.

The growing and aging of the population is putting demands on the health care field and therefore providing a surplus of openings in the job market for qualified health professionals. This career guide helps those interested in pursuing a health-related career find out more about career opportunities and discover how to go about getting those jobs. Part 1 presents an overview of the field and discusses the education needed for health care positions. Part 2 discusses the skills needed to work in health-related fields and the importance between developing a trusting relationship between health care workers and patients. Part 3 deals with the job search processes, such as networking, finding job openings, and writing a résumé. Part 4, which constitutes more than one-half of the work, outlines the various job opportunities in the health care field. More than 80 careers, organized into 5 groups, are discussed here. These include diagnosing and treating practitioners, associated health-care personnel (e.g., nurses, pharmacists), adjunctive health care personnel (e.g., anesthesiologists, laboratory technicians), rehabilitative personnel (e.g., physical therapists), and affiliated personnel (e.g., health educators). Each of the 80 careers presented has information on education, a list of schools offering a degree or certificate in the area, rate of growth of career opportunities, salary range, work setting, and an overview of what the professional does on a daily basis. The five appendixes provide additional information on alternative health care careers, admissions tests, addresses for allied health professional organizations, job search resources, and Websites for health organizations.

This volume will serve as a good starting point for those seeking introductory information into health care careers. The information presented here is straightforward and easy to understand; however, more research may need to be done for those seriously considering a career choice in one of the 80 professions listed. This resource will be useful in high school and undergraduate academic libraries as well as many public libraries.

—**Shannon Graff Hysell**

C, P

79. Wolfinger, Anne. **The Quick Internet Guide to Career and Education Information.** 2000 ed. Indianapolis, Ind., JIST Works, 2000. 154p. illus. index. $16.95pa. ISBN 1-56370-622-9.

The Quick Internet Guide to Career and Education Information is an easy-to-use directory and sourcebook of career and college Internet Websites. After reading the introduction one gets the feeling this book is intended for Internet users new to the information highway. It begins with simple instructions on how to use the Internet, along with tips on which search engines to use, how to send e-mail, and e-mail etiquette. The bulk of the work is divided into nine chapters on using the Web to find information on college and financial aid, distance learning, career exploration, job openings, career clearinghouses, labor market resources, military careers, self-employment, and contract and freelance work. After a short introduction the book lists Website URLs that are intended to be useful to students or job-seekers. Each Website is given a one-paragraph summary. A seven-page glossary at the end of the book covers Internet terms such as Boolean logic, FTP, and modem. The book concludes with an index.

This Internet directory bypasses the problem of out-of-date Web addresses by supplying readers with a Website to register with for free address updates, new listings, and a newsletter from the author. At such a reasonable price, this directory will be a worthwhile purchase for both public and academic libraries.—**Shannon Graff Hysell**

Dictionaries and Encyclopedias

C, P

80. **Encyclopedia of Careers and Vocational Guidance.** 11th ed. Holli R. Cosgrove, ed. Chicago, Ferguson, 2000. 4v. illus. index. $159.95/set. ISBN 0-89434-274-6.

A long standard in career reference, the 11th edition uses much of the same information from the 10th edition (1997), but updates it with various trends and adds more career fields, notably those that have popped up in response to the Internet.

The first volume describes 91 career fields corresponding to 68 industry profiles from the 10th edition. Much of the information included in the history, structure, and outlook sections comes from the 10th edition. A new feature in the articles is a glossary sidebar to explain some of the industry's jargon. As in the last edition, each article ends with a list of associations to contact for more information. These lists have been updated and revised extensively.

For example, the article on accountants lists 4 groups to contact, only one of which was in the 10th edition. The first volume concludes with several indexes. The job title index is repeated in each of the volumes.

The remaining volumes describe 684 specific careers. Again, the text is very similar to the earlier edition, although some of the headings have changed (i.e., from "Nature of Work" to "The Job" and from "Methods of Entry" to "Starting Out") in an effort to communicate more informally.

The most obvious change in the set is the design and typeface. The print is smaller, but various type sizes, fonts, and shading are used to offset any problems in the readability of the set. Numbers are represented by numerals, not words. Black-and-white pictures are used throughout to illustrate various fields and careers. Some of the pictures are reused from the 10th edition and, in some cases, reinforce stereotypes—male boss, female secretary. One odd caption and picture in the librarian article describes a cataloger tracking the library's books and shows him flipping through a drawer full of microfiche. Surely, microfiche catalogs have not been widely used in a decade.

Clearly, there are still improvements to be made for the 12th edition, but in the meantime, the work is solid and should be part of most libraries' career collections. [R: BR, Jan/Feb 2000, pp. 74-75; Choice, April 2000, p. 1444]—**Juleigh Muirhead Clark**

Directories

C, P

81.   Crispin, Gerry, and Mark Mehler. **CareerXroads: The Directory to Job, Résumé and Career Management Sites on the Web.** 5th ed. Kendall Park, N.Y., MMC Group, 2000. 435p. illus. $26.95pa (with disc). ISBN 0-9652239-2-2.

The World Wide Web has become a great aid for those many job-seekers. There are numerous agencies, consultants, newsletters, and résumé distribution sites that are designed specifically with the job-seeker in mind. Unfortunately, with all of the resources currently available it is often confusing for those unfamiliar with how to use them and who they are designed for.

CareerXroads has the job-seeker in mind as it attempts to explain the different types of services on the World Wide Web as well as rates them. The first several short chapters of the book describe typical resources available to recruiters and job-seekers and explain how to use the directory. One of the most useful chapters is titled "Tips and Advice from Experts in the Field," which discusses such topics as Internet recruiting strategies, how to write an online job description, and preparing a scannable résumé, among other useful topics. After these short chapters there is a directory of the 500 best job and résumé sites on the World Wide Web. This section constitutes the bulk of the work. The entries are listed in alphabetical order and include the Website address, the physical address, whether they charge a fee to post or see résumés or job descriptions, the site's job specialty, and whether the site will distribute résumés to employers or jobs to job-seekers. Each of the 500 sites also has a short description that further explains how the site works. The final section lists Websites by several different categories: "Master List," "Best of the Best," "Career Management," "College," "Corporation Staffing Pages," "Diversity," "Jobs for a Fee or for Free," "Location: International and Regional," "Meta-Links," "Push" (sites that will forward a résumé or job description), "Résumés for a Fee or for Free," and "Specialty & Industry." All of the sites listed here in bold typeface are among the top 500 reviewed earlier in the book.

This book will be extremely valuable in reference collections in academic and public libraries. Because job seeking on the World Wide Web is only going to grow in popularity, there will be many patrons with questions on the topic and this resource is a wise choice to consult.—**Shannon Graff Hysell**

Handbooks and Yearbooks

P

82.   **Grievance Guide.** 10th ed. Washington, D.C., BNA Books, 2000. 464p. $55.00pa. ISBN 1-57018-217-5.

The goal of this book, which was first published in 1959, is to help both management and labor advocates understand and anticipate possible rulings in labor arbitration. While arbitration awards do not set binding precedent, most arbitrators take them into consideration. Rulings tend to follow a general pattern. In this volume, BNA tracks those general patterns in several categories: discharge and discipline (both general and specific);

safety and health; seniority and its application; leaves of absence; promotions; vacations; holidays; health and welfare benefits; management rights; union rights, strikes, and lockouts; union security; checkoff; and wages and hours. The 10th edition includes rulings in new areas such as sexual harassment, drug testing, AIDS, off-duty misconduct, and job evaluation.

In each of these categories key materials have been compiled from BNA's Labor Relations Reference File. Each category includes an overview, summaries of cases with issues and distinctions noted, a policy guide summary, and an application of policy summary with examples and guidelines.

This book is an invaluable guide for both labor and management. It provides a wide range of examples in the most common areas of grievance, giving both sides a quick reference to rulings and the rationale behind those rulings.—**Joanna M. Burkhardt**

C, P, S

83. **Occupational Outlook Handbook.** 2000-01 ed. Lanham, Md., Bernan Associates, 2000. 554p. illus. index. $49.00pa. ISBN 0-16-050250-0.

This government document, published by the Bureau of Labor Statistics, has been published on an annual basis for the last 50 years. The *Occupational Outlook Handbook* is arranged in related occupational clusters: executive, administrative, and managerial occupations; professional and technical occupations; marketing and sales; administrative support, including clerical occupations; services, mechanics, installers, and material-moving occupations; and handlers, equipment cleaners, helpers, and laborers. Each entry describes the occupation, training, and education required; advancement possibilities; earnings; job outlook; and sources of additional information from professional organizations and associations.

Career and job search information is provided through the chapters entitled "Tomorrow's Jobs." This chapter outlines projections of the labor force, economic growth, and industry and occupational employment from 1998 to 2008. The chapter titled "Sources of Career Information" lists national, state, and local information for careers, education and training programs, and financial aid information.

The *Occupational Outlook Handbook* remains the best source for up-to-date and reliable career information. This source should be a standard for schools, college and university, and public and special libraries.

—**Kay M. Stebbins**

MANAGEMENT

C, P

84. **The IEBM Dictionary of Business and Management.** Morgen Witzel, ed. London, International Thomson Business Press; distr., Albany, N.Y., Thomson Learning, 1999. 329p. $24.95pa. ISBN 1-86152-218-5.

This new dictionary is an offshoot of the publisher's six-volume *International Encyclopedia of Business and Management* (1996). With more than 7,500 terms, this is one of the most comprehensive business dictionaries available. However, the definitions are very brief—in most cases only one or two lines of text. All major areas of business are covered: accounting, economics, finance, human resource management, industrial relations, information technology, international business, management information systems, manufacturing operations, marketing, and organizational behavior. Acronyms are included, with cross-references to the definition. In the introduction, the editor, clearly identifies the limitations of the dictionary. For example, current "jargon" terms are not included, nor are those terms that are linked to specific business sectors or countries. This will be a useful edition to most business reference collections, although libraries that own Jerry Rosenberg's *Dictionary of Business and Management* (see ARBA 95, entry 187), which also contains over 7,500 terms, might not need this one.

—**Thomas A. Karel**

5 Education

GENERAL WORKS

Bibliography

C, P

85. Aby, Stephen H. and James C. Kuhn IV, comps. **Academic Freedom: A Guide to the Literature.** Westport, Conn., Greenwood Press, 2000. 225p. index. (Bibliographies and Indexes in Education, no.20). $75.00. ISBN 0-313-30386-X.

The pursuit of knowledge and truth in research, writing, and teaching is a cornerstone principle of modern higher education in the United States. It is a hard-won freedom that has often been abridged and reinterpreted. Because academic freedom has been an evolving issue and affects controversies in many sectors of higher education, the academic freedom literature may be found in a variety of disciplines. This volume provides excellent access to this literature through nearly 500 books, chapters, articles, reports, and Websites. All entries are annotated. Most of the entries are from 1948 (the date of the publication by the American Association of University Professors of the Statement of Principles on Academic Freedom and Tenure) and onward, but some older studies have also been included.

The comprehensive approach to the topic is suggested by chapters that cover philosophy, history, current issues and general trends, culture wars, religion, tenure, international activities, and World Wide Web sites. The entries are uniformly well written. Name and subject indexes round out this important volume. This work is strongly recommended for all academic libraries and for those collections that cover education and first amendment freedoms. [R: Choice, Sept 2000, p. 100]—**Arthur P. Young**

P, S

86. **Educator's Guide to Free Science Materials 2000–2001.** 41st ed. Kathleen Suttles Nehmer, ed. Randolph, Wis., Educators Progress Service, 2000. 233p. index. $33.95pa. ISBN 0-87708-339-8.

The fact that the 2000–2001 version of this book is in its 41st annual edition is an indicator of its acceptance by the educational community. The version reviewed here is for science, but there are 14 other subjects as well. Resources listed include a broad range of items classroom teachers find useful and interesting: information sheets, charts, posters, booklets, brochures, film strips and films, videos (to both borrow and keep), replicas of uranium fuel pellets, and even a rocket kit. They are accessible by mail, by telephone, and by Website, where many can be downloaded directly. Some are even available as classroom sets. Front matter includes an introduction and useful information about interacting with sponsors to obtain and evaluate information. The body of the text is an alphabetic listing by title of materials arranged within nine categories: aerospace education, biology, chemistry, environmental education, general science, lesson plans, nature study, physics, and teacher reference. Each entry includes a short description, availability, appropriate grade level, running time (for films, videos, and such), date, terms (such as "borrower pays return postage"), and how to contact the source. The book is user-friendly, with indexes provided by title, subject, source, and "What's New."

The instability of sources of free materials can by measured by the fact that of 1,147 entries in this edition more than 618 are new and, conversely, over 600 of the entries in last year's edition are no longer available. To help deal with this problem, the editors contact each entry annually to ensure the availability of their resources. New items are highlighted within the listings. Although the list is updated, some of the resources are not; some 16mm films are over 30 years old.

The book is an excellent resource, as far as it goes. A complete listing of every free teacher resource for science would be too expensive and thick to produce; and it would be out-of-date by the time it was completed. The *Educator's Guide* is a great place to begin, but teachers should be aware of many other sources as well.

This book could be one of the most significant expenditures a science department could make. A science department, at any grade level (kindergarten through college), could make excellent use of this resource. The two biggest drawbacks might be finding the time to access all the sources and finding a place to store the materials when they arrive.—**Craig A. Munsart**

C, P, S

87.   O'Brien, Nancy Patricia. **Education: A Guide to Reference and Information Sources.** 2d ed. Englewood, Colo., Libraries Unlimited, 2000. 189p. index. (Reference Sources in the Social Sciences Series). $37.50. ISBN 1-56308-626-3.

This 2d edition is a decade apart from the 1st edition. Sources in this guide include items published from 1990 through 1998. It updates the 1st edition with more recent information while maintaining the same purpose— that is, to provide information about the key reference and information resources in the field of education. One of the significant differences between the 1st and 2d editions of this guide is the type of material selected for inclusion. Besides the inclusion of Internet resources that were not available when the 1st edition was published, many journal titles are being listed in this guide due to the increasing reliance on journals as a source of information.

The guide is divided into 14 categories based on the different aspects of education, such as general education sources, educational technology and media, higher education, and multilingual and multicultural education. Special education, career and vocational education, comparative and international education, and educational administration and management are also covered. Under each category, the resources are arranged by material type, including bibliographies; dictionaries and encyclopedias; directories and almanacs; guides, handbooks, and yearbooks; indexes and abstracts; statistical sources; World Wide Web and Internet sources; journals; and biographies. Each entry provides not only a description of the source, but also a summary of the contents. Author, title, and subject indexes are listed at the end of this guide, which add more access points to this well-compiled sourcebook. The guide is for librarians, faculty, students, and researchers who are seeking information on every aspect of education. [R: TL, Dec 2000, p. 44]—**Xiao (Shelley) Yan Zhang**

Directories

P, S

88.   **Educational Opportunity Guide 2000: A Directory of Programs for the Gifted.** Durham, N.C., Duke University Talent Identification Program, 2000. 317p. index. $15.00pa. ISBN 0-9639756-6-8.

This Duke University Talent Identification Program publication is especially beneficial to parents, teachers, administrators, and mature gifted students. More than 400 programs for talented youths are featured in a state-by-state arrangement. The 2000 edition of the *Educational Opportunity Guide* provides information on both academic year and summer programs and highlights opportunities for significant student challenges in the fine arts, science, math, computers, and governor's schools as well as outdoor and wilderness camps and international travel-study experiences. Two bonus features are state and national contacts for advocacy of gifted students and descriptions of academic competitions and activities. Each entry provides critical data such as program name, geographic location, dates of operation, admissions criteria, cost, applicable grade levels, financial aid, and contact information.

The majority of the program entry descriptions are sufficient to provide parents, mentors, and middle and secondary students with enough information that wise enrollment decisions can be made. One of the chief values of the directory is that it provides information not within easy reach of most readers. For example, information on the Junior Statesman Summer School Program at Yale University and the Minority Introduction to Engineering

Program at the United States Coast Guard Academy are highlighted. *Educational Opportunity Guide 2000* yields a fine, comprehensive overview of diverse, challenging, and exciting programs for gifted students of all ages.

—**Jerry D. Flack**

P, S

89. **The Handbook of Private Schools.** 80th ed. Boston, Porter Sargent Publishers, 1999. 1336p. illus. index. $95.00. ISBN 0-87558-140-4. ISSN 0072-9884.

A directory of private K-12 schools can be valuable both to parents of school-age children and to prospective teachers. This handbook includes descriptions of more than 1,500 independent schools in all 50 states, with descriptions ranging from single to multiple paragraphs. The book is arranged into three major sections: "Leading Private Schools," "Private Schools Illustrated," and "Concise Listing of Schools." "Leading Private Schools" includes detailed descriptions of almost 800 schools. These entries are grouped by one of eight regions of the country, then by state, and then alphabetically by city and school. For each school users can find typical directory information, as well as Web addresses, e-mail contacts, enrollment, endowment, tuition, size of the physical plant, number of teachers, and recent graduation numbers, among other details. In addition, there is a paragraph or more description that often focuses on the school's founding, curriculum, and extra curricular activities.

"Private Schools Illustrated" includes, for over 200 schools, multipage announcements that have been provided and paid for by the school. These entries are grouped according to categories for coeducation schools, girls' schools, boys' schools, the underachiever, and schools abroad. The final section, "Concise Listing of Schools," provides briefer descriptions, with some of the same directory information, for 760 additional schools. These entries are arranged by categories for boarding and day schools, then by region and state. There are supplemental indexes not only to the schools and display advertisements, but also to support agencies and firms, such as educational consultants, insurers, fundraisers, teacher agencies, and others.

The schools identified here are, by and large, fairly expensive with tuition generally ranging from $4,000 to over $20,000 per year. While some may offer scholarship support, this directory is nonetheless for a more affluent clientele. Parochial or religious-affiliated schools are included selectively, although no criterion is given. Still, this annual is an excellent source for both public libraries and for colleges with teacher education programs.

—**Stephen H. Aby**

Handbooks and Yearbooks

P, S

90. **School Violence.** Denise M. Bonilla, ed. Bronx, N.Y., H. W. Wilson, 2000. 258p. index. (The Reference Shelf, v.72, no.1). $35.00pa. ISBN 0-8242-0982-6.

The 34 documents in this collection explore the current phenomenon of violence in U.S. schools—its nature, causes, effects, and possible prevention. They are primarily reprints of articles from newspapers and magazines that are popular rather than scholarly in nature but, nevertheless, are considered reliable, authoritative, and objective (e.g., *U.S. News and World Report*, *The Nation*, *The New York Times*). Each article averages three or four pages in length. Only one lists sources used in the article's preparation. The original publication dates of these selections range from mid-1998 through the beginning of 2000. Many were inspired by or a reaction to the tragic shootings at Columbine High School in Littleton, Colorado, in April 1999.

The work is divided into five parts, with each containing five to nine articles plus an introduction by the editor that summarizes the contents and point of view of each selection. The first section contains general articles on the various types of school violence, their frequency, and their perpetrators. The second and largest section examines possible explanations for school violence, such as lack of gun control; video games; lack of parental responsibility; and psychological, gender, and biological factors. The third discusses the effects of school violence on such areas as gun legislation and stricter legal policies regarding behavior and their impact on individual rights. The fourth looks at the role of the media in reporting incidence of violence and related issues like accuracy and bias. The last examines violence in higher education, including the problems related to hazing by campus organizations. The book concludes with a 2-page bibliography of books, a section containing abstracts of about 40 related articles, and a single author/subject index.

Because of its comprehensiveness, authority, and depth this is certainly an outstanding reference on this timely topic and should be valuable in reference collections in high school as well as college and public libraries. Although Deborah L. Kopka's *School Violence* (see ARBA 98, entry 277) bears the same title, it complements rather than duplicates the material in Bonilla's work. It is basically a resource manual with annotated lists of organization and print sources, a review of programs and agencies state-by-state, plus chronologies and biographical sketches. Both are welcome additions to library collections needing material on this topic.—**John T. Gillespie**

COMPUTER RESOURCES

P, S

91.   **Educator's Guide to Free Computer Materials & Internet Resources 2000–2001.** 18th ed. Kathleen Suttles Nehmer, ed. Randolph, Wis., Educators Progress Service, 2000. 352p. index. $39.95pa. ISBN 0-87708-332-0.

Using the Internet effectively has become a new concern for teachers at every grade level. How can the busy classroom teacher find time to locate Websites in the subject being taught or discover Websites that offer unusual resources? The *Educator's Guide to Free Computer Materials & Internet Resources 2000–2001* provides more than 1,900 resources on the Internet in 16 curriculum areas at levels pre-K to adult. Areas of interest to the teaching professional, such as computer education, going online, lesson plans, programming, teacher reference sources on the Web, Web design, and desktop publishing, are an additional bonus.

Each entry is listed by subject and then its practical use in the classroom is described. For example, a teacher trying to enrich a unit on the American Indian will be able to find sites describing the Cherokee and Inuit languages, the Native Olympic games, totem poles and their stories, buffalo-skin art, and 17 additional Native American sites. Who should use the site, suggested grade level, format, e-mail address, and a source complete the entry. There are 1,200 new sites for this edition and new entries are marked. All entries are indexed by title, subject, and source, with a "What's New" section completing the book.

The *Educator's Guide to Free Computer Materials & Internet Resources* will be a practical addition to the elementary and high school library, department resource collection, computer laboratory, and individual classroom teacher. Teachers can use the guide effectively to find sites that will enrich their own teaching and as a source for students in their classroom.—**Carol D. Henry**

P, S

92.   Heide, Ann, and Linda Stilborne. **The Teacher's Complete & Easy Guide to the Internet.** 2d ed. Toronto, Trifolium Books, 1999. 354p. index. $29.95pa. (w/CD-ROM). ISBN 0-8077-3779-8.

This update of an award-winning guide, a favorite for teachers everywhere, is as well done as its predecessor was. *The Teacher's Complete & Easy Guide to the Internet* is an invaluable resource in this era of growing enthusiasm for use of the Internet as a teaching tool. Experienced Web-surfers can find many new ideas in these pages, while the information is presented clearly enough for a neophyte to feel comfortable venturing into this new realm. Each chapter is a blueprint for teaching, containing ideas from successful teachers for employing the Internet with the students, creating lesson plans with goals and objectives, as well as providing "teaching tips" to help avoid the pot holes that lurk on the information highway.

There are project ideas explained, suggestions for designing other projects, and addresses of Websites that are helpful in the projects or that demonstrate similar work completed by other classes. Other parts of the volume contain equally valuable information on technology, acceptable use policies, and Web publishing.

Included with the book is an accompanying CD-ROM. This valuable resource contains more than 1,000 live educational links, a beginner's help file, and lesson plan links. Often books containing directories of Internet addresses are of questionable value due to the ephemeral nature of so many links. However, the other information and helpful material in this guide make it an extremely useful tool for today's teacher. This title is recommended for the reference or circulating collections of any library that serves teachers.—**Nancy P. Reed**

P, S

93.   McElmeel, Sharron L., and Carol Smallwood. **WWW Almanac: Making Curriculum Connections for Special Days, Weeks, and Months.** Worthington, Ohio, Linworth, 1999. 218p. index. (Professional Growth Series). $34.95pa. ISBN 0-938865-78-1.

Librarians and teachers will find this a practical, useful resource for using the World Wide Web to investigate special days, explore issues, and discover information about authors. Organized by month, the user can browse in search of a familiar holiday, such as New Year's Day. When January gets cold and snowy, the students might enjoy observing National Soup Month.

Professionals in year-round schools will appreciate the abundance of opportunities during the summer, such as American Rivers Month in June, Space Week in July, and Friendship Day in August. Although Websites for Day of the Dead are missing, there is a sample of cultural observations—Black History Month, Native American Month, Yom Kippur, and Kwanzaa, to name a few.

The final chapter, "Quick Links," proves especially useful. It includes links for the states, presidential birthdays, and authors. Lists are presented twice: chronologically and alphabetically. A lengthy, detailed index completes this economical supplement. One can only hope the authors are already working on an updated edition for next year. [R: SLJ, July 2000, p. 131; TL, Dec 2000, p. 45]—**Suzanne I. Barchers**

C, P, S

94.   Miller, Elizabeth B. **The Internet Resource Directory for K-12 Teachers and Librarians.** 2000/2001 ed. Englewood, Colo., Libraries Unlimited, 2000. 462p. index. $27.50pa. ISBN 1-56308-839-8.

Published annually, this directory presents a sample of some of the best Internet resources for educators, school library media specialists, students, and parents. All entries are selective and evaluative, rather than comprehensive. Resources are organized by curriculum areas. Annotated entries help users determine the more useful resources for their specific information needs and suggest ways to integrate resources into the curriculum. Libraries Unlimited provides monthly updates to all entries on their Website (http://www.lu.com). Each month, all URL addresses in the directory will be checked, with any changes noted. This directory is designed to help educators plan lessons that are enriched with up-to-date and accurate online information that complements and enhances traditional information resources. It can also be used by parents and students. Students can learn from experts, tap into major library collections and scientific databases, and communicate with other students around the world. The directory is divided into 11 chapters, each addressing a different area of the K-12 curriculum. Two chapters contain professional information as well as lesson plans and general information specific to education, K-12 schools, and the school library media center. The "Reference" chapter focuses on resources that can be used across the curriculum. Included are resources for educators, the arts, computer science, foreign language studies, language arts, mathematics, science, applied arts and sciences, social studies and geography, reference, and the school library. Overall, this is an excellent resource for discovering and using Internet resources in the field of education.—**Janet Mongan**

ELEMENTARY AND
SECONDARY EDUCATION

S

95.   **Random House Webster's Student Notebook Writers' Guide.** New York, Random House, 2000. 90p. $4.99pa. ISBN 0-375-71951-2.

This work will be a perfect addition to any middle or high school library. With its inexpensive price and easy-to-understand text it will serve many students with questions about the English language and authorship. The work covers such topics as parts of speech; phrases and clauses; how to construct sentences; how to relate a shift in tense, voice, or mood; words that are commonly misused and misspelled; rules of punctuation; how to write a research paper; and how to prepare citations. The layout of the work is straightforward and the text is easy to understand—just the kind of thing student's need while writing a paper. On the inside of the front cover and the back cover there are citation styles for both the MLA style and the APA style. This work will be useful for both students and teachers at the middle and high school levels.—**Shannon Graff Hysell**

C, P

96.   Weil, Danny. **Charter Schools: A Reference Handbook.** Santa Barbara, Calif., ABC-CLIO, 2000. 211p. index. (Contemporary Education Issues). $45.00. ISBN 1-57607-245-2.

     While not truly a reference book, Weil has written an excellent introduction to charter schools, including how they are distinguished from and compare to other educational innovations and reforms; controversies that surround the charter school concept; how the concept has been implemented in various settings; and organizations, agencies, and sources of information on this topic. An introduction, a chronology, and a list of selected resources are included, along with chapters on curriculum and instructional approaches; charter schools and the law; politics and the charter school challenge; teachers' unions and charter schools; and organizations, associations, and government agencies. These chapters cover the major subtopics that undergraduates are likely to be interested in. Appendixes include a comparison of state standard development and charter school requirements, lists of state testing requirements and admissions policies, and a discussion of teacher professionalism. Sections are succinct and well written. The wealth of information and Weil's evenhanded discussion of the issues involved in developing and administering charter schools makes this a particularly valuable book for students beginning their research in this area. It is recommended for circulating collections in all libraries serving education undergraduate programs.—**Rosanne M. Cordell**

P, S

97.   Whiteley, Sandy, comp., with Kim Summers and Sally M. Walker. **The Teacher's Calendar School Year 2000–2001: The Day-by-Day Directory to Holidays, Historic Events, Birthdays and Special Days....** Chicago, Contemporary Books, 2000. 268p. illus. index. $19.95pa. ISBN 0-8092-2521-2.

     This book is a treasure trove of useful information. Beginning with August and ending in July, this thorough and practical resource provides teachers, school librarians, and public librarians with an invaluable guide to a wide variety of events. The calendar covers presidential proclamations; national holidays and state days; religious observances; historic events; birth anniversaries; astronomical phenomena; sponsored events; and various special days, weeks, and months.

     Many entries are brief, giving just enough information to inspire educators or students to research the entry more fully. Other entries include contacts, addresses, Websites, and the like. Sidebars that provide more detail and curricular recommendations range from topics such as National Inventors Month to the anniversary of Mark Mcwire's 70 home runs. The authors waste no space, even using the inside cover to explain how to use the book. The appendixes are particularly rich, featuring lists such as religious calendars, a perpetual calendar, facts about the states, facts about Canada, facts about the presidents, abbreviations, book awards, and a bibliography. The impressive index—nearly 24 pages long—makes this a user-friendly resource.

     School librarians and teachers should not delay in purchasing this book, even if the year is well under way. Most of the information will be useful for several years. However, it is hoped the compiler will update it annually.

—**Suzanne I. Barchers**

HIGHER EDUCATION

Directories

P, S

98.   **Barron's Best Buys in College Education.** 6th ed. By Lucia Solórzano. Hauppauge, N.Y., Barron's Educational Series, 2000. 756p. index. $16.95pa. ISBN 0-7641-1345-3.

     Choosing a college is a big decision, both academically and financially. With several thousand institutions to select from and an average tuition fee of about $15,400 (1999–2000), the choice is difficult. The choice will be much better, claims the editor of this guide, if readers utilize their book to find the "best buys" in American undergraduate education. They identify 282 such institutions and for each they present a 2- to 3-page profile, covering tuition and other fees, student body composition, academic programs and facilities, and campus life. The institutional profiles also include the more substantive but very intriguing indications of "rate of return" (percentage of dropouts); "payoff" (what percentage of students did what after graduating); and "bottom line" (summary, conclusions, and advice to prospective enrollees).

Barron's Best Buys has been published every two years since 1990; this is the 6th edition. Such frequency of publications suggests that, whatever doubts the reader may have about the editors' ability to accurately determine the best buys in college educations, their book has been a success in that it continues to find a large audience. It is now the well-established authority in its field and the modest price makes each new edition worth getting. For the 1.5 million students making a choice of college, *Barron's* is itself a "best buy."—**Samuel Rothstein**

C, P

99.   **Barron's Guide to Graduate Business Schools.** 11th ed. By Eugene Miller. Hauppauge, N.Y., Barron's Educational Series, 1999. 812p. index. $16.95pa. ISBN 0-7641-0846-8.

Barron's profiles more than 630 U.S. and Canadian schools that offer graduate business programs in this guide. Each profile states the school's name, address, telephone number, admission contact, Web address, and a short institutional history. The student body statistics include the school's retention rate, while the faculty section describes credentials and average class size. The library and computer lab facilities are discussed. Monetary factors are enumerated in the sections on cost and financial aid. Academics are covered in the sections on admissions, programs offered, course requirements, and average GMAT of accepted applicants. The placement section states the number of companies recruiting on campus, the degrees most in demand, the average and the range of starting salaries, and the percentage of graduates employed within three months of graduation. Preceding the profiles is a sample GMAT, a narrative about pursuing an MBA, and how to choose an institution to fit one's needs. This is a must-have resource for any library that has patrons who are considering graduate business studies.
—**Holly Dunn Coats**

C, P

100.   **Barron's Guide to Law Schools.** 14th ed. Hauppauge, N.Y., Barron's Educational Series, 2000. 566p. index. $16.95pa. ISBN 0-7641-1396-8. ISSN 1062-2489.

This guide delivers a great deal more than its title suggests. There are nine introductory chapters by Pace University law professor Gary A. Munneke under the general rubric "Choosing a Law School." These cover topics such as deciding whether to enter the legal profession, types of courses to take as an undergraduate, what the law school experience is like, career opportunities in law, and trends affecting the practice of law.

Following that is a section on the Law School Admission Test, including sample questions. The largest section provides profiles of individual ABA-approved law schools (schools not approved by ABA are covered briefly at the end). The information is presented both in tabular form, to facilitate quick comparisons, and in two-page spreads for each school. The coverage is thorough and logically organized; of particular interest are the statistics on each school's placement record. Regional maps showing school locations are also helpful—except that the University of Maryland is shown at College Park rather than Baltimore. Overall, this is a splendid and inexpensive guide to the process of preparing for legal education that all academic and public libraries ought to acquire.
—**Jack Ray**

C, P

101.   **Barron's Guide to Medical and Dental Schools.** 9th ed. By Saul Wischnitzer and Edith Wischnitzer. Hauppauge, N.Y., Barron's Educational Series, 2000. 625p. index. $18.95pa. (w/CD-ROM). ISBN 0-7641-7375-8.

Barron's Guide to Medical and Dental Schools is now in its 9th edition. This edition also includes a CD-ROM designed to create personalized contact lists that match individual preferences and test scores to the college profiles included in the guide. The real strength of this resource is the vocational guidance and background information essays included in the introductory section and chapters interspersed throughout the guide. About two-thirds of the 600-plus pages of the guide provide career guidance, demographics for the fields, high school and college preparation, testing requirements and sample MCAT questions, information on the application process, admission, and financing a medical education.

Special sections address concerns of women and minorities entering medicine or dentistry. The text is readable and engaging, and the authors have thoughtfully considered all aspects of entering medical school and planning a medical career. Essays are often supported by research, such as in the essay on rejection, which provides encouraging advice on alternatives and statistics from a research study that found that many rejected applicants do eventually achieve their goal to pursue a medical career.

Appendixes include worksheets to self evaluate readiness for medical school and a medical career, sample application materials and essays, lists of professional organizations and Websites, and forms to stay on schedule through college and organize the time consuming and detailed process of applying to medical or dental schools. Any library serving community members or high school and undergraduate students considering medical or dental careers will find this a useful publication.—**Lynne M. Fox**

P, S
102. **Barron's Profiles of American Colleges 2001.** 24th ed. Hauppauge, N.Y., Barron's Educational Series, 2000. 1622p. index. $25.00pa. (w/CD-ROM). ISBN 0-7641-7294-8. ISSN 1065-5026.

This 24th edition of *Barron's Profiles of American Colleges* includes data from nearly 1,700 accredited colleges and universities in the United States and Canada. More than 1,300 pages in this 1,622-page volume consists of 1,000-word entries on each of the institutions of higher learning. The entries, which are arranged alphabetically by state of institution, include brief statements about some 20 items dealing with college and student life. These categories include such areas as housing, sports, programs of study, admission standards, financial aid, computer facilities, and graduation rates. At the top of each entry is a box that contains statistical information, such as the school's enrollment, student and faculty ratios, entrance examination scores, academic reputation, and tuition and room and board expenses. The statistical data for these entries was collected during the fall of 1999.

Barron's Profiles of American Colleges also includes about 300 pages of miscellaneous information that is designed to assist prospective students with the selection and application process. A section on finding financial aid is also included. This volume comes with a CD-ROM for Windows and Macintosh that includes brief profiles on the schools and computerized help with the preparation of application forms and letters.

Although this volume is cumbersome, it contains a wealth of information that will both assist and bewilder those prospective high school graduates who are searching for the college of their dreams. The book, complete with CD-ROM, is well worth its $25 price tag.—**Terry D. Bilhartz**

C, P
103. **College Blue Book.** 27th ed. [CD-ROM]. New York, Macmillan Reference USA/Gale Group, 1999. Minimum system requirements: IBM or compatible 486. CD-ROM drive. Windows 95. 16MB RAM. SVGA monitor. $250.00. ISBN 0-02-865306-8.

This valuable reference tool continues a tradition of high quality coupled with ease of use, and continues to be a mainstay resource for counselors, librarians, and students. Compiled here are the responses from 18,000 questionnaires sent to colleges; universities; community and junior colleges; trade, technical, and proprietary schools; state departments of education; and all sources that provide financial aid scholarships for students.

From the main page, users have the option of searching any of three main categories: colleges, occupational schools, or scholarships. Users can search by city, state, region, type, cost, major, general areas of study, or a straight alphabetical listing. Occupational schools can be searched in the same fashion. Scholarships can be searched by key terms, level of study or general area of study, or alphabetically by name.

Profiles of institutions include a directory of information, a general description, entrance requirements, annual costs, collegiate and community environments, deadlines, enrollment figures, housing information, library holdings, degrees conferred, and a variety of other brief information that might be of use to a prospective student. Scholarship entries include address and contact information; number, amount, and type of award; eligibility requirements; and appropriate additional information. Tips for advanced searching and printing, and a variety of help screens are available to assist the user.

This product is highly recommended for the breadth of useful information provided, and for ease of use. It should be in every academic, public, and high school library.—**Edmund F. SantaVicca**

C, P, S
104. **Higher Education Directory, 2000.** Mary Pat Rodenhouse and Constance Healy Torregrosa, eds. Falls Church, Va., Higher Education Publications; distr., Lanham, Md., Bernan Associates, 2000. 812p. index. $57.00pa. ISBN 0-914927-29-9. ISSN 0736-0797.

This annual publication, which began in 1983, contains basic information on postsecondary, degree-granting institutions accredited by national, regional, professional, and specialized agencies recognized as accrediting bodies by the U.S. Secretary of Education and by the former Council on Postsecondary Accreditation/Commission on Recognition of Postsecondary Accreditation. Descriptions are based on information gathered in 1999. It includes such institution changes as additions, deletions, mergers, and name changes.

Four indexes—key administrators, accrediting bodies, Federal Interagency Commission on Education (FICE) number, and school name—are cross-referenced to the main institutional listing arranged by state, territory, or possession of the United States. Information provided about each institution includes Carnegie Classification, contact information, size, calendar system, programs offered, accreditation, FICE number, and names of administrators. E-mail addresses have been added for administrators who chose to have them included.

An academic reference librarian could expect to use this source on a regular basis. The price makes it affordable.
—**Lois Gilmer**

P, S

105.   Oldman, Mark, and Samer Hamadeh. **The Best 106 Internships.** 8th ed. New York, Princeton Review/ Random House, 2000. 406p. $21.00pa. ISBN 0-375-75637-X. ISSN 1073-5801.

According to the authors, internships have gone from a résumé-enhancing tool to their current status as an essential stepping stone to career success. Further, more college students are interning than ever before. If this is indeed so, then an informative guide to securing the internship that is right for the individual is truly needed. This guide is written by two highly educated and experienced people who are nationally recognized experts on the subject. They state in the introduction that not all internships are created equal and present a set of criteria that were used to discern the best internships "from the duds." For those who are exploring internships, these criteria alone help to clarify the value of a good internship.

It seems that finding the right internship has many of the same tasks as finding the right college program—it requires a commitment of time for both the research and the application process. This volume can be of great assistance in both areas. Each of the 106 entries provides easy-to-read information on selectivity, compensation, quality of life, location, field, duration of the internship, prerequisites for the internship, deadlines, and the most important "busywork meter" icon. Addresses are also given for obtaining further information. Please note that there are 32 appendixes covering everything an applicant might want to know, such as if casual dress is allowed, internships with minority programs, internships by interest, and good prospects for permanent employment.

The 106 internship programs included in this resource provide more than 20,000 internship opportunities. The top 10 internships for 2001 are Academy of Television Art & Sciences, The Coro Foundation, CNN, Hewlett-Packard, Inroads, Northwestern Mutual Financial Network, Proctor & Gamble, Summerbridge National, The Supreme Court of the United States, and the *Washington Post*. These 10 companies offer about 4,500 internship positions. The industrious and selective student should be able to learn a great deal about internships from this reference book and more than likely obtain a first-class internship.—**Karen D. Harvey**

Financial Aid

C, P

106.   Blum, Laurie. **Free Money for Graduate School.** 4th ed. New York, Checkmark Books/Facts on File, 2000. 298p. index. $35.00. ISBN 0-8160-4278-0.

This volume delivers a concise, user-friendly, and reasonably priced resource that provides information on more than 1,000 grants and scholarships for graduate study. The author begins with a brief, straightforward, and commonsense introduction, covering the basics of searching for funding for graduate education. This small and useful reference is divided into the major broad categories of academic study and the index lists more specific subject categories or academic disciplines. Sections also include sources of funding for special groups, including women, ethnic minorities, and foreign nationals, as well as information regarding study and research abroad.

The format of the entries is convenient, with the address, telephone number, and Website address listed for each funding organization. Entries include a brief description of the award, restrictions, dollar amount, application information, deadline, and contact name. An industrious graduate student who is seeking financial support has the information needed to follow through.

The expenses associated with graduate education are escalating. Tuition, books, computers, and the general cost of student living require financial assistance for nearly all students. And, although any assistance is always helpful, it almost seems that the student needs to search for the more substantial grants or scholarships—books alone usually cost more money than a significant number of the entries provide.—**Karen D. Harvey**

P, S

107.   Clark, Andy, and Amy Clark. Breslow, Karen, ed. **Athletic Scholarships: Thousands of Grants—and over $400 Million—for College-Bound Athletes.** 4th ed. New York, Checkmark Books/Facts on File, 2000. 338p. index. $35.00. ISBN 0-8160-4308-6.

This book could be worth thousands of dollars to the right readers. High school students (of both sexes) with athletic ability and adequate grades can obtain substantial college and university scholarships if they know how and where to apply. *Athletic Scholarships* will provide them with the necessary guidance.

The introduction leads readers through the application process and includes suggestions on how to prepare résumés, how to write letters (samples provided), and, most importantly, how to make the best impression on coaches and recruiters. Next, there are state-by-state listings of the institutions, which show what scholarships are available and provide directory information. The last part lists the academic institutions by sport, which is particularly useful when a sport is less common, such as badminton, racquetball, or riflery.

The fact that this book is in its 4th edition is strong evidence of its intrinsic value. It also has clear typeface, a sturdy binding, and a reasonable price.—**Samuel Rothstein**

P

108.   **GrantFinder: The Complete Guide to Postgraduate Funding Worldwide, Social Sciences.** New York, St. Martin's Press, 2000. 504p. index. $40.00. ISBN 0-312-22894-5. ISSN 1526-0909.

Derived from *The Grants Register 2000* (see ARBA 2000, entry 258), this directory provides key information needed to identify and apply for approximately 1,000 postgraduate grants in the social sciences. These grants, from organizations in dozens of countries, can be applied toward such activities as graduate study, post-doctoral work, professional development, and research.

The volume is divided into four sections: Grants, Subject and Eligibility Guide to Awards, Index of Awards, and Index of Awarding Organizations. The section on grants is arranged alphabetically by the names of the granting organizations. For each organization there is an address, phone number, fax number, e-mail address, Web address, and contact name, as well as a brief description of the organization. Following this are descriptions of the organization's grants, arranged alphabetically. Each grant description includes the subject areas covered, eligibility requirements, level of study, purpose, type of grant, number of awards, frequency of award, value of the grant, length of study, country of study, application procedure, closing date, and additional information. The guide to awards by subject and eligibility lists grants by broad subject category and subcategory, then by geographic restrictions on the grants. The indexes to awards and awarding organizations are straight alphabetical listings by award name and organization name, respectively.

Two issues are worth noting in evaluating this source. First, it duplicates a subset of entries found in the parent volume, *The Grants Register 2000*. If users own that volume, there is no need to buy this derivative volume. Alternatively, a library could selectively purchase some of the specific volumes (i.e., social sciences, science, medicine, and arts and humanities) at $40 each and spend less than the cost of the parent volume at $125. Second, this volume claims to be a "complete guide to postgraduate funding" in the social sciences. However, without any indication of how this comprehensiveness is achieved, users may not want to rely exclusively on this directory. That said, *GrantFinder* is useful, well organized, and recommended for public and academic libraries.

—**Stephen H. Aby**

P, S

109.   Leider, Anna. **The A's and B's of Academic Scholarships.** 22d ed. Alexandria, Va., Octameron, 2000. 191p. $9.00pa. ISBN 1-57509-057-0.

Many colleges try to woo good students with merit-based scholarships. This directory lists only such awards given by colleges themselves, and not those made by other organizations. It claims to cover 1,200 colleges and 100,000 awards.

The arrangement is alphabetical by state, and then by the names of individual schools. All the information is in tables and mostly provided by codes and abbreviations. It is necessary to read the introductory material carefully to figure out what it all means. But this format has enabled the publisher to pack a lot of useful information about the size of awards, eligibility, other criteria, and restrictions into a compact work. An opening section provides information on what academic scholarships are and how they differ from need-based financial aid. There are also useful tips on how to qualify for them and other financial packages. This is a useful college-planning tool at a reasonable price. It complements other college directories.—**Christine E. King**

P, S

110.   Schlachter, Gail Ann. **Directory of Financial Aids for Women 1999–2001.** El Dorado Hills, Calif., Reference Service Press, 1999. 568p. index. $45.00. ISBN 0-918276-80-2.

This title (whose earlier edition was reviewed in ARBA 99, entry 773) remains a well-organized, comprehensive, and easy-to-use guide for women seeking financial aid for undergraduate to postgraduate studies. Information on over 1,700 scholarships, fellowships, loans, grants, personal grants-in-aid, awards, and internships designed primarily or exclusively for women is given in the directory. The main section describes each funding source and lists sponsoring agency, address, purpose, eligibility, financial data, duration, limitations, number awarded, and deadline. Programs that supply more than one type of assistance are listed in all relevant subsections. The directory also provides indexes by program title, sponsoring agency, residency, tenability, subject, and calendar along with brief instructions for optimal use of each index.

The introductory section is quite thorough. Besides providing the obligatory purpose and sample entry explanation, it includes the extent of updating in this edition (it was completely updated with every item checked before inclusion), plans to update the directory in two years, and a list of other related publications. This work is highly recommended for all public, high school, and college libraries. [R: Choice, Feb 2000, p. 1075; C&RL News, April 2000, p. 323]—**Michele Russo**

P

111.   Schlachter, Gail Ann, and R. David Weber. **Financial Aid for African Americans 1999–2001.** El Dorado Hills, Calif., Reference Service Press, 1999. 516p. index. $37.50. ISBN 0-918276-76-4.

The new edition of this work reflects the addition of 300 new entries and the revision and updating of 75 percent of the continuing programs listed. It is part of a four-volume set on minority funding that includes separate volumes on Asian, Hispanic, and Native American funding sources. This work is intended for students in high school as well as those interested in graduate and professional development, counselors, librarians, and researchers. It is a convenient one-volume source for funding opportunities.

There is a detailed introduction that describes how information was gathered through mail and phone calls, and how to use the directory to locate information on 356 scholarships, 325 fellowships, 50 loans, 448 grants, 74 awards, and 237 internships. The main section of the work contains entries arranged by the type of financial aid, and then within the section it is alphabetically arranged by the title of the program. Listings include an entry number, information on whom to contact, address, telephone number, and a Website address. There is also a description of the purpose of the program, who's eligible and what criteria they need to meet, financial data about the award's amount and time frame, duration of the program, any special features or items to note, any limitations on the award, the number of awards given out during a certain time frame, and the deadline for application. An annotated bibliography of about 57 general financial aid sources, subdivided into the different types of financial aid, is also provided. There are several very useful indexes arranged alphabetically. Indexes for program title and sponsoring organization are coded to reflect the type of financial aid category the program falls within and the entry number. A residency index identifies the residency requirements of a program and is arranged alphabetically by corresponding city, state, province, region, country, and continent, and then is subdivided by type of financial aid with *see also* references provided. A tenability index identifies the geographic region where the program may be used and is also arranged alphabetically by corresponding city, state, province, region, country, and continent, and then subdivided by type of financial aid with *see also* references provided. The subject index is alphabetically arranged by subject or program emphasis with *see* and *see also* references. The calendar index is arranged by type of financial aid and then chronologically by month, including those that can be applied for at any time.

This work is a very valuable and useful standard for those seeking a comprehensive collection of financial aid sources for African Americans. It is recommended for all libraries. [R: Choice, Feb 2000, p. 1075]—**Jan S. Squire**

P, S

112.   Schlachter, Gail Ann, and R. David Weber. **High School Senior's Guide to Merit and Other No-Need Funding 2000–2002.** El Dorado Hills, Calif., Reference Service Press, 2000. 400p. index. $27.95. ISBN 0-918276-87-X.

Written for the many high school seniors whose family income is too high to meet financial need–based scholarship requirements, but who lack sufficient funds to pay for a college education (and for the counselors and librarians serving them), this excellent directory contains a wealth of information about possible sources of support. Over 1,100 entries organized into 4 categories—sciences, social sciences, humanities, and any subject area—constitute the major section of this book, providing a great deal of information (including purpose, eligibility, deadlines, address, e-mail, and Website location) about each award-granting program. There are also two other useful sections, one about sources of information on educational benefits organized by state and another about other literature and Websites where additional information is available. All three sections are clearly formatted and easy to use, but should users wish to search using indexes, there are six excellent ones: program title, sponsoring organization, residency, tenability, subject, and calendar.

All in all, Schlachter and Weber have done an exemplary job of organizing an enormous amount of information that could be priceless to all students who believe they may not have the financial means to go to college. It belongs in all libraries patronized by them and those who care about their futures.—**G. Douglas Meyers**

P, S
113.   Schlachter, Gail Ann, and R. David Weber, with the staff of Reference Service Press. **Scholarships 2000.** 2000 ed. New York, Kaplan Books/Daplan Educational Centers and Simon & Schuster Trade Paperbacks, 1999. 584p. index. $25.00pa. ISBN 0-684-86612-9. ISSN 1090-9052.

Kaplan Books has long been in the business of preparing students for all levels of standardized testing. Savvy and affluent students can take a Kaplan course to increase the likelihood of being admitted to the program of their choice. Readers are often unaware, however, that Kaplan publishes books that help potential students find the right school and then find the means to finance it. This is the purpose of the book being reviewed. This book, along with the other Kaplan books, is published with the help of References Service Press. They are a company specializing in financial aid directories, of which *Scholarships 2000* is one of several.

The compilers acknowledge that there is a good deal of federal funding available for students, but the purpose of the directory is to identify private sources exclusively supporting college studies. Additionally, they claim the scholarships listed include the biggest and best funding programs that are truly scholarships and not loans. The first section gives the prospective scholarship applicant some worthwhile guidelines and advice to consider. Sample letters are included and a timetable is offered. It is a section that is worth perusing. The largest section is the directory itself. It is divided between scholarships unrestricted by subject area and subject sections (i.e., humanities, social sciences, and sciences). Each entry contains typical directory information, including Web and e-mail addresses and fax information. Additionally, the eligibility requirements for the scholarships and financial data are given. There are several indexes by subject, sponsoring organization, and tenability.

These types of books provide large amounts of information, but the question arises how valuable it is. For those potential scholarship-seekers whose high school counselors or college financial aid officers are not particularly helpful, this might be a worthwhile source.—**Phillip P. Powell**

P, S
114.   Vuturo, Chris. **The Scholarship Advisor: Hundreds of Thousands of Scholarships Worth More Than $1 Billion.** 2000 ed. New York, Princeton Review/Random House, 2000. 907p. $25.00pa. ISBN 0-375-75468-7.

This easy-to-read book lists 4,327 scholarships and is essentially written for students and their parents who are looking for financial aid. It includes listings for the moderately successful student, and the author states that there are hundreds of scholarships available for those who are not "the most brilliant students, the neediest of the needy, or the most spectacular athletes."

There are many scholarship books available on the market. One advantage of this one lies in the first seven chapters that walk the student and parent through the process of understanding what the different kinds of financial aid are and the implications of each one on future earnings. The chapters address the background the student needs to create or have in order to be successful in receiving financial aid, the search process for identifying different kinds of scholarships, the application process (including writing several kinds of essays), and answering other application questions. Also discussed is preparing for an interview, and what happens if you receive or do not receive the award, and there is a special chapter geared toward graduate students.

Chapter 8 starts with the alphabetic listing of the scholarships available and a corresponding chronological entry number. Following the alphabetic list are several indexes. It might have helped to have these more defined with a running title or a new chapter for clarity. The first portion of the list is the majors and academic interests scholarships that are broken down into categories, such as banking, biology, European history, and library science. There are indexes on career interests, hobby and leisure activities, having less than a 3.0 GPA, minority students, ethnic background, religious affiliation, students with disabilities, and college-specific scholarships and work experience.

Chapter 9 is a list of the scholarships in alphabetic and numerical order. Included in each brief entry is the award type, level of study, amount, number of awards, deadlines, requirements for the applicant, and contact information (address, telephone number, and Website and e-mail addresses). There are two appendixes at the end of the book. One provides sample forms, including letters and applications, and the other is a list of state and territory aid agencies. This book is recommended for school, public, and academic libraries.—**Jan S. Squire**

Handbooks and Yearbooks

C, P

115.   **The Grants Register 2001.** 19th ed. Sara Hackwood, ed. New York, St. Martin's Press, 2000. 1018p. index. $130.00. ISBN 0-312-23142-3. ISSN 0072-5471.

The new edition of this standard work will more than live up to users' expectations. The design and arrangement of the directory is similar to previous editions—two sections that the awards are listed in (first in an alphabetic listing by the awarding organizations and second in a listing by subject that is further subdivided by eligibility requirements). Three indexes are also provided: an alphabetic list of the awards, a list of discontinued awards, and a list of the awarding organizations.

Approximately 3,500 awards are listed from more than 1,200 organizations. A typical description of an award (or a scholarship, fellowship, grant, or program) includes the following information: subjects, eligibility, level of study, purpose, number of awards offered, frequency, value (monetary as well as any benefits or perks), the country of study, application procedure, and closing date. Complete contact information is given for the organizations, including e-mail and Website addresses. One of the great advantages of searching a comprehensive volume like this, as opposed to a direct search of a Website, is the ease of browsing through the offerings of a specific organization, or within a subject area. Similar compilations are available from other publishers, such as the *Directory of Research Grants* (see ARBA 2001, entry 859), but none is quite as comprehensive or as well organized. This guide is recommended for all academic libraries.—**Thomas A. Karel**

P, S

116.   Phifer, Paul. **College Majors and Careers: A Resource Guide for Effective Life Planning.** 4th ed. Chicago, Ferguson, 2000. 258p. illus. index. $16.95. ISBN 0-89434-278-9.

A useful guide for the high school student, this work allots approximately 2 pages to profile each of 61 college majors or careers, ranging from education to philosophy, and from geology to legal and protective services. Each profile includes five sections, the first of which lists high school courses that are pertinent or possible prerequisites to further study. This is followed by a list of related occupations, with an indication of type of degree usually needed to enter that occupation. A third section lists leisure activities of those typically involved in this subject area or career, while a fourth section provides a bulleted list of skills that employers will expect. A final section lists values and attributes associated with those who enter the field in question.

Although these college major and career profiles comprise two-thirds of the volume, they are prefaced by a list of clusters of careers, a basic introduction by the author, and an explanation of how to use the guide. A suite of 38 questions and answers, aimed at further clarifying questions asked by many high school students, supplements the main body of the text. Appendixes include brief descriptions of selected occupations, definitions of skills that are identified in the main entries, and definitions of terms used to describe values and personal attributes. A full index concludes the work.

In addition to its value for students, the work functions as a useful handbook for counselors, parents, and others involved in advising or career counseling. It is highly recommended for high school, public, community college, and other academic libraries.—**Edmund F. SantaVicca**

INTERNATIONAL EXCHANGE PROGRAMS AND OPPORTUNITIES

P

117.   **Academic Year Abroad 2000/2001: The Most Complete Guide to Planning Academic Year Study Abroad.** Sara J. Steen, ed. New York, Institute of International Education, 2000. 690p. index. $44.95pa. ISBN 0-87206-249-X.

This volume provides a valuable overview of programs abroad. The Institute of International Education has 80 years of experience in assisting students and scholars in studying abroad. The Institute is responsible for administering the U.S. government's Fulbright program of scholarships and manages 250 programs for private agencies and foundations, including those such as the World Bank and The MacArthur Foundation. They disperse $100 million in funds. There are 2,500 programs listed in this year's guide, 75 percent that are sponsored by U.S. educational institutions and the rest by foreign universities, foundations, and other organizations. The book is arranged geographically and includes indexes on sponsors, fields of study, special options, cost ranges, and duration. This is a valuable resource for students and scholars and will help advisors and counselors in preparing students to explore the greater educational opportunities in the world.—**Linda L. Lam-Easton**

P, S

118.   **Vacation Study Abroad 2000/2001.** 50th ed. Sara J. Steen, ed. New York, Institute of International Education, 2000. 512p. index. $42.95pa. ISBN 0-87206-250-3.

The year 2000 coincides with the 50th anniversary edition of the Institute of International Education's (IIE) guide to summer and short-term study courses. Together with its companion volume, *Academic Year Abroad*, it is the most comprehensive annual directory on international study available. IIE is a nonprofit organization that has been promoting international exchange programs for 80 years and manages the Fulbright Program for the U.S. Department of State. *Vacation Study Abroad* provides information on more than 2,000 programs in 70 countries. Summer programs can vary in length from one week to several months. The short courses are offered the rest of the year. About 60 percent of the programs are sponsored by U.S. colleges and universities, and the rest by foreign universities, language schools, and other organizations. Many of the programs combine study with travel.

The arrangement of the work is first by geographical region and then alphabetically by country, city, and sponsoring organization. Each entry provides details about site, dates, subjects, eligibility, credit, language and format of instruction, costs, housing, deadlines, and contact information. A helpful preface provides practical tips and additional resources to consult. There are extensive indexes to sponsoring institutions, consortia, fields of study, options for those who are not undergraduates, cost ranges, and durations. This source belongs in all library collections, as its audience includes adult learners and teenagers as well as college students.—**Christine E. King**

P, S

119.   ***Yale Daily News* Guide to Summer Programs 2000.** By Sara Schwebel and the staff of the *Yale Daily News*. New York, Kaplan Books/Kaplan Educational Centers and Simon & Schuster Trade Paperbacks, 1999. 378p. illus. index. $22.00pa. ISBN 0-684-84213-0.

The idea behind this book for high school students is that if they do something interesting with their summer, they will learn something, have fun, and look good on college applications. Useful advice about the merits of a summer experience, the application and interview process, and how to decide which one is appropriate form the first two chapters. The directory of over 500 programs is arranged into chapters that cover seven broad categories of academic, study abroad, community service, outdoor adventure, athletic, arts, and leadership offerings. Traditional summer camps are not included for the most part.

Each section starts off with information on what to expect and how to make it work. For instance, there are hints on how to audition on tape or in person for performing arts programs, and warnings about the physical demands required in many community service programs. Black-and-white photos throughout show students engaged in various activities, and quotations from student participants are highlighted in numerous sidebars; both serve to pique the reader's interest. Individual entries give the program's address, e-mail, URL, program name, location, subject areas, description, dates, duration, and cost. There are also data about financial aid, academic credit, eligibility requirements, application process and deadline, and the average number of applicants and participants. Some families might want to know how long a program has been operating, so perhaps a starting year could be included in future editions. A final chapter notes how to make the college connection from a summer program, be it obtaining letters of recommendation or listening to counselors' advice.

There are five indexes by name of organization, by subject, by cost (some no-cost programs are included), by location (international and U.S.), and by duration. Unfortunately, only the organization name index gives page numbers, so it must always be consulted after using one of the other indexes to find the program listing. There are a couple of caveats for using this directory. The author does not state criteria for inclusion, and although many of the names are certainly familiar (e.g., Amigos de las Americas, National Outdoor Leadership School, Rhode Island School of Design), others may not be. Also, users should be aware that hundreds of worthwhile programs are omitted from the directory (e.g., Bates Dance Festival and the University of Maine Pulp and Paper Foundation's Introduction to Engineering). *Peterson's International Directory of Summer Opportunities for Kids and Teenagers* (Peterson's, 1999), the National Association for Gifted Children (www.nagc.org), and even a Yahoo! search for K–12 summer programs could be used to supplement the information here. Nevertheless, this is a good, inexpensive guide to get high school students started and will be used in any public or school library where it finds a home.—**Deborah V. Rollins**

NONPRINT MATERIALS
AND RESOURCES

C, P, S

120.   **The Complete Sourcebook on Children's Software 2000, Volume 8.** Warren Buckleitner, Ann Orr, and Ellen Wolock, eds. Flemington, N.J., Children's Software Revue, 2000. 1v. (various paging). illus. $61.95pa. (w/CD-ROM). ISBN 1-891983-04-0.

The 8th edition of *The Complete Sourcebook on Children's Software* continues to provide a valuable source of computer programs for children. As with previous editions, the reviews are well presented and easy to read. The work begins with a brief section entitled "A Study of the Children's Software Market," which provides both an interesting overview of statistics concerning software publication for children and selection criteria for the present volume. The editors point out that 4,005 titles were in print on the U.S. market as of December 31, 1999, and that the number of new titles being published has actually dropped slightly from 1998. The introduction is followed by an alphabetical list of more than 700 titles, with about 400 receiving a "feature review." (These reviews were first published in a special newsletter.) Each entry provides the title of the program, the platform it runs on, what it teaches, the name of the producer, address, telephone number, and an indication of the recommended age level range. In addition, the editors rate each item based on a five-star rating—"Dud," "Poor," "Fair," "Good," and "Excellent." The section with featured reviews provides the basic information along with a picture of the outside of the software box and a detailed annotation. The featured reviews tend to be the four- and five-star items. In addition, there are listings of "The Best Software: By Subject," "The Best Software: By Grade Level," "Software Listing by Computer Platform," and a "Directory of Children's Software Producers."

Although there are other sources of software for children, including *Learn* (MENU Publication, 1989) and *Software for Schools: A Comprehensive Directory of Educational Software Grades pre-K Through 12* (R. R. Bowker, 1987), *The Complete Sourcebook on Children's Software* is by far the most complete and comprehensive listing. It is highly recommended for all school, public, and academic libraries, and for collection development personnel in schools.—**Robert L. Wick**

C, P

121.   **Educational Media and Technology Yearbook, Volume 25.** 2000 ed. Robert Maribe Branch and Mary Ann Fitzgerald, eds. Englewood, Colo., Libraries Unlimited, 2000. 354p. illus. index. $70.00. ISBN 1-56308-840-1. ISSN 8755-2094.

Published in cooperation with the ERIC Clearinghouse on Information and Technology and the Association for Educational Communications and Technology, the latest *Educational Media and Technology Yearbook* (EMTY) covers a variety of topics, with an emphasis upon applications that are interactive and learner-centered. The 33 contributors are, for the most part, faculty and librarians from U.S. institutions.

The first part contains 11 essays on major issues; 7 are research summaries that were previously published as ERIC Digests. Titles include "The Benefits of Information Technology," "Internet Relay Chat," "Information Literacy," and "Building and Maintaining Digital Reference Services." The four unique articles cover trends in IT, a survey of doctoral research in educational technology, development programs for faculty, and the National Library of Education's GEM (Gateway to Educational Materials) project. The second and third parts are new features for EMTY, focusing on technology centers and institutes for learning (with two articles on exemplary programs) and school library media (with five entries, including such topics as criticizing media- and Web-based instruction). Six profiles of leaders in media and technology, usually emeritus faculty who remain active in the field, form the fourth part. The fifth part lists organizations and associations in the United States and Canada. Each entry provides contact information, including Websites, statement of purpose, membership statistics and costs, meeting dates, and publications. A classified list for the U.S. breaks groups down into such categories as child- and youth-related organizations, distance education, museums and archives, and so on. The sixth part has annotated entries by states for graduate programs in IT, educational media and communications, and school library media, with information current as of early 1998. The classified list can help narrow a search to 1 of 20 specialties, such as human performance, instructional design and development, or computer education.

A representative, annotated bibliography of journals, books, ERIC documents, journal articles, and non-print media from 1998 and early 1999 forms the seventh part. Entries were chosen to reflect the instructional technology field as it is today. Among the 15 subject categories are computer-assisted instruction, libraries and media centers, professional development, and telecommunications and networking. There are some problems here—the section on educational research lists *Current Index to Journals in Education* and *Resources in Education*, the two print indexes that are also available as ERIC, the free searchable database known to (and probably preferred by) almost every educator. Yet there is no description of the ERIC database or the URL for accessing it. And the hodgepodge of entries that may jump from a journal title to a periodical index to an association to an article citation is difficult to sort through at times. An index, the thoroughness of which leaves a lot to be desired, concludes the volume. For instance, a check under reference does not lead to the article on digital reference services, and information literacy does not lead to pages in the bibliography listing materials on that topic. There is also no headword for dissertations, although there is an essay about them in the book. Despite these shortcomings, the EMTY will remain a standard in most academic libraries, since it provides an annual snapshot of the state of this ever-changing field.—**Deborah V. Rollins**

P
122.   **Educator's Guide to Free Videotapes 2000–2001: Elementary/Middle School.** Kathleen Suttles Nehmer, ed. Randolph, Wis., Educators Progress Service, 2000. 351p. index. $34.95pa. ISBN 0-87708-346-0.

P
123.   **Educator's Guide to Free Videotapes 2000–2001: Secondary Edition.** 47th ed. Kathleen Suttles Nehmer, ed. Randolph, Wis., Educators Progress Service, 2000. 330p. index. $34.95pa. ISBN 0-87708-334-7.

Educators Progress Service now publishes 15 different annual guides to free materials. Until the 2000 edition, only one guide to videotapes was published, covering all levels. This has now been split into the new elementary and middle school edition with 1,554 videos, and the secondary edition with 1,321 videos (829 new listings) for use with high school and adult audiences. There is some overlap in titles, but it is not extensive. The editor notes that thousands of letters are written to companies every year in order to keep the information about availability accurate and up to date. If a company does not respond then last year's information is omitted. Most videos must be borrowed with the borrower paying postage one way or both ways. Hints on writing letters of request are found in the front matter. A guide for evaluating industry-sponsored educational materials, developed by the National Association for Industry-Education Cooperation, may be photocopied and completed in order to give feedback to sponsoring organizations about the value of their materials in the classroom. Needless to say, borrowers will want to preview items for content, bias, and appropriateness.

Entries are arranged in broad subject categories relevant to educators, such as career education, fine arts, home economics, safety education, and social studies. Each entry gives the title, a brief description, suggested grade levels, language, production date, running time, borrowing terms (including how far in advance request must be made), and address and contact information for the organization. Indexes by title, detailed subject, and source (company or organization) conclude each volume. There are slightly more than 90 sources of videos in each volume, ranging from government agencies (e.g., the Environmental Protection Agency and the National Agricultural Library) to embassies, organizations (e.g., the Latin American Curriculum Resource Center and Korean Cultural Service), and corporations (e.g., Maytag and Pendleton Woolen Mills). Educators with limited local video collections will find useful materials here to supplement their curriculum. These guides are recommended for school libraries as well as public, academic, and state agency libraries that support education programs.

—Deborah V. Rollins

6 Ethnic Studies and Anthropology

ANTHROPOLOGY AND ETHNOLOGY

C, P

124. **Cultures of the World.** Melvin Ember and Carol R. Ember, eds. New York, Macmillan Reference USA/ Gale Group, 1999. 1249p. illus. index. (Macmillan Compendium). $125.00. ISBN 0-02-865367-X.

This work is excerpted from the previously published 10-volume *Encyclopedia of World Cultures* (see ARBA 97, entries 318–320; ARBA 95, entries 397 and 398; ARBA 94, entries 395 and 396; ARBA 93, entry 413; ARBA 92, entries 334 and 335). Although the extraordinarily comprehensive coverage of world cultures has been pared down by presenting only a representative selection of the original articles, each of the original articles that does appear is complete and unabridged. The 253 entries average approximately 4,500 words, organized by regions, including an appendix of American (i.e., United States) immigrant cultures. For accuracy and utility, nothing compares to it. Most of the accounts are by scholars (primarily anthropologists) who have worked for decades with the peoples they chronicle. Each entry systematically treats geography, demography, language, history, economy, kinship and the family, sociopolitical organization, religion, and art, and provides a bibliography. Although the emphasis is decidedly on traditional cultural practices and beliefs, there is no sense of timelessness; each entry is firmly placed within the sweep of historical forces affecting the relevant peoples. In the larger, multicultural nation-states (e.g., Russia, China, Brazil, the United States) the populations covered include the majority cultures and many of the smaller minority or tribal groups. Two significant problems should be noted. First, there is no discussion of how these "cultures" are constituted or were chosen; in some cases they are merely the peoples living in a given country or territory, in others they are linguistically or ethnically defined. Second, and most disturbing, there are no maps. Given the presence of wide margins, photographs, and sidebars, this seems a glaring omission. This work is probably too advanced for most elementary and junior high school students, but for any high school, college, or public library without the original 10-volume *Encyclopedia of World Cultures*, this seems indispensable as a source of accurate, contemporary, and highly sophisticated summaries of the lives of the peoples with whom we share the planet.—**Glenn Petersen**

C, P

125. **Encyclopedia of Human Evolution and Prehistory.** 2d ed. Eric Delson, Ian Tattersall, John A. Van Couvering, and Alison S. Brooks, eds. New York, Garland, 2000. 753p. illus. maps. index. (Garland Reference Library of the Humanities, v.1845). $175.00. ISBN 0-8153-1696-8.

This thoroughly updated edition of a distinguished reference book (last reviewed in ARBA 89, entry 336) contains nearly 800 articles written by 54 international, but largely U.S., contributors. The articles are divided between shorter specific articles and longer integrative articles, including articles on concepts and methods, localities and sites, fossils, primate taxa, tool types, archaeological industries, and eminent deceased and living anthropologists. There are also long, integrative articles on major regions such as Western Asia. A new editor, an archaeologist, has been added to help correct the 1st edition's emphasis on paleontological/biological topics over archaeological/ cultural topics—yet, this bias is still somewhat apparent. Although a few, mainly general, articles on later prehistory are included, archaeological coverage is largely Paleolithic.

The articles are clear and jargon-free, but the necessary technical terminology is likely to present difficulties to the novice reader. The editors have not imposed any theoretical uniformity, and the articles, while never polemical, reflect a variety of sometimes conflicting points of view. Thus, this feature reflects the current liveliness of the field. This book is essential for all academic libraries and for large, and many medium-sized, public libraries. [R: BL, 1 Sept 2000, p. 176; Choice, Dec 2000, p. 685]—**Frederic F. Burchsted**

ETHNIC STUDIES

General Works

C, P

126.   **Gale Encyclopedia of Multicultural America Primary Documents.** Jeffrey Lehman, ed. Farmington Hills, Mich., Gale, 1999. 2v. illus. index. $145.00/set. ISBN 0-7876-3990-7.

Despite a title implying coverage of the Americas, this two-volume set is in reality a resource for ethnic groups found in the United States. Originally designed as a companion to the 2d edition of the *Gale Encyclopedia of Multicultural America* (see ARBA 96, entry 387), but capable of being used independently, this reference contains 210 primary documents intended to illuminate the experiences of 90 national, religious, or Native American groups.

Primary documents are defined broadly to include approximately 20 different types of documents, ranging from autobiographies, political cartoons, photographs, and speeches to recipes. Each of the documents, alphabetically arranged by group, is preceded by a commentary that is designed to provide context. If more than one document is provided for a particular group, then they are arranged chronologically from first to last. Each of the documents concludes with a citation to the original source. Approximately 80 illustrations, including maps, are included to supplement the documents. A general index provides access to the data at the conclusion of volume 2.

This is a unique resource that provides information that is not easily retrievable, and should thus be considered for both public and academic libraries. For maximum effect, however, it should be used in conjunction with its companion publication. [R: SLJ, May 2000, p. 88; BL, Aug 2000, pp. 2195-2196; VOYA, Aug 2000, pp. 211-212]—**John R. Burch Jr.**

P

127.   **A Nation of Peoples: A Sourcebook on America's Multicultural Heritage.** Elliott Robert Barkan, ed. Westport, Conn., Greenwood Press, 1999. 583p. index. $99.50. ISBN 0-313-29961-7.

This book presents 27 new essays on ethnic groups who are a significant presence in the United States. Written for the most part by scholars who are themselves of the ethnicity they describe, they examine the history of the group's immigration, its demography, settlement patterns, cultural impact, interethnic relations, and progress toward assimilation. The introduction by editor Barkan puts these essays in the context of recent multicultural debates in U.S. education and society. Each chapter is concluded with a brief and useful bibliographic essay, as is the entire volume. The appendixes include immigration and naturalization tables. Most of these essays are excellent and anthropologist Alice Kehoe's essay on American Indians is superb—eloquently written, comprehensive, and insightful. Barkan has done a fine job compiling and editing these essays. Each of these well-written essays addresses common subjects and concerns, giving this volume a unified theme and consistency lacking in many edited monographs. The book's greatest failure is its inadequate and inconsistent index (e.g., cross-references for Latvians but not for Lebanese) that severely hampers its usefulness as a reference tool. Some will also quibble with who is and is not included (e.g., Mormons but not Appalachians or Brazilians) or which groups are treated individually in a full chapter (e.g., Cubans) and which ones get briefer treatment in collective chapters (e.g., Haitians in the chapter on West Indians and Caribbeans). However, with the major exception of the inferior index, this is a well-conceived, carefully constructed, and quite useful book.—**Fred J. Hay**

Africans

C, P

128.   **Encyclopedia of African Peoples.** By the Diagram Group. New York, Facts on File, 2000. 400p. illus. maps. index. (Facts on File Library of World History). $55.00. ISBN 0-8160-4099-0.

This eye-catching resource on African cultures, history, and geography offers users information on more than 1,000 ethnic groups and all 53 countries in Africa. The arrangement of the text is somewhat confusing because it is not one large alphabetic listing but has four main sections, some alphabetic and some not. Preceding these sections are 10 pages of maps and explanations dividing Africa into 5 geographic areas: North, East, West, Central, and Southern.

Section 1, "The Peoples of Africa," comprises most of the book, with 200 pages of alphabetically arranged descriptions of the continent's ethnic groups. According to the foreword, "ethnic group" is used to refer to people who are linked by a common language, history, religion, and cultural and artistic legacy. The coverage is often detailed. For example, the four-page entry for *Maasai* includes two maps, a timeline, and paragraphs on history, language, ways of life, industry, tourism, housing, diet, clothing, social structure, religion, and dancing. There are 12 excellent illustrations: shield designs, cattle branding, cattle breeding, implements, children and adults in traditional costume, and battle dress of the Maasai. Cross-references are well supplied. When ethnic groups in this book are compared to the Encyclopedia Britannica, some offer more detail but some offer less, and sometimes with differing information. Section 2, "Culture and History," offers a more "almanac" approach, with a hodgepodge of interesting and fun details including pictorial histories and chronologies for each of the five African geographic areas. A historical area spotlights entries like "Birthplace of Humanity," "Christianity in Ethiopia," and four pages on "Apartheid." Section 3, "The Nations," is a fact sheet for each of the 53 countries. Section 4, "Biographies," gives short paragraphs (alphabetically arranged) on 300 famous Africans. An improved glossary and index would make this handsome book even handier. [R: LJ, 1 April 2000, p. 88; Choice, Sept 2000, p. 104; BR, Nov/Dec 2000, p. 73; SLJ, Nov 2000, p. 90; RUSQ, Fall 2000, p. 83]—**Georgia Briscoe**

C, P

129.   **Peoples of Africa.** Tarrytown, N.Y., Marshall Cavendish, 2000. 11v. illus. maps. index. $329.95/set. ISBN 0-7614-7158-8.

Divided into 11 books, this reference begins with an introductory essay giving a general overview of African history. The series proceeds with individual entries focusing on each country's history, political evolution, cultural development, and geographic distinctions. Each nation is showcased with an article illustrating its uniqueness and connects the reader to the people of that geographical entity by providing information on the economy, music, dance, arts, cuisine, religion, language, and daily activities of the populace. Maps, photographs, timelines, sidebars, and even recipes highlight each country's contributions to the world's experience. The diversity of the region is portrayed and the reader is readily engaged.

Readers learn many interesting insights into the continent. For example, only 42 percent of the Angolan population is literate. Burkina Faso has an international reputation for its Pan-African film festival. And, Ceuta was the first European colony in Africa and is still governed as a territory by Spain.

Features include a glossary of definitions for the key concepts covered in each volume. There is a comprehensive index by general topic as well as additional indexes by individuals, national holidays, geographic features, arts, festivals, food, religion, and sports. Referrals for further reading are also given. This set is a well-written secondary education resource for a little-understood and under-appreciated part of the world.

—**Adrienne Antink Bien**

Arab Americans

P, S

130.   **Arab American Encyclopedia.** Anan Ameri and Dawn Ramey, eds. Farmington Hills, Mich., U*X*L/Gale, 2000. 310p. illus. index. $42.00. ISBN 0-7876-2952-9.

P, S

131.   Hall, Loretta. **Arab American Voices.** Farmington Hills, Mich., U*X*L/Gale, 2000. 233p. illus. index. $42.00. ISBN 0-7876-2956-1.

The publication of these two titles completes U*X*L's Arab American Reference Library series, whose focus is Americans whose ancestry can be traced to one of the 21 Arab countries that are members of the League of Arab States. Each book in the series, which began with the publication of *Arab American Biography* (see ARBA 2000, entry 272), is designed as a unique title even though a cumulative index is available if the three parts of the series are purchased as a set.

Arab American Encyclopedia was compiled by the Arab American Center for Economic and Social Services (ACCESS). The encyclopedia is divided into 19 sections focusing on such diverse topics as health and environmental issues, family and gender roles, and literature. Also used are sidebars, a timeline, and a glossary to supplement the text. The glossary, though, is short on necessary details such as the differences between the Shi'a and the Sunni Muslims. Bibliographic citations for further research are included both at the end of each section and in a short three-page bibliography. Many of the items suggested for further research are published by academic presses and seem much too advanced for the target audience of middle to high school students. The outstanding index that concludes the book is much more detailed than is usually evident in a work aimed at school-age children.

Arab American Voices is a compilation of 27 previously published primary sources, some of them excerpted, that are arranged into several sections. Each of these sections begins with an overview of the topic to provide context and concludes with bibliographic citations for further research. Libraries interested in this title might also want to consider the *Gale Encyclopedia of Multicultural America: Primary Documents* (see entry 126). The books in the Arab American Reference Library series are all recommended for public and school libraries. These titles fill a niche that has long been neglected in juvenile reference sources. [R: BL, July 2000, p. 2055; SLJ, Aug 2000, p. 127; BR, Sept/Oct 2000, p. 71]—**John R. Burch Jr.**

Asian Americans

P

132.   Do, Hien Duc. **The Vietnamese Americans.** Westport, Conn., Greenwood Press, 1999. 148p. illus. index. (The New Americans). $39.95. ISBN 0-313-29780-0.

The Vietnamese American issues the author treats are elders who would rather be back home; the first generation who find good in both cultures commercializing their folk festivals, trying to learn English to fulfill their and our values of health, prosperity, and happiness; and the next generation who are integrating, or quite to the contrary have neither Vietnamese nor American acculturation, and become frightening delinquents. The author's social science doctorate prepares him to analyze and make conclusions based on wide reading, interviews, and observations in southern California.

Although federal and nongovernmental organization's money have brought over two million Vietnamese refugees stranded by war, Americans, whose ethnic migrations centuries or decades earlier, have not welcomed them. Basic networks of an integrated work place and education established in the United States—by those earlier refugees—do sustain new populations. The author believes America is now a mosaic, not a melting pot. The work includes minimal black-and-white pictures, a good bibliography, and an index. There are no maps or sidebars.

—**Elizabeth L. Anderson**

P

133.   Tong, Benson. **The Chinese Americans.** Westport, Conn., Greenwood Press, 2000. 248p. illus. index. (The New Americans Series). $39.95. ISBN 0-313-30544-7. ISSN 1092-6364.

The Chinese were the first Asians to arrive on America's shores in the 1780s. Historically, Chinese Americans have been the largest and most prominent Asian American group; however, the 2000 U.S. census will most likely show that they are now slightly outnumbered by Filipino Americans. This new and authoritative treatment of their immigrant experience deserves our serious consideration.

This volume is part of Greenwood Press's New Americans Series. The series foreword states that "these volumes are designed for high school students and general readers"; however, this particular volume's sophisticated style and treatment make it more appropriate for college students and teachers as well as the educated reader.

In chapter 1 the author provides the necessary background information on Chinese culture and society during the late Qing Dynasty (1644–1912). His discussion of Chinese geography, language, society, philosophy and religion, politics, and dynastic history places Chinese American immigration in a suitable context. The next 5 chapters consider the Chinese American experience chronologically, with coverage emphasizing post-1945 developments.

Within each chapter the author identifies and explores major social and economic themes rather than giving a straightforward historical narrative. He is particularly good on the role of women, labor, and economic issues, and on U.S. immigration legislation and anti-Asian laws. In chapter 7, Tong discusses the arts and Chinese Americans, including such topics as their images in film, fiction, poetry, theater, television, documentaries, visual arts, and music. His insights on feminist perspectives are especially helpful. Chapter 8, "Chinese American Families and Identities," concludes the main body of the work. Here are valuable sections on gangs and juvenile delinquency, gay men and lesbians, and interracial marriage. An appendix, "Noted Chinese Americans," concludes the work. It contains 15 short biographies of prominent contemporary figures, such as March Fong Eu, Maxine Hong Kingston, Maya Lin, Gary Locke, Yo-Yo Ma, and I. M. Pei.

The work is heavily documented with extensive chapter notes and a selected unannotated bibliography. There are no Internet Website citations in either of these sections. There are 14 black-and-white photographs, which are interesting but of average quality.—**Marshall E. Nunn**

Blacks

Bibliography

C

134.   Walters, Ronald W., and Cedric Johnson. **Bibliography of African American Leadership: An Annotated Guide.** Westport, Conn., Greenwood Press, 2000. 279p. index. (Bibliographies and Indexes in Afro-American and African Studies, no.41). $57.50. ISBN 0-313-31314-8.

Compiled in part to stimulate the pursuit of African American leadership studies from theoretical, strategic, and organizational angles, *Bibliography of African American Leadership* (BAAL) provides annotated citations to approximately 2,000 books, articles, unpublished graduate theses, and audiovisual resources; primary collections are not listed. Although the authors stress the importance of the theoretical over the biographical material (featuring leaders of black people as opposed to leaders who happen to be black), roughly two-thirds of the citations fall in the latter category. The nonbiographical chapters cover broad issues, such as local leadership studies, ideologies and social movements, leadership organizations, and general critical appraisals. Scholars will find these particularly useful. The authors make no claim to comprehensiveness, but rather stress the most significant material relating to "leadership" conceptually. The theoretical chapters are best viewed as literature reviews, in that the arrangement (including the index) does not point well to specific topics. One minor point, however, is that the audiovisual chapter could easily (and more practically) have been integrated into the earlier chapters, particularly the biographical sections.

Even with the above caveats, BAAL is a welcome and much-needed addition to the literature of African American leadership studies and will serve scholars as an excellent companion to Ronald Walters and Robert C. Smith's *African American Leadership* (SUNY, 1999) and Marable Manning's *Black Leadership* (Columbia, 1998). It is highly recommended for all political studies collections. [R: Choice, Dec 2000, p. 692]—**Anthony J. Adam**

Biography

C, P

135.   Warren, Wini. **Black Women Scientists in the United States.** Bloomington, Ind., Indiana University Press, 2000. 366p. illus. index. $35.00. ISBN 0-253-33603-1.

This unique work contains biographies of more than 100 black women scientists in a wide range of fields, including astronautics and space science, biology, chemistry, medicine, physics, and zoology, among many others. Working on this volume for more than six years, Warren, a professor of American studies, has both mined the existing biographical literature and done an enormous amount of original research.

In the introductory chapter, Warren critically examines the scholarship on blacks in several works, including Vivian Ovelton Sammons's *Blacks in Science and Medicine* (see ARBA 92, entry 351). She also discusses her own research methodology to produce this work—an expansion of her dissertation. Arranged alphabetically by scientist, the entries range from one paragraph to several pages. The profiles are extensively footnoted, often including useful annotations. This illustrated and well-bound volume concludes with a selective bibliography of publications by the women profiled in the work and also a general bibliography of books, archives, and multimedia sources.

The author's meticulous and diligent research—locating personal and family papers and conducting interviews throughout the country—has certainly ensured that this volume is now the classic biographical source on this topic. An outstanding reference source, this work should serve as a model for future biographical dictionaries of relatively unknown scientists. [R: Choice, Sept 2000, p. 98]—**Donald Altschiller**

Dictionaries and Encyclopedias

C, P

136.   Altman, Susan. **Encyclopedia of African-American Heritage.** 2d ed. New York, Facts on File, 2000. 353p. illus. index. (Facts on File Library of American History). $40.00. ISBN 0-8160-4125-3.

Alphabetically arranged entries provide an introduction to the African diaspora as they chronicle both the history of Africans on their ancestral continent as well as those who were captured and sold as slaves. Although there is a concentration on indigenous Africans in the United States, also included is information about descendants of Africans who were involuntary and voluntary immigrants to other parts of the world. Entry subjects include ethnic groups, individual personalities, political movements and organizations, countries and tribes of Africa, events, and more. While most entries are relatively short (three or four paragraphs to one page), some are much longer, such as the lengthy overview of the criminal justice system of the United States as it applies to African American history and the article on education, which includes important court decisions. Biographical entries include intellectual, political, military, scientific, and educational leaders as well as musicians, artists, literary figures, and athletes. Special features include numerous captioned photographs and historical drawings; charts, chronologies, and maps; cross-references within articles; guide words at the top of each page; bold headings for each entry; and *see* references when applicable. There is an extensive bibliography and a comprehensive index.

This is a very readable and easy to use encyclopedia, which will be of use in secondary school and public libraries for both research and browsing. Of particular interest are the articles on African tribes, information that is often hard to find in smaller libraries.—**Dana McDougald**

Indians of North America

Atlases

C, P, S

137.   Waldman, Carl. Illustrated by Molly Braun. **Atlas of the North American Indian.** rev. ed. New York, Facts on File, 2000. 385p. illus. maps. index. (Facts on File Library of American History). $45.00; $21.95pa. ISBN 0-8160-3974-7; 0-8160-3975-5pa.

Originally published in 1985 (see ARBA 86, entry 380) this revised edition is 109 pages longer. The arrangement remains the same as the prior edition—seven chapters from Paleo-Indians to contemporary Indians. Most of the sections have a few added or revised paragraphs. For example, in the chapter dealing with Paleo-Indians, Waldman added a section addressing a seaborne migration theory that is slowly gaining acceptance among North American archaeologists. As in the previous edition, it remains true that there is significantly more text than maps for an atlas, but there are 14 new maps. One of the improvements of this edition is that the maps are now black and white rather than several shades of brown. In most cases, revision involves a new map related to a new section, such as the material and map for the Poverty Point complex in the lower Mississippi River Valley or the material and map related to pre-contact trade in North America. The chronology has substantial new entries for 1985–1998. There are several entries for 1999, including one for the creation of Nunavut as a new Canadian territory for the Inuit people. There is also a single entry for 2000 (the issuance of the Sacajawea dollar coin).

The contemporary Indians chapter, as expected, contains the most new material with a long section on Indian gaming, and one on "Indian Country" and what that term does and does not mean. This revised edition is a worthwhile purchase even if readers do have the original edition. [R: VOYA, Oct 2000, p. 300; SLJ, Aug 2000, p. 136; BL, 1 Sept 2000, p. 172; BR, Nov/Dec 2000, p. 74]—**G. Edward Evans**

Biography

P, S

138.   **American Indian Portraits.** New York, Macmillan Reference USA/Gale Group, 2000. 395p. illus. index. (Macmillan Profiles). $80.00. ISBN 0-02-865491-9.

Designed for the high school and middle school markets and part of the Macmillan Profiles series, this is an interesting biographical mix of past and present prominent Native American individuals. Of the 156 entries for individuals, 66 were written specifically for this volume. The balance came from the 1996 edition of the *Encyclopedia of the American West* (see ARBA 97, entry 415) and were edited to match the format of the Profiles series. Approximately one-third of the entries are for individuals living today. Selection of contemporary individuals appears to have focused on providing a range of professions—Sherman Alexie (writer), Vine Deloria, Jr. (academic and writer), R. C. Gorman (artist), John Echohawk (lawyer), LaDonna Harris (economic development), Wilma Mankiller (politician and activist), Russell Means (activist and actor), Wes Studi (actor), and Maria Tallchief (ballerina). Entries range from one to as much as three pages.

An appendix provides three or more additional resources for each person, including some Internet sites for a few of the contemporary persons. There is also a general section dealing with Native American biographical works. A glossary of terms and an index conclude the volume. One interesting, as well as frustrating, aspect of the collection is the insertion of special explanatory material for a few (20) of the individuals. For example, in the entry for Dennis Banks there is a half-page sidebar describing the American Indian Movement (AIM) of which Banks was one of the cofounders. Another contemporary example is in the entry for Reuben Snake, Jr., which has a discussion of peyote and the Native American Church. On the historical side there is an extended section on the Sand Creek Massacre in the Black Kettle entry. What is useful is these additional sections provide a broader context for understanding the importance and place of the individual in history or Native American affairs. What is frustrating is that all the entries could have benefited from such a contextual placement. While length and thus price may be a factor in limiting such material, perhaps fewer individuals and more context would be desirable.

The other frustrating aspect is, some of the additional material is too general to provide a full understanding of the issues. For example, the material on AIM might leave the reader thinking it was still rather active on the national level. This problem could have been addressed by having additional resources listed for the contextual topics as well as for the persons covered. While the book's main market is high schools and middle schools, it is very likely to receive extensive use in a public library reference collection. This is a very sound purchase for such libraries. [R: BL, 15 Oct 2000, p. 478]—**G. Edward Evans**

Dictionaries and Encyclopedias

P

139.   Baxter, Paula A., and Allison Bird-Romero. **Encyclopedia of Native American Jewelry: A Guide to History, People, and Terms.** Phoenix, Ariz., Oryx Press, 2000. 242p. illus. index. $65.00. ISBN 1-57356-128-2.

While the need for a reference filled with interesting and useful information about Native American jewelry certainly cannot be disputed, it is worthy to note that this book is also unusually engrossing to read. The preface, which outlines the challenges facing those who seek to understand the development of Indian jewelry as craft and as art, is extraordinarily useful, particularly for those who are not familiar with Native American history and cultures. This encyclopedia addresses the development of native jewelry-making as a significant post-European contact craft or art form and focuses on native-made jewelry from the period after 1776, with emphasis on works of the nineteenth and twentieth centuries. The parameters that guide the organization of the encyclopedia and the criteria for inclusion are clearly presented.

Information is presented in four main categories: "People," "Materials and Forms," "Techniques," and "Designs and Motifs." The introduction presents concise essays on these four main entry categories, providing an overview and historical, technological, and economic context for the material. Much of the information has not been previously published, adding to the utility of the reference. Entries (400 to 1,000 words) often provide references for further reading as well as Websites that allow further exploration of a particular subject. A guide to selected topics introduces the book and an appendix that lists U.S. and Canadian museums and cultural institutions holding significant collections or presenting important exhibits of Native American jewelry is provided. An extensive bibliography, artist index, and subject index are also included. Black-and white photographs are interspersed throughout the text and it is truly unfortunate that they are not more abundant and, when appropriate, in color. Better photography would truly enhance readers' understanding of designs. The authors of this work carry academic and experiential credentials that allow readers to have confidence in the organization of this volume and the information provided in the essays and entries. Scholars, collectors, and consumers alike will appreciate the convenience and credibility of this reference.—**Karen D. Harvey**

C, P
140. Hirschfelder, Arlene, and Paulette Molin. **Encyclopedia of Native American Religions.** updated ed. New York, Facts on File, 2000. 390p. illus. index. (Facts on File Library of American History Series). $65.00. ISBN 0-8160-3949-6.

"Updated edition" is the correct label for this volume. Locating what is new in the main text is something of a challenge. There is a new general index of names, places, and ceremonies that supplements the revised subject index of the 1992 edition (see ARBA 93, entry 432). There are also additional entries in the further reading section. Overall, this edition is 23 pages longer, but the typeface appears somewhat smaller so the actual total increase in new material is greater than the page count might suggest. The basic format remains the same as in the previous edition. A person might be somewhat misled by the marketing material—both a flyer included in the review copy and a mailed flyer covering both this and several other Native American titles from Fact on File. For example, the marketing material uses the phrase "updated edition features" and lists seven items. One of the items relates to legal decisions regarding prisoners' religious rights. Some people might take that to mean this is a new subject area in the updated edition. The reality is that the topic existed in the first version and what took place was the addition of one new entry under that topic. A side-by-side review of five sections of the two versions showed there were a few new entries in each section, such as "Bear Dance, Calif." and "Stillday, Thomas, Jr." Since the first edition appeared, several other works have come on the market dealing with some of the same subject matter; for example, *Dictionary of Native American Mythology* (see ARBA 94, entry 418), *Encyclopedia of Native American Healing* (see ARBA 97, entry 340), and *Encyclopedia of Native American Shamanism* (see ARBA 2000, entry 308). For information on a wide variety of people, ceremonies, and issues related to Native American religions, this is still the best source. If the reference budget is tight and one has the earlier edition in the collection, no harm would be done by passing on this update. However, if one passed on the 1st edition, one should give serious consideration to purchasing this one. [R: BR, Sept/Oct 2000, p. 76]—**G. Edward Evans**

Italians

C, P
141. **The Italian American Experience: An Encyclopedia.** Salvatore J. LaGumina, Frank J. Cavaioli, Salvatore Primeggia, and Joseph A. Varacalli, eds. New York, Garland, 2000. 735p. illus. index. (Garland Reference Library of the Humanities, v.1535). $110.00. ISBN 0-8153-0713-6.

The Italian American Experience brings together the expertise of 166 scholars devoted to furthering the study of Italian Americans. Like the four editors of this volume, many of the contributors are members of the American Italian Historical Association.

This unique volume contains more than 400 entries that explain the contributions and relationship of Italian Americans to art, history, religion, Italian organizations, archival depositories, literature, pop culture, politics, sports, military history, and science and technology. The entries vary in length from several pages to merely half a page. Each is provided with a bibliography at the end of the entry and many have *see also* cross-references. There are many entries of prominent individuals, but more often individuals can be found in broader entries such as "Explorers," "Movie Actors and Actresses," and "Politics." There are photographs of many of the more prominent individuals. A thorough index concludes the work.

This work is unique in its content and scholarly in its compilation. It will be useful in many academic and public libraries. [R: LJ, 1 Feb 2000, pp. 73-76]—**Shannon Graff Hysell**

Latin Americans

P, S

142. **Latino Americans.** New York, Macmillan Library Reference/Simon & Schuster Macmillan, 1999. 465p. illus. index. (Macmillan Profiles). $100.00. ISBN 0-02-865373-4.

In the preface to *Latino Americans*, the editors note that the Latino population in the United States is projected to be more than 40 million by 2010, making it the largest minority group in the country. As one of the newest publications in the Macmillan Profiles series, *Latino Americans* seeks to bring "the heritage of this multifaceted community to life" (p. xi). The reference work is targeted at the young adult audience, and contains more than 180 profiles of notable men and women of Latino origin, from the sixteenth century to the present. Most of the entries have been extracted from other reference works, including the *Encyclopedia of Latin American History and Culture* (see ARBA 97, entry 349), the *Dictionary of American Biography* (see ARBA 99, entry 33 for a review of the CD-ROM version), and the *Encyclopedia of the American West* (see ARBA 97, entry 415). Macmillan's editors and writers have updated and adapted entries for the young adult audience, and 43 new entries were commissioned specifically for this work.

Each entry includes a timeline to place the figure in a historical context, along with highlighted quotations by or about the person. Definitions of specialized or more difficult vocabulary are included in the margins, and a separate glossary of other terms is found at the back of the book. Entries vary in size, from a single paragraph to more than six pages, and seem to be well balanced between historical and contemporary figures. At the back of the book, the editors included a master timeline of key events in Hispanic American history, a list of sources for the volume's entries, and a suggested reading list organized by the names of the persons covered in the book. There is also a combined name, subject, and place of birth index. Although *Latino Americans* is easy to use, it would be more helpful to place the article source and suggested readings at the end of each entry instead of separately at the back of the book. The decision to include Latin Americans and those of Latin American heritage living in the United States is understandable given Macmillan's goal of providing a sense of the overall cultural experience. However, the book's subjects range from explorer Ponce de Leon to movie star Jennifer Lopez, and at times this compromises the thematic focus of the work. Focusing specifically on persons whose lives reflect the interactions between Latin American and U.S. cultures might have made for a tighter work, especially given the existence of the reference book *Latin American Lives* (see ARBA 2000, entry 322), which serves as a more complete biographical tool for learning about Latin American historical figures. Such questions of scope aside, *Latino Americans* is an informative and easy-to-use resource for the young adult level, and can serve as a useful tool for teaching and learning about this important and growing group within the United States.—**Pamela M. Graham**

Norse

P, S

143. Haywood, John. **Encyclopaedia of the Viking Age.** New York, Thames and Hudson, 2000. 224p. illus. maps. $34.95. ISBN 0-500-01982-7.

Haywood, a British historian and Fellow of the Royal Historical Society of Great Britain, has produced this reasonably priced, well-written, concise, and up-to-date reference source with answers to basic questions relating to nearly all aspects of Viking history and life in the period from 789 to 1100 C.E. Haywood has carefully incorporated findings from late twentieth-century archaeological digs. That evidence suggests that the Vikings engaged in interesting peaceful activities as well as in violent raids. Entries range widely from battles to women and family life. British spelling is sometimes disconcerting. A useful, short introduction summarizes the causes of the Viking Age and provides clear maps of the Vinland voyages, Viking Age Scandinavia, and Viking Age British Isles.

Middle school and high school readers seeking more scholarly information than that provided in the many juvenile books about the Vikings will have no trouble using the convenient alphabetic subject index to the more than 400 encyclopedia entries. College students and faculty members will find both the suggested reading titles given at the end of many entries and the more extensive list of selected primary and secondary sources printed at the end of the volume helpful. All readers will enjoy the black-and-white illustrations with accompanying explanatory text. The work is especially handy for the chronological table for 1–1500 C.E. and the chart of Viking kings and rulers for 700–1100 C.E. Libraries needing additional maps may wish to consider Haywood's *The Penguin Historical Atlas of the Vikings* (1995). [R: Choice, Nov 2000, p. 499; BL, 15 Oct 2000, p. 478]

—**Julienne L. Wood**

7 Genealogy

GENEALOGY

Bibliography

P

144. Kemp, Thomas Jay. **Genealogist's Virtual Library: Full-Text Books on the World Wide Web.** Wilmington, Del., Scholarly Resources, 2000. 268p. $70.00; $27.95pa. (w/CD-ROM). ISBN 0-8420-2864-1; 0-8420-2865-Xpa.

Kemp, a prolific author of genealogical books and articles, also compiles the *Genealogy Annual: A Bibliography of Published Sources* (1995 ed.; see ARBA 98, entry 361). Materials in this volume are divided into three sections. In the section on family histories entries are arranged alphabetically by surname. Entries in the section on local histories are alphabetical by state and subdivided by locality. And the section on general subjects includes ethnic and religious groups and foreign countries. For each item, full bibliographic information is provided, as well as the URL for the online version. There are no annotations. Rather than using cross-references or an index system with sequential numbers, books are listed under as many surnames or localities as necessary. For example, full bibliographic information for the book *Long Island Genealogies* appears under all 59 surnames that are included in its very long subtitle.

Although Kemp claims to include only free items, there are links to many city directories from Primary Source Media that are available only by subscription. Even though the volume's subtitle indicates that materials included are full-text books, Kemp also includes many research guides, pamphlets, and journals. Some of these are not really full-text, either offering only selective articles online or merely their tables of contents (e.g., the *American Historical Review*). Many of the books and serials that Kemp includes are not exactly genealogical (e.g., the Area Handbooks from the Library of Congress Website, six of whose titles are given incorrectly). The relevance of including references such as Information Today and Library Journal is questionable.

Included is a companion CD-ROM containing the entire book in PDF format, along with a copy of Adobe Acrobat Reader 4.05 (which is also available for free on the Internet) to read the PDF file. The advantage of the CD, of course, is that all the URLs are hypertext links that can be clicked on, rather than having to manually type them into a Web browser. Although there are now numerous books on genealogical Websites, such as Kemp's *Virtual Roots: A Guide to Genealogy and Local History on the World Wide Web* (see ARBA 98, entry 366) and *Genealogy Online* (McGraw-Hill, annual), this volume is unique and belongs in all genealogical collections. [R: LJ, 1 April 2000, p. 93; C&RL News, Nov 2000, p. 946]—**John A. Drobnicki**

Handbooks and Yearbooks

P

145.   Greenwood, Val D. **The Researcher's Guide to American Genealogy.** 3d ed. Baltimore, Md., Genealogical Publishing, 2000. 662p. illus. index. $29.95. ISBN 0-8063-1621-7.

It is good to have a new edition of this work. Greenwood manages to make research in American genealogy understandable. The book is divided into two parts, one covering background to research and the other covering records and their use. The first part includes discussions on understanding genealogical research, understanding the evolution of handwriting, the calendar, symbols used in records, and the evaluation of evidence. Greenwood then introduces research tools, giving a chapter discussion on the library and reference materials. The work deals successfully with organizing the research, corresponding with others, and discussing the purposes of family history beyond genealogy. Greenwood has greatly expanded the chapter on computers in genealogy. In fact, it was the great changes in computer technology that motivated him to bring out this edition since the other basics he discusses have not changed much.

The second part has chapters on compiled sources and newspapers, vital records, census returns, probate records and basic legal terminology, wills, land records, governmental as well as local records, court records, property rights of women (a new chapter), church records, military records, and cemetery and burial records. This is a wonderful resource; however, Greenwood should have taken the time to update his references since some of the publications cited are no longer published. This will be useful in any collection needing information on basic genealogical research. [R: LJ, 1 Feb 2000, p. 73]—**Robert L. Turner Jr.**

P

146.   Kemp, Thomas Jay. **International Vital Records Handbook.** 4th ed. Baltimore, Md., Genealogical Publishing, 2000. 601p. $34.95pa. ISBN 0-8063-1655-1.

How does one get official vital records? That is a question asked nearly every day by many people in search of birth, death, marriage, and divorce records. This work will help answer that question. It tells how and where to obtain the needed records, including the price charged in local currency. A copy of the actual request form is included when available. Many entries now have URLs for Web pages and e-mail addresses for the office where this information can be obtained.

This work is divided into three parts based on geography. The first is the United States, the second is U.S. Trust Territories, and the third lists information for nearly 200 International countries. In nearly every entry there is a reminder that the Family History Library of Salt Lake City has microfilmed many of the original and published vital records and that these records can be obtained on microfilm from any Family History Center of the Church of Jesus Christ of Latter-Day Saints.

This work will save much time and effort, avoiding needless delays because users do not know where to get the record needed or which form to use. It will be useful in most reference collections. [R: LJ, Dec 2000, p. 110]
—**Robert L. Turner Jr.**

PERSONAL NAMES

P

147.   Altman, Nathanial. **The Little Giant Encyclopedia of Names.** New York, Sterling Publishing, 1999. 511p. $9.95pa. ISBN 0-8069-6509-6.

The Little Giant Encyclopedia of Names is a fascinating compilation of first and last names found primarily in North America, with the focus mainly on first names. It examines the origins and meanings of the given names of the vast majority of individuals living in the United States today, as well as those residing in Canada, the United Kingdom, Australia, and New Zealand.

The work begins with an essay on given names, their various sources, and the reasons for choosing them, such as religion, family roots, to honor others, euphony, literary names, fashion, and spiritual and psychological qualities. In the main portion of the encyclopedia, names are listed in boldface print with their ethnicity noted in parentheses and a brief definition of its origin and meaning. Cross-references to other variations and nicknames are also indicated in bold typeface. Names that are appropriate for both boys and girls are marked by an asterisk.

The encyclopedia also contains several lists of the 40 most popular boys' and girls' names for each decade from the 1930s through the 1990s along with an additional list for the 100 most popular names for 1997. Lists are also provided for the 50 most popular African, African-American, Chinese, French, German, Indian, Irish, Italian, Japanese, Muslim, Russian, and Spanish names.

Overall, the encyclopedia covers a great number of popular and not-so-popular names given in English-speaking countries. But, it is obvious that there are many names not included in the collection. Also, some variations of names are difficult to locate unless the reader knows which name it is derived from. Nevertheless, this is a useful reference for readers looking for a baby name or the origin and meaning of their own name.

—**Cari Ringelheim**

8 Geography

GEOGRAPHY

General Works

Atlases

P

148. **America: A Celebration of the United States.** Skokie, Ill., Rand McNally, 2000. 208p. illus. maps. index. $39.95. ISBN 0-528-84174-2.

With splendid photographs and detailed maps, this atlas from Rand McNally provides the rare combination of reference information and enjoyable reading. *America: A Celebration of America* offers readers a unique perspective on the different regions and cultures of the United States. This atlas is unique in that its sections are not divided into the typical categories of perfunctory state lines; instead it is divided by regions based on the areas' similarities in geography, culture, and history. The regions studied include "New England and the Adirondacks," "Metro New York," "Mid-Atlantic Coast," "Appalachian Mountains," "Coastal Southeast," "The South," "Midwest and Great Lakes," "Great Plains," "Heart of Texas," "Southwest and Great Basin," "Mountain West," Pacific Northwest," "Coastal California to the Sierras," "Hawaii," and "Alaska." Each section provides thorough descriptions of the region's history, culture, geography, and features. It also provides a detailed map of the entire region as well as smaller maps indicating the important features (e.g., Central Park in New York City, site of the Revolutionary War). Interspersed within the larger text are sidebars that give more information on things unique to the region discussed (e.g., luaus in Hawaii, music of the southern states). The book concludes with an index to regional maps.

The maps and information provided in this book are of excellent quality and will be used by researchers and browsers alike. This will be a useful addition to public libraries.—**Shannon Graff Hysell**

P, S

149. **Dorling Kindersley Children's Atlas.** updated ed. New York, DK Publishing, 2000. 176p. illus. maps. index. $24.95. ISBN 0-7894-5845-4.

This newly updated edition of the popular *Dorling Kindersley Children's Atlas* features more than just detailed maps; it gives an overview of the geography, vegetation, and climate of the Earth in easy-to-understand terms that children will relate to. A team of 20 cartographers and researchers created this atlas with the latest cartographic information and digital technology. The resource begins with a 12-page introduction to the Earth as a whole, discussing the Earth in space, landscapes, climate, people's relationship to the planet, and a guide to using the atlas. Because the clientele is based in the United States there is a special section on North America, which covers North America's physical traits, environment, history, people, and politics. Following this the seven regions of the world are featured: North America, Central and South America, Europe, Africa, North and West Asia, South and East Asia, and Australasia and Oceania. For each region the major countries are featured and information on their climate, history, industry, and people are provided. The photographs and maps are beautiful (typical of DK Publishing) but the information is scattered and inconsistent. A glossary of terms and an index conclude the volume.

This atlas will be popular in elementary and middle school libraries as well as public libraries children's reference collections. At only $24.95 there is a lot of valuable information provided along with the excellent maps.—**Shannon Graff Hysell**

P

150.   **Dorling Kindersley World Atlas.** 3d ed. New York, DK Publishing, 2000. 354p. illus. maps. index. $50.00. ISBN 0-7894-5962-0.

This atlas portrays each continent, and the countries within that landmass, as an integrated whole with the interdependencies of its parts recognized. A profusion of narratives and illustrations tell the story of daily life as it varies across the globe. Brief political and economic summaries are given for every mapped area. In addition to landscape details and political boundaries, the annotations provide insights as to cultural development, economic activity, and natural resources. Photographs are sprinkled throughout the volume and bring alive the depicted countries and regions. For example, when studying the section for eastern Canada, the reader not only notes the correct location of the Bay of Fundy, but also sees a photograph of the bay's shoreline at low tide and learns that the tides in this bay are among the highest in the world. All map place-names are in the native language of that country. Maps are also provided for the world's oceans.

The index-gazetteer offers additional background material. The geographic comparison tables list data such as square miles, rainfall, gross national product, language usage, and so on. A thumbnail sketch is presented for each country, with population, religion, currency, literacy, and caloric consumption information. The names used on all 450 maps are listed alphabetically and identified by language and type of geographic feature. There is also a glossary of geography terms from abyssal plain to weathering. Maps are easy to find either through the comprehensive index, the table of contents, or the key to map pages. This reference goes beyond traditional expectations of an atlas. This is an eye-pleasing and user-friendly resource to better understand the world in which humans live, work, and travel.—**Adrienne Antink Bien**

S

151.   **Facts on File Children's Atlas.** updated ed. By David Wright and Jill Wright. New York, Facts on File, 2000. 96p. illus. maps. index. $18.95. ISBN 0-8160-4433-3.

This is an updated version of previous editions (see ARBA 99, entry 412; ARBA 94, entry 447; ARBA 92, entry 400; and ARBA 88, entry 455). The oversized volume has maintained the same organizational format of nine sections that include information on the planet Earth, continents and land areas, and quiz questions. Except for color enhancements and updated political boundaries, the maps are basically unchanged from the previous edition. Statistics have also been updated; however, much of the text is unchanged.

Each geographic area or topic is covered in a two-page spread. A large map, photographs, a fact box, entertaining quizzes, and brief text fill the two pages. Population, topography, culture, religion, and climate are mentioned in each section. End pages are illustrated with flags from various countries. An extensive index and answers to questions found throughout the book conclude the atlas. The volume is colorful and attractive but it does not provide in-depth information on the geographic areas. The volume is more of an introductory geography book than an atlas, and coverage is uneven. The United States gets six pages while the former Soviet Union is covered in two pages entitled, "Russia and Neighbors." A listing of the republics, their capitals, and populations would be helpful. Although an intended audience is not given, the amount of text and reading level would make it suitable for grades 3–6.—**Elaine Ezell**

C, P

152.   **Goode's World Atlas.** 20th ed. John C. Hudson and Edward B. Espenshade Jr., eds. Skokie, Ill., Rand McNally, 2000. 371p. maps. index. $34.95. ISBN 0-528-84336-2.

This is the 20th edition of the venerable *Goode's World Atlas* and features Hudson, a professor of geography at Northwestern University, as the new editor. Remaining true to its predecessors, this edition continues the tradition of providing excellent maps and tabular information that will provide answers to many reference questions. Since five years have elapsed since the last edition, special attention has been paid to update both the thematic maps and the political maps.

The work is divided into three parts: world thematic maps, regional maps, and geographic tables and indexes. The world thematic maps provide information on topics such as vegetation, birth and death rates, agricultural products, manufacturing, and energy production. New thematic maps in this edition include ocean environments, distribution of fowl, and forest exploitation. The regional maps divide the world into continents and provide both thematic and political maps. New maps in this section include the Indian-Pacific Ocean floors, the Atlantic Ocean floor, the Arctic Ocean floor, U.S. grain trade, and updates on all of the political maps. The geographic tables section includes eight pages of new tables in addition to the updating of most of the other tables to represent the latest data available.

As it has been in the past, the 20th edition of *Goode's World Atlas* will remain a tried and trusted friend for the reference librarian. This edition deserves to be in every library and is a bargain at its price of $34.95.

—**Gregory A. Crawford**

C, P

153.   **Hammond World Atlas.** 3d ed. Maplewood, N.J., Hammond, 2000. 312p. maps. index. $69.95; $95.00 (executive edition). ISBN 0-8437-1352-6.

The 3d edition of the *Hammond World Atlas* is 11-by-14¼ inches in size. The map scales vary from 1:12,000,000 to 1:500,000, with most of the maps in the 1:1,000,000 to 1:3,000,000 range. The volume is broken down into six sections: "Interpreting Maps," "A Quick Reference Guide," "Global Relationships," "The Physical World," "Maps of the World," and "Statistical Tables and Index."

The "Interpreting Maps" segment provides a history of mapmaking from ancient times to the present. It also explains map scales and projections and gives useful information on using the atlas. An alphabetic listing of continents, countries, states, provinces, and territories, with the size, population, and capital of each, is available at "A Quick Reference Guide." The "Global Relationships" section includes thematic maps, charts, and graphs showing the relationships between people and the environment. Coverage includes demographic trends, population distribution and growth, global energy production, assessing the consequences of pollution, comparing GNP per capita, and literacy and life expectancy. Fifteen pages of terra scape maps can be found in the "Physical World" components. Shaded relief maps depict the Earth's surface and the ocean's floor three-dimensionally.

In the section on "Maps of the World," there is a balance of political and topographic maps, which were generated from a computer database structured by latitude and longitude. Included also are map projections of the continents and 60 inset maps featuring metropolitan areas and special areas. "Statistical Tables and Index" rounds out the atlas. In this section one can find the dimensions of the world's largest mountain peaks, longest rivers, and the largest lakes and islands. This section also includes the population of countries and major cities, foreign geographical terms, and "Index of the World." The "Index of the World" contains 110,000 entries.

In sum, the maps are colorful and fresh with clear, easy-to-read type, and are easily accessible through the master index, the "Quick Reference Guide," or the locator map. This work is recommended for all libraries as well as for the home. [R: BL, 1 May 2000, p. 1684]—**Earl Shumaker**

P, S

154.   **National Geographic Atlas of Natural America.** Washington, D.C., National Geographic Society, 2000. 304p. illus. maps. index. $40.00. ISBN 0-7922-7955-7.

When one hears "National Geographic" they think first of exquisite maps, and then of nature photography that sets the highest standards. This atlas delivers both. It is a guide to many of the best natural areas in the United States and Canada, and it is a celebration of North America's natural beauty. This book is a reference work any library will be proud to display.

More than 125 locations are covered in this atlas using over 100 maps and 160 color photographs. The maps are detailed enough to use on the road, but with their muted colors and shaded relief, they are also art worthy of the accompanying photographs. The images themselves are flawless, the type that make you wonder how long the photographer stood in that spot waiting for the best light, the perfect stance of the mountain goat, or just the right swirl of mist. These photographs have considerably evolved in style and content over the decades that National Geographic has been constructing such volumes. No longer do we see dozens of the proverbial happy campers frolicking in the national parks. Now we have to look hard to find a single human being, and when he or she is found they are invariably a small colored dot or a tiny silhouette. Nature itself is the subject now. Not necessarily how we enjoy it.

Such well-illustrated, glossy, large-format books often suffer an ironic fate because they are so attractive: they stay on that coffee table to be occasionally paged through and admired, but they are not often read. That would be a pity in this case because the writing is superb. It is part history, part travel advice, part natural science, and part advocacy for preserving these precious wild areas. It is well-crafted prose to match the spectacular art. This is a book to treasure.—**Mark A. Wilson**

C, P, S
155. **The New International Atlas.** 25th ed. Skokie, Ill., Rand McNally, 1999. 1v. (various paging). maps. index. $150.00. ISBN 0-528-83808-3.

A giant among large-format atlases, this latest edition of a key reference tool provides a wealth of information regarding world geography and cultures. With over 250 pages of color maps, and another 200 pages of gazetteer and index information, this atlas is more than comprehensive in its treatment of the Earth. A work of continuous revision, the maps and data reflect the latest measurements and revisions discovered within the past year.

Introductory sections are written in five languages (English, French, German, Portuguese, and Spanish) and all place-names presented on maps are in the local official language. New to this edition are thematic maps that focus on world climates, religious languages, environmental changes, populations, and economics. Maps follow each other in a logical fashion; and new design elements render many of these maps almost three-dimensional in nature. Through a combination of color schemes, print, and contour, maps are clear and comprehensible. A section of metropolitan maps includes maps of 65 major cities, all of which are drawn at the same scale and allow for comparison.

Supplementing the maps are various tables that provide data on population and population density, area, and capital cities and political status of countries. There are also listings of the largest cities within each country, a 7-page glossary of geographic terms, and a full index that provides map numbers and latitude and longitude for over 160,000 sites.

High school, public, and academic libraries will want to include this title in their atlas collections, primarily for its scope, clarity, and high quality of execution. This atlas is a handsome and impressive volume.
—**Edmund F. SantaVicca**

C, P
156. **Oxford Atlas of the World.** 8th ed. New York, Oxford University Press, 2000. 304p. maps. index. $75.00. ISBN 0-19-521684-9.

This book begins with statistical tables for all the world's countries and territories showing land area, population, capital cities, and annual income. Oceans, mountains, rivers, islands, and lakes are listed in kilometers and miles. Satellite images for various cities and geographic areas are showcased with additional photographs from space scattered throughout the volume. Introductory essays discuss geology, climate, environment, population, languages, religions, agriculture, minerals, cities, energy, trade, and political conflicts.

Following this background material, city maps are given for 67 major urban areas in sufficient detail for travel planning. The resource continues with 176 physical and political maps for each continent and its countries portraying landforms, terrain contours, roads, railroads, canals, airports, and major towns and cities. National borders are noted, as well as de facto boundaries where there are territorial disputes. Each map has a locator diagram, page numbers for adjacent areas, longitude, latitude, and the scale and projection used. Maps are easily located either through the table of contents or the comprehensive index that is sorted by geographic features and cities, with latitude, longitude, and grid references. Both English and local names are used on the maps as well as in the index. This atlas is a useful reference for research projects or to browse for the pleasure of learning more about the world. [R: LJ, Jan 01, p. 92]—**Adrienne Antink Bien**

C, P, S
157. **Oxford Encyclopedic World Atlas: A–Z Country-by-Country Coverage.** 5th ed. New York, Oxford University Press, 2000. 280p. maps. index. $45.00. ISBN 0-19-521589-3.

Now in its 5th edition, this atlas continues to be a quality, comprehensive atlas that includes additional information normally found in almanacs and gazetteers. The work is divided into three sections. The first section of the volume, "World Statistics," consists of eight pages of statistics on all countries and territories in the world. Population, capital, annual income in United States currency, and area in kilometers and miles are given in an alphabetic arrangement by country. A list of the principal cities and metropolitan areas, arranged by country and then by size from the largest, follows with the most recent census or estimated population figures. The final table in this section gives physical dimensions of continents, oceans, and other landforms.

The 2d section is 32 pages of maps. Physical, political, economic, population and wealth, climate, and vegetation maps are provided for each continent. The maps are colorful, with detailed relief mapping, and the accompanying charts and tables are easy to read.

The final section of the volume comprises the main body of the book. It is an alphabetic list of each country. Full-color topographical maps with illustrated settlements and major communication routes are provided for each. Information given includes the flag with a summary of its origin, geography, climate, history, politics, economy, and statistics. Most countries are covered in one page but larger countries that are more significant world leaders receive more extensive coverage. China is given five pages and the United States is given six pages.

An index to the country maps concludes the volume. The names of all the principal places and features on the country maps are indexed. Each name is followed by the country or region in which it is located and the letter-number grid to assist in easily locating the feature on a map. A pronunciation guide, a list of abbreviations, and instructions on how to use the atlas are also included. End pages feature full-color world maps. This is an excellent geographical resource for home and library use. [R: LJ, Jan 01, p. 92]—**Elaine Ezell**

S

158.   **Rand McNally Children's Millennium Atlas of the United States.** Skokie, Ill., Rand McNally, 2000. 109p. illus. maps. index. $16.95. ISBN 0-528-84204-8.

Aimed at children aged 8 to 12, these atlases are richly illustrated and fun to read. Both provide brightly colored and easy-to-read maps. Color photographs illustrate the history and culture of various regions. The main maps show principal cities, highest peaks, rivers, and other features. Both works also include an index to major places.

The world atlas is arranged by continent, with a full chapter devoted to each of the seven continents. There is also a millennium timeline and an introduction to the basics of maps and cartography. Along with political maps there are also physical maps and thematic maps for populations, climates, and economies. A guide to each country's flag along with information on size, population, and capital cities and a glossary are also included.

The U.S. atlas opens with a map illustrating what life was like in the area now known as the United States of America in the year 1000. Next, individual state maps denote major cities, lakes, rivers, highest peaks, and national parks. Each of these maps is accompanied by various information about the state, including a historical timeline and a sidebar illustrating the state's flag, bird, flower, and much more.

Both works are educational and entertaining for children and adults. While larger atlases will provide more in-depth information, these works provide basic informational data for a reasonable price. They will be very appealing to young learners and a good addition to juvenile reference collections.—**Cari Ringelheim**

C, P

159.   **Rand McNally Millennium World Atlas.** Skokie, Ill., Rand McNally, 1999. 1v. (various paging). maps. index. $70.00. ISBN 0-528-84175-0.

Rand McNally's latest atlas presents the world as it enters a new century in both maps and reference material. A section on how to use the atlas provides historical information, defines common terms associated with maps and geography, and explains the use of the index and how topography is indicated. Before giving an overview of the world today, the past century is presented in a timeline of facts and illustrations that are divided into seven categories: exploration and mapping; science and inventions; agriculture, industry, and trade; nature, weather, and the environment; culture and the arts; population and politics; and philosophy, religion, and learning. Each category is divided into 100-year increments.

The timeline is followed by 2-page spreads that cover 19 topics related to our current world that include the solar system, weather topics, environmental concerns, and population. The text is detailed and well illustrated with charts, graphs, and photographs. The topics complement the categories in the timeline.

The main body of the volume is 176 pages of digitally created maps divided into regional maps that are grouped by continent and metropolitan maps of over 60 urban areas. Most of the maps are physical. However, political maps of the counties of the world and each continent except Antarctica are included. Elevation tints, shaded relief, and clear text make the maps easy to read. Small locator maps in the margins provide the user with a visual orientation of where the specific area is in relation to larger landmasses. A 30-page section of metropolitan maps follows. These maps use a scale of 1:300,000.

World information tables provide political information that includes population, area, and the capital of each country as well as the population of major cities. The inside back cover has detailed index maps that key maps to the pages they appear on. The index has 92,000 names of places and geographic features. The entries are keyed to the maps by both an alphanumeric map reference number and a pair of precise latitude and longitude coordinates.

The addition of reference material often found in gazetteers and almanacs makes the atlas useful for purposes other than just maps. The large size of the volume is enough to make the maps easy to read without being overwhelmingly cumbersome and difficult to handle. This is a high-quality atlas that will be beneficial in the home, school, and public or university libraries.—**Elaine Ezell**

P, S

160.   **The 21st Century World Atlas.** Naples, Fla., Trident Press International; distr., Bronx, N.Y., H. W. Wilson, 2000. 751p. maps. index. $125.00. ISBN 1-888777-93-1.

Remarkable in both its scope and execution, this comprehensive atlas includes more than 400 thematic maps of the world, beginning with the geopolitical framework of the continents and the oceans and including satellite images, digital image models, and bathymetric representations. Additional sections focus on climatology, geology, and biogeography; demography and social indicators; basic economic activities; and industry, commerce, and transport. Complementing these are more than 500 thematic country maps, arranged into five broad sections: Africa, America, Asia, Europe, and Oceania.

Descriptive text accompanies the maps and provides the current cultural, political, social, and economic situations for most countries and the larger land or water masses being illustrated. Distributed throughout are more than 300 satellite images and reference maps, more than 200 digital terrain models, and more than 1,700 graphs indicating the most recent statistical data available. The whole is supplemented by a place-name index that includes over 60,000 entries referenced through an effective page and grid system—providing easy access to specific geographical information. A short preface and introductory guide provide succinct information regarding scope, projections, images, and other facets of production.

Printed in Italy, this atlas is visually stunning in its use of color, line, and page layout. Perhaps most notable is the placement of digital terrain models against a solid black background, effectively creating a dramatic approach to representation, clarity, and learning.

For its scope and execution, this atlas should be in all strong geography collections and in all academic libraries. Public and high school libraries also would be wise to invest in this work, as it provides for easy access and ease of understanding—qualities not readily found in all atlases.—**Edmund F. SantaVicca**

P, S

161.   **The World Book Atlas.** Chicago, World Book, 2000. 1v. (various paging). illus. maps. index. $49.00. ISBN 0-7166-2650-0.

The World Book Atlas is a large-size, general world atlas incorporating maps of the world and illustrative materials from Rand McNally and *Goode's World Atlas* (see entry 152). An introductory section contains articles and color photographs on oceans and mountains, rivers and streams, lakes and ponds, forests and grasslands, polar caps, and world time zones. There are also pages describing how to use the atlas and an index map and legend.

The main body of the atlas covers approximately 144 pages of maps, most of which are physical maps emphasizing terrain, landforms, and elevation. There are political maps of the world for each of the continents except for Antarctica. Map scales range from 1:2,500,000 to 1:30,000,000, and a bar scale with each map is expressed in both miles and kilometers. Another scale accompanying each map identifies in feet the meters all of the elevation and depth categories that appear on the map. The atlas appears to be up to date with recent name changes, such as Congo, Czech Republic, and Slovenia presented correctly. The majority of the maps are presented in double-paged spreads, which is problematic because the book does not lie flat enough to see the information on the inside without straining the binding.

The index includes approximately 54,000 names of places and geographical features that appear on the reference maps. Each name is followed by the name of the country or continent in which it is located, an alphanumeric map reference key, and a page reference. All abbreviations used in the index are defined in the list of abbreviations at the beginning of the index.

This is a reasonably priced atlas that is quite adequate for searching world locations and would be a good choice for both school and home use. The binding is sturdy, the print is easy to read, and the maps are current. The extensive index, legends, and latitude and longitude grids make locating a place or geographical feature fast and easy.—**Dana McDougald**

Dictionaries and Encyclopedias

C, S
162.   **Philip's Geography Dictionary.** 2d ed. New York, Sterling Publishing, 2000. 240p. illus. maps. index. $12.95pa. ISBN 0-540-07824-7.

First published in Great Britain, this single-volume dictionary purports to deliver "comprehensive coverage of the major terms used in physical, human and environmental geography" (introduction). It provides definitions for over 1,500 geographical entries covering themes as diverse as the atmosphere, weather and climate, coastal formation, geomorphology, and settlement and economic development. In addition, this specialized dictionary covers scales, organizations, treaties, and famous scientists. However, Gunnar Myrdal and J. H. von Thunem may not be everyone's first choice when thinking of famous scientists. Fifty gray-tone diagrams and maps, along with boxed tables and plentiful cross-references, illustrate the definitions. A list of illustrations is handy for quick reference. This work should definitely be considered for collections supporting strong geography and earth science units at high school and college levels.—**Esther R. Sinofsky**

P, S
163.   **The World Book Encyclopedia of People and Places.** Chicago, World Book, 2000. 6v. illus. maps. index. $229.00/set. ISBN 0-7166-3797-9.

This six-volume encyclopedia provides articles on the nations of the world. Each country's entry summarizes its history, geography, economy, culture, and politics. Many of the listings also give additional information on the nation's environment, major cities, arts, natural resources, industry, religion, indigenous peoples, and so on. Features include photographs, fact boxes with key socioeconomic data, maps, and timelines. Of particular interest is a pie chart showing each nation's average caloric intake compared to the recommended daily allowance. For example, this graphic shows that the population of Bhutan consumes 107 percent of the recommended daily intake of 2,345 calories.

The cumulative index is detailed and indicates topics by subject, such as the Masai Steppe, the Punic Wars, and Voltaire. Plus, there are subheadings under each country's name, such as agriculture in Chile. This is a useful general-interest reference. [R: BR, Sept/Oct 2000, p. 66; RUSQ, Winter 2000, pp. 193-194]

—**Adrienne Antink Bien**

9 History

ARCHAEOLOGY

C, P

164.   **The Atlas of World Archaeology.** Paul G. Bahn, ed. New York, Checkmark Books/Facts on File, 2000. 208p. illus. maps. index. $39.95. ISBN 0-8160-4051-6.

This handsome atlas is comprehensive both geographically and chronologically. It is divided into three parts. The first picks up the emergence of the earliest hominids and traces their spread and development through the last ice age. The second focuses on the development of framing, kiln and forge, early city and state societies, and writing. The third, and by far the most lengthy section, divides the globe into five areas and describes cultural development, from hunter-gatherer through early farmers to the rise of organized states and empires.

The focal point of each section is a series of clear maps denoting the appropriate archaeological sites for each period and a well-written general text. There are also excellent color photographs to illustrate the test and a series of chronological charts illustrating the development of various human enterprises, like stages and tool making. A brief selected bibliography and an index are included.

There are some puzzling aspects of the work though. There is a beautiful two-page photograph of part of the Lascaux cave, but Lascaux does not appear in the index, text, or any map. Chauvet and Altimira are also not shown on the maps, although they are mentioned in the text. The majority of places sited on the maps would not be familiar to the level of reader who would use this atlas, while the sites just mentioned would be. The maps avoid anachronistic thinking by forcing the reader to look in the right time period for any site they are seeking.
—**Robert T. Anderson**

C

165.   **Medieval Archaeology: An Encyclopedia.** Pam J. Crabtree, ed. New York, Garland, 2001. 426p. illus. maps. index. $135.00. ISBN 0-8153-1286-5.

Crabtree, an associate professor of anthropology at New York University, and 118 additional experts, drawn from both North America and Europe, have produced an authoritative resource on the field of medieval archaeology. Defining the medieval period broadly, from 500 to 1500, this work focuses primarily on the geographic region ranging from Italy to Scandinavia and Poland to Iceland. An entry for Novgorod, Russia, is also included, even though it does not fit into the geographic region noted.

Preceding the signed entries is a two-page preface defining the field of medieval archaeology, a list of contributors, a list of sites by country, and a subject guide. There are approximately 150 alphabetically arranged entries that range in length from 2 paragraphs to several pages. Although written by specialists in the field, the text is not filled with technical jargon that would make it inaccessible to lay readers. The entries are cross-referenced and conclude with bibliographic citations. Black-and-white photographs, maps, and drawings supplement the text. The work concludes with an index that contains article titles in bold typeface.

While this title is authoritative, it is not comprehensive due to the exclusion of entries for the Balkans and Byzantium. For information on Byzantium, librarians should consider *The Oxford Dictionary of Byzantium* (see ARBA 92, entry 510) that remains the most authoritative reference work on the subject. There is no comparable work currently available on medieval archaeology, thus this over-priced title is highly recommended for academic libraries supporting programs in archaeology or European history.—**John R. Burch Jr.**

AMERICAN HISTORY

General Works

P, S

166.   **American Civil War: Almanac.** By Kevin Hillstrom and Laurie Collier Hillstrom. Edited by Lawrence W. Baker. Farmington Hills, Mich., U*X*L/Gale, 2000. 251p. illus. maps. index. $155.00/set; $45.00/vol. ISBN 0-7876-3823-4.

P, S

167.   **American Civil War: Biographies.** By Kevin Hillstrom and Laurie Collier Hillstrom. Edited by Lawrence W. Baker. Farmington Hills, Mich., U*X*L/Gale, 2000. 2v. illus. index. $155.00/set; $45.00/vol. ISBN 0-7876-3821-8.

P, S

168.   **American Civil War: Primary Sources.** By Kevin Hillstrom and Laurie Collier Hillstrom. Edited by Lawrence W. Baker. Farmington Hills, Mich., U*X*L/Gale, 2000. 176p. illus. index. $155.00/set; $45.00/vol. ISBN 0-7876-3824-2.

Tackling the American Civil War is always a daunting task because it is such a huge conflict and so much has been written on the subject. One of the latest contributions is U*X*L/Gale's American Civil War Reference Library to which these 4 volumes belong.

The *Almanac* provides a concise overview of the war, including its causes and the Reconstruction period. Two volumes of *Biographies* present 60 life stories of important Civil War people. The last volume, *Primary Sources*, contains 14 accounts of people who experienced various aspects of the war. The books are well designed, with a handy timeline in the front, numerous photographs, interesting sidebars, and suggests for further reading.

Because of its single-volume length, the almanac is a concise history of the war with few first-person accounts in the text. Although the major battles are briefly described, others such as the Crater are not even mentioned. Indexing glitches are also present: there are no entries for "casualties," "illness," or "disease" in the index, yet a sidebar dealing with these important subjects is on pages 182 to 183. There is also no index entry for "prisons" or "Andersonville," which are very important subjects that should be in any Civil War overview (although they are described in *Biographies*).

It is admirable to want to include lesser-known personalities in *Biographies*, such as Winslow Homer or Mary Boykin Chesnut, but with only 60 available slots it would have been more useful to include those who actually shaped the Civil War, such as George Armstrong Custer. *Primary Sources* would be better if there were less introductory material for each first-person narrative, with the authors getting to the narrative more quickly and making room for other accounts. For example, the section on Frank Holsinger contains seven pages of analysis and three pages of his eyewitness descriptions.

All this sniping aside, the American Civil War Reference Library does a good job of presenting the basic facts of the Civil War. It is a valuable resource for middle school and high school students, especially in libraries that have limited or outdated Civil War material. [R: BR, Sept/Oct 2000, pp. 66-67]—**Mark J. Crawford**

P, S

169.   **American Revolution: Almanac.** By Barbara Bigelow and Linda Schmittroth. Edited by Stacy A. McConnell. Farmington Hills, Mich., U*X*L/Gale, 2000. 195p. illus. maps. index. (U*X*L American Revolution Reference Library). $155.00/set; $45.00/vol. ISBN 0-7876-3795-5.

P, S

170.   **American Revolution: Biographies.** By Barbara Bigelow and Linda Schmittroth. Edited by Stacy A. McConnell. Farmington Hills, Mich., U*X*L/Gale, 2000. 2v. illus. index. (U*X*L American Revolution Reference Library). $155.00/set; $45.00/vol. ISBN 0-7876-3792-0.

P, S

171.   **American Revolution: Primary Sources.** By Barbara Bigelow and Linda Schmittroth. Edited by Stacy A. McConnell. Farmington Hills, Mich., U*X*L/Gale, 2000. 264p. illus. index. (U*X*L American Revolution Reference Library). $155.00/set; $45.00/vol. ISBN 0-7876-3790-4.

Four volumes make up U*X*L's American Revolution Reference Library. The first volume, *American Revolution: Almanac*, presents an overview of the war. Its first chapters give information about the colonies, daily life during colonial times, and the political situation. Subsequent chapters detail the course of the rebellion as it built toward inevitable war and then follow the war itself, giving information on specific battles or political developments. Each chapter is followed by a bibliography of further sources, including Web sources.

The second and third volumes of the set are titled *American Revolution: Biographies*. In these volumes, both well-known and lesser-known players on the revolutionary stage are profiled. Information on Betsy Ross, Thomas Jefferson, Ethan Allen, and George III is presented here. The student can also find information on such unknown but fascinating characters as Simon Girty, an uneducated, rough frontiersman who acted as interpreter during negotiations with the Ohio Indian tribes as efforts were made to ensure their neutrality. There is also information on Mary Katherine Goddard, the printer and publisher of the *Maryland Journal* during the revolutionary years who was chosen by the Continental Congress to print the first copies of the Declaration of Independence containing the names of all the signers.

Excerpts from various pertinent contemporary documents, along with commentary, make up the fourth volume, *American Revolution: Primary Sources*. The Stamp Act, the Intolerable Acts, and the Declaration of Independence are all excerpted and discussed. Also included are excerpts from letters and speeches of the time. These are also from a mix of such luminaries as Benjamin Franklin and Thomas Paine and more ordinary Americans who left a record of their thoughts.

All four volumes are well illustrated with engravings of the period, maps, and portraits. Numerous sidebars sprinkled throughout the text give students a snapshot of a specific moment or theme. Preliminary material in each volume includes a timeline of the war and a glossary of terms. Also included is a section that presents ideas for class discussion. These themes and questions will also help an ambitious, independent student think more deeply on various topics.

Both general and specific questions can be addressed through the almanac. Students wanting an answer to a specific question can probably find it through the chronologically arranged chapters, or in the biographies. Those wishing for more in-depth information about a particular event can read one or several chapters. This would be a useful source for middle school libraries, particularly for its coverage of lesser-known participants in the American Revolution. [R: VOYA, Dec 2000, p. 373; SLJ, Nov 2000, pp. 87-88]—**Terry Ann Mood**

P, S

172.   **Colonial America: Almanac.** By Peggy Saari. Edited by Julie L. Carnagie. Farmington Hills, Mich., U*X*L/Gale, 2000. 2v. illus. index. (U*X*L Colonial America Reference Library Series). $185.00/set; $45.00/vol. ISBN 0-7876-3763-7.

P, S

173.   **Colonial America: Biographies.** By Peggy Saari. Edited by Julie L. Carnagie. Farmington Hills, Mich., U*X*L/Gale, 2000. 2v. illus. index. (U*X*L Colonial America Reference Library Series). $185.00/set; $45.00/vol. ISBN 0-7876-3760-2.

P, S

174.   **Colonial America: Primary Sources.** By Peggy Saari. Edited by Julie L. Carnagie. Farmington Hills, Mich., U*X*L/Gale, 2000. 297p. illus. index. (U*X*L Colonial America Reference Library Series). $185.00/set; $45.00/vol. ISBN 0-7876-3766-1.

Middle school students are the target audience for this five-volume set on Colonial America. Two volumes titled *Almanac*, two titled *Biographies*, and one titled *Primary Sources* make up the set. All of the volumes are arranged attractively, are heavily illustrated, and have numerous sidebars interwoven into the main text, which present short bursts of information on specific topics. The format should appeal to the intended age group, who have grown up with hypertext and have become accustomed to jumping from one spot to another.

The two almanac volumes set the stage and place colonial times in context. Volume 1 contains chapters on such topics as Native Americans, Spanish exploration, and social and political issues. Volume 2 concentrates more on daily life in the colonies, with chapters on religion, family life, education, science and medicine, and arts and culture.

Biographies of both well-known and lesser-known people of the period are in the two biography volumes. As one might expect, John Rolfe is here, as are Powhaten and Pocahontas. Also included are Eliza Lucas Pinckney (a plantation manager in South Carolina who cultivated indigo), John Smibert (the first portrait painter in colonial America), and Catherine (Kateri) Tekakwitha (a Mohawk who was a Catholic nun and is now a candidate for sainthood).

Primary Sources, the final volume, gives young students a taste of what doing original research is like, presenting contemporary documents for them to read. To ease the process of reading often arcane language, support material accompanies each document. A section entitled "Things to remember when reading [name of document]" is included, as is a glossary of unusual words, and a section called "What Happened Next?" that leads the student forward in time.

Like its counterpart from U*X*L on the American Revolution (see entries 169, 170, and 171), this should satisfy both students wanting brief information on a specific topic and those willing to make a deeper exploration of the times and events that shaped Colonial America. [R: BL, July 2000, p. 2056; SLJ, Nov 2000, p. 96]

—**Terry Ann Mood**

P, S
175. **Westward Expansion: Almanac.** By Tom Pendergast and Sara Pendergast. Edited by Christine Slovery. Farmington Hills, Mich., U*X*L/Gale, 2000. 254p. illus. maps. index. (U*X*L Westward Expansion Reference Library). $120.00/set; $45.00/vol. ISBN 0-7876-4862-0.

P, S
176. **Westward Expansion: Biographies.** By Tom Pendergast and Sara Pendergast. Edited by Christine Slovery. Farmington Hills, Mich., U*X*L/Gale, 2000. 200p. illus. index. (U*X*L Westward Expansion Reference Library). $120.00/set; $45.00/vol. ISBN 0-7876-4863-9.

P, S
177. **Westward Expansion: Primary Sources.** By Tom Pendergast and Sara Pendergast. Edited by Christine Slovery. Farmington Hills, Mich., U*X*L/Gale, 2000. 200p. (U*X*L Westward Expansion Reference Library). $120.00/set; $45.00/vol. ISBN 0-7876-4864-7.

This three-volume set is designed to bring the American West alive for middle school and high school students. *Westward Expansion: Almanac* offers an overview of the events that took place leading up to the migration west as well as the events that shaped this time period's history. It is arranged into 11 chapters covering such topics as territorial expansion to 1812, driving the Native Americans further west, the gold rush, wars with the Native Americans, religion in the west, and technology of the wild west. This volume also offers a timeline of events, a glossary of terms to know (e.g., *Continental Divide, Homestead Act of 1862*), and research and activity ideas. Each chapter contains black-and-white photographs; sidebars on interesting facts, battles, and characters; resources for further information (books and Websites); and a list of sources used in compiling the chapter.

Westward Expansion: Biographies focuses mainly on the interesting characters of the west. Each 2,000-words essay is presented in alphabetic order and includes such people as Buffalo Bill, George Custer, Wyatt Erp, Annie Oakley, Levi Strauss, Daniel Boone, Lewis and Clark, and John Deere. The *Primary Sources* volume features personal accounts from many of the people who experienced the expansion westward first hand. These include journals, autobiographies, and letters.

These volumes are best suited for school libraries and larger public libraries. The information will appeal to children and young adults.—**Shannon Graff Hysell**

Atlases

C, S

178.   Hamilton, Neil A., Jon Keith Brunelle, Beth Scully, and Rebecca Sherman. **Atlas of the Baby Boom Generation.** New York, Macmillan Reference USA/Gale Group, 2000. 250p. illus. maps. index. $130.00. ISBN 0-02-865008-5.

To characterize the "baby boomers," those Americans born during the population explosion from 1946 to 1964, the authors of this excellent atlas use the word "kaleidoscopic." The term is appropriate, for the boomers are certainly diverse. They consist of whites, blacks, Hispanics, and Native Americans; men and women; rich and poor; radicals, liberals, and conservatives; and straights and gays. Add to this the fact that boomers born in 1946 have experienced circumstances quite different from those born in 1964, a contributing factor to the transition from the youthful idealism of student radicals in the 1960s to the crass materialism of "yuppies" in the 1980s, and one can easily appreciate the risk of generalizing about the "baby boomer generation." Even so, the authors point to several unifying themes. Although not all prosperous, the boomers were all children of a prosperous era; although not all indulged in drugs, they were familiar with the drug culture; they all grew to maturity in a culture obsessed with youth, as evidenced by teen movies and magazines and the ever-present rock-n-roll; they were influenced by the nation's move to suburbia; and they shared the thrill of the Apollo missions and the dismay of the political assassinations and the violence at Kent State and in Vietnam.

The purpose of this study is to show how this generation shaped and in turn was shaped by the developments of this tumultuous period. And to accomplish this the authors follow the boomers in successive chapters decade by decade from the 1940s through the 1990s, examining such recurring issues as population and family, education, economics, the bomb (the Cold War and the threat of nuclear destruction), the television, and technology. Additional features in each chapter are a chronology of the decade, biographical sketches, and some treatment of events unique to that time, such as "The Birth of Cool" in the 1950s and Watergate in the 1970s. Replete with an abundance of photographs, drawings, charts, graphs, several statistical appendixes, a brief bibliography, and a thorough index, this study will be of value to anyone interested in contemporary American culture. High schools and universities should add it to their reference collections. [R: VOYA, Dec 2000, p. 374; BR, Jan/Feb 01, pp. 72-73]—**John W. Storey**

Bibliography

C

179.   Cole, Garold L. **Civil War Eyewitnesses.** Columbia, S.C., University of South Carolina Press, 2000. 271p. index. $39.95. ISBN 1-57003-327-7.

The 1st edition of this bibliography earned high accolades from reviews in library and historical periodicals and this excellent update is sure to earn equally fulsome praise. Cole, an emeritus professor of librarianship from Illinois State, includes 596 firsthand accounts on the American Civil War from books and articles published between 1986 and 1996. Entries were originally produced in diaries, journals, letters, or memoirs written by soldiers, sailors, civilians, and foreign observers. Cole divides the entries into three parts. Both the first part on the North and the second part on the South are further divided into military and civilian sections. The third part covers anthologies, studies, and foreign travelers and is further subdivided into sections for the North, South, and general accounts. Within each section, entries are listed alphabetically. Each entry includes the name of the author, editor (if known), publisher or journal, date, and pagination as well as rank, unit, dates of writing, original form (diary letters and so on), major battles the author participated in, and civilian occupation. The annotations are long, detailed, well written, informative, and evaluative. Most take up a third to a half of a page. The excellent index covers personal names, battles, concepts (such as religion, food, and disease), and states. Regiments are indexed under the name of the state. Cole has produced a model historical bibliography. This should be a mandatory acquisition for any library serving serious Civil War scholarship. [R: Choice, Sept 2000, pp. 100-102]—**Patrick J. Brunet**

Dictionaries and Encyclopedias

P, S
180.   **The Civil Rights Movement.** Hackensack, N.J., Salem Press, 2000. 2v. illus. index. (Magill's Choice). $95.00/set. ISBN 0-89356-169-X.

The editors draw from four other Magill publications and add new material to pull together a good quick reference. The two hardbound volumes, the size of nonfiction trade books, will answer basic questions of fact and date and will serve as a starter source. The table of contents reveals an eclectic choice of entries, most pertaining to the struggle for civil rights by African Americans; a very few pertain to Indians and Mexicans (the word "Hispanic" does not appear in the entry titles). Length varies from a half page to six pages. Some sample entries are "Census, U.S.," "Colored Women's League," "Conservative theorists," "Grovey v. Townsend," "Gullah," "Intelligence and race," "Psychology of racism," "Simpson, O. J., trial," "Slave revolt," and "Universal Negro Improvement Association." Only a very few persons appear by name in the body of the text, but a section of biographical sketches appears at the end. Entries are clearly written and accessible to good high school students. Some entries are followed by a list of "Core Resources," and most have *see also* suggestions. This is a useful chronology. [R: SLJ, Aug 2000, p. 128; BR, Nov/Dec 2000, p. 78]—**Edna M. Boardman**

P
181.   **Historical Dictionary of the 1960s.** James S. Olson and Samuel Freeman, eds. Westport, Conn., Greenwood Press, 1999. 548p. index. $95.00. ISBN 0-313-29271-X.

P
182.   **Historical Dictionary of the 1970s.** James S. Olson, ed. Westport, Conn., Greenwood Press, 1999. 414p. index. $89.50. ISBN 0-313-30543-9.

Covering the 1960s and 1970s, these two volumes not only chronicle some of the more tumultuous times in this nation's past, but also highlight, unintentionally, the artificiality of imposing a particular image or pattern on specific decades. History does not come neatly packaged decade by decade, and these two works, taken together, offer ample evidence of that fact. For instance, doubts about those deeply held American convictions referred to by Olson in the 1970s—freedom and equality for all people, the difficulty of severely abusing political power in the balanced system fashioned by the Founding Fathers, the ability of America's capitalistic economy to sustain growth and prosperity, and a commitment to global freedom and prosperity—had their roots in earlier periods, especially so in the case of African Americans.

Although a chronology for each decade, an adequate index, and an alphabetic arrangement make the material readily accessible, there are some questions about the content itself. A number of figures, such as Billy Graham, would seem to fit about as well in either decade. Does Muhammad Ali really merit over three pages, while the antiwar movement and the 1973–1974 Arab oil embargo receive only one? If the Russian invasion of Afghanistan of 1979 warranted coverage, although its repercussions came later, why not at least some mention of the founding of the Moral Majority in 1979? And finally, there appears to be a disproportionate emphasis on movies and television series. Such concerns aside, students would probably find these studies useful. They do offer a quick overview of important segments of American history, and for that reason libraries should consider adding them to their reference collections. [R: BL, 15 April 2000, pp. 1574-1576]—**John W. Storey**

P
183.   Olson, James S. **Historical Dictionary of the 1950s.** Westport, Conn., Greenwood Press, 2000. 353p. index. $79.95. ISBN 0-313-30619-2.

The *Historical Dictionary of the 1950s* heavily emphasizes popular culture and politics. At least 50 percent of its 450 entries, most of which are relatively brief, cover television programs, film stars, movies, rock and roll singers, radio broadcasts, sports stars, celebrities, and miscellaneous events like the Hula Hoop fad. Another large percent of the entries are devoted to politics, such as the Cold War, the Korean War, anti-Communism, and American foreign policy. The remaining entries include biographical sketches of influential intellectuals, musicians, Supreme Court judges, and religious figures, as well as entries on economic trends, medical and scientific developments, legal cases, and literature and plays. A chronology and selected bibliography are also included.

Inevitably, in a work of this sort, some major entries will be omitted, and this dictionary is no exception. It is weak on 1950s intellectuals, artists, and women. It neglects such central thinkers as Lewis Mumford, Ralph Ellison, Reinhold Niebuhr, Will Herberg, B. F. Skinner, and Arthur M. Schlesinger Jr. It also ignores "The New York School" of art, and provides no entries for the abstract expressionists Willem de Kooning, Jackson Pollack, or Robert Motherwell. And, it provides no entries for such female luminaries as Mary McCarthy, Diana Trilling, Margaret Mead, Georgia O'Keeffe, Tillie Olsen, Dorothea Lange, and Agnes DeMille. Despite these omissions, this dictionary provides a solid introduction to the period, making it a useful tool for undergraduates.

—**E. Wayne Carp**

P, S

184.   Schneider, Dorothy, and Carl J. Schneider. **Slavery in America: From Colonial Times to the Civil War.** New York, Facts on File, 2000. 458p. illus. maps. (Eyewitness History Series). $65.00. ISBN 0-8160-3863-5.

Another title in the Eyewitness History series, this volume is designed for an audience ranging from the high school student to the serious historian. Arranged into 12 chapters that span from the early slave trade in Africa (1441) to the demise of slavery in the United States (1865), this remarkable compendium includes a variety of primary source materials focused on the development and evolution of slavery in North America. Each of the 12 chapters begins with a narrative that describes the historical context of the facts presented. This is followed by a detailed chronology and excerpts from memoirs, diaries, letters, newspapers, advertisements, and speeches of slaves and others involved in the institution of slavery.

Comprehensive in scope, the volume treats slavery in Canada, the relationship between Native Americans and African slaves, abolition and the movement to end slavery, and the latest scholarship on women slaves and female slave owners. Also included are extensive appendixes covering major documents, biographies of more than 100 individuals who are important in the history of slavery, a glossary of terms, a bibliography for further study, and a full index for easy access to information. Numerous black-and-white photographs complement the major text.

A reference volume in its own right, this work can also be used to chart pertinent lesson plans, design instructional modules that develop critical thinking skills, or simply be used as an informative narrative regarding an important aspect of African American and United States history. High school libraries and public libraries will not want to hesitate in adding this work; academic libraries should consider the advantage of having so much primary source information brought together between two covers. This work is highly recommended. [R: LJ, 1 Sept 2000, p. 196]—**Edmund F. SantaVicca**

S

185.   Thompson, Peter. **Dictionary of American History: From 1763 to the Present.** New York, Facts on File, 2000. 540p. index. (Facts on File Library of American History). $65.00. ISBN 0-8160-4462-7.

Arranged in an A to Z format, the book covers many of the important people, places, and events that shaped U.S. history. The text is brief and informative. Topics range from broader-scale economic and social issues to more specific subjects, such as generals, politicians, battles, and acts of legislation. The appendixes are especially useful and include maps that show the growth of the United States, government documents, presidents, and Supreme Court justices. A subject index and recommendations for further reading are also included.

Thompson, a scholar of American history, has pulled together 1,200 entries he feels are the most important. Creating a dictionary of American history is always a daunting task—what is important enough to include and what is not? It is easy to quibble about what is missing. For example, not all Native American tribes are listed. Minor mistakes can also be found, such as the battle of Bad Axe River during the Black Hawk War was fought in Wisconsin, not Illinois.

This sniping aside, the book is a solid presentation of U.S. history. Entries, however, would be more useful with references to specific sources. The recommended reading section could also have been greatly expanded. A timeline showing the sequence of events would also have been beneficial. The *Dictionary of American History* is useful as a starting point for high school and college students and general readers who are exploring U.S. history. Its use as a research tool is limited because of its lack of sources for individual entries.—**Mark J. Crawford**

S

186.   Volo, James M., and Dorothy Denneen Volo. **Encyclopedia of the Antebellum South.** Westport, Conn., Greenwood Press, 2000. 390p. illus. index. $65.00. ISBN 0-313-30886-1.

The scope of this work includes the social, cultural, political, and economic aspects of life in the southern United States before the war's onset and the beginning of the Southern Confederacy. The authors, a historian and a teacher, also co-authored a previous book, *Daily Life in Civil War America* (see ARBA 2000, entry 425). Almost 300 entries in just over 350 pages comprise the body of this reference book. Each entry includes several bibliographic suggestions, along with lists of related entries and suggested readings. Boldfaced terms are used liberally throughout this volume and serve as cross-references. Over 45 drawings, maps, period posters, charts, and black-and-white photographs supplement the text. Following A to Z entries is a "Chronology of the Antebellum Period" spanning the years 1781 to 1865, covering major political events leading up to and through the American Civil War.

There are numerous entries under the general topic "Slaves" but only one entry for the general topic "Women," so coverage is somewhat uneven. Because some entries might be difficult to find, the 12-page index provides needed access points and cross-references. Still, this is the only reference work devoted solely to the Antebellum South, and it goes a long way to help dispel the mythology about the lives of pre-Civil War southerners as perpetuated by such works as *Gone with the Wind*. In truth, life was much more complex; volatile political and cultural changes percolated beneath that ostensibly "genteel" exterior.

Encyclopedia of the Antebellum South is a unique and valuable reference source. Previous references, such as the 1,421-page *Encyclopedia of Southern History* (see ARBA 81, entry 444) by Roller and Twyman, or Wilson and Ferris's 1,634-page *Encyclopedia of Southern Culture* (see ARBA 90, entry 491) cover the southern states throughout their 200-plus years of history. Although this encyclopedia is intended for juvenile readers, it is a fine tool for all beginning history students. It is recommended for junior high and high school libraries as well as public and undergraduate college libraries, preferably to be used in conjunction with the more comprehensive works mentioned above. [R: Choice, Sept 2000, pp. 109-110]—**Linda D. Tietjen**

Handbooks and Yearbooks

P, S

187.   Russell, David Lee. **The American Revolution in the Southern Colonies.** Jefferson, N.C., McFarland, 2000. 367p. maps. index. $55.00. ISBN 0-7864-0783-2.

History books give limited space to the battles and events that took place in the South during the American Revolution. In this historical account, the author sets out to "present a comprehensive account of the events" that took place in the Southern colonies that significantly impacted the American Revolution. The role of these colonies was important to the war and several firsts of the American Revolution took place in the South, which include the first declaration of an unconstitutional nature over the Stamp Act in Virginia and the first armed resistance to the Stamp Act in Wilmington, North Carolina.

Before documenting these events, a historical account of the origins of Georgia, Maryland, North Carolina, South Carolina, and Virginia is given. This account begins with the English settlers in 1585 and is important in understanding the viewpoints of both the Southerners and the English government. Not only are the origins of the colonies covered but also the beginnings of slavery in the colonies. The author traces the slavery topic throughout the book. The number of slaves, conditions, runaways, and the theft of slaves by the British are discussed in detail.

The 20-year period from 1763 to 1783 is the main focus of the volume. The year 1783 is noted as the year the British changed their economic and political policies regarding the American colonies. The French and Indian War had ended, and the British looked to the Americans for financial relief in paying the debt. The year 1783 marked the official signing of the declaration of sovereignty and independence for the colonies. Russell devotes a chapter to the events following the surrender at Yorktown, including the problems of withdrawal and loyalists and slaves desiring to leave the colonies.

Place-names are spelled as they were in the 1700s. Historical maps interspersed throughout the volume aid the researcher. Biographical sketches of 53 principal leaders in the Revolution follow the text. These sketches provide a summarization of their lives after the war until their death. American, British, and French individuals are included. A lengthy notes section by chapter, bibliography, and detailed index complete the work. This is a scholarly work recommended for historians and high school, public, and university libraries.—**Elaine Ezell**

AFRICAN HISTORY

P, S

188.   Beck, Roger B. **The History of South Africa.** Westport, Conn., Greenwood Press, 2000. 248p. maps. index. (The Greenwood Histories of the Modern Nations). $35.00. ISBN 0-313-30730-X.

The author of this work, who teaches African and world history at Eastern Illinois University, has written quite a nice little monograph on South African history in only about 200 pages. Given the complexity of the topic, this is no mean feat. Although it begins with the prehistoric period, it is current enough that it can discuss not only the development of the post-apartheid constitution, but even the post-Mandela era. As one might expect, however, the twentieth century garners half the book, and three-fourths of that is taken up with the period following the establishment of the apartheid state in 1948.

This book is, of necessity, startlingly terse at times. Yet, that is not meant to be a criticism since it was written as an introductory text, especially for students, probably of high school or college age. It is also quite suitable as a reference work. It has a good index, a list of notable people in the history of South Africa (58 in all), a glossary of terms (32 of them, primarily Afrikaans and African words), and a brief bibliographic essay that probably could have been expanded somewhat. Also included are a timeline of historical events and a list of abbreviations.

There are no illustrations and the maps are few and at best adequate. More maps, especially in the beginning of the text, would have been helpful. On the other hand, the initial chapter discusses South Africa today, its geography, population, economic conditions, mass media, and much more to set the stage for what follows. Overall, the text is well written, easy to follow, and a good place to start for readers who have no prior knowledge of South African history. This work is recommended for most libraries, but especially high school, college, and public libraries.—**Paul H. Thomas**

C, P

189.   Oyewole, Anthony, and John Lucas. **Historical Dictionary of Nigeria.** 2d ed. Lanham, Md., Scarecrow, 2000. 599p. (African Historical Dictionaries, no.40). $64.00. ISBN 0-8108-3262-3.

This is a much expanded and revised edition of what was a well-received and important reference book when first published in 1987 (see ARBA 88, entry 540). For this 2d edition, Oyewole has been joined by John Lucas, an assistant professor at Pierce College in Washington.

This edition is much larger than the original. The number of pages devoted to the dictionary itself has expanded 60 percent and the bibliography is 35 percent larger, although there appear to be few titles that were published after the early 1990s. The introduction is also larger—primarily to reflect on all that has happened in Nigeria since 1987. One criticism of this series, though, is the lack of helpful maps. This issue's one map is almost useless.

Many of the items added to the dictionary for this edition are for people and events that update the political turmoil in Nigeria. For example, the first entry is for Sani Abacha, the military dictator from 1993 to June 1998. Entries for new states created since 1987 and more entries on women as well as more biographical entries in general can also be found in this edition. In addition, many of the entries from the 1st edition have been updated or deleted. There appear to be more entries dealing with Northern Nigeria and greater attention paid to cultural affairs. The Nigerian musical genre known as "Highlife" is now listed under "Music, Highlife," but unfortunately is lacking a reference from "Highlife."

Given the scope and quality of this work, and that there is nothing else quite like it, as well as the importance of Nigeria in African affairs, this work should be part of any reference collection dealing with Africa.

—**Paul H. Thomas**

C, P

190.   Saunders, Christopher, Nicholas Southey, and Mary-Lynn Suttie. **Historical Dictionary of South Africa.** 2d ed. Lanham, Md., Scarecrow, 2000. 375p. (African Historical Dictionaries, no.78). $85.00. ISBN 0-8108-3646-7.

Updating the 1983 edition and taking account of apartheid's end, this work will strongly interest those collecting information on South Africa. The work begins with a preface, a foreword, a table of contents, a brief five-page introduction, and a list of acronyms and abbreviations. The 22-page chronology covers earliest times through January 1998. One table gives population numbers (male, female, and total) under four racial categories between 1904 and 1991. Another table shows the 1996 population by province and by gender. Maps show the country in the 1890s, provinces from 1910 to 1994 and post-apartheid, and Bantustans. The 289-page dictionary contains alphabetic entries ranging from a short paragraph to a couple of pages. Extensive cross-references between articles and *see* references from unused terms facilitate use.

Citations in the 83-page selective bibliography are arranged under 9 main subjects with 40 subdivisions. Materials are from secondary English-language scholarly sources accessible to North American and British readers. Journal articles and monographs are included, but not unpublished works. Suttie's introduction indicates that the shift in historical work on South Africa from political and economic issues toward broader social and cultural ones since minority rule ended is a major bibliographic shift from the 1st edition. With all of the changes that have occurred since the publication of the 1st edition in 1983, this major work of reference and scholarship will be a must acquisition for serious collections on South African history and current affairs.

—**Nigel Tappin**

ASIAN HISTORY

C, P

191.   Copper, John F. **Historical Dictionary of Taiwan (Republic of China).** 2d ed. Lanham, Md., Scarecrow, 2000. 269p. maps. (Asian/Oceanian Historical Dictionaries, no.34). $49.50. ISBN 0-8108-3665-3.

Much has happened in Taiwan in the political arena since the publication of the 1st edition of this work in 1993 (see ARBA 95, entry 137). This 2d edition brings the historical chronology up to the end of 1998. During this later period, opposition parties gained strength, the voice of Taiwan independence became louder, the power of the ruling Kuomintang party became weaker, direct presidential elections were held, and the tension between China and Taiwan over the one-China policy heated up. Following the growing economic prosperity in Taiwan, there was an increasing deterioration in social order.

This new edition follows much the same format as the first one. The main part of the concise dictionary consists of a chronology of important events, an introduction, a dictionary, and two appendixes (one a list of presidents and premiers since 1949 and the second a compilation of key statistics, along with a fairly extensive topical bibliography). The author of this historical dictionary has written many books on Taiwan and China and is one of the recognized scholars on the subject. It is a useful addition to any library's reference collection on international affairs. [R: Choice, Sept 2000, p. 102]—**Hwa-Wei Lee**

EUROPEAN HISTORY

General Works

Atlases

C, P

192.   Konstam, Angus. **Atlas of Medieval Europe.** New York, Checkmark Books/Facts on File, 2000. 191p. illus. maps. index. $35.00. ISBN 0-8160-4469-4.

In his work, *Atlas of Medieval Europe*, Konstam has provided readers with a valuable guide to studying the history and culture of Medieval Europe. This book has many valuable points. For instance, its coverage extends beyond Western Europe to the Middle East as well as Eastern and Southeastern Europe. A timeline charts crucial events across the bottom of the pages. The coverage extends to history, art, religion, literature, economics, politics, and other subjects. Konstam's focus topics call attention to key issues in the study of this era. As with its predecessor (see ARBA 84, entry 330), the maps in this work are colorful and offer the reader a firsthand account of key battles and movements. The introduction's discussion of "The Medieval Myth" will serve readers well. Konstam's use of excellent contemporary illustrations and the genealogical table in the back are also useful.

However, the book has several flaws that need to be pointed out. First, this work needs a gazetteer and a bibliography. Also, the chronology might have been placed at the front of the book. Finally, it seems as if the Early Middle Ages (400–1100 C.E.) were quickly glossed over to get to the High and Later Middle Ages and the Renaissance. Despite these points, Konstam has provided scholars with a useful reference tool, especially for the High and Later Middle Ages in addition to the Renaissance. His work is recommended for public, community college, and academic (undergraduate) libraries.—**David J. Duncan**

Biography

C

193.   Kamen, Henry. **Who's Who in Europe 1450–1750.** New York, Routledge, 2000. 321p. (Who's Who Series). $29.95. ISBN 0-415-14727-1.

This work is intended to serve as a ready-reference for those searching for information on notable Europeans of the early modern age, 1450 to 1750. It is written mainly for history scholars, although the author notes in the introduction that he has decidedly tried to include those from all disciplines. The author thoroughly explains his criteria for inclusion in this biography as well as gives an explanation of how names are presented in the volume. Each of the 1,000 biographies listed here are one to two paragraphs in length and include birth and death dates and a brief history of their life as well as their contributions to European history. The entries are well written and will be easily understood by the intended audience. This work is relatively inexpensive for a reference book of this caliber. It would be a worthwhile purchase in academic libraries. [R: Choice, Sept 2000, p. 88]

—**Shannon Graff Hysell**

Chronology

P

194.   **The Holocaust Chronicle: A History in Words and Pictures.** Lincolnwood, Ill., Publications International, Ltd., 2000. 765p. illus. maps. index. $35.00. ISBN 0-7853-2963-3.

This volume serves several purposes. First, it is a chronology of the Holocaust covering 1933 to the summer of 1999, which runs along the bottom of each page. In addition, it is both an introduction and a pictorial history of that tragic event. For each year, there is a thematic overview (for example, "Machinery of Death" for 1940, and "Mass Murder" for 1941), as well as many briefer pieces on specific topics of a few paragraphs in length ("Janusz Korczak"; "Art as Resistance"). The final chapter, titled "The Aftermath," discusses some of the more controversial topics, such as Christian culpability, the Swiss banks, and the Goldhagen thesis. The strong point of the book is its abundance of illustrations; there are several hundred archival black-and-white photographs, including portraits of ordinary people and prominent Nazis, stark photographs of executions and war images, and examples of Nazi propaganda. Other features include a glossary of 90 terms, an overall bibliography, an index, and color maps. There is an appendix of statistical tables, which includes a table of concentration camps, but, curiously, not one for extermination camps. Although the book is the product of six contributing writers and a consultant (all of whom are specialists in the field), there is no indication as to which writer is responsible for which chapter(s). There is a companion Website (http://www.holocaustchronicle.org), which offers the complete text of the book, but only some of the photographs (due to copyright restrictions). Robert A. Michael's *The Holocaust: A Chronology and Documentary* (Jason Aronson, 1998) also offers a day-by-day chronology, but it lacks the illustrations and essays of this book. This volume will be ideal for students and the general public as well as for browsing; and, since it is a not-for-profit venture, it is certainly a bargain. [R: BL, 15 Oct 2000, pp. 484-485]—**John A. Drobnicki**

Dictionaries and Encyclopedias

C

195.   Bennett, Martyn. **Historical Dictionary of the British and Irish Civil Wars 1637–1660.** Lanham, Md., Scarecrow, 2000. 253p. (Historical Dictionaries of War, Revolution, and Civil Unrest, no.14). $65.00. ISBN 0-8108-3661-0.

The author of the *Historical Dictionary of the British and Irish Civil Wars 1637–1660* is a faculty member at Nottingham Trent University teaching early modern, British, Irish, and American history. He is an English civil war expert with a number of other publications in this area. The title under review was also published by Fitzroy Dearborn in 2000. The book's purpose is to guide readers in this period of British and Irish history, covering the run up to the war and the aftermath. It provides information on the military and political aspects, but also on the economic, social, and religious consequences. The book contains a map with battle sites and dates, a chronology of events, an introduction, the dictionary itself (including names of people, battles, concepts, places, institutions, names of documents), and a bibliography. The introduction is a readable synthesis, suitable for high school students and above. There are no further readings at the ends of the entries, which is a drawback as most entries are only a paragraph long. The unannotated bibliography contains primarily twentieth-century, secondary works that will be readily accessible in most U.S. libraries, except for the wealth of local history studies. In all cases, the entry relates the person, place, or concept directory to the civil war and its events and concerns. Although one can usually find much more information about many of the concepts and persons in other works, one will not find the depth of information related to the civil war in other comparable dictionaries, such as the *Historical Dictionary of Stuart England, 1603–1689* (see ARBA 97, entry 442) by Ronald Fritze, William Robison, and Walter Sutton. There are also a lot of entries for persons and places connected with the civil war that do not appear in the latter work at all. However, one would think that because religion played such a large role in the conflict that the entries on Catholicism, Presbyterianism, and Puritanism would be fully done in Bennett's work, but this is not the case. These entries are much better in the other work. The work under review shines for its attention to civil war details. And, in this aspect, the work has no peer. This is a labor of love on the author's part, as this is where his expertise lies. There is more detail here than most libraries will need on the subject in their reference departments; this is for comprehensive British history collections, for libraries of military schools, and other libraries where public interest in the British and Irish civil wars is particularly keen, where it will be the last word on the subject.—**Agnes H. Widder**

C, P

196.   **The Encyclopedia of Eastern Europe: From the Congress of Vienna to the Fall of Communism.** Richard Frucht, ed. New York, Garland, 2000. 958p. maps. index. (Garland Reference Library of Social Science, v.751). $95.00. ISBN 0-8153-0092-1.

More than 200 contributors have lent their expertise to this excellent reference volume. Each of the over 1,000 alphabetically arranged articles, which range in length from several sentences to many pages, is signed and includes suggestions for further reading. Topics covered include major cities and geographic territories, historical events and concepts, political leaders, authors, literary works, political parties, trade unions, and prominent universities. Social and cultural subjects are also included, such as art, music, cinema, and women. Users are guided by *see* and *see also* references as well as a thorough index, and there are 16 black-and-white maps. As with any work of this size and scope, questions will be raised about omissions of both fact and content. For example, the Baltic countries, which have historic ties to the region, are not included, and the article on Slovak nationalist leader Andrej Hlinka fails to mention anything about either his or his party's anti-Semitism. Although there are long articles on each country, it would have been more convenient if all the relevant articles were grouped together. For example, to use Poland as an illustration, both "Polish Culture" and "Polish Literature" appear under "P," but "Communist Party of Poland" and "Economic Development in Poland" appear, respectively, in "C" and "E," which does not facilitate browsing. This volume provides much more information (for a longer time period) than Joseph Held's *Dictionary of East European History Since 1945* (see ARBA 95, entry 560) and belongs in all reference collections. [R: BL, 1 Oct 2000, p. 374; LJ, July 2000, pp. 76-78; Choice, Oct 2000, pp. 293-294; RUSQ, Winter 2000, p. 185]—**John A. Drobnicki**

C

197.　Pope, Stephen. **Dictionary of the Napoleonic Wars.** New York, Facts on File, 1999. 572p. maps. (Facts on File Library of World History). $65.00. ISBN 0-8160-4243-8.

The era of the Napoleonic Wars has faded in the public memory—apart from the legions of readers of Patrick O'Brian. All too often Napoleon I is left out of Western civilization classes, despite the tremendous influence he had on the development of modern Europe. Pope's *Dictionary of the Napoleonic Wars* is a lesson in just how important these few decades were for the world, the Western world in particular. In articles covering both broad and narrow subjects (e.g., naval artillery, French Revolution, Waterloo) Pole provides an exhaustive array of information. The articles cover military, political, economic, and social aspects of the period. Most are brief—a few paragraphs or a column at most—but they are clear and informative. Although the entries lack bibliographic information (which would have been helpful to those in search of further detail), they are elaborately cross-referenced. Pope has included a detailed chronology of the years from 1792 to 1815 (also cross-referenced) and 30 maps. The maps illustrate important battles at sea and on land, and some of the continental-sized changes wrought by the Corsican adventurer. The book will be a handy reference for those in need of basic information, and is a pleasure to browse as well. [R: Choice, Sept 2000, pp. 106-108; BL, 1 Sept 2000, p. 175]—**Victor L. Stater**

C, P

198.　Rozett, Robert, and Shmuel Spector. **Encyclopedia of the Holocaust.** New York, Facts on File and Jerusalem, Israel, Yad Vashem, The Holocaust Martyrs' and Heroes' Remembrance Authority, 2000. 528p. illus. index. $95.00. ISBN 0-8160-4333-7.

Following 8 general essays on the Jewish experience before, during, and after the Holocaust, the editors present nearly 700 articles covering people, places, organizations, documents, and camps. The individual entries do not contain suggested readings, but there is a basic overall bibliography. Articles range in length from one to two sentences to a few pages, with the majority several paragraphs. Co-published by Yad Vashem, Israel's official Holocaust remembrance authority, the book has a slight bias toward inclusion of people and topics of interest to an Israeli audience. For example, Gideon Hausner (the chief prosecutor at the Eichmann trial) is included, but not Robert Jackson (the chief prosecutor at the Nuremberg IMT).

There are *see, see also*, and cross-references. Other features include a chronology (1920–1945) as well as an abundance of black-and-white archival photographs. Although the articles are up-to-date—including an entry covering the recent David Irving/Deborah Lipstadt libel trial—several entries do not have the detail that one expects in an encyclopedia. For example, the article on Polish courier Jan Karski does not mention that in 1944 he wrote an important book helping to publicize the Final Solution (Story of a Secret State). Further, the article on Franz Stangl does not mention that extensive interviews with him formed the basis of Gitta Sereny's book, *Into That Darkness.* Similarly, it does not serve the reader well to describe Itzhak Katzenelson's diary as an important document and then not give its title (*Vittel Diary*). Nevertheless, this is a fine one-volume source and should be strongly considered by libraries that do not own Israel Gutman's *Encyclopedia of the Holocaust* (see ARBA 91, entry 520), which remains the standard source.—**John A. Drobnicki**

Handbooks and Yearbooks

C, P

199.　**The Columbia Guide to the Holocaust.** By Donald Niewyk and Francis Nicosia. New York, Columbia University Press, 2000. 473p. maps. index. $45.00. ISBN 0-231-11200-9.

With so many new books on the Holocaust published every year, authors and editors are attempting to distinguish their works by offering features different from the rest. Such is the case with this volume by historians Niewyk and Nicosia, which consists of several valuable books in one. The authors begin by offering a well-written historical overview of the Holocaust, before moving into a balanced discussion of controversies and interpretations on topics such as intentionalists and functionalists, Jewish resistance, and bystanders and perpetrators. The 3d section is a chronology covering 1918 to 1993, while the 4th is an encyclopedia providing information on 54 people, 41 places, 59 terms, and 29 organizations, which (due to obvious space constraints) is much too small to cover all the requisite persons and terminology. For example, there are no entries for either Martin Bormann or Rudolf Hess. The volume's 5th section is a valuable 150-page guide to resources (subdivided by subject headings), consisting of annotated bibliographies of both print and electronic materials (including primary and secondary sources, selected music recordings, and Websites); an annotated filmography; and a list of Holocaust-related organizations, museums, and memorials, which provides addresses, telephone and fax numbers, and e-mail and URL addresses. Finally, there are 2 appendixes containing tables of statistics and 11 black-and-white maps, as well as an overall index.

Because this book is a combination monograph, dictionary, encyclopedia, and handbook, it is not fair to compare it with other books, since it obviously will not cover as many persons and events as Jack R. Fischel's *Historical Dictionary of the Holocaust* (see ARBA 2000, entry 493), or contain as many entries as Israel Gutman's *Encyclopedia of the Holocaust* (see ARBA 91, entry 520) or *Dictionary of the Holocaust: Biography, Geography, and Terminology*, by Eric Joseph Epstein and Philip Rosen (see ARBA 99, entry 528). Nevertheless, it is an impressive volume, and the authors have succeeded in providing a handy one-volume, multipurpose guide to the Holocaust.

—**John A. Drobnicki**

French

C, P

200.   Haine, W. Scott. **The History of France.** Westport, Conn., Greenwood Press, 2000. 260p. maps. index. (Greenwood Histories of the Modern Nations). $35.00. ISBN 0-313-30328-2.

A first examination of the 260-page text makes one think that the title *The History of France* is a presumptuous one for such a succinct treatment of such a rich history like that of France. When a book of this size begins its coverage with prehistoric times, it becomes difficult to address, in a single volume, one of the most eventful histories of the world, and one that has constituted the research subject of so many scholars worldwide. In a 4-page "Bibliographic Essay" (pp. 243–246) the author acknowledges that "the list of histories of France is almost endless." A basic OCLC search performed on 11 November 2000 with the key words "France" and "history" yield 208,667 items. When the search was restricted to materials in the English language, 47,589 documents were retrieved. When the search was further narrowed to publication year "1999–2001" and document type "books," a number of 8,397 items were retrieved. Clearly, the history of France continues to be a hot topic.

A closer examination of the volume reveals that it is part of the Greenwood Histories of the Modern Nations series, which has featured many other countries, such as Brazil, Mexico, Nigeria, Portugal, Poland, and South Africa, among others. The series "is intended to provide students and interested lay people with up-to-date, concise, and analytical histories of many nations of the contemporary world" (p. viii). Therefore, this is an unpretentious look into French history that highlights only major events and prominent figures. The appendix, "Notable People in the History of France," lists a total of 45 names of writers, politicians, kings, and presidents. This book provides a compact history of France, however, it would need supplementation as a course textbook.

The volume consists of 12 chapters. The first chapter represents a country study, where France's geography, climate, flora, fauna, population, economy, religion, and political system are presented. The subsequent chapters broadly cover distinct periods of French history, such as the Roman conquest, the Merovingian dynasty, Charlemagne's empire, the Capetian and Carolingian rules, the Absolute Monarchy, the Revolution, the Napoleonic era, the two World Wars, and the Republican age. The third, fourth, and fifth Republics received in-depth treatment, each having an entire chapter devoted to the specific events and key players of the period. The post-Charles de Gaulle presidencies (Georges Pompidou, Valéry Giscard d'Estaing, François Mitterrand, and Jacques Chirac) are analyzed not only from political, but also from economic, social, and cultural perspectives. The author's research draws on recent sources published in French or English. He also points the reader to significant resources on French history and society available on the World Wide Web.

Haine's master's thesis and doctoral dissertation, both from the University of Wisconsin, Madison, focused on social issues specific to late nineteenth-century France. *The History of France* is Haine's second book. His first book, *The World of the Paris Café: Sociability Among the French Working Class, 1789–1914*, was published in 1996 by Johns Hopkins University Press.—**Hermina G. B. Anghelescu**

German

C, P

201. Nicholls, David. **Adolf Hitler: A Biographical Companion.** Santa Barbara, Calif., ABC-CLIO, 2000. 357p. illus. index. $55.00. ISBN 0-87436-965-7.

Adolf Hitler: A Biographical Companion is a first-rate encyclopedic resource encompassing the key elements of Hitler's life and times. Topics include biographical profiles of significant individuals in Hitler's life, ranging from Josef Goebbels and Dwight D. Eisenhower to Albert Speer. There are concise articles about both Allied and Axis nations, as well as analytical discussions of more abstract concepts like "Cinema," "Radio," and "Total War." The essays are well written, if short, with excellent cross-references to related entries and suggestions for further readings. The essays, while covering a broad range of topics, consistently focus on how the topic in question affected either Germany or Hitler, giving the entire volume a coherence it might otherwise lack in the hands of a less-disciplined author. The book is well illustrated and nicely bound on acid-free paper. There is an erudite introduction that provides the reader with an overview of Hitler's rise and fall. A detailed chronology of Hitler's life is included as well as an outstanding bibliography that includes all of the sources referred to in the "Suggestions for Further Readings." The back of the book includes selections from primary source documents, which cover such topics as "Hitler's Worldview," "The Beer Hall Putsch," "Mein Kampf: Lebensraum and Russia," and "Racial Science." Perhaps the only shortcoming is that the book lacks maps, a serious oversight in a book dealing with World War II. On the whole, this is an outstanding reference resource that is highly recommended for any library. [R: LJ, 1 Nov 2000, p. 72; BL, 1 Jan 01, p. 992]—**Philip G. Swan**

Irish

C, P

202. Bew, Paul, and Gordan Gillespie. **Northern Ireland: A Chronology of the Troubles 1968–1999.** rev. ed. Lanham, Md., Scarecrow, 1999. 471p. index. $45.00. ISBN 0-8108-3735-8.

The 1st edition of this work, published in 1993, covered the troubles from 1968 to 1992. This volume carries the story to May 1999; otherwise the work is the same. The primary author, Paul Bew, is a professor of politics at Queen's University, Belfast; the co-author, Gordon Gillespie, is a professor of politics and of sociology at the same institution. Bew, alone and with colleagues, is the author of some 11 other books on nineteenth- and twentieth-century Ireland and Northern Ireland in our library, which are much used by students writing papers on the Northern Irish problems in this period.

Northern Ireland: A Chronology of the Troubles, 1968–1999 is a fine work arranged by year and within the year chronologically by date, providing paragraph-length entries on happenings in Northern Ireland essentially day by day. It is a fine substitute for newspapers of the period 1968–1999, if the library has no subscription to papers from Northern Ireland, which few of do. Current daily news is now available on the Internet from Belfast from several newspapers. The book has simple but clear maps of Northern Ireland, Belfast, and Derry. There is a six-page summary chronology at the back covering the entire period, and a six-page unannotated bibliography. Some of the major events, such as Bloody Sunday and the Belfast Agreement, have page-length essays devoted to them. The authors of this work teach at an institution in Northern Ireland and are thus in a better position to know the facts of the situation over a long period of time than authors located elsewhere. This volume is essential for libraries with patrons who want to study the situation in Northern Ireland in the late twentieth century.—**Agnes H. Widder**

Polish

C, P

203. Biskupski, M. B. **The History of Poland.** Westport, Conn., Greenwood Press, 2000. 236p. index. (The Greenwood Histories of the Modern Nation). $35.00. ISBN 0-313-30571-4.

Biskupski, a professor of history at St. John Fisher College who has written extensively on twentieth-century Polish and diplomatic history, synthesizes 1,000 years of Polish history into one succinct volume. Although he does cover pre-partition Poland in one chapter, the bulk of the book covers the years 1795 to the present. Writing clearly and concisely and never shying away from controversy, Biskupski offers very balanced treatments of many sensitive issues such as Poland's relations with its Jews. Unlike some writers, the author does not blindly praise or condemn, offering fair and balanced assessments of, among others, Roman Dmowski, Jozef Pilsudski, and Woodrow Wilson. Especially valuable is Biskupski's bibliographic essay where he points out the strengths, weaknesses, and biases of the vast secondary literature. Although this book is ideal for circulating collections or as a textbook, it does not appear to have been designed as a reference book—it contains a glossary of only 31 words in addition to brief biographical profiles of 42 notable Poles. Libraries seeking more comprehensive reference volumes should consider *Historical Dictionary of Poland, 966–1945* by Jerzy J. Lerski (Greenwood Press, 1996), and *Historical Dictionary of Poland, 1945–1996* by Piotr Wróbel (see ARBA 2000, entry 461).

—**John A. Drobnicki**

Russian

C

204.   Raymond, Boris, and David R. Jones. **The Russian Diaspora 1917–1941.** Lanham, Md., Scarecrow, 2000. 273p. $45.00. ISBN 0-8108-3786-2.

It is estimated that from 1917 to 1922, that is, after the revolutions and the Civil War, some 1.5 to 2 million people left Soviet Russia. In addition, approximately 7 million Russians found themselves living in newly independent states, which had previously belonged to the Russian Empire. *Russian Diaspora* deals with those Russians, who left Soviet Russia in a mass exodus between 1917 and 1922. Although the chronological parameters in the title are 1917 to 1941 the authors do not explicitly state why they chose the latter date. It was, of course, in 1941 that Germany attacked the Soviet Union, but the Russian/Soviet emigration had dwindled down to a trickle in the 1930s and, in fact, during the same period considerable return traffic was taking place, to which the authors only obliquely refer. Most of the exiles of the major wave belonged to the privileged classes—artists, scientists, aristocrats, army officers, and so forth.

This book concentrates on those Russian exiles who, after the emigration, gained worldwide recognition in their fields. The introduction outlines the history of pre-Revolutionary Russia and Russian emigration in general terms. Separate sections are devoted to the various countries or continents where the Russian exiles immigrated. The sections describe the reception of the refugees in those countries and their attempts to resist the assimilation and to maintain the Russian culture, education, religion, and other organized activities, while also analyzing the political disagreements among them. The main section is an alphabetically arranged biographical dictionary of the names of some 200 accomplished Russian emigrants.

The entries vary from $\frac{1}{2}$ to $1\frac{1}{2}$ pages and include references to sources on the subject's life and activities. The third section consists of sources used, a general bibliography, and country-specific sources and studies, mostly in English or Russian, on the Russian emigration. The authors intended the work for "the nonspecialist student" of Russian history and culture. One hopes that the authors, or someone else, will produce a sequel to the work in hand to cover the subsequent waves of Russian/Jewish emigration.—**Leena Siegelbaum**

United Kingdom

C, P

205.   Black, Jeremy. **Historical Atlas of Britain: The End of the Middle Ages to the Georgian Era.** Herndon, Va., Sutton Publishing, 2000. 204p. illus. maps. index. $39.95. ISBN 0-7509-2128-5.

Seldom do readers find a historical atlas of this scope and size that gives more than a mere outline of its subject. This work is an exception. Not only does it give users the facts, they also experience the feel of what the events meant to the historical evolution of Britain during the covered time. These events are brought to life both by Black's detailed knowledge of the period and a lively style that knows what needs explanation and what does not. Then there are the illustrations and maps.

The illustrations give a studied blend of portraits of the most important characters of the period and paintings of houses, castles, and events that reflect the history. The colors are vibrant and even the black-and-white reproductions stand out on the heavy paper of this physically well-constructed title.

Of note are the four dozen maps. Rather than completely reconstructing events from a modern point of view, Black uses many maps drawn during the period to illustrate towns, battles, and points of historical interest. Of course, there are maps showing invasion routes and points of economic change, but the reproduction of historical renderings give this title a unique flavor of how contemporaries would have viewed their country during the time.

There are also a narrative bibliography that describes and points to both the best historical and secondary sources to broaden the readers understanding of the period and a detailed index for ease of use. Black has given users a wonderful and attractive place to start their journey through the heart of the history of Great Britain.

—**Kennith Slagle**

LATIN AMERICA AND THE CARIBBEAN

C, S

206.   Foster, Lynn V. **A Brief History of Central America.** New York, Facts on File, 2000. 326p. illus. maps. index. $35.00. ISBN 0-8160-3962-3.

Facts on File's history of the seven countries of the isthmus between Mexico and Colombia is a serious, complex digestion of its geography, economy, politics, and wars. An extensive bibliography of English titles grounds the text, but there are no footnotes to facilitate the reading, leaving the sources unclear. Foster's strengths are her coverage of ecology, democracy, education, the welfare of the lower classes, unification of the area, and peace. Yet, her coverage of difficult weather, volcano and earthquake threats, colonization, economic development, and dictators make many pages painful to read. She does not think drugs or communism were ever a major problem. Rather it is the hustling of European and North American business ventures that disrupted a relatively adequate indigenous lifestyle and caused wars and poverty.

The long index is helpful, as is the glossary for the regularly used Spanish vocabulary. Nearly every other page turn brings up a picture; a box of quotations; or a chart of statistics about education, religion, language, and so on. High school students with high reading competence and a stomach for horror can read this work. It would make a valuable textbook for college courses.—**Elizabeth L. Anderson**

P, S

207.   Kirkwood, Burton. **The History of Mexico.** Westport, Conn., Greenwood Press, 2000. 245p. maps. index. (The Greenwood Histories of the Modern Nations). $35.00. ISBN 0-313-30351-7.

This book is an excellent review of key economic, historical, political, and social events that shaped the country and people of Mexico. Beginning with the first known inhabitants, dating back to 35,000 to 50,000 B.C.E., the author highlights major events up to 1998; however, the emphasis is on recent times. There are 11 chapters that represent different periods, such as the Conquest, wars of Mexican independence, and the Mexican Revolution. Each chapter is followed by a very brief bibliography. Of more importance, however, is the short bibliographic essay at the end of the book that provides an excellent starting point for in-depth analyses. Besides the narrative, the book includes a timeline, 1 map, and 24 brief biographies. Although the author is a historian specializing in Mexico, the book is written for the layperson. This is an important book in the series of national histories because it provides a readable history of the United State's neighbor to the south. The book is reasonably priced and is recommended for school, public, and academic libraries.—**Karen Y. Stabler**

MIDDLE EASTERN HISTORY

C, P

208.   Baines, John, and Jaromir Malek. **Cultural Atlas of Ancient Egypt.** rev. ed. New York, Checkmark Books/Facts on File, 2000. 240p. illus. maps. index. $50.00. ISBN 0-8160-4036-2.

The *Cultural Atlas of Ancient Egypt* comprises a revision of the authors' well-known *Atlas of Ancient Egypt*. The redigitized maps show many details and descriptions that do not appear in the earlier book. Place-names now include modern, classical, and ancient Egyptian, omitting the biblical that was often used previously. Some illustrations are new, others are presented from a different view, and some newer photographs of archaeological activity have been substituted for older images.

The authors have also thoroughly reviewed the text, revising it to include new information and current thinking on many matters. Very significantly, they have revised the dates for the historic periods and for the dynasties and kings prior to dynasty 26, as well as suggesting there are no absolutely firm dates prior to that dynasty. In addition, they have changed the dating terminology from B.C. to B.C.E. and A.D. to C.E. Finally, the bibliography has been considerably revised and updated. The revisions present in this edition suggest that it belongs in any private, public, school, college, and university library that serves people interested in ancient Egypt.

—**Susan Tower Hollis**

C, P, S

209.   **Dictionary of the Ancient Near East.** Piotr Bienkowski and Alan Millard, eds. Philadelphia, University of Pennsylvania Press, 2000. 342p. illus. maps. index. $49.95. ISBN 0-8122-3557-6.

This work covers the ancient Near East (Mesopotamia, Anatolia, the Levant, and the Arabian Peninsula) along with relevant materials from the biblical world and ancient Egypt, from prehistory through the middle of the first millennium. Topics of discussion include places, both ancient and modern people (e.g., Flinders Petrie), deities, narratives, and much more in clear, concise, and informative entries. For example, A. R. Millard's discussion of the ancient, putative king Gilgamesh not only places him within the Sumerian king list, discussing his evolution to receiving offerings as an underworld deity, but also outlines the hero's presence in Sumerian poems and in the epic about him that is so well known throughout the ancient Near East. The same scholar presents a similarly clear discussion of the three different Sargons, leaving the reader with a good understanding of each king as an individual.

Every entry concludes with an appropriate brief bibliography, largely, though not exclusively, citing English-language resources. A number of these bibliographic entries refer to modern multivolume works such as the four-volume *Civilizations of the Ancient Near East* (see ARBA 96, entry 159) or the five-volume *Oxford Encyclopaedia of Archaeology in the Ancient Near East* (see ARBA 98, entry 429). These reference works may be present in college and university libraries and some large public libraries, but are unlikely to be readily available otherwise. Thus, this volume, lavishly illustrated with photos and some maps and written by well-known and well-qualified scholars, provides a reasonable reference for both the interested layperson and public and school libraries. [R: BL, 15 Oct 2000, p. 478; Choice, Oct 2000, pp. 308-310]—**Susan Tower Hollis**

S

210.   Harris, Geraldine, and Delia Pemberton. **Illustrated Encyclopedia of Ancient Egypt.** Lincolnwood, Ill., Peter Bedrick Books/Contemporary Publishing, 1999. 176p. illus. $29.95. ISBN 0-87226-606-0.

This authoritative and entertaining one-volume reference work is an excellent introduction to the world of Ancient Egypt for young students. While its over 200 entries are written for children age 9-12 years of age, older students may also find it useful for ready reference.

The authors, lecturers in Egyptology at Oxford University and the British Museum, effectively communicate their knowledge of the life and times of Ancient Egypt in such a way as to capture the imaginations of their intended audience. The encyclopedia is beautifully illustrated with a predominance of color photographs. A majority of the illustrations depict items that are part of the British Museum collections.

Entries vary in length from one line to two pages, with an average entry approximately a quarter to half a page. The well-researched and well-written entries highlight key terms in bold typeface. Each topic highlighted in this way has its own separate entry in the encyclopedia. Following these cross-references is sometimes difficult. For example, the single-line entry for the Nile highlights the word "Egypt." A reader going to the entry for Egypt will not immediately find the information relating to the Nile in the entry since it does not appear in bold typeface. An index is also available.

A novel means of access is provided through thematic "trails." Selected entries are classified using topics such as "Myth and Magic" or "Egypt and its Neighbors." A listing of the thematic trails and the corresponding entries related to each may be found in the beginning of the book. Every trail is identified by an icon, which appears at the beginning of each entry that is a part of the trail. Using the icon for a particular trail, a reader may browse the encyclopedia looking for entries displaying a particular icon to locate information on a topic.

This encyclopedia is an admirable reference source that provides a wealth of information on Ancient Egypt. School libraries and children's collections will find it a worthwhile purchase. [R: SLJ, Nov 2000, pp. 90-92]

—**Elizabeth M. Mezick**

P

211. Moussalli, Ahmad S. **Historical Dictionary of Islamic Fundamentalist Movements in the Arab World, Iran, and Turkey.** Lanham, Md., Scarecrow, 1999. 401p. (Historical Dictionary of Religions, Philosophies, and Movements, no.23). $75.00. ISBN 0-8108-3609-2.

This volume is part of a group of 17 dictionaries on religions, philosophies, and movements. The focus is on recent movements, groups, and leaders within what has come to be known as Islamic fundamentalism. The main part of the dictionary contains brief biographies of leaders, thinkers, and ideologues like al-Afghani and Hasan al-Banna and explanations of terms like "Feda'iyan-i Islam" and "martyrdom," all from the point of view of Islamic fundamentalism. Entry to terms is made easy for both expert and neophyte as all entries are extensively cross-referenced with concepts and doctrines listed according to their translated meaning in English (e.g., "al-hurriyya" is listed under "freedom"). Well-known Arabic terms such as "jihad" and "Hamas" are presented in their transliterated form. The dictionary includes major and minor figures, legal and illegal organizations, and radical and moderate individuals. Making the dictionary even more useful is a chronology of formative events in the development of nineteenth- and twentieth-century fundamentalism. There is also an introductory essay on the development and role of Islamic fundamentalism in the Middle East with explanations of the fundamentalist interpretation of legislation, revolution, and consensus. An extensive, select bibliography with material in both Arabic and English covering the Middle East from Morocco to Iran and Turkey is also included. The dictionary should be accessible to experts and beginners and thus should be located in all libraries where access to information on Islamic fundamentalism will be called for. [R: Choice, April 2000, p. 1450]—**David L. White**

WORLD HISTORY

Atlases

P, S

212. Farrington, Karen. **Historical Atlas of Expeditions.** New York, Checkmark Books/Facts on File, 2000. 189p. illus. maps. index. $35.00. ISBN 0-8160-4432-5.

From antiquity to the present, man has gone exploring for trade, wealth, power, and religious conversion—but above all, out of curiosity. In this reference, biographical essays tell the story of global discovery. It is amply illustrated with photographs, drawings, and timelines but there is limited use of maps. The author begins with early voyages throughout the Ancient world and moves on to explorations before 1600. This account includes interesting individuals, such as Ibn Battuta who traveled all over the medieval Arab world and Willem Barents who was the first European to survive an Arctic winter. The book continues with individual sections for explorations to each continent after 1600. These chapters expand the reader's awareness beyond the usually discussed explorers.

Students are introduced to new names, such as Nain Singh who mapped Tibet for the British in the 1860s while posing as a Buddhist monk; Mary Kingsley who collected zoological specimens during the 1890s in present-day Nigeria, Cameroon, and Gabon; and Fridtjof Nansen who used ice pack drift to travel the Arctic from 1893 to 1895. The narrative also points out changing motivations for exploration. By the end of the twentieth century the world's geography was generally known and explorers turned their attention to wildlife preservation and archaeology. Also interesting is the changing use of technology. Although the men and women profiled are predominately of European origin, the abundance of less well-known figures, from the West as well as the East, is a key strength of this well-written chronology of humans' quest for knowledge about the world and its diversity. [R: LJ, 1 Nov 2000, p. 70]—**Adrienne Antink Bien**

P, S

213. Konstam, Angus. **Historical Atlas of Exploration 1492–1600.** New York, Checkmark Books/Facts on File, 2000. 191p. illus. maps. index. $35.00. ISBN 0-8160-4248-9.

For 20 years, Facts on File has produced cultural and historical atlases combining the best of maps and illustrations with historical accounts. Konstam's *Historical Atlas of Exploration 1492–1600* carries on this tradition in splendid fashion.

This work has many strengths. Konstam's historical account includes every nation of the period, its respective interests, and the issues surrounding its colonizing efforts. The important figures' biographical sketches give perspective to their actions. Important factors such as ocean currents, the ships, the navigational instruments, and techniques enlighten the reader to the environment in which these events occurred. The work's balanced analysis of European, Asian, African, and Native American cultures is commendable. The timetables at the bottom of each section's first page assist the reader in tracking these events' development throughout the period. The author also blends his maps between contemporary and modern versions. The cultural and archaeological depictions add yet another dimension to the work's account. The index and alphabetic list of explorers are a nice addition.

However, the work has two weaknesses. First, Konstam should have included a gazetteer with his index. Second, a section of further reading materials should be here as well. Despite these issues, the *Historical Atlas of Exploration* should be included with the other Facts on File atlases. Like its counterparts, it provides an apt introduction to its chosen subject field for years to come. This work belongs in public, high school, junior college, college, and university libraries. [R: SLJ, Nov 2000, p. 92]—**David J. Duncan**

Biography

C, P

214. **World Leaders of the Twentieth Century.** Hackensack, N.J., Salem Press, 2000. 2v. illus. index. $95.00/set. ISBN 0-89356-337-4.

A recent entry in the Magill's Choice series, this 2-volume set chronicles the lives of 111 political leaders, most of whom were (or are) heads of state either through election or coercion. Only 15 of the biographies are new, while the rest are taken from Salem Press's Great Lives from History: American series, British and Commonwealth series, Twentieth-Century series, and *Dictionary of World Biography: The 20th Century* (see ARBA 2000, entry 479). For the most part, the original text was not changed, although the biographies for those still living have been brought up-to-date and recent titles have been added to the brief bibliographies at the end of each essay. As with most Magill titles, the language is clear and easy to understand.

The countries most heavily represented are the United States, Great Britain, and the Soviet Union, although leaders from 44 other countries are included. The broad geographical coverage definitely enhances the reference value of the set. Of the 111 entries, 5 are devoted to women: Indira Gandhi, Elizabeth II, Golda Meir, Margaret Thatcher, and Corazon Aquino.

Each entry is 2,000–3,000 words long and each follows the same format: a listing of birth and death dates and places, a brief paragraph summarizing the significance of the person, a section on his or her early life, another on his or her life's work, and an overview of the individual's contribution. The leaders are presented alphabetically, followed by an appendix listing them by country and a subject index.

Recommended for middle- through undergraduate-level students. For libraries owning the original sets, this purchase is not essential. [R: Choice, April 2000, pp. 1450-1452]—**Hope Yelich**

Chronology

P, S

215. **Children's History of the 20th Century.** New York, DK Publishing, 1999. 344p. illus. index. $29.95. ISBN 0-7894-4722-3.

This compilation of historical twentieth-century information is designed specifically with children and young adults in mind. The short, news-like articles, which are accompanied by brilliant photographs, will appeal to children ages 8 through 14. The book begins with an overview of the century, which features quotes from children with their thoughts on such topics as war, the environment, and the future. Following this introduction, each year in the twentieth century is featured on one page. The book highlights political, technological, and pop cultural hits of that year. The book is arranged in typical DK Publishing style—the layout is not uniform but instead has entries arranged sporadically throughout the text, with different font sizes and both illustrations and photographs. At the bottom of each page is a timeline that highlights newsmakers from each month. Throughout each decade there are pages discussing important features of the decade, such as the Depression in the 1930s, women at war in the 1940s, the feminist fight of the 1970s, and the end of the Cold War in the 1990s. A section titled "Life in the 21st Century" focuses on the new millennium and how human life will change as a result of new technologies such as Internet shopping, videophones, and high-tech homes. The last section of the work chronologically lists people who are famous in the areas of entertainment, science, sports, politics, and music, as well as famous criminals. An index concludes the work.

Children will enjoy browsing through this book so filled with interesting historical facts. School libraries and public libraries will do well to add this to their collections.—**Shannon Graff Hysell**

P, S

216.   Davidson, Edward, and Dale Manning. **Chronology of World War Two.** London, Cassell; distr., New York, Sterling Publishing, 1999. 286p. illus. maps. index. $29.95. ISBN 0-304-35309-4.

In their previous book, *Who Was Who in the Second World War*, the authors collected the biographies of 500 leading figures of the conflict. This volume provides a day-by-day chronology of the most important events of the war from September 1, 1939, through September 1, 1945, including every combatant nation. The accessible format lists each date in bold along the left followed by the entries, which vary from a few sentences to several paragraphs. Brief two- or three-word topical headings in the margins denote what is treated more thoroughly in the entries. The volume contains maps of all the theaters, a good index, and a few pictures in the center section. The picture section is so scant, however, that it would have been better not to include it.

Many World War II chronologies, both more specific and as part of larger collections, already exist. If a library already owns John S. Bowman's *Facts About the American Wars* (see ARBA 99, entry 471), with its extensive coverage of World War II, this particular volume is not necessary. However, it is quite inexpensive, which makes it an easy acquisition.—**Joe P. Dunn**

S

217.   **Millennium Year by Year.** 2000 ed. New York, DK Publishing, 2000. 896p. illus. maps. index. $29.95. ISBN 0-7894-6539-6.

An entertaining blend of historical fact and editorial journalistic narrative, this volume should help many high school students better understand the cultural highlights and achievements of civilizations around the world—past and present. The basic arrangement is chronological by year (or clusters of years) and the format is that of a basic tabloid newspaper, with approximately 10 major stories per year. Most of the stories average 150 to 200 words, and at least one-half are accompanied by color or black-and-white illustrations. Also included is a sidebar that highlights other major events of the year. Each article has a dateline and location of the story. A full index complements the volume, while a brief five-page chronology chart of the entire millennium prefaces the work. No introduction or criteria for inclusion are to be found anywhere.

For the individual who simply wants an overview of a decade or other extended period, this volume will serve as a good general introduction. However, the interrelationships of historical events and achievements are not to be found between the pages of this work. It is a selected chronology of events, enhanced by a bit of prose and illustration. As such, the armchair historian, trivia buff, and others will find the work of some interest and curiosity. Easily readable, this volume could certainly be used effectively within the contexts of school curricula in the area of world civilization. It is recommended for its readability and illustrations.—**Edmund F. SantaVicca**

P, S

218.   Shaw, Antony, and Ian Westwell. **World in Conflict 1914–1945.** Chicago, Fitzroy Dearborn, 2000. 416p. illus. maps. index. $125.00. ISBN 1-57958-212-5.

Unquestionably, World War I and World War II are the defining events of the first half of the twentieth century. Shaw and Westwell look at these two wars not as discrete catastrophic happenings, but as one continuum. The interwar period of 1918–1939 was not a time of peace, but instead was marked by civil wars, localized territorial disputes, and colonial campaigns that all contributed to the five-decade record of death and misery.

This book begins on June 28, 1914, with the assassination of the Archduke Ferdinand and continues day by day in a diary format to September 2, 1945, when the Japanese signed the surrender treaty on board the USS *Missouri*. Major political and military events for each date are given. Notations include battles on land, sea, and air as well as on all fronts across the globe. The profusion of photos brings to life the human toll suffered and viscerally connects the reader with the people who lived through those perilous times. There are frequent sidebars focusing on the pivotal leaders, decisive weapons, and key strategies that shaped these five decades. Features include maps, a detailed index, and a bibliography, along with brief biographies for many generals, admirals, and politicians. [R: Choice, Oct 2000, p. 313]—**Adrienne Antink Bien**

S

219.   **Timelines on File: Nations and States.** By Diagram Group. New York, Facts on File, 2000. 1v. (various paging). illus. index. $125.00; $390.00/set with binder. ISBN 0-8160-4307-8; 0-8160-4277-2/set.

S

220.   **Timelines on File: The Ancient and Medieval World (Prehistory–1500 CE).** By The Diagram Group. New York, Facts on File, 2000. 1v. (various paging). illus. maps. index. $125.00; $390.00/set with binder. ISBN 0-8160-4304-3; 0-8160-4277-2/set.

S

221.   **Timelines on File: The Expanding World.** By The Diagram Group. New York, Facts on File, 2000. 1v. (various paging). illus. maps. index. $125.00; $390.00/set with binder. ISBN 0-8160-4305-1; 0-8161-4277-2/set.

S

222.   **Timelines on File: The 20th Century.** By The Diagram Group. New York, Facts on File, 2000. 1v. (various paging). illus. maps. index. $125.00; $390.00/set with binder. ISBN 0-8160-4306-X; 0-8160-4277-2/set.

The four volumes in *Timelines on File* are intended for use by teachers to introduce world history in a chronological manner. The introduction states that the set "is designed to encourage chronological thinking, historical comprehension, and issues analysis." The Diagram Group has written and arranged the volume to meet the requirements of the National Standards for World History.

Nations and States is arranged in eight sections, covering North American history, Central American and Caribbean history, South American history, European history, African history, Middle Eastern and Western Asian history, South and East Asian history, and Australian history. *The Ancient and Medieval World* covers general world history and Middle and Near East, European, American, and African history. It includes timelines with brief explanations as well as maps and illustrations. *The Expanding World* covers the same areas and also discusses advances in religion, science and technology, and the arts. *The 20th Century* discusses the major historical events within this past century as they occurred around the world.

Either purchased as individual volumes or as the set, this work will be most valuable for middle and high school libraries. Teachers of world history can use the chronologies in their classrooms to demonstrate the history of events and where they happened.—**Shannon Graff Hysell**

Dictionaries and Encyclopedias

P, S

223.   **A Dictionary of World History.** New York, Oxford University Press, 2000. 697p. maps. (Oxford Paperback Reference). $16.95pa. ISBN 0-19-280105-8.

This affordable A to Z desk reference is one of 92 published or forthcoming books in the Oxford Paperback Reference Series (OPRS). It has more than 4,000 entries covering prehistory through 1999. The small size of this one-volume work, coupled with the breadth of the topic, leads to a relatively narrow definition of world history. Political, military, and geographic entries are well covered. However, cultural, technological, and ecological entries are scant and inconsistent. For example, no entries exist for Michelangelo, Rabindranath Tagore, Wagner, or Kurosawa. Yet inexplicably, there are entries for two literary figures named Alexandre and Dumas. But an examination of other titles available in the OPRS indicates these topics have probably been left out for other works in the series.

Each entry is relatively short with accurate information. Overall, the dictionary not only strikes a decent balance in the coverage of ancient and modern topics, but also seeks to represent each continent evenly. Biographical entries include birth and death dates, and ruling political and military figures predominate. Dates are given for major events when appropriate. All current nation-states are represented; entries provide a physical description, history, economy, and a few statistics. Spot maps help locate each country. Further, line maps are used to highlight events or nations that cover large geographic areas, but they have limited value and focus on Western topics. As the preface states, 25 such maps are included, but a publicity flyer erroneously lists 50. A few cross-references are found, but more could have been added. Many comments made in the review of another OPRS title, *A Dictionary of Twentieth Century World History* (see ARBA 98, entry 504), are also appropriate here. Unfortunately, no pronunciation guide is provided, and the length of each entry does not indicate overall importance. For instance, the Falkland War measures four inches, but the Soviet Union receives only two-and-a-half inches.

When considering cost, size, paper quality, and number of titles available in the series, *A Dictionary of World History* is undoubtedly intended as a desk reference, and as such it could be quite useful. [R: Choice, Jan 01, p. 882]—**Allen Reichert**

C, P

224.   **Encyclopedia of Prisoners of War and Internment.** Jonathan F. Vance, ed. Santa Barbara, Calif., ABC-CLIO, 2000. 408p. illus. index. $65.00. ISBN 1-57607-068-9.

Being a prisoner of war (POW) has to be almost as strange as being in combat. Complete and multiple complex subcultures evolve in the prison camps just so people can survive with some semblance of sanity and society. Civilians can just as easily get caught up in this infernal mechanism as military personnel. The term "internment" is frequently applied to their situation, especially if they were diplomats being held in an enemy country or military personnel being held in a formally neutral country. Things were much worse than those portrayed in popular movies like *The Great Escape* or *The Bridge on the River Kwat*. These conditions vary due to time period, location, the group imprisoned, and who is doing the imprisoning.

A vast literature has grown up to report this experience, and there is a lot of interest in the subject. The more than 270 signed and alphabetically arranged entries found here include bibliographic references for further reading. Some of the topics covered include movies, religion, places, important people, events, organizations, larger conflicts, and general themes. Obviously, most of the entries concern the two world wars of the last century, when incredible situations were experienced by huge numbers of people. (The introduction states that it is estimated that one person in every thousand was interned at some point during World War II.) There have been many wars where the treatment of prisoners really did not vary, so representative examples are examined to discern some general features. The same condition holds true for different societies; to try to include every little thing would have led to a monster of a book with a lot of repetition. The Holocaust is obviously similar in some respects with the POW experience, but it is fully covered in many other reference books and is not dealt with here.

This reference tool is provided with a table of contents, cross-references, a separate six-page bibliography, and an index. The illustrations are all interesting and not generally well known. At the end of the book the reader can find extracts from the texts of the 1929 and 1949 Geneva Conventions, the 1907 Hague Convention, and the U.S. Army "Lieber Code," all of which govern the conduct of prisoner of war activities. This subject involves the fields of ethics, sociology, and psychology as well as military history. Among the 85 contributors are three self-identified POWs. One wishes that more than eight people from outside the Anglo-American world (who were identified as such by their locations) had been able to contribute, especially POWs, as their observations might have been different from those normally available in the United States. However, the majority of written works in this country have been on the Anglo-American and European experiences. The title under review is suitable for the reference collections of all public, high school, and academic libraries. [R: LJ, 1 Nov 2000, pp. 66-70]—**Daniel K. Blewett**

C, P

225.   **Encyclopedia of the Vietnam War: A Political, Social, and Military History.** Spencer C. Tucker and others, eds. New York, Oxford University Press, 2000. 578p. index. $45.00. ISBN 0-19-513524-5.

The one-volume condensation of Tucker's superb three-volume *Encyclopedia of Vietnam* (see ARBA 99, entry 527) is remarkable for its ability to include almost all of the original 900 articles, although in a smaller font. The articles, which seek to place the Vietnam War in its fullest context, are notable for their geopolitical range, covering the political, diplomatic, and military policies of the United States, French, Vietnamese, Laotian, Cambodian, Chinese, and Russian protagonists. They are also notable for their historical depth, reaching far back in the nineteenth- and early twentieth-century history with articles, for example, on French colonial administrator Charles Marie Le Myre de Vilers and the Viet Nam Quoc Dan Dang (Vietnam National Party).

This edition provides a full bibliography, rather than the selected version in the original. But there is a price to be paid. Missing from this edition are the striking full-page illustrations of the original; the appendix with its five statistical tables of U.S. deaths, casualties, and aircraft sorties; and a chronology of events in Vietnam through April 1973. Nevertheless, this work is an essential acquisition for libraries, scholars, and military enthusiasts who do not own the three-volume work, especially since it is offered at such a reasonable price. [R: Choice, Nov 2000, pp. 511-512]—**E. Wayne Carp**

P, S

226.   **Encyclopedia of World History.** New York, Facts on File, 2000. 524p. illus. maps. $85.00. ISBN 0-8160-4249-7.

This reference provides alphabetic entries for key political, social, economic, philosophical, religious, artistic, and cultural events across world history. Notations range from Acropolis, an ancient Mycenaean hilltop fortress, to Emilio Zapata, the Mexican revolutionary. Equal attention is paid to both Western and non-Western nations. Expanded profiles are included for 200 countries and numerous major historical figures.

This volume is amply illustrated with photographs, maps, and drawings. As an appendix, a chronology outlines key historic, scientific, and artistic milestones by continent from 15,000 B.C.E. to the present. This allows the reader to track common themes across the globe. The chronology is followed by listings of emperors, monarchs, prime ministers, and presidents for many countries. Population, religious affiliation, and language preference statistics are also given. This volume is a useful secondary school resource to enable students to understand the facts and interfaces of world history.—**Adrienne Antink Bien**

P, S

227.   **The Kingfisher History Encyclopedia.** New York, Larousse Kingfisher Chambers, 1999. 491p. illus. maps. index. $39.95. ISBN 0-7534-5194-8.

This large-format reference for elementary and middle school students is designed to be a starting point for further exploration on historical topics. With its profuse and colorful illustrations, both photographic and artist-rendered, it is also an enjoyable book to browse.

Rather than alphabetic, the arrangement is chronological with 10 major sections covering each historical period. Beginning with the ancient world (40,000–500 B.C.E.) and ending at 2000 C.E. with the end of apartheid, and the encyclopedia also contains a look toward the world's future. Unlike some historical reference works, a bias toward Euro-American subject matter appears to be absent—the Eastern Hemisphere gets its due in this work. Two pages, occasionally one, are devoted to each major topic. In such space, the main text is necessarily quite general, but annotated maps, captioned illustrations, and sidebars provide related items of interest. A full timeline runs across each spread with a red bar that highlights the period covered. With its global focus, this encyclopedia would have benefited from a two-page map of the world to help place the regions covered in relation to each other.

At the end of the book, a ready-reference section offers tables of dates, historical figures, and facts. The index boasts approximately 3,500 topics and subtopics, making lookup easy. All in all, this encyclopedia should find a place in school and public libraries. [R: BL, 15 Dec 99, p. 799; BR, Jan/Feb 2000, p. 78]—**Lori D. Kranz**

P, S

228.   **ResourceLink: 17th-Century World History.** [CD-ROM]. Santa Barbara, Calif., ABC-CLIO, 2000. Minimum system requirements (Windows version): Pentium-compatible processor at 75MHz. Four-speed CD-ROM drive. Windows 95. 16MB RAM. 10MB hard disk space. SVGA monitor (640x480). Windows Media Player. Adobe Acrobat Reader 2.1. Mouse. Minimum system requirements (Macintosh version): 68040 processor at 25MHz. Double-speed CD-ROM drive. MacOS 7.5.3. 16MB RAM. 10MB hard disk space. SVGA monitor (640x480). QuickTime 2.5. Adobe Acrobat Reader 2.1. $79.00 (standalone); $199.00 (lab-pack); $389.00 (network). ISBN 1-57607-141-3.

Part of ABC-CLIO's ResourceLink series, *17th-Century World History* is appropriate for middle school and lower-level high school students. This interactive product supplies primary source documents (many in abbreviated form), short biographies, encyclopedic entries (the longer ones having short bibliographies for further research), maps, images, and a glossary.

Installation (and un-installation) is easy. To do a search, users can choose from the 739 resources—some images, some text—using a combination of keyword searching and choices from two pull-down menus. The first menu lists "topics" (culture, economy, environment, government, law, population, society, or "all"), while the second lists "types" of information (biographies, documents, events, glossary, maps, organizations, photos, quotes, tables, or "all"). Boolean operators are not used. While students can easily collect and export information to create reports or multimedia presentations, there are no attributions for the images—including paintings that are somewhat anachronistically listed as "photos"—except for those linked to an entry on an artist. Also, intended users might have trouble distinguishing between similar terms, such as Holland (30 entries), the Netherlands (62 entries), and Dutch (86 entries). The online user's manual is more useful in detailing how to manipulate the information than how to find it.

There is a good balance of information between Western and non-Western countries, women and men, primary and secondary sources, and cultural and political history. Despite the limited number of entries and the drawbacks noted, this is a useful adjunct to other forms of study for seventeenth-century world history. [R: LJ, July 2000, p. 156]—**Hope Yelich**

P, S

229. **ResourceLink: 18th-Century World History.** [CD-ROM]. Santa Barbara, Calif., ABC-CLIO, 2000. Minimum system requirements (Windows): Pentium-compatible processor at 75MHz. Four-speed CD-ROM drive. Windows 95. 16MB RAM. 10MB hard disk space. SVGA monitor (640x480). Windows Media Player. Minimum system requirements (Macintosh): MacOS 7.5.3 or later. 68040 processor at 25MHz. Double-speed CD-ROM drive. 16MB RAM. 10MB hard disk space. SVGA monitor (640x480). QuickTime 2.5. Adobe Acrobat Reader 2.1. Mouse. $79.00 (standalone); $199.00 (lab-pack); $389.00 (site license). ISBN 1-57607-140-5.

The primary audience for this tool is high school and middle school teachers and librarians who need to have simple, clear, and easy-to-use resources in support of a world history classroom curriculum. This latest resource in a new series presented by the publisher includes over 900 text and image entries that explore and explain the various cultures, events, people, discoveries, and inventions that became known as the Age of Enlightenment. Statistics, summaries of events, quotations, glossary terms, organization profiles, and primary documents are included. Social and political movements as well as religious developments are summarized and brought together through a sophisticated search engine capable of customizing searches by format and general subject categories. Visual materials include photographs, engravings, paintings, and maps that the user can zoom in or out of at will.

Students can also customize search results and create multimedia portfolios and presentations suitable for the classroom. They are also able to edit, add, export, or delete resources. Whether for use in the classroom or the library setting—or possibly as a circulating item—this resource should receive enthusiastic reception on the part of its users. Its interactive capabilities will enhance both the teaching and learning processes. The product may be purchased as a stand-alone item or for use on a network.—**Edmund F. SantaVicca**

C, P, S

230. **Trade, Travel, and Exploration in the Middle Ages: An Encyclopedia.** John Block Friedman, Kristen Mossler Figg, and Scott D. Westrem, eds. New York, Garland, 2000. 715p. illus. index. (Garland Reference Library of the Humanities, no.1899). $135.00. ISBN 0-8153-2003-5.

This encyclopedia is a compendium of far-ranging topics centered on trade, travel, and exploration of the Middle Ages. Books in which the venerable medieval scholar John Friedman is involved tend to be erudite, yet eminently readable. Associate editor Scott D. Westrem and collaborating editor Gregory G. Guzman join Friedman and co-editor Kristen Mossler Figg in coordinating this huge project. The result is a specialized and valuable reference work—a first of its kind.

The 435 signed articles comprising this work were researched and written by 177 international subject experts. Articles are arranged in A to Z, dictionary-style format, from "Abagha," a thirteenth-century Persian regional khan, to "Zoroastrianism." Over 125 illustrations and maps complement the entries, each of which concludes with a brief bibliography of 3 to 10 suggestions for additional reading.

This 715-page work, which took more than 6 years to assemble, covers the time period from 100 B.C.E. to roughly 1500 C.E. Its focus is on interdisciplinary topics from a non-Eurocentric perspective. Much of the research used to write the articles is in French, German, Italian, and other languages. It would be extremely time-consuming for a student, general reader, or even a trained scholar to locate and gather such information piecemeal and then translate. This book gathers much heretofore-elusive historical information into one convenient volume.

Articles include details of the daily life of medieval travelers, explorers, and merchants, reflected in such titles as "Inns and Accommodations," "Use of the Magnetic Compass," "Costume, Oriental," and "Women in Mongol Society." Architecture, religion, and literature as well as extensive geographic references, including maps, are also covered. Selected explorers, such as Marco Polo, Christopher Columbus, and John Mandeville (under "Mandeville's Travels"), receive detailed analyses.

This encyclopedia is very browser friendly, which is good, since the arrangement of entries is often inverted, something a casual user might not expect (e.g., "Spice Trade, Indian Ocean," or "Navigation, Arab"). The detailed back of the book index is therefore welcome, as is an 11-page list of subject areas following the table of contents.

Teachers and librarians will want to examine this work for possible inclusion in their curricula and collections. It is unequivocally recommended for the history reference areas of high school, public, and academic libraries, although, sadly, smaller libraries will find the cost prohibitive at $135. [R: BL, 15 Dec 2000, p. 846; LJ, Jan 01, p. 94]—**Linda D. Tietjen**

Handbooks and Yearbooks

P, S

231.   **Ancient Civilizations.** Danbury, Conn., Grolier, 2000. 10v. illus. maps. index. $319.00/set. ISBN 0-7172-9471-4.

The staff at Grolier has put together a resource on ancient people and places that is fun and informative. Each of the 80-page volumes in this 10-volume set contains around a dozen articles dealing with ancient civilizations and peoples (Babylonia, Japan, Vikings), archaeological sites and the people who inhabited them (Angkor Wat, Machu Picchu, Ur), and related topics (archaeology, marriage and families, tools and technology). The articles range in length from 2 to 15 pages, with the vast majority between 4 and 6 pages. The volumes are profusely illustrated with photographs, drawings, and maps, all of excellent quality and appropriately placed. In addition to the articles, each volume has a timeline spanning 6500 B.C.E. to 1600 C.E., a glossary specific to the volume, a brief reading list (also volume-specific), and an index to the set.

Though most of the articles are relatively brief, they cover the topics well, if not thoroughly, and are clearly written. At the end of each are one or more cross-references. Thus readers can expand their knowledge of a particular aspect of the ancient world and, at the same time, begin to see the bigger picture. Sprinkled throughout are insets that, although related to the articles in which they are found, are enjoyable to read on their own. Titles include "The Origin of Dice," "How Do We Know What They Ate?," "Plaster People of Pompeii," and "The Use of Zero."

Designed to meet the needs of younger readers, this set will also appeal to some older readers who know little or nothing about ancient civilizations and peoples and want to gain a minimum understanding without being bored. This set is recommended for school and public libraries. [R: BL, 1 Sept 2000, p. 172]—**Craig W. Beard**

P, S

232.   **Ancient Civilizations: Almanac.** By Judson Knight. Edited by Stacy A. McConnell and Lawrence W. Baker. Farmington Hills, Mich., U*X*L/Gale, 2000. 2v. illus. maps. index. (U*X*L Ancient Civilizations Reference Library Series). $115.00/set; $45.00/vol. ISBN 0-7876-3982-6.

P, S

233.   **Ancient Civilizations: Biographies.** By Judson Knight. Edited by Stacy A. McConnell and Lawrence W. Baker. Farmington Hills, Mich., U*X*L/Gale, 2000. 254p. illus. index. (U*X*L Ancient Civilizations Reference Library Series). $115.00/set; $45.00/vol. ISBN 0-7876-3985-0.

Students, middle school and above, are the target audience of this 3-volume set covering 12 ancient civilizations and biographies of 38 people who influenced those cultures. Beginning with ancient Egypt, the two almanac volumes include Mesopotamia, Israel, Phoenicia, Syria, Arabia, Asia Minor, Persia, India, China, the Americas,

Africa, Greece, and Rome. The entry for each country covers its location, history by time period (dynasty, empire, kingdom), political system, religion, and any significant contributions to civilization. There is also an overview of the country's modern history and an explanation of archaeological discoveries. A list of sources to consult for further information follows each chapter and includes books, motion pictures, and Websites.

The biography volume includes well-known historical figures such as Aristotle, Alexander the Great, and Confucius and also lesser-known people like the Indian emperor Asoka and the Celtic woman warrior Boadicia. Biblical personalities such as Jesus, David, Paul, and Moses are included along with philosophers, artists, and rulers. Each of the three volumes has a glossary, a timeline, an index, a pronunciation guide, and suggestions for research topics and activities.

Students using the set to research an ancient culture will find everything they need. Not only can they find information on the details of a specific civilization but also comments on the similarities between cultures, the impact of geography on economics, religious rituals, and political developments over time. Information is well organized and the vocabulary and sentence structure make it easy to access and understand. Words are usually defined within the text of the entry and phonetic pronunciation is given. Sidebars and information boxes highlight other "words to know" and topics of special interest. Upper elementary, middle school, and public libraries will find this set a good value and an outstanding reference source. [R: BR, Sept/Oct 2000, p. 67; SLJ, Nov 2000, p. 92]—**Marlene M. Kuhl**

S

234.   **DK Great Wonders of the World.** By Russell Ash. Illustrated by Richard Bonson. New York, DK Publishing, 2000. 64p. illus. index. $19.95. ISBN 0-7894-6505-1.

This volume focuses on the Seven Wonders of the World and how they came to be known as such. Each of the seven wonders is presented in a two-page spread with color illustrations and sidebars. The author then compares them with other great structures of the time (in order to provide context for the reader) and other similar structures present today. For example, the discussion of the great pyramid at Giza explains in detail the structure of the pyramid, how it was built, and gives examples of other great pyramids (e.g., the Pyramid of the Magician, the Great Temple of Tenochtitlán, Transamerica Pyramid). The book also discusses the statue of Zeus at Olympia, the Mausoleum at Halicarnassus, the Hanging Gardens of Babylon, the Colossus of Rhodes, the Pharos at Alexandria, and the Temples of Artemis at Ephesus in the same format. The final pages list other wonders, such as palaces and castles, "Weird Wonders" (the leaning tower of Pisa), engineering wonders, inventions, and natural wonders (e.g., the Great Barrier Reef, the Northern Lights). The illustrations and photographs, along with the entertaining text, make this resource most suitable for middle school and high school libraries.—**Shannon Graff Hysell**

S

235.   Ferguson, Rebecca N. **The Handy History Answer Book.** Farmington Hills, Mich., Visible Ink Press/ Gale, 2000. 572p. illus. index. (Handy Answer Book Series). $19.95pa. ISBN 1-57859-080-9.

Part of Visible Ink's Handy Answer Book Series, this new title features answers to almost 1,000 "frequently asked" questions about historical events and persons. It is organized into 14 chapters comprising broad areas such as religion, exploration and settlement, political and social movements, medicine and disease, and science and invention. The chapters are subdivided into more specific categories; for example, the chapter on culture and recreation is broken down into written language, education, literature, the various visual and performing arts, radio and television, games, and sports. The responses vary in length from one to four paragraphs. Most illustrations are in black and white, and there is a 16-page center section of color photographs. The index is adequate. Ferguson intends her book as a resource for "brushing up" on topics of Western history. Considering its reader-friendliness, she has succeeded well.—**Lori D. Kranz**

P, S

236.   **History of the Modern World.** Tarrytown, N.Y., Marshall Cavendish, 2000. 10v. illus. maps. index. $459.95/set. ISBN 0-7614-7147-2.

This beautiful 10-volume set is a compendium of world history covering the time period between the Medieval and Renaissance eras through the end of the twentieth century. Volume 1 discusses that very transition, since there is no one discernible event or demarcation line signaling the end of the Medieval era and the beginning of the Renaissance in any given country or region.

The publisher aptly picks up where Henk Dijkstra left off in his 1996 12-volume *History of the Ancient and Medieval World* (see ARBA 98, entry 501). The venerable Marshall Cavendish Corporation, a company specializing in quality reference works, publishes these two sets that are encyclopedic in scope and depth. The set avoids traditional historical myopia by featuring some in-depth coverage of Asia, South America, Africa, and other frequently ignored areas of the world. For example, in volume 6, "The Changing Balance of Power," there are chapters, averaging 10 pages, covering "Nineteenth Century Japan," "Revolution in South America," and "The Scramble in Africa." Now, if women warranted more than 33 pages of this 1,421-page reference work, perhaps in a future edition it might indicate a reparation of another persistent and pernicious historical conceit—that women were somehow not very involved in "history," or that what they did was not worthy of documenting.

Still, this in-depth work offers an impressive analysis of over eight centuries worth of conventional history and highlights major events and trends, worldwide, for that period. The 10 volumes contain over 1,500 color and black-and-white photographs as well as maps, charts, and timelines to complement the text. Volumes 1 through 9 each conclude with a timeline, glossary, bibliography, and index specific to that volume. Volume 10 provides comprehensive topical indexes for the entire set: arts and culture, customs and everyday life, government and politics, wars and battles, and 5 separate geographical indexes. The approach to world history is thematic, geographic, and chronological. Although a strict dictionary A to Z arrangement is sacrificed, the topics are covered in a way that flows logically and cohesively.

The 10-volume *History of the Modern World* is recommended for high school and public libraries as well as junior college libraries, although its cost will be prohibitive for smaller libraries. Even though it classes under "juvenile," bibliographers for undergraduate libraries might consider its purchase for its concise, easy-to-read, thoroughly indexed, and geographically comprehensive overview of modern world history.—**Linda D. Tietjen**

P, S
237. **Slavery Throughout History: Almanac.** By Theodore L. Sylvester. Edited by Sonia Benson. Farmington Hills, Mich., U*X*L/Gale, 2000. 263p. illus. maps. index. (Slavery Thoughout History Reference Library). $120.00/set; $45.00/vol. ISBN 0-7876-3176-0.

P, S
238. **Slavery Throughout History: Biographies.** By Theodore L. Sylvester. Edited by Peggy Saari. Farmington Hills, Mich., U*X*L/Gale, 2000. 235p. illus. maps. index. (Slavery Throughout History Reference Library). $120.00/set; $45.00/vol. ISBN 0-7876-3177-9.

P, S
239. **Slavery Throughout History: Primary Sources.** By Judson Knight. Farmington Hills, Mich., U*X*L/Gale, 2000. 168p. illus. index. (Slavery Throughout History Reference Library). $120.00/set; $45.00/vol. ISBN 0-7876-3178-7.

Slavery Throughout History: Almanac is the first of three volumes in the Slavery Throughout History Reference Library series. It provides an overview of the institution of slavery from its inception among the "earliest permanent settlers in Mesopotamia (perhaps as early as 3500 B.C.E.) to the present day" (p. xiv). The entries, narrative in form, run approximately 25 pages each. Chapter titles include "Slavery in Ancient Mesopotamia, Egypt, and Israel"; "Colonial Latin America"; "Slave Life in Antebellum America"; and "Slavery in the Twentieth Century." A glossary is provided as well as a timeline of events related to slavery and a general historical timeline. Graphics are provided in each chapter—photographs, illustrations, and maps. This volume also includes an index and a bibliography.

Many of the 30 men and women in the 2d volume, *Biographies*, are famous figures from the African Diaspora related to slavery. They include Sally Hemmings, Harriet Tubman, and Nat Turner. In addition, a number of well-known white abolitionist leaders are included. True to its billing, however, this volume provides a broad world scope of important historical figures, such as Moses, Aleksandr Solzhenitsyn (slave in Soviet labor camps), Haksun Kim (comfort woman [prostitute] for the Japanese military), and Hammurabi (King of Babylonia). Readers are likely to encounter many people who are new to them as individuals of importance related to slavery.

Each entry includes a number of graphics: photographs, illustrations, or maps, as well as a sidebar with an interesting fact. The text is straightforward and concise. In addition, a phonetic pronunciation is provided for names that may be difficult to pronounce. At the end of each entry is a further reading section and a bibliography.

There are an index and a "Words to Know" section, along with a timeline of events as well as a separate timeline for other historical events.

The 3d volume, *Primary Resources*, allows students to study 20 full or excerpted speeches, diary entries, newspaper accounts, novels, poems, memoirs, and other materials related to slavery. It includes Hammurabi's code of laws regarding slavery, slave narratives, abolitionist speeches, legislation, and much more. This series is recommended for public and secondary schools.—**Leslie R. Homzie**

P, S

240.   **World War II: Almanac.** By George Feldman. Farmington Hills, Mich., U*X*L/Gale, 2000. 2v. illus. maps. index. (U*X*L World War II Reference Library Series). $155.00/set; $45.00/vol. ISBN 0-7876-3830-7.

P, S

241.   **World War II: Biographies.** By Kelly King Howes. Christine Slovey, ed. Farmington Hills, Mich., U*X*L/Gale, 1999. 288p. illus. index. (U*X*L World War II Reference Library). $155.00/set; $45.00/vol. ISBN 0-7876-3895-1.

P, S

242.   **World War II: Primary Sources.** By Barbara C. Bigelow. Christine Slovey, ed. Farmington Hills, Mich., U*X*L/Gale, 2000. 229p. illus. maps. index. (U*X*L World War II Reference Library Series). $155.00/set; $45.00. ISBN 0-7876-3896-X.

These three titles complete the Gale/U*X*L World War II Reference Library Series. The *Almanac* volumes provide in-depth information and current commentary on World War II. The 2 volumes provide 17 chapters covering subjects such as the war's background (beginnings in Europe), its expansion, American's entry into the war, the U.S. home front, and occupied Europe. These chapters also discuss the Holocaust, impact of the war, the Allied and Axis sides, the war's turning points, D-Day, defeat of Germany, war against Japan and its defeat, spies and scientists, the arts and propaganda, and the post-war world.

Each volume includes a reader's guide, timeline, words to know, research and activity ideas, where to learn more, and an index. The "Words to Know" section is a useful glossary for World War II units. The "Research and Activity" section is a boost for teachers and students looking for project ideas. Over 150 black-and-white photographs and maps enhance the text, as do the numerous sidebars that highlight individuals and facts. Despite a few proofing errors, this is an excellent title to add to World War II reference collections.

The *Biographies* volume focuses on 31 people who played key roles in World War II. These include such well-known figures as Winston Churchill, Charles de Gaulle, Dwight D. Eisenhower, Adolf Hitler, Douglas MacArthur, George S. Patton, and Joseph Stalin. The biographies are generally 8 to 10 pages in length and feature photographs, interesting sidebars, and resources to consult for further research (e.g., books, periodicals, Websites).

The *Primary Sources* volume provides 16 full or excerpted documents, such as speeches and memoirs from soldiers, nurses, and Holocaust survivors. Documents from Winston Churchill, Franklin D. Roosevelt, Adolf Hitler, Ruth Minsky Sender, Ernie Pyle, and Stephen E. Ambrose, and many more are included. Over 70 black-and-white photographs illustrate the text and maps help explain the logistics of the war.

This volume also includes a reader's guide, a timeline, a list of words to know, and an index. Each chapter begins with an introduction to set the stage for the reproduced document and concludes with a list of where to find more information. Sidebars and boxed information further help clarify the text. Bold typefaced words in documents are defined in the margin. As always with such a limited collection of documents, readers can quibble over what was selected. But this work does provide secondary students with some key primary resources for their research needs. All in all, these three titles, like others in the Gale/U*X*L Reference Library Series, deserve a place in reference and circulating collections for grades 6 through 12. [R: SLJ, Aug 2000, p. 128]

—**Esther R. Sinofsky**

10 Law

GENERAL WORKS

Bibliography

C, P
243.   Matthews, Elizabeth W. **Law Library Reference Shelf: Annotated Subject Guide.** 4th ed. Buffalo, N.Y., William S. Hein, 1999. 213p. index. $48.50. ISBN 1-57588-501-8.

This annotated bibliography of law and general reference sources lists more than 400 titles, of which about one-half would be found in the reference collection of any medium-sized public, academic, or law library. The list is not meant to represent an entire reference collection, but only the ready-reference collection in the average law library. Almost all sources are in print format, with a notation about availability in online or CD-ROM versions. Brief annotations describe the most useful aspects of the reference works.

The table of contents and body are organized alphabetically by subject. The index is by author and by title, although occasionally a subject heading is included for clarity. Because the titles of most reference books are descriptive of their subjects, the arrangement of the index is sufficient for the size of the bibliography.

Few sources of local information are listed because so many are unique to a locality. However, future editors may be able to list more. Good additions, for example, would be *Carroll's Municipal Directory* and *Carroll's County Directory* (Carroll Publishing, annuals) to complement *Carroll's State Directory* that is already included in the bibliography. Also, a comment by the editor about possible sources of local information—bar associations, local rules of courts, and so forth—could be helpful.

Naturally, the bibliography's strength is its legal sources. The number of international and foreign-language works is impressive for a ready-reference collection. No current, directly comparable bibliography can be found. *Law Library Reference Shelf* is recommended for all law libraries and for any library with a significant law collection.—**Nancy L. Van Atta**

Dictionaries and Encyclopedias

C, P
244.   Collin, P. H. **Dictionary of Law.** 3d ed. Middlesex, England, Peter Collin; distr., Chicago, Independent Publishers Group, 2000. 398p. $15.95pa. ISBN 1-901659-43-7.

The 3d edition of the *Dictionary of Law* contains over 7,500 words and phrases used in British, American, and European Union law. However, as in the previous editions, the emphasis of this work is definitely on British terms, spellings, and usage. For example, whenever the spelling of a term varies between British and American English, the British term is used as the entry's heading. The American term is mentioned in the entry, but no cross-reference is provided for the American term within the body of the work. The terms and phrases chosen for inclusion range from very formal (including many Latin terms) to prison slang. In addition to definitions, each entry provides the user with the part of speech and, new to this edition, pronunciation (using the International Phonetic Alphabet). Many of the entries also provide examples of the words used in context. Furthermore, numerous comments on legal practice are provided after appropriate terms. These comments are readily identifiable throughout the work because a border surrounds the text. While these comments are interesting and potentially quite useful, the emphasis is on British rather than American legal practice.

This edition does display some noteworthy improvements from the previous edition. In addition to providing the pronunciation of each term and defining European Union terms for the first time, the layout of this work has improved tremendously. This edition's attractive and easy-to-read format stems from the use of a bigger font size and borders to distinguish the text of the legal comments from the text of the entries. Because this work emphasizes British legal terms, though, it is recommended only for collections with an interest in this area.

—**Karen Selden**

C, P

245.   Kelly, Robert J. **Encyclopedia of Organized Crime in the United States: From Capone's Chicago to the New Urban Underworld.** Westport, Conn., Greenwood Press, 2000. 358p. illus. index. $59.95. ISBN 0-313-30653-2.

One of a group of broad-based reference works in historical and analytic criminology (the voluminous 1989 *Encyclopedia of World Crime* and Carl Sifakas's 1999 *The Mafia Encyclopedia* among them), Robert Kelly's new tome takes a more focused approach emphasizing the developmental history of American organized criminal efforts, imported and homegrown, from 1860 to the 1990s. The author has written and edited four previous books on hate crimes and criminal social evolution, most relevantly the 1994 *Handbook of Organized Crime in the United States* (Greenwood Press), whose contributed essays on formally structured illegal operations outside the traditional *mafiosi* make it a precursor of the present volume. While the bulk of the entries are biographies of individuals, articles on Russian organized crime, Colombian drug cartels, tongs, organized crime and the media, and crime commissions provide updated background on newly visible groups and historic underworld precedents. Suggested readings of books and articles drawn from the literatures of biography, history, and criminology are appended for each essay. A bibliography of selected reference works, general treatments of organized crime, memoirs and biographies, feature films, and government reports provides a valuable resource for collection development. This work is most useful for public libraries; college and university reference collections supporting undergraduate and graduate programs in criminal justice, history, and political science; and law libraries. [R: BR, Sept/Oct 2000, p. 80; Choice, Nov 2000, p. 512; C&RL News, Nov 2000, p. 945]—**Robert B. Marks Ridinger**

P

246.   **Random House Webster's Dictionary of the Law.** By James E. Clapp. New York, Random House, 2000. 528p. $17.95pa. ISBN 0-375-70239-3.

Handy legal dictionaries, which are useful for laypersons, are popular items in American society where law touches all aspects of modern life. This 6-by-9-inch dictionary is of intermediate size. It has more than 8,500 terms—in comparison to other pocket dictionaries with 2,500 entries and the classic 7th edition of *Black's Law Dictionary* (West Group, 1999) with 25,000 entries.

The text is easy to read and the definitions are easy to understand. The author seeks to present the vocabulary of law in a way that provides not just each term's meaning in isolation but also an understanding of its place in the larger legal picture. It includes the latest legal terms, such as "cyberpiracy," "identity theft" and "Twinkie defense." Many of the entries have supplemental notes that provide additional information on usage, history, pronunciation or "false friends" (where the legal meaning differs from the ordinary meaning). Cross-referencing is good and the introductory "Guide to the Dictionary" is helpful and easy to use.

Appendixes in 57 pages include a guide to the U.S. Constitution, full text of the U.S. Constitution, an outline of U.S. government agencies, an outline of international organizations (including the United Nations and the European Union), and a selected list of legal Internet metasites. This book offers great value for anyone who needs legal definitions; however, most attorneys will want an additional, more extensive legal dictionary in their libraries.—**Georgia Briscoe**

Directories

C, P

247.   Biehl, Kathy, and Tara Calishain. **The Lawyer's Guide to Internet Research.** Lanham, Md., Scarecrow, 2000. 350p. index. $35.00pa. ISBN 0-8108-3885-0.

This is a remarkably well-organized and thorough guide to the Internet for legal professionals. It is far more than a classified list of Websites; the authors present a very clear introduction to online computing in general, including the basics of browsers, mail readers, newsreaders, plug-ins and other applications, and managing bookmarks. Following is general advice on setting up an online law library, with specific recommendations for legal megasites, such as FindLaw, to bookmarks and strategies to pursue when a URL no longer connects. From there the authors devote separate chapters on finding various types of legal information: case law, statutes, and regulations; court information and rules; government forms; international, federal, state, and local resources; journal and legal news sources; and other legal professionals. There is also a chapter on finding information by topic (e.g., taxation, family law, intellectual property). Every site that is listed has an annotation of at least one or two paragraphs. There is a good index as well as a detailed table of contents for easy access. And to top it off, the authors have a Website of their own (http://www.fortunaworks.com) where readers can go to find "virtual pocket parts" in order to update the book's information. This is a valuable resource not only for lawyers but for any library where research in legal or government sources is of importance.—**Jack Ray**

Handbooks and Yearbooks

P

248.   Elias, Stephen, and Richard Stim. **Patent, Copyright, & Trademark.** 4th ed. Edited by Beth McKenna. Berkeley, Calif., Nolo Press, 2000. 496p. $34.95pa. ISBN 0-87337-601-3.

This book can serve as a ready-reference for those seeking information on how to protect their intellectual property. The four basic types of intellectual property law are covered here: trade secret law, copyright law, trademark law, and patent law. The book begins with an explanation of exactly what intellectual property is and how it can be protected by law. It discusses how these laws intersect with one another as well as which types of creative works are covered by which law (if any). The book is then broken down into the four laws covered herein. Each law is given an overview with a definition and examples of infringement, a set of definitions, sample forms, and statutes. Although still considered a gray area of intellectual property law, this book also discusses how the Internet affects these laws.

This book provides basic information on what to many is a confusing topic. It will serve as a starting point for many researchers. Although the authors do suggest that readers with further questions may want to consult a legal professional, this will give readers a basic understanding. *Patent, Copyright, & Trademark* will be useful in public libraries.—**Shannon Graff Hysell**

P, S

249.   Hempelman, Kathleen A. **Teen Legal Rights.** rev. ed. Westport, Conn., Greenwood Press, 2000. 299p. index. $49.95. ISBN 0-313-30968-X.

Teen Legal Rights addresses nearly every concern teenagers may have concerning their rights in the United States. The book is arranged in a question-and-answer format and covers such topics as teens' rights involving driving, school, at home, on the job, when parents divorce, one's sexual life, alcohol and drugs, crime, discrimination, and how to take matters into a court of law. The author writes in an easy-to-understand style and often cites court cases and the U.S. Constitution in her explanations. At the end of each chapter are lists for further reading and organizations. This work will be useful in high school libraries and larger public libraries. The layout of the table of contents and the comprehensive index will make this volume valuable at the reference desk. [R: BR, Nov/Dec 2000, p. 79]—**Shannon Graff Hysell**

P

250.   **The MVR Book Motor Services Guide.** 2000 ed. Tempe, Ariz., BRB, 2000. 303p. (Public Record Research Library). $19.50pa. ISBN 1-879792-58-3.

P

251.   **The MVR Decoder Digest.** 2000 ed. Tempe, Ariz., BRB, 2000. 321p. (Public Record Research Library). $19.50pa. ISBN 1-879792-59-1.

   The MVR Book Motor Services Guide and *The MVR Decoder Digest* are companion volumes that comprehensively outline the motor vehicle records and laws for the 50 states. The *Guide* deals specifically with privacy restrictions, access procedures, and regulations of vehicle records, while the *Digest* translates the codes and abbreviations of violations and licensing categories that appear on vehicle records. The *Guide* lists each state alphabetically and includes what information appears on the driver's license, insurance requirements to be held by drivers, privacy and access as they relate to drivers' records, and how license plates are distributed. At the beginning of each state's description is an address where questions can be submitted as well as telephone numbers and a Website address. The *Digest* lists each state alphabetically as well and defines terms listed on each driver's license, what codes on a traffic violation mean, and how many points (if any) the violation is worth. Because each state holds its own laws concerning vehicle violations, these volumes will be extremely helpful in all public libraries.

—**Shannon Graff Hysell**

P

252.   Yarbrough, Tinsley E. **The Burger Court: Justices, Rulings, and Legacy.** Santa Barbara, Calif., ABC-CLIO, 2000. 346p. illus. index. (ABC-CLIO Supreme Court Handbooks). $65.00. ISBN 1-57607-179-0.

   The Burger Court is part of the ABC-CLIO Supreme Court Handbooks series and covers the years during which Warren Burger served as the Chief Justice—1969 to 1986. Each title in the series follows the same format: an overview of the court's social and political context, a biography of each justice on that court, a review of the major decisions, and a concluding chapter discussing the impact of the court on law and society. Each chapter concludes with a bibliography of further reading. Every title in the series also includes a section describing significant laws, people, and events of the period not discussed in the main text; an annotated bibliography; a table of cases; and an index. In addition, this work has a chronology of case law with annotations. Several statistical charts show dissent rates, voting blocs, and voting on issues such as civil liberties.

   Yarbrough's thesis that the Burger Court has been unfairly labeled a mere transition between the "liberal" Warren Court and the "conservative" Rehnquist Court is built up throughout the book. His discussion of the jurisprudence of the justices—examining not only their majority opinions and dissents but also the influence of their personal background, speeches, and writings—shows a court that has its own identity. Rather than dismiss this court as directionless, Yarbrough demonstrates, court analysts should recognize that the Burger Court set many important precedents—especially in criminal law and civil rights law—that endure today. The difficulty in pigeon-holing this court does not lie in the inability to build a collegial, cohesive court, he concludes, but in the unprecedented number of complex issues, such as abortion, that the Burger Court faced.

   Yarbrough's writing style is informal, making the book pleasant and comfortable reading for lay readers, the intended audience. *The Burger Court* would be a valuable reference book for undergraduate and public libraries. Law libraries may also wish to add this engrossing eulogy to their collections.—**Nancy L. Van Atta**

CRIMINOLOGY AND CRIMINAL JUSTICE

Biography

P

253.   Bobit, Bonnie. **Death Row: Meet the Men and Women of Death Row.** 9th ed. Chicago, Independent Publishers Group, 1999. 311p. index. $24.95pa. ISBN 0-9624857-8-0.

   As of 1999, 3,555 men and women convicted of murder were awaiting execution in American prisons. As the debate over capital punishment rages on, states like Texas and Florida continue to execute prisoners in record numbers. If polls are to be believed, a majority of Americans seemingly favor the death penalty under certain circumstances.

First published in 1989 as a listing of convicted murderers currently awaiting execution in American prisons, the 9th edition of this collection of death row profiles and allied facts does not advocate either position. Instead the author supplements hundreds of death row profiles with well-written essays on a variety of topics, including a history of capital punishment, letters from death row inmates, and reflections from the families of victims.

Expanded death row profiles in the form of case studies are offered on eight individuals, including John William King, the white supremacist convicted of the dragging death of a black man in Texas in 1998. Interspersed throughout this coverage are sidebars that contain relevant information. The entry on King provides statistics on lynching in America and brief discussions of hate crimes and racism in prison.

Still, the sources primary reference value lies in its alphabetic listing of inmates currently awaiting execution. A typical entry includes a photograph and supplies information on the inmate's gender, race, and state where incarcerated. The brief essay (100 to 200 words) accompanying the entry reports on the crime and its legal dispensation. Also of great interest is a list of executed inmates as of May 31, 1999, that follows the same format as those awaiting execution. This work is fascinating and useful, but the lack of a general index will hamper its reference value in libraries.—**David K. Frasier**

Dictionaries and Encyclopedias

P

254. **Encyclopedia of Women and Crime.** Nicole Hahn Rafter, ed. Phoenix, Ariz., Oryx Press, 2000. 361p. illus. index. $65.00. ISBN 1-57356-214-9.

Historically, crime and its control have been a dominantly male enterprise. Beginning principally in the 1970s, a growing number of feminist criminologists began to direct attention to women as offenders, as justice system personnel, and as victims of crime. By the end of the twentieth century a formidable literature on women and crime had developed. This encyclopedia is further acknowledgment of the breadth and depth of recent scholarship on women as criminals, victims, and law enforcers or adjudicators. It claims to be the first comprehensive encyclopedia devoted to this topic.

A useful topic finder at the beginning of this encyclopedia provides users with an efficient map of the terrain covered. One series of entries addresses offenders, offenses, and theories of offending. Forms of crime where women are especially well represented—such as shoplifting and prostitution—are highlighted here. For other types of crimes, such as domestic violence and homicide, patterns of female involvement are addressed. While the crimes of females have been explained by some of the same theories applied to male crime, a feminist criminology imposes an alternative framework on the understanding of female crime. A series of entries on juvenile delinquency address the differential treatment of juvenile females relative to males. And some entries describe specific classes of offenders (e.g., call girls) or notorious offenders (e.g., Barbara Perry's informative and entertaining piece on Bonnie Parker of Bonnie and Clyde).

Women have been especially vulnerable to certain forms of victimization, such as rape and domestic violence, and another series of entries covers many aspects of victim proneness among women as well as the increasingly influential victims' rights movement. Another series of entries addresses policing, courts, and case processing as they relate to women. Since the early 1970s women have become a significant presence on police forces. Women in court proceedings have all too often had negative experiences. An entry on rape shield laws addresses the legal device that has been widely adopted to diminish the likelihood of rape victims being humiliated as witnesses in rape trials.

Entries relating to punishment and treatment address some of the particular issues that arise when women go to prison and when women gain employment in the correctional system. Entries here range from co-correctional prisons to sexual abuse of prisoners. Entries on the treatment of prisoners include one on incarcerated mothers.

Finally, some entries specifically focus on patterns of crime, victimization, and criminal justice system responses in Australia, Britain, and Canada—most of the entries focus on the American situation. Altogether, this encyclopedia is sure to prove indispensable to the growing number of students of women as criminals, as criminal justice personnel, and as victims before the system of criminal justice. The contributors include many well-known women criminologists and feminist criminologists. A variety of figures and tables enhances the usefulness of this volume, as does a bibliography of sources cited.—**David O. Friedrichs**

Handbooks and Yearbooks

P

255. **City Crime Rankings: Crime in Metropolitan America.** 6th ed. Kathleen O'Leary Morgan and Scott Morgan, eds. Lawrence, Kans., Morgan Quitno Press, 1999. 400p. index. $39.95pa. ISBN 0-7401-0003-3. ISSN 1081-6453.

This work presents rankings and analyses of crimes in cities with a population over 75,000 and all metropolitan areas of the United States for 1998 with comparisons to earlier years. Data are based on the information submitted to the FBI through the Uniform Crime Reporting (UCR) program. Statistics were not available, however, from 29 cities and areas, including the Chicago metropolitan area—one that would undoubtedly be important for crime statistics. Thus, comparisons with some cities or areas in earlier editions are not possible. The crimes tracked under the UCR program and used for rankings in this volume include violent crimes of murder, rape, robbery, and aggravated assault; property crimes of burglary, larceny, and theft; and a separate category for motor vehicle theft.

The work is divided into two main sections: metropolitan area crime statistics and city crime statistics. Preceding these listings is a preface, a table of contents, and an introductory section on the safest cities and safest metropolitan areas followed by an overview of 1998 crime statistics. The section ranking safest cities and metro areas presents the editors' analyses of which areas are safest and least safe. The editors point out that these are not taken from any government agency. In fact, government officials have expressed concern regarding the validity of such rankings because crime levels are affected by many different factors, including population density, composition of the population (particularly the concentration of youth), economic conditions, and the strength of local law enforcement agencies. For this reason it is important to read the introductory statement on the methodology used by the editors in compiling these rankings.

The main sections are followed by appendixes containing population statistics for 1994, 1997, and 1998; descriptions of which cities are included in different metropolitan areas; a county index; and summaries of national, metropolitan, and city crime statistics. Although there is no index, the table of contents lists each table of rankings in numerical page order and follows a pattern of overall crime first and then each category of crime for both of the main sections.

While finding this type of information is relatively simple, readers should be reminded that even for cities and areas that are part of the UCR program, many fail to submit their statistics and others are not part of the program. Thus, comparisons are somewhat skewed. For those seeking statistics on different kinds of crimes in certain cities, this is a valuable and easy-to-use reference tool. For any in-depth research, however, readers should probably seek original sources.—**Lucille Whalen**

C, P

256. Henderson, Harry. **Capital Punishment.** rev. ed. New York, Facts on File, 2000. 300p. index. (Library in a Book). $39.95. ISBN 0-8160-4193-8.

This book is indispensable for anyone doing research on capital punishment. Chapter 1 introduces the death penalty debate and includes an overview of the leading arguments in the debate about the death penalty's moral and legal justification. There is also a substantive section on the legal issues, including the cruel and unusual punishment clause of the Eighth Amendment, that define the debate. Chapter 2 reviews the legal issues involved in the debate, including an excellent overview of the aggravating and mitigating circumstances that states employ to reach judgments that are not arbitrary and haphazard. This chapter also contains a brief summary of capital punishment for each of the 38 states that have capital punishment statutes. The chapter ends with a selection of representative Supreme Court death penalty cases from 1968 to 1993.

Chapter 3 offers a chronology of important dates (from 1700 to 2000) in the history of capital punishment. Chapter 4 contains a biography of some of the important names that occur in the death penalty debate. Chapter 5 provides a brief glossary of capital punishment terms. Chapter 6 presents an indispensable guide to research on the death penalty, including numerous Internet addresses. Chapter 7 presents an outstanding annotated bibliography divided into 12 sections, including reference works, punishment and deterrence, race and the death penalty, execution of the innocent, and international and historical works. Chapter 8 lists organizations and agencies, along with their Web addresses, that have been involved with capital punishment issues. There are four appendixes, including capital punishment statistics, polls and surveys, and an overview of research studies. This book belongs in every reference collection.—**Michael A. Foley**

C, P

257.   Henderson, Harry. **Gun Control.** New York, Facts on File, 2000. 297p. index. (Library in a Book). $39.95. ISBN 0-8160-4031-1.

On Mother's Day, May 14, 2000, an estimated 750,000 people marched on Washington, D.C., while thousands of others across the nation supported the Million Mom March with rallies in their own towns. The National Rifle Association, fronted by president-elect Charlton Heston, countered the anti-gun message with increased lobbying and a series of television infomercials. There is perhaps no issue in American politics more controversial or divisive than gun control. Henderson, a professional writer, has produced a strong entry in the Facts on File Library in a Book series that serves as an unbiased starting point for studying and researching this volatile issue.

Similar in focus to Earl R. Kruschke's 1995 book *Gun Control: A Reference Handbook* (see ARBA 97, entry 510), this guide presents a concise overview of the topic, its debatable issues, and a historical survey of the various state and federal laws that govern firearms. A chronology of important events relating to gun issues is given along with a brief biographical section of 29 past and present key players in the gun debate.

The book's reference value, however, is found in a well-structured section on how to research gun control issues. The section provides topically arranged information on several Internet resources as well as on the traditional print reference sources. The extensive annotated bibliography is particularly useful. Appendixes include data on recent research studies, polls, landmark legal cases, federal and state constitutional provisions, and the text of the Brady Handgun Violence Prevention Act. The work also includes a serviceable index and is recommended for undergraduates.—**David K. Frasier**

P, S

258.   **Police in Society.** Terence J. Fitzgerald, ed. Bronx, N.Y., H. W. Wilson, 2000. 240p. index. (The Reference Shelf). $35.00pa. ISBN 0-8242-0983-4.

Serving as a compilation of articles previously published, this volume is a handy one-stop reference tool for students and others interested in researching current trends and or social issues within the society. This particular title is part of a series, and one of six separately numbered issues—each on a different topic—that appears annually in one complete volume. In addition to articles, each of the topical numbers also includes excerpts from books, addresses on current issues, and studies of social trends.

This compilation on the police force is divided into five chapters, each providing three to six articles on one of the following subtopics: defining the police, the role and functions of police in the community, misconduct by police, the relationship between justice and the police, and the globalization of law enforcement. Works included here are authoritative, current (within the last year), easy to read, and thought-provoking. A brief bibliography complements the work and is supplemented by a valuable annotated bibliography of periodical articles for further reading. An index is also included.

High school students and college freshmen will be the heaviest users of both this volume and this series. Public libraries with limited funds for periodical resources should strongly consider purchasing the entire series, and keeping it up to date. This work is recommended for its ease of access, scope of materials, and balanced treatment of the topic.—**Edmund F. SantaVicca**

HUMAN RIGHTS

Dictionaries and Encyclopedias

C, P, S

259.   Maddex, Robert L. **International Encyclopedia of Human Rights: Freedoms, Abuses, and Remedies.** Washington, D.C., Congressional Quarterly, 2000. 404p. illus. index. $125.00. ISBN 1-56802-490-8.

Congressional Quarterly enjoys a well-deserved reputation based on the quality of their research publications. This encyclopedia reinforces that reputation. A six-page table of contents alphabetically lists all of the topics addressed. In addition, there is a six-page list of the subject categories that divide the book according to "Concepts" (e.g., Apartheid, disabled persons, minorities), "Documents" (e.g., Charter of the United Nations, Declaration on the Right of Peoples to Peace, the International Bill of Human Rights), "Human Rights Agencies" (e.g., Human Rights Committee, International Criminal Court, the United Nations), "Nongovernmental Organizations" (e.g., Human Rights Internet, Oxfam International, Physicians for Human Rights), and "Biographies" (e.g., Cesare Beccaria, Eleanor Roosevelt, Desmond Tutu). All entries offer clear, coherent, and brief explanations of each subject as well as additional information where applicable. For example, at the end of the entry on "Families," the reader is directed to relevant documents, court decisions, sources of information, further reading, and a list of related entries in the encyclopedia itself. The entries on Beccaria and Aristotle, however, offer information only on further reading and related entries. The entries are relatively short, so users should not expect an extensive presentation on any topic. (There are slightly over 400 entries treated in 382 pages.) But for any initial research, this reference is exceptional. The beginning researcher will know where to go next for further information. The book concludes with a comprehensive index. The *International Encyclopedia of Human Rights* is highly recommended.

—**Michael A. Foley**

P

260.   Utter, Glenn H. **Encyclopedia of Gun Control and Gun Rights.** Phoenix, Ariz., Oryx Press, 2000. 376p. illus. index. $62.50. ISBN 1-57356-172-X.

This one-volume encyclopedia is a valuable source of the viewpoints and activities of organizations, individuals, and governments (U.S. and international) involved in either gun rights or gun control. An essay summarizes the issues and lists organize the 300 entries into broad headings, such as court cases, nicely supplementing the detailed index. A chronology and bibliography are included.

The encyclopedia entries are each 500 to 1,000 words. The coverage is current and includes, for example, the attack on Columbine High School. The text provides ample statistics. Cross-references to related entries appear at ends of entries, as do suggestions for further reading (which often include a Website). Generally, two books are recommended, one for each side of an issue. Utter describes all views honestly and without judgmental language or labels. The best way to demonstrate the author's objectivity is that his personal position, if he has one, is impossible to discern.

The charts are excellent and show that the facts can surprise. For example, table 13 shows "What Felons Look for in a Handgun" (p. 323). The single most important factors are, first, firepower, and second, that the product is well made. The factors one might have predicted are only a third-place tie—concealable and untraceable.

The appendixes provide a table summarizing state constitutional gun ownership rights, a chart of state gun ownership regulations, and a directory of organizations and agencies that includes Web addresses. A comparable encyclopedic work could not be found. This work is strongly recommended for all libraries: academic, law, public, and junior and high school. [R: LJ, 1 Mar 2000, p. 78; Choice, Sept 2000, p. 109; VOYA, Dec 2000, p. 374]

—**Nancy L. Van Atta**

Handbooks and Yearbooks

C, P

261.   Bales, Kevin. **New Slavery: A Reference Handbook.** Santa Barbara, Calif., ABC-CLIO, 2000. 225p. index. (Contemporary World Issues). $45.00. ISBN 1-57607-239-8.

Most Americans today acknowledge that slavery existed for many centuries in different countries of the world, including the United States, but believe it was abolished in the nineteenth century. Many would be surprised to learn that millions of slaves can be found today in almost every country—the large majority concentrated in developing countries, but exploited also in Europe, the United States, and Japan. The author of this work points out that because the nature of slavery has changed, it is difficult to find a standard definition of slavery. In some 300 international treaties, the term is never defined in exactly the same way. However, after a careful discussion of the basic characteristics of slavery, namely that there must be violence or a threat of violence and there must be a loss of free will, the author provides a working definition of this social and economic relationship that includes the different types of slavery that exist today.

As part of the Contemporary World Issues series, this volume follows the familiar pattern in arrangement. The lengthy introduction describes all kinds of slavery, both historically and in its many present day forms, including examples of modern slavery. The second chapter presents a chronology of slavery from 6800 B.C.E. to the present, with emphasis on the key events of the past century. A chapter on biographical sketches of those fighting slavery, some of whom had been slaves themselves, follows. The fourth chapter, one of the most helpful sections of the book, discusses facts and documents. It includes excerpts from international laws and conventions, but more importantly, many documents containing actual testimony or evidence depicting different types of modern day slavery. The last three chapters are devoted to resources: organizations concerned with abolishing slavery in all its forms; print resources, most of which come from abolition groups rather than from academics or professional writers; and nonprint resources, including not only video and audio tapes, but also exhibits, photographs, posters, and other types of useful aids. A glossary and index are found in the appendix.

This volume presents much valuable information on a topic that is generally little known, but the author makes it clear that it is meant to be only a starting point for those who want to understand slavery as it exists today. It is hoped that the many resources given will lead people to further study. The author has done an excellent job of presenting this material; the writing is concise and clear and the organization and index, even within an established pattern, make the information easily accessible. This small volume should be useful in both academic and public libraries.—**Lucille Whalen**

C, P

262.   **The Right to Die Debate: A Documentary Debate.** Marjorie B. Zucker, ed. Westport, Conn., Greenwood Press, 1999. 303p. index. (Primary Documents in American History and Contemporary Issues). $49.95. ISBN 0-313-30522-6.

This book is an annotated collection of readings for use in high school and undergraduate classes. The 138 readings represent conflicting viewpoints about suicide, assisted suicide, and euthanasia. Almost one-half of the readings date back to the 1990s, and nearly all to the twentieth century. The authors are doctors, attorneys, moralists, philosophers, journalists, and individuals who have faced the issues in their personal lives.

Topics include the impact of medical advances on attitudes toward death, the euthanasia movement, the use of living wills and health care proxies, court decisions, religious perspectives, treating patients who have never been able to express their wishes, medical futility, and palliative care. Some essays are followed by suggested readings for further research. Sample forms for living wills and the selection of a health care proxy are reproduced.

The index is usually helpful; however, occasionally a topic is indexed under a broader heading than a student might guess. For example, Jack Kevorkian's name is not indexed, but his work is discussed in sections about assisted suicide and he is listed in the timeline.

A similar collection of essays is *Last Rights? Assisted Suicide and Euthanasia Debated* (William B. Eerdmans, 1998) by Michael M. Uhlmann. However, Uhlmann's book of fewer but longer selections would be less helpful for high school classroom use.

This book is an impressive and valuable collection that never promotes a particular position on the issues. *The Right to Die Debate* is recommended for high school, college, and public libraries. [R: BR, May/June 2000, p. 82]—**Nancy L. Van Atta**

P, S

263.   Yount, Lisa. **Physician-Assisted Suicide and Euthanasia.** New York, Facts on File, 2000. 282p. index. (Library in a Book). $39.95. ISBN 0-8160-4021-4.

The books in this series are designed to give researchers and students basic information about the topic at hand and then the tools to do further research. This volume addresses the topic of euthanasia, or physician-assisted suicide. As with all works in this series, the topic is timely and one of popular interest. The work is divided into three parts. The first gives an overview of the topic and explores such themes as the laws surrounding euthanasia, a 15-page chronology, a biographical listing of key players in the history of euthanasia (e.g., Hippocrates, Jack Kevorkian), and a glossary of terms. Reference information is mainly found in part 2, which features a section on how to research the right-to-die debate, a 62-page annotated bibliography (with books, magazines and journals, Internet sites, and other media), and directory information of relevant organizations and agencies. Part 3 consists of 6 appendixes that feature congressional acts on the subject and court cases that ruled on issues related to euthanasia. An index concludes the volume.

The works in this series will be useful in high school and undergraduate libraries because they walk students through the topic and offer tips for further research. This volume is on a particularly timely issue.

—**Shannon Graff Hysell**

11 Library and Information Science and Publishing and Bookselling

LIBRARY AND INFORMATION SCIENCE

Reference Works

Bibliography

C, P

264.   **On Account of Sex: An Annotated Bibliography on the Status of Women in Librarianship, 1993–1997.** Betsy Kruger and Catherine A. Larson, eds. Lanham, Md., Scarecrow, 2000. 304p. index. $65.00. ISBN 0-8108-3725-0.

Women constitute the majority in the profession of librarianship. Despite their overwhelming numbers, women on average are still paid less than men for comparable work, and continue to be greatly underrepresented in senior administration positions. This is reason enough to continue the focus on the status of women in librarianship with another annotated bibliography in the series, which began in 1977. Like the previous bibliographies in the series, this volume is a product of the American Library Association's Committee on the Status of Women in Librarianship.

The format of the 1993–1997 bibliography differs markedly from the previous three bibliographies (see ARBA 94, entry 949, for a review of the book listing years 1987–1992). Instead of a single long list of annotated citations, this bibliography is classified into 14 broad subject areas. This arrangement makes the bibliography both easier to use and more pleasing in appearance. The categories in the bibliography are biography and autobiography, career development and satisfaction, education, employment issues, gender issues in librarianship, image of librarians, information technology, leadership and management, library associations, library history, salary and pay equity, sexual discrimination and harassment, training and development, and women librarians as authors. Each category is preceded by a brief scope note that describes the content of that section. An author, a geographic, and a subject index provide additional access points to the content of the bibliography.

Libraries who have purchased the previous three bibliographies will definitely want to add this volume to their shelves. It will also be useful to any library that serves women's studies programs.—**Elaine F. Jurries**

C, P

265.   Slade, Alexander L., and Marie A. Kascus. **Library Services for Open and Distance Learning: An Annotated Bibliography.** Englewood, Colo., Libraries Unlimited, 2000. 344p. index. $75.00. ISBN 1-56308-745-6.

Library Services for Open and Distance Learning is a compilation of 764 references to works on library services for distance education. All the entries in this edition were published in the 1990s and the edition carries forward coverage of the 2d edition, which was published in 1995. Entries included in the edition were identified through searches in a variety of databases as well as by recommendations from a list of contributors representing many institutions and countries. Entries are primarily from the United States, the United Kingdom, and Australia; however, many other countries are represented, including considerable coverage of Canada, India, and South Africa.

Library Services for Open and Distance Learning is divided into 10 chapters covering general works, the role of libraries, organization, planning and regulatory issues, electronic resources and services, instructions issues, interlibrary cooperation, library surveys, user studies, and library case studies. Within each chapter, entries are arranged by year in reverse chronological order and then in alphabetical order by author name. Several chapters are divided by subheadings and the last three chapters are divided by country or geographic region. A typical entry includes a full bibliographic citation with a descriptive abstract prepared by one of the two authors. Abstracts are concise yet provide enough information to understand the setting, scope, and results of the original work. Studying a variety of abstracts at random gives the reader a good perspective on the state of library services for distance education. The volume includes an author index, a geographic index, an institution index, and a subject index. In addition, there is an excellent introductory section that not only describes the arrangement, terminology, and methodology of the volume, but also provides an excellent overview of the state-of-the-art library services available for distance education programs.

Library Services for Open and Distance Learning would be an excellent addition to academic library collections, particularly those that support library science or education curricula. It provides an excellent overview of the library services and programs being developed in support of distance education throughout the world. [R: BL, 1 Dec 2000, p. 756; LJ, 15 Sept 2000, p. 121; RUSQ, Winter 2000, p. 195]—**Sara Anne Hook**

P, S
266.   Wood, Irene. **Culturally Diverse Videos, Audios, and CD-ROMs for Children and Young Adults.** New York, Neal-Schuman, 1999. 276p. index. $35.00pa. ISBN 1-55570-377-1.

Multicultural books receive a lot of attention in review sources but videos, audiocassettes, and CD-ROMs do not always receive the attention they deserve. Media provides unique instructional opportunities that books cannot. This book contains entries for more than 900 audiovisual materials covering a variety of cultures in the United States.

The book is divided into video, audio, and CD-ROM sections. Titles must be technically excellent and culturally accurate to be included. Each entry lists basic bibliographic information, age range, and a brief description. Dates for each item can range from the 1970s to the late 1990s. Media for kindergarten to high school levels are included. A distributor index provides valuable contact information for ordering the media items listed.

Videos are included if they provide a unique and accurate view of the culture and a view of life that shows that children may be different but they do share common experiences. The audio titles are divided into music, storytelling, and audio books. The audio books are unabridged readings of books about ethnic traditions and experiences. The CD-ROM section only has about 15 multicultural titles but it also has a short listing of software books in French, German, Japanese, and Spanish.

Those who contributed to this book have impressive credentials that show they have the expertise and the interest to make thoughtful selections. Librarians and teachers will find their job of selecting and using culturally diverse media easier because of the work of the author and contributors. [R: VOYA, Oct 2000, p. 304]
—**Suzanne Julian**

Directories

C, P
267.   Cibbarelli, Pamela R., comp. **Directory of Library Automation Software, Systems, and Services.** 2000-2001 ed. Medford, N.J., Information Today, 2000. 354p. index. $89.00pa. ISBN 1-57387-088-9.

This new edition of a publication that has been in existence since 1983 is a necessity for any library considering automating its system or changing automation vendors. Written in directory format, the book holds a wealth of information on automation software, retrospective conversion services, automation consultants, database hosts, and CD-ROM and portable database distributors.

The major portion of the text consists of an alphabetic listing of software available. To be included the software must meet the following criteria: it must be targeted to the library market, be marketed and currently installed in the United States, and be commercially available. Each entry contains a wealth of information about the software. For example, the text states whether each program considered accepts bar code format, and if so, which format. This is an invaluable piece of information if users are converting from one system to another.

The other sections of the directory are equally helpful. The database distributors included are those providing databases of interest in the automation of libraries, ranging from book jobbers to serial databases. Also included is a bibliography of articles concerning library automation and a listing of Websites that deal with the subject. Any librarian involved in library automation will find this useful book invaluable. It is highly recommended.

—**Nancy P. Reed**

P, S

268.   Mandel, Mimi. **Teen Resources on the Web: A Guide for Librarians, Parents, and Teachers.** Fort Atkinson, Wis., Alleyside Press/Highsmith Press, 2000. 120p. index. $17.95pa. ISBN 1-57950-042-0.

Aimed at librarians, parents, and teachers who work with students in grades 6 through 12, this title covers over 900 Websites selected for their value and interest to teens on more than 90 teen-related topics. Mandel has eliminated difficult-to-use, slow-loading, or information-weak sites and focuses on user-friendly, professionally produced, and content-packed Websites. Of the book's three chapters, the first two are very brief discussions of Internet basics such as e-mail, newsgroups, mailing lists, chat rooms, etiquette tips, search engines, and basic questions and answers about common problems. The third chapter comprises the bulk of the book, with over 900 Websites arranged by subject from activism to dance, holidays, politics, and Website design. Three appendixes cover "Netiquette" (Web etiquette), safety in cyberspace, and over 900 U.S. college URLs. There is also an index to the Websites and a dedicated Web page offering current links to all the Websites listed in the book. Entries include a brief review, specific highlights, URL, source or authority, and how the Website helps a teenager. When available, special features such as downloadable free shareware are mentioned. Subjects are cross-referenced for ease in locating Websites. This is an excellent resource for building links to vetted sites. The dedicated Web page for current links increases its usefulness as an up-to-date tool. This work complements titles such as Miller's annual *The Internet Resource Directory for K–12 Teachers and Librarians* (2001/2002 ed.; see entry 94). [R: BR, Jan/Feb 01, p. 68]—**Esther R. Sinofsky**

C, P

269.   Prytherch, Ray, comp. **Harrod's Librarians' Glossary and Reference Book.** 9th ed. Brookfield, Vt., Ashgate Publishing, 2000. 787p. $165.00. ISBN 0-566-08018-4.

In compiling the newest edition of *Harrod's Librarians' Glossary and Reference Book*, Prytherch combined the traditional and innovative features of librarianship. This work has its strengths. The entries pertain to librarianship's important terms, organizations, and concepts. As an innovative procedure, Prytherch added European bibliographic societies and important Websites in addition to various metadata, HTML, and JavaScript formats. The definitions related to traditional librarianship are to be appreciated as well. However, the work has its problems. The traditional items' definitions remain identical in both the 8th and 9th editions. The virtual items' addresses limit this work's currency. This text also could have included more international definitions despite the compiler's stated intention.

Prytherch's efforts to update this classic work are commendable. He has brought this work up-to-date with the library profession through the addition of digital formats and services. Despite the added continental booksellers to the entries, more balance is needed in this regard. Also, the traditional items' entries need rewriting. Despite the fact that the 9th edition is almost 100 pages longer than its predecessor, this weakness could persuade many libraries to wait for the promised 10th edition. However, for library reference collections, *Harrod's Librarians' Glossary and Reference Book* remains a vital resource. It is recommended for all libraries. [R: C&RL News, April 2000, pp. 323-324]—**David J. Duncan**

Handbooks and Yearbooks

P, S

270.   Beasley, David. **Beasley's Guide to Library Research.** Toronto, University of Toronto Press, 2000. 206p. index. $30.00; $12.95pa. ISBN 0-8020-4782-3; 0-8020-8328-5pa.

Beasley's Guide to Library Research is a revision of David Beasley's 1988 book *How to Use a Research Library*. This updated work provides the reader with a basic overview of how to locate and use materials in a research library. Working from an understanding that procedures are basically the same in all research libraries, with only minor differences, many examples are taken from the New York Public Library where Beasley worked as a reference librarian for 28 years. The guide's goal is to help the researcher to "apply the most efficient methods of library research to find the bibliographic tools most useful" to his or her own particular needs.

The guide is written in a clear style and each section is organized in a self-contained fashion so that the reader can jump forward to a particular area of interest outlined in the table of contents. Such topics as what a research library offers, where to begin, strategy, online searching, when not to use online retrieval, interlibrary loan, catalogues and how to use them, tools of research (e.g., bibliographies, indexes), government publications, and even a section on "librarians and how to deal with them" are just some of the areas covered by the guide. An appendix containing brief summaries of some of the world's major research libraries and search methods to use in each is included.

More coverage of the electronic library, especially in the chapters on "Catalogues and How to Use Them" and "Tools of Research" would have made the book more valuable to researchers. However, the guide provides useful information to library users that should enable them to make better use of their time in research libraries.

—**Frances C. Wilkinson**

P

271.   Hillard, James M., with Bethany J. Easter. **Where to Find What: A Handbook to Reference Service.** 4th ed. Lanham, Md., Scarecrow, 2000. 307p. $45.00. ISBN 0-8108-3402-2.

In this 4th edition, useful reference sources are listed under 618 primarily Library of Congress subject headings. The book lists selected basic sources of mainly books, with some serials. A new feature of this edition provides an occasional Web address, especially for U.S. government agencies and organizations such as the American Association of Retired Persons. Bibliographic information for books includes author, title, edition, publisher, and year. Serial entries contain title, publisher, frequency, and date title began. Brief annotations for most titles identify content. Some titles are listed under more than one heading (e.g., the *CRB Commodity Yearbook* can be found under "Commodities," "Paper," "Petroleum," and "Steel"). An entry under "Periodicals—Indexes" lists paper and CD-ROM versions of 11 H. W. Wilson periodical indexes, but it omits the Web versions that also are available.

This book will be particularly helpful for beginning reference librarians, paraprofessionals, and student assistants who provide service at reference desks. It also serves as a kind of inexpensive abridgment of Robert Balay's *Guide to Reference Books* (see ARBA 97, entry 8) for smaller libraries that may not be able to afford Balay's work. [R: RUSQ, Fall 2000, p. 99]—**O. Gene Norman**

P, S

272.   Peterson, Carolyn Sue, and Ann D. Fenton. **Story Programs: A Source Book of Materials.** 2d ed. Revised by Stefani Koorey. Lanham, Md., Scarecrow, 2000. 359p. illus. index. (School Library Media Series, no.10). $29.50pa. ISBN 0-8108-3207-0.

This work is a handbook of information designed to help users in conducting story programs for young children. It contains story programming sources and sample materials developmentally suited for infants, toddlers, preschoolers, primary-level children, and families. This edition contains the text of complete story programs, including finger plays, songs, physical activities, and creative dramatics. There are also flannel board stories with fully traceable patterns, and puppet scripts with patterns accompanied by complete directions for making 11 different types of puppets. To further aid users, the authors have included ideas for themed story programs and an annotated listing of picture books that work well in story programs.

In this 2d edition the authors have added sections that deal with before-and-after aspects of story programming. The first includes information on planning a program, age-appropriate material selection and child development, length and timing of story programs, indexing and record-keeping techniques, and tips on advertising programs. There is also information on story program elements and variety and ideas regarding the physical location of programs, including program setup and book displays. The second section offers guidelines on judging programming success and information on program evaluation. This section also includes a menu of choices for answering tricky questions encountered during story programs as well as advice on dealing with crowd-control issues. Another new section is on selecting, learning, and performing told stories without props.

This is a worthwhile purchase for all storytellers, including teachers, librarians, and parents. It is a good source for ideas and materials. The patterns for puppets and flannel board stories can also be used as craft projects for young learners.—**Cari Ringelheim**

P, S

273.   **Sears List of Subject Headings.** 17th ed. Joseph Miller, ed. Bronx, N.Y., H. W. Wilson, 2000. 770p. $65.00. ISBN 0-8242-0989-3.

The commitment of this library science classic to continue suggesting subject headings for small- to medium-sized libraries remains unchanged. To make it more contemporary and socially aware, however, it has incorporated several important revisions. The most notable of which is the global replacement of Indians with Native Americans. Other revised or updated headings attempt to reflect either current usage (computer monitors for video display terminals) or cataloging practices (world history is now subdivided by century). Most new headings added to this edition—proposed by librarians, vendors, and Wilson indexers—represent the disciplines of computers (cyberspace), personal relations (stalking), politics (postcolonialism), and popular culture (violence in mass media).

Like the 16th edition (see ARBA 98, entry 580), the Dewey Decimal Classification numbers come from the 13th abridged edition. The latest edition also continues the practice of listing the entries by direct form rather than inverted on the theory that most library users search for multiple-word terms in the order in which they naturally occur in the language—a valid assumption unless those same users are used to LCSH. The short time span between editions reflects the editor's successful attempt to keep up with the rapidly changing nomenclature environment.—**Lawrence Olszewski**

Libraries

College and Research Libraries

C, P

274.   Baldwin, David A., Frances C. Wilkinson, and Daniel C. Barkley. **Effective Management of Student Employment: Organizing for Student Employment in Academic Libraries.** Englewood, Colo., Libraries Unlimited, 2000. 334p. index. $45.00pa. ISBN 1-56308-688-3.

This work reflects the authors' 50 years of combined experience as supervisors of student employees. Intended as "a foundation in the principles of supervision and . . . a handbook for the day-to-day problems that arise" (p. xviii), this book manages to achieve thoroughness and detail while retaining balance and clarity of presentation.

The authors address the major problem for those who manage student workers in college and university libraries, including the importance of training programs to improve supervisors' performance as an alternative to a sink-or-swim formula. The book clearly defines the roles and functions of both supervisors and employees, then offers specific techniques, problem-solving tips, and self-administered tests to help supervisors develop their potential. The 14 chapters cover several aspects of student employment in libraries, from hiring and training to performance evaluation and labor law. The authors do a particularly good job explaining student job classifications and the financial aid packages available to students as employees. Over 40 one-page examples illustrate a systematic approach to job descriptions and a useful glossary of terms and acronyms supports the explanation of financial aid. Each chapter ends with a bibliography of recent books, articles, and government publications, many dealing specifically with libraries as workplaces. A detailed table of contents, a list of figures, job descriptions, tables and tests, an FAQ section, and an index make it easy to find needed information.

The authors' detailed presentation and assessment of training methods will confirm for supervisors why they have been doing some things right and suggest ways to do an even better job. This book would be a useful addition to any library's human resources office as a tool for student supervisors. [R: RUSQ, Fall 2000, p. 97; JAL, Nov 2000, p. 439]—**Steven W. Sowards**

P, S

275.   Deese-Roberts, Susan, and Kathleen Keating. **Library Instruction: A Peer Tutoring Model.** Englewood, Colo., Libraries Unlimited, 2000. 212p. index. $46.00pa. ISBN 1-56308-652-2.

Peer tutoring has received a lot of attention in education literature. Applying it to library instruction has been carried out as well by a variety of writers in library science periodicals. However, few books have been dedicated to peer tutoring in libraries. *Library Instruction* is the most significant book published on this topic in the past 20 years and it does an excellent job introducing and modeling the idea.

The book begins with two thin chapters that give overviews of both the history of library instruction and a look at peer tutoring in institutions of higher education. The strength of the book is that it gives a model for establishing peer tutoring programs in library instruction. Chapters on the foundations of a peer tutoring program and how to establish one follow. These chapters give good ideas in the areas of recruiting tutors, training them, and evaluating the program. The meat of this work is a detailed model curriculum for what to teach peer tutors. Seven sessions are outlined and could easily be adapted by a higher education institution for their own program.

This work also provides details for using peer tutoring in the K-12 setting along with two appendixes. One appendix covers the College Reading Learning Association International Tutor Training Certification Program and provides a lengthy directory of institutions that are certified. Yet, this section probably could have been left out of the book as it provides little original content. However, the second appendix is a real gem as it provides the documents that the authors used at the University of New Mexico in their peer tutoring program. These documents are of a uniformly high quality and should be easy for any institution to adapt. This guide is a strong book that will provide most of the information needed to establish and run a peer tutoring program. It is strongly recommended.

—**Michael Lorenzen**

Public Libraries

C, P

276.   Evans, G. Edward, Anthony J. Amodeo, and Thomas L. Carter. **Introduction to Library Public Services.** 6th ed. Englewood, Colo., Libraries Unlimited, 1999. 500p. index. (Library and Information Science Text Series). $60.00; $45.00pa. ISBN 1-56308-632-8; 1-56308-633-6pa.

Library educators will welcome this new edition of a textbook to be used with beginning library and information science students to make them aware of the public services in all types of libraries. This is the 6th edition of the work originally done by Marty Bloomburg. Among the public services included are reference, library instruction, interlibrary loans, circulation, reserves, special collections, serials, media, and government publications. Security issues as they relate to all services are given in a separate chapter.

New to this edition is the inclusion of the technological information in the context of each service. Also, the chapter on the various types of libraries has been omitted and the information concerning the way services differ between them has been incorporated under the description of each service. The review questions and suggested reading lists have been updated and some Websites have been added. Especially useful is the list of the readings under the types of libraries.

The editors as well as the authors of each chapter (professional librarians, professors of library and information science, and professional library support staff) have attempted and succeeded in making the information as meaningful and current as possible. Because every aspect of library public services seems to have been adequately covered in this work, it is recommended as an up-to-date textbook for library and information science courses in both graduate and undergraduate programs as well as for training purposes within libraries. [R: JAI, July 2000, pp. 291-292]—**Sara R. Mack**

School Library Media Centers

S

277.   Bacon, Pamela S. **100 Library Lifesavers: A Survival Guide for School Library Media Specialists.** Englewood, Colo., Libraries Unlimited, 2000. 317p. index. $37.50pa. ISBN 1-56308-750-2.

100 Library Lifesavers: A Survival Guide for School Library Media Specialists gives tips and tools for busy school library media specialists who serve primary through high school grades. Along with 10 other contributors, Bacon's witty, nicely encouraging, and informative suggestions are compiled from her own experiences of being a very busy librarian. The lifesavers, covering a range of topics, are summarized in the front of the book. The author has also indicated an interest level for each lifesaver—the majority being intended for all levels.

The book covers many areas of interest that are beneficial for a new school library media specialist or an experienced one. The areas of interest include a Book Buck behavior management technique, suggestions for professional refresher or certification classes, many suggestions for interacting with teachers, inventive ways to promote the library and reading, as well as some skills checklists and lessons. Some of the many administrative management tips deal with managing the collection, purchasing new materials, directing student assistants, keeping everything organized, and how to handle other library tasks. The ideas, most of which the reader could put to use this afternoon, have been tested in the field and are not time consuming but time saving. The 8½-by-11 book has reproducible pages as well as information on how to contact the places and people mentioned in the book. There is also a bibliography. *100 Library Lifesavers* is a very useful source, easy to read, enjoyable, supportive, and helpful. [R: BR, May/June 2000, pp. 77-79; VOYA, Aug 2000, p. 216; SLJ, June 2000, p. 179]

—**Karen Browne Ohlrich**

S

278.   Clyde, Laurel A. **Managing InfoTech in School Library Media Centers.** Englewood, Colo., Libraries Unlimited, 1999. 290p. illus. index. $32.50pa. ISBN 1-56308-724-3.

School library media specialists looking for a thorough, basic overview of managing technology in its various aspects in their school library media center (SLMC) will find this an excellent resource. It is exceptionally thorough and respectful of its audience. Technical terms are defined in the text to aid immediate understanding. Clyde takes a clear look at the different kinds of technology and their usefulness. The aspects of information technology treated include the management of information technology (e.g., facilities, personnel, maintenance, issues, circulation, networks), using information technology in the management of the SLMC itself (e.g., inventory, budgeting and accounting, the materials catalog, disaster prevention), collection assessment, access to information and consideration of its many electronic formats, uses of e-mail, recreational uses, and shaping a technology plan and implementing it. Although the word "book" does not appear in either the detailed table of contents or the index, and only occasionally in the text, the intent of the author is to focus the content of the book, not to deny the book's continued value. Clyde provides chapter bibliographies (including URLs), a Web page evaluation worksheet, and a list of software and hardware systems. She offers assistance in managing this now commonplace but still problematic part of today's school environment. [R: BR, Sept/Oct 2000, p. 73; BL, Aug 2000, p. 2151; TL, June 2000, p. 43]—**Edna M. Boardman**

S

279.   Duncan, Donna, and Laura Lockhart. **I-Search, You Search, We all Search to Research: A How-To-Do-It Manual for Teaching Elementary School Students to Solve Information Problems.** New York, Neal-Schuman, 2000. 159p. index. (How-To-Do-It Manuals for Librarians, no.97). $45.00pa. ISBN 1-55570-381-X.

This work is a teaching manual for elementary school teachers and librarians collaborating on teaching a research unit. Duncan and Lockhart's manual is the latest of several works based on the I-Search method of teaching research skills developed by Ken Macrorie, which emphasizes personal information problem solving. Duncan and Lockhart's manual is divided into five sections representing the five steps of the I-Search method. Each section contains a brief discussion of the theoretical basis for that step, lessons to accomplish that step, the types of activities the authors have used with their classes, and anecdotes about the authors' experiences. An individual lesson includes sections on materials and advanced preparation, the objective, an anticipatory set (examples), input and modeling, guided practice, independent practice, and closure. A bibliography, an appendix of student papers (brief project reports rather than formal research papers), and an index conclude the manual.

Although not as cleanly laid out as most textbook teachers' manuals, this work will be useful to its intended audiences—mainly students in undergraduate and graduate elementary education or library/information study programs; elementary school administrators, team leaders, curriculum directors, and subject coordinators; and practicing elementary teachers and librarians, who are either new to this information problem-solving method or are looking for additional ideas for implementing the I-Search method. Unfortunately, this reviewer could not find a notice giving permission to reproduce for classroom use the numerous copy-ready forms and information sheets, a regrettable lack in a work of this kind. This book is recommended for school library professional collections or circulating collections in academic libraries supporting education or library and information science programs.—**Rosanne M. Cordell**

S

280.   **Learning and Libraries in an Information Age: Principles and Practice.** Barbara K. Stripling, ed. Englewood, Colo., Libraries Unlimited, 1999. 375p. index. (Principles and Practices Series). $39.00pa. ISBN 1-56308-666-2.

This volume is intended for practicing library media specialists. It provides school librarians with tested research and theory that will assist them in addressing the educational needs of students in an age where resources are many and filters are few. The goal of the Principles and Practice Series is to implement a philosophy and a system for library service that will enhance student achievement.

The contributors in this collection of essays stress that library media specialists, in conjunction with classroom teachers, can best teach students the skills they need to become information literate, that is, to learn how to become knowledgeable information consumers, deriving meaning from the resources at their disposal. The editors of this volume have synthesized much research on education and libraries, including learning theories of prominent scholars (e.g., Jean Piaget, B. F. Skinner), models for creating learning environments where students employ both practical library skills and evaluative skills to complete assignments, and the challenge of learning in a hi-tech context where technology is changing how we learn (e.g., linear learning vs. hypertextual learning). The final chapter contains an excellent annotated bibliography of core titles from educational literature, which will acquaint library media specialists with some of the best research done on instructional strategies, standards, and assessment.

This volume encourages creating a learning community made up of parents, teachers, and library media specialists, who must focus on encouraging students' curiosity and discouraging didactic instruction. Librarians and teachers should act as facilitators of learning, allowing students' questions and concerns to guide classroom instruction.

Each essay has a detailed bibliography, including valuable Web addresses. There is also a useful index at the end of the volume. The essays are well-written, if somewhat dry at times, and should be required reading for anyone entering the field of education—teachers and librarians alike. Those working in school libraries will recognize the challenges ahead of them, and hopefully some of the ideas presented here will be inspiring and give renewed meaning to their work. Those entering the field of education should be motivated by the opportunities available to them to improve student learning in the future. [R: VOYA, Oct 2000, p. 303; BR, May/June 2000, p. 79; SLJ, June 2000, p. 179; JAL, Mar 2000, p. 150; BL, 15 Mar 2000, p. 1393; LJ, 15 Feb 2000, p. 204]

—**Paula Crossman**

S

281.   Small, Ruth V., and Marilyn P. Arnone. **Turning Kids on to Research: The Power of Motivation.** Englewood, Colo., Libraries Unlimited, 2000. 199p. illus. index. (Information Literacy Series). $26.00pa. ISBN 1-56308-782-0.

This is not a reference book, but a how-to-teach-reference-skills book. Small and Arnone focus on how "a student's motivation can affect his or her success in learning and using information skills" and they persuasively argue for a "systematic approach for applying motivational principals" to the teaching of reference skills (p. xv). In other words, lackluster, dull lessons on the research process turn off many students to the entire research process. In order to fully engage students in the research process, library media teachers must design motivation into their information skills instruction.

Divided into five chapters, each chapter ends with a "chapter challenge" (i.e., quiz on the chapter), answers to the challenge, reflection points (i.e., a page for jotting down notes and ideas related to the chapter), and references. The 1st chapter provides an overview of information literacy and motivation (e.g., how motivation fits into information literacy and motivational goals and theories). The 2d chapter covers the start of the research process, including generating interest in the research process and 7 motivational moments. The 3d chapter moves on to the middle of the research process and discusses how to maintain interest in the process and how to promote the value of information skills, including 6 motivational moments. The 4th chapter focuses on the end of the process, with promoting satisfaction in research accomplishments and 5 motivational moments. The 5th chapter brings it all together with discussions of creating a constructionist learning environment. "What Would YOU Do?" sections are scattered throughout the last four chapters. This is excellent supplemental reading for students in school library programs and for library media teachers seeking new insights into motivating students to complete their research assignments. [R: BR, Nov/Dec 2000, p. 76; VOYA, Oct 2000, pp. 303-304; TL, Oct 2000, p. 44]—**Esther R. Sinofsky**

P, S

282.   Snyder, Timothy. **Getting Lead-Bottomed Administrators Excited About School Library Media Centers.** Englewood, Colo., Libraries Unlimited, 2000. 184p. index. (Building Partnerships Series). $27.00pa. ISBN 1-56308-794-4.

Written from the perspective of an administrator, the author assesses the status of education and library media centers today, while also providing insightful suggestions to meet new and old challenges. Although libraries are directly linked to academic achievement, educational leaders do not always focus upon, nor use to the greatest extent, that which brings proven results. Snyder turns negative situations into challenges and offers a fresh outlook on meeting the somewhat impossible demands of education and library media centers today. He recognizes the various titles that library professionals carry today, from the traditional term librarian to library media specialist, and uses them interchangeably without any intention to give preference or offend. He is on target in recognizing the many factors and attitudes toward education today and the need to defend and save library media centers.

The book is divided into three parts. The first part recognizes the current climate in education, describes the various personality characteristics of administrators and library media specialists, and gives examples of individuals who faced specific challenges and dealt with them. The second part is the longest section of the book and perhaps the most critical in achieving the desired results. Snyder describes common successful themes and the components of good planning. Here, the reader learns to establish an objective and assess an administrator's background, goals, and leadership and learning styles. Taking assessment of one's own resources, including a self-analysis, is also shown to play a significant role in achieving goals. Timelines, implementation strategies, and the equally important evaluation provide steps in the successful accomplishment of goals. Examples and the actual situations of two library media specialists illustrate the topics within the section.

The final section is a listing of specific suggestions to consider in building relationships with administrators, teachers, parents, and students. The suggestions for what to do and what not to do for achieving credibility are insightful and helpful not only to those entering the profession but also to veteran educators needing to assess and to perhaps make changes. The final chapter recognizes the need for balance between the demands of educational life and librarians' goals and needs, as well as those of their families.

Although administrators appreciate employees that go beyond the basic fulfillments of the position and give in extra ways, Snyder states throughout the book the need for balance in goals and time commitments. He also provides examples and suggestions of how to meet the increasing demands of education. The reader could easily read the brief summaries at the end of each chapter and the list of strategic ideas, but in doing so they would miss the anecdotes and examples that make the narrative insightful and a pleasurable read. Useful checklists, outlines, and surveys are provided to assist the reader in implementing the suggestions. The index is detailed to easily assist in locating a topic. This is an insightful and suggested read for all library professionals in education. [R: BR, Jan/Feb 01, p. 78; SLJ, Nov 2000, p. 156; BL, 15 Oct 2000, p. 449]—**Elaine Ezell**

P, S

283.   Thompson, Helen M., and Susan A. Henley. **Fostering Information Literacy: Connecting National Standards, Goals 2000, and the SCANS Report.** Englewood, Colo., Libraries Unlimited, 2000. 257p. index. (Information Literacy Series). $37.50pa. ISBN 1-56308-767-7.

Information literacy is defined by the authors as "the ability to access, evaluate, and use information from a variety of sources for both academic and personal reasons and to effectively communicate this knowledge to others" (p. 229). This book, which can be used for staff development, includes various information literacy standards developed by states and organizations; background information, explanations, articles, and links to national curriculum guidelines; techniques for teaching problem-solving and critical thinking skills; and instructions about designing information literacy lessons for all types of students. These components are then put together into examples of lesson plans that encourage researching, thinking, evaluating, and communicating. A lesson plan model is provided that may be used to outline a single lesson or a unit of study.

Chapters are divided into logical components with bold headings. At the end of each chapter are a summary, notes, and sometimes a bibliography for further reading. A "Checklist of Information Literacy Goals, Objectives, and Strategies" is an excellent tool to help teachers and librarians develop a systematic plan to ensure that all of the necessary skills and objectives are being taught and practiced.

Appendixes include charts comparing the K-4 national math, science, history, English, and fine arts standards with the AASL/AECT Information Literacy Standards for Student Learning. Also included are transparency masters designed to help library media specialists introduce and explain the concepts and components of a school-wide information literacy program. A comprehensive index provides easy access to topics covered. [R: SLJ, July 2000, p. 131; BR, Sept/Oct 2000, pp. 75-76; TL, June 2000, p. 42]—**Dana McDougald**

P, S

284.   Woolls, Blanche. **The School Library Media Manager.** 2d ed. Englewood, Colo., Libraries Unlimited, 1999. 340p. index. $50.00. ISBN 1-56308-772-3; 1-56308-702-2pa.

Woolls' 2d edition of *The School Library Media Manager* is more than complete; it is all-inclusive, detailed, and most informative. Tied in with the 1998 *Information Power: Building Partnerships for Learning* (AASL, 1998), the book covers a breadth of topics. Pre–graduate school students to seasoned school librarians will find the book helpful and filled with necessary information that is well researched from a variety of numerous and excellent resources. The resources are listed at the end of each chapter.

The book starts with an overview of becoming and being a school library media specialist with the necessary details outlined. The next 10 chapters discuss what is involved with managing a library media center program as a library administrator in a school. Woolls talks about all of the facets of management without overwhelming readers, who will find, instead, that they are given enough information to make decisions based on what they have read. There are additional chapters about instituting evaluations of the program, being involved in professional organizations, serving in a leadership position in a school, and collaborating as an instructional partner with the teachers. The exercises at the end of each chapter will guide the readers' personal inquiry into the area of the chapter's focus. Library school students would be well served to answers these questions. The appendix has 12 varied entries of interest to readers.

The School Library Media Manager is a must read for those coming into the profession so that they gain a better understanding of all that is involved. It is also a must read for experienced school librarians to find out about new methods, areas of interest, and ideas for managing a school library media program. [R: TL, Jan/Feb 2000, p. 45]—**Karen Browne Ohlrich**

P, S

285.   Zweizig, Douglas L., and Dianne McAfee Hopkins, with Norman Lott Webb and Gary Wehlage. **Lessons from Library Power: Enriching Teaching and Learning.** Englewood, Colo., Libraries Unlimited, 1999. 281p. index. $35.00pa. ISBN 1-56308-833-9.

Lessons from Library Power is the result of the evaluation of the Library Power program that has been implemented in 19 communities across the country. Library Power is an effort to improve teaching and learning by increasing library collections, librarians, and their integration into the total instructional program of a school.

This evaluation focuses on implementation processes and effects in local sites. Some readers may find fault with the work in that it does not measure improved student learning as an outcome variable. The authors acknowledge this fact and provide a rationale for the design. Data were collected through a variety of surveys, teacher logs, library collection maps, and other instruments that are included in the appendixes as resources.

Lessons from Library Power is a valuable resource for those who wish to implement Library Power or who wish to conduct an educational program evaluation. It will also be beneficial to those who are involved in any type of school change initiative. The discussions of the program components and implementation processes for Library Power in clearly titled chapters can serve as a guide for the many local school practitioners looking for specific guidance on school change. For instance, a chapter is dedicated to a discussion of the interaction of Library Power with multiple school change initiatives currently operating in schools.

Researchers from the University of Wisconsin, nationally known for their expertise in integrated instruction, school restructuring, and library/information sciences, conducted the evaluation. Their insights and advice throughout the report are applicable to a wide range of school change issues. [R: BR, May/June 2000, p. 80; SLJ, July 2000, p. 131]—**Glen W. Cutlip**

Special Topics

Cataloging and Classification

C, P

286.   Scott, Mona L. **Conversion Tables.** 2d ed. Englewood, Colo., Libraries Unlimited, 1999. 3v. $75.00pa./set. ISBN 1-56308-596-8.

Scott has revised and refined these volumes, perhaps due to the scathing review the last edition received in ARBA (see ARBA 94, entry 630). There are now three instead of two volumes. The first volume provides LC numbers in strict order immediately followed by Dewey and a subject heading. This process is duplicated for the Dewey numbers in the second volume and the subject headings in the third volume. Scott indicates which editions of the *Dewey Decimal Classification* (21st), *Library of Congress Subject Headings* (1996), and *Library of Congress Free-Floating Subdivisions* (1994) she used as her reference tools and why.

In the front of each volume is an identical complete introduction. It includes a description of the structure of tables and instructions for use of the tables. Unfortunately the LC references seem a bit dated. Hopefully the CD version will be kept up-to-date. A looseleaf format would still have been preferred to the bound volumes. Scott still asserts that some conversions can be completed successfully from the tables or they will lead users to the appropriate one in the schedules. As indicated in the previous review, this "action may be inadvisable. . . . Some problems arise from the different intellectual arrangements of the two classification systems and from the extreme brevity of entries." Yet, *Conversion Tables* remains an authoritative cataloging tool. [R: LJ, July 2000, p. 149]—**Nadine Salmons**

Collection Development and Evaluation

C, P

287.   Evans, G. Edward, with Margaret R. Zarnosky. **Developing Library and Information Center Collections.** 4th ed. Englewood, Colo., Libraries Unlimited, 2000. 595p. index. (Library and Information Science Text Series). $69.50; $49.50pa. ISBN 1-56308-706-5; 1-56308-832-0pa.

A comparison of the 4th edition of this book with the 3d edition reveals the following major changes. The old chapter 4 on selection process theory has been eliminated and replaced by information on selection process in practice that was previously in the fifth chapter. The old chapters on serials and electronic materials have been substantially revised and expanded. Also extensively revised are the chapters on government information and evaluation. The first chapter on the information age and society is essentially unchanged. The second chapter on information needs assessment makes a distinction by type of library or information center that was not in the previous edition. Otherwise, this chapter is also essentially unchanged. Yet it is useful for anyone doing a user survey. The chapters on collection development policies; producers of information materials; and censorship, intellectual freedom, and collection development are essentially unchanged. A section on Internet filtering has been added to the latter. References, charts, and examples used have been updated in all four chapters. The chapter on legal issues focuses on the important issue of copyright.

Users may question how much can really be new in the chapters on producers of printed materials, audiovisual materials, acquisitions, and distributors and vendors, but procedures and expectations of client and information suppliers do change and all are effected by new efficiencies as a result of improved methodologies and information systems. Throughout this edition, even when chapters have not been extensively revised, there are frequently minor changes in wording and emphasis with the result that the subjects appear to be more reflective of current developments. Relevant URLs are used where appropriate throughout this edition.

This is an excellent book of important topics sometimes relegated to the backburner in the information age. The more "seamless" presentation of topics makes it far superior to the 3d edition. [R: RUSQ, Fall 2000, pp. 96-97; LJ, 15 Mary 2000, p. 131]—**Robert M. Ballard**

Copyright

C, P

288.   Talab, R. S. **Commonsense Copyright: A Guide for Educators and Librarians.** 2d ed. Jefferson, N.C., McFarland, 1999. 292p. index. $39.95pa. ISBN 0-7864-0675-5.

Talab provides readers of *Commonsense Copyright: A Guide for Educators and Librarians* with a compass to navigate through the maze of copyright law. In this 2d edition, she includes issues around new technology, the Internet, and the Bill of Rights and Responsibilities for Electronic Learners (appendix G). What could be a dry narrative full of legal terminology turns out to be a readable guide full of examples that illustrate specific materials and uses.

Of special interest to librarians is part 4, "Library Use of Copyrighted Materials." Here the reader will find a thorough discussion of library reproduction rights in both for-profit and nonprofit arenas, library networks, library video use, and library software/Internet use. Each of these sections, as well as other chapters, contain usage examples—a can do list, a cannot do list, tried and true procedures, situations to be aware of, and tips to follow to prevent illegal activities. Many Internet addresses are provided (in addition to print resources) for those who want to explore a given topic in more depth.

There is acknowledgement that copyright in digital formats changes rapidly. To facilitate the interpretation of these issues the author includes the text of the American Library Association Digital Millennium Copyright Act Guide (appendix O). This guide helps the reader understand new issues surrounding copyright and new technology. Electronic publishing, multimedia, and distance education are highlighted in the copyright primer, as are the four fair use criteria and the three fair use tests.

The book is highly recommended for reference departments in all types of libraries. It contains valuable examples of copyright use for students, researchers, educators, administrators, and librarians. [R: VOYA, Aug 2000, p. 219]—**Laura J. Bender**

Information Science and Information Systems

C, P

289.   Osborne, Larry N., and Margaret Nakamura. **Systems Analysis for Librarians and Information Professionals.** 2d ed. Englewood, Colo., Libraries Unlimited, 2000. 261p. illus. index. (Library and Information Science Text Series). $50.00pa. ISBN 1-56308-693-X.

Systems Analysis for Librarians and Information Professionals is a concise and well-written overview of systems analysis. There are many books available on systems analysis, but few offer such a practical and interesting overview of this topic as this work. In addition, although systems analysis seems to always be applied to computers, this book demonstrates that systems analysis is a technique that can be applied to all types of problems, including modest manual processes that are commonly found in libraries. The authors also illustrate some of the pitfalls and dangers in systems analysis and the need to keep the political and financial realities in mind when attempting to facilitate operational changes through this technique.

The first three chapters provide an excellent beginning framework for the rest of the text, covering the purpose of systems analysis, the historical development of systems analysis, and the human element (including ethics and organizational commitment). The remaining 12 chapters are arranged in a sequence that corresponds with the steps in a typical systems analysis project. These chapters are also held together by an ongoing case study that applies principles and techniques of systems analysis to the serials department of a university library along with a series of discussion questions that could be used in the classroom. There are some other exercises blended into several of the chapters with the answers provided in an appendix. Chapters concentrate on the practical rather than the theoretical aspects of systems analysis. The text is easy to read, logically organized, and is supplemented by useful illustrations. Each chapter has a short but carefully selected list of references. One appendix is a list of tasks for a sample systems analysis project, while another is a Java program for determining sample size. There is also an index for the volume.

This work is an excellent resource for librarians in any type of library. In addition, it is useful as either a textbook or supplemental reading for many courses in librarianship or information science. Chapters on flow-charts, flow diagrams, and other modeling tools will be a particularly good introduction for those who do not have a background in the use of these techniques. [R: JAL, Nov 2000, p. 443]—**Sara Anne Hook**

PUBLISHING AND BOOKSELLING

Directories

C

290.   **Directory of Small Press/Magazine Editors & Publishers 2000–2001.** 31st ed. Len Fulton, ed. Paradise, Calif., Dustbooks, 2000. 331p. $23.95pa. ISBN 0-916685-81-0.

This directory's information is culled from the well-known standard reference work, titled the *International Directory of Little Magazines & Small Presses* (36th ed.; see ARBA 2001, entry 687). The *Directory of Small Press/Magazine Editors & Publishers* provides the names and contact information of small press and magazine editors and publishers listed in the larger work. This volume also states that it includes legitimate editors and publishers who are classified as "self publishing" and who were perhaps not listed in the larger work.

The entries are alphabetically arranged by the person's last name. Contact information is provided in each entry, including the name of the company or the publication title (indicated by italicized capital letters) that the person is affiliated with, street address, telephone and fax numbers, and e-mail and Website addresses. Cross-references are also provided for persons who are located at the same company. This is a nice companion volume to the larger directory, and would be useful in academic and public libraries as well as in any library where the contact information is needed.—**Jan S. Squire**

C

291.   **Literary Market Place 2001.** 61st ed. New Providence, N.J., R. R. Bowker, 2000. index. $249.00pa./set. ISBN 0-8352-4346-X. ISSN 0000-1155.

This 2001 edition of *Literary Market Place* marks the 61st year of this publication. This book is well known among libraries, booksellers, and publishers for its up-to-date information and complete listings. This latest edition has almost 14,000 entries, 300 of which are listed for the first time. Of those 14,000 entries, 3,461 are publishers from the United States and Canada.

The arrangement of this edition remains the same as past editions. Volume 1 provides information on book publishers; editorial services and agents; associations, events, courses, and awards; and books and maga-zines for the publishing trade. Electronic publishers are now listed in with book publishers, which is new to this edition. Volume 2 provides information on advertising, marketing, and publicity companies associated with publishing; book manufacturing; sales and distribution; and services and suppliers. For each entry the name, address, telephone and fax numbers, e-mail and Website addresses, key personnel, ISBN prefix, number of titles published annually, and ordering information in provided. Several indexes are located throughout the volumes that facilitate ease of use: a company index, personnel index, index to sections, and index to advertisers.

This work, along with its international counterpart *International Literary Market Place* (see ARBA 2001, entry 688), continues to offer the most up-to-date information on publishers and the publishing industry. It will be of great use in public and academic libraries. The work is also available on CD-ROM (see ARBA 2000, entry 589, for a review) or the World Wide Web at http://www.literarymarketplace.com.—**Shannon Graff Hysell**

12 Military Studies

GENERAL WORKS

Dictionaries and Encyclopedias

C, P

292. **Dictionary of Military Terms.** Richard Bowyer, ed. Chicago, Fitzroy Dearborn, 1999. 214p. $45.00. ISBN 1-57958-156-0.

Bowyer's dictionary provides definitions of a few thousand military terms and terms of common use with military applications. In some cases there are additional notes (as in the entry explaining the difference between "detention" and "imprisonment"), but most are brief and written in easily understood English. Appendixes include British and American uses of phonetic alphabets, structure and pronunciation of units of time, military ranks, and sample orders. The only illustrations are a page of military grouping symbols.

A similar publication is the U.S. Department of Defense's (DOD) *Dictionary of Military Terms* (3d ed.; Stackpole Books, 1995). It includes terms approved by the DOD and for use by NATO, and is also focused on British and American terminology. For the most part the DOD's definitions are more informative, substantive, and useful; the volume is better edited; and it is available on a Website (http://www.dtic.mil/doctrine/jel/doddict/). However, there are many terms unique to each publication. Bowyer's *Dictionary of Military Terms*, for example, includes more abbreviations (even common forms), is more up-to-date, and provides definitions for military equipment. Bowyer's work would have benefited from better editing, but it is nevertheless useful. In short, these sources serve to complement each other in a comprehensive collection serving military, defense, and public policy studies. [R: Choice, Oct 2000, p. 308]—**Kenneth W. Berger**

C

293. Purcell, L. Edward, and Sarah J. Purcell. **Encyclopedia of Battles in North America: 1517 to 1916.** New York, Facts on File, 2000. 383p. maps. index. $60.00. ISBN 0-8160-3350-1.

This encyclopedia covers nearly 400 alphabetically arranged battles in Mexico, Canada, and the United States—from Francisco Hernández de Córdoba's battle against the Maya at Champoton, Mexico in 1517 to Major Frank Tompkin's fight against the forces of Pancho Villa in Parral, Mexico, almost 200 years later. Small encounters are excluded, as well as those that little information is available for (e.g., pre-European, Native American conflicts). But, the definition of "battle" is flexible enough to include encounters not found in other standard works, such as Mark M. Boatner's *The Encyclopedia of the American Revolution* (David McKay, 1966) and *The Civil War Dictionary* (rev. ed.; David McKay, 1988).

Each entry is headed with the name of the battle; any alternate names; and the place, date, and name of the larger conflict (e.g., American Revolution). The text describes the battle; its context, outcome, and significance; and the military figures, units, geographic locale, and casualties. Entries also feature brief bibliographies for further reading. Supplementary features include a glossary of military terms, dozens of maps (up to a full page in size), several appendixes (battles listed alphabetically, chronologically, and by war, and a directory of battlefield sites), an extensive bibliography, and a subject index. This is an accessible, reasonably priced, and comprehensive military history reference work that is appropriate for all school, public, and academic libraries' history collections. [R: LJ, July 2000, p. 79]—**Kenneth W. Berger**

13 Political Science

POLITICS AND GOVERNMENT

United States

Biography

C, P

294.   **The American Presidents.** rev. ed. Frank N. Magill, John L. Loos, and Tracy Irons-George, eds. Hackensack, N.J., Salem Press, 2000. 813p. illus. index. $115.00. ISBN 0-89356-224-6.

This work remains committed to providing comprehensive biographical portraits of each American president, but the revised edition is intended to build on the 1st in several important ways. First, profiles have been commissioned for Presidents George Bush and William Clinton. In addition, the essays on recent presidents Richard Nixon, Gerald Ford, Jimmy Carter, and Ronald Reagan have been updated to reflect new research devoted to evaluating their terms in office. The bibliographies accompanying each profile have also been updated to reflect new scholarship produced in the past 10 years. The revised edition includes additional photographs, illustrations, and textual sidebars, including the Monroe Doctrine, the Gettysburg Address, and the Declaration of Independence. The most useful enhancement is the inclusion of several new appendixes. These include the complete text of the U.S. Constitution; a chronology of key events by administration; election results from 1798 to 1996; lists of vice presidents, first ladies, and cabinet members; and an informative directory of presidential libraries with highlights on holdings, contact information, and Website addresses. The volume concludes with a glossary of terms and a name and subject index.

Overall, this revised work is a useful reference guide that is most appropriate for student researchers. The essays are well written, the bibliographies are up-to-date, and the appendixes enhance the value of a single-volume resource on the presidency. However, most of the factual information is readily available elsewhere (i.e., *The Presidency A to Z* [2d ed.; see ARBA 2000, entry 634]). This volume is recommended for those libraries needing a comprehensive, one-volume reference guide to the presidency. However, the information contained herein is mostly superfluous for those libraries that already own multiple guides to the American presidency. [R: BL, 1 Mar 2000, p. 1257; BR, May/June 2000, p. 70]—**Robert V. Labaree**

C, P

295.   **Who's Who in Congress 2000, 106th Congress.** Washington, D.C., Congressional Quarterly, 2000. 343p. illus. $17.95pa. ISBN 1-56802-556-4. ISSN 1054-9234.

Congressional Quarterly's *Who's Who in Congress 2000* is a compact biographical directory displaying essential information on the members of the U.S. Senate and House of Representatives. This volume enables patrons and reference librarians to quickly access what Congressional Quarterly states is the most often-requested information about our national legislators. The edition covers the 2d session of the 106th Congress, and a new edition is issued every March.

Along with short biographical entries, a small official photograph, constituency, and committee membership, one receives each legislator's contact information (including Website and e-mail address) and the names of important staff members. In addition, each legislator's entry is supplied with the annual ratings each has received from four important special interest groups—the AFL-CIO, Americans for Democratic Action, the American Conservative Union, and the United States Chamber of Commerce. Congressional Quarterly also supplies the entries with the results of their voting studies, giving percentages for the frequency of members' support for his or her party's bills or those supported by the president.

The arrangement and format make this handbook easy to use. All the congress members appear first by chamber and then alphabetically, with two entries per page. The appendixes include the lists of the Congressional Leadership, the legislators by state, and committee memberships, giving the biographical entries multiple access points.

The volume also lists roll calls of key votes, allowing one to judge the actions of the members. The delineation of the bills in question, however, is cursory, and proper judgment of the votes cast should be suspended until the particulars of each bill are discovered elsewhere. This volume, instead, is suitable for quick information. It may have been designed as a program for lobbyists, political reporters, and spectators of the bicameral institution, but its elegance and usefulness will find it a home in every public, school, and academic library. This volume should be placed in an easily accessible area, as it provides ready-reference and will likely provoke political participation and stimulate voter turnout.—**David E. Michalski**

Dictionaries and Encyclopedias

C, P

296.   Harold, Bass F., Jr. **Historical Dictionary of United States Political Parties.** Lanham, Md., Scarecrow, 2000. 389p. (Historical Dictionaries of Religions, Philosophies, and Movements, no.29). $69.50. ISBN 0-8108-3736-6.

As number 29 in the Historical Dictionaries of Religions, Philosophies, and Movements series from Scarecrow Press, this work provides brief biographical entries on all of the presidents and vice presidents, anyone who has received presidential votes in the Electoral College, key national party leaders, and important congressional members who have in some way contributed to shaping the political party system in the United States. The dictionary also includes definitions of conceptual terminology, such as "loyal opposition," that have evolved from the institution of party politics. However, the dictionary is most useful in defining technical terminology and characteristic idioms, such as "rump session," concerning all aspects of the political party system. These entries are particularly effective in deciphering the jargon embedded in the political process by giving concise definitions, often in historical context. The dictionary is supplemented with several useful features, including a short list of common acronyms, a chronology of key events, and an introductory essay that outlines the development and impact of the party system on the overall political landscape of the United States. The introduction is well written and succeeds in placing the subsequent entries in a broad historical context. The volume concludes with 14 appendixes that are primarily lists of key political and party leaders (i.e., floor leaders of the House of Representatives, 1899-2000) and a selective but thorough bibliography of reference works, general texts, and scholarly books and journal articles subdivided by topic. Both the appendixes and the bibliography contribute to the usefulness of this work. Overall, this is an excellent resource that provides a comprehensive framework for understanding the history of the party system in the United States and is highly recommended.—**Robert V. Labaree**

Handbooks and Yearbooks

P, S

297.   **Congressional Quarterly's Desk Reference on the Presidency.** By Bruce Wetterau. Washington, D.C., Congressional Quarterly, 2000. 311p. index. (Desk Reference Series). $49.95. ISBN 1-56802-589-0.

According to the book's preface, the purpose of this quick reference guide is "to provide an uncomplicated look at the whole American presidency and vice-presidency." Similar to the previous five volumes in Congressional Quarterly's series of question-and-answer reference books on the American system of government, information is given in the form of questions accompanied by answers that are usually between one or two paragraphs long, although many entries include useful charts or lists of data. The questions range from the factual ("Who was the first president born as an American citizen?") to the trivial ("Which states produced the most presidents?"), but all include succinct information that is not otherwise easily attainable in many cases.

The 500 questions and answers are arranged under 6 headings and further subdivided into more precise categories. For example, within the chapter on presidential powers and duties are questions and answers concerning the role of the president as commander in chief. The criteria for selecting the questions are based on frequently asked questions about the presidency, but no other details are described as to how information was identified for possible inclusion. Access to information is further facilitated by a comprehensive subject and name index as well as cross-references after many questions and answers that lead the reader to related entries. The guide also includes a brief bibliography of further reading about the American presidency.

There is a wealth of information embedded in this reference guide, but its presentation, style, and arrangement are obviously intended to assist the general nonresearcher, secondary school student, or lower-level undergraduate. Nevertheless, for these audiences the book succeeds in being informative and useful.—**Robert V. Labaree**

Europe

C, P

298.   Butler, David, and Gareth Butler. **Twentieth-Century British Political Facts 1900–2000.** 8th ed. New York, St. Martin's Press, 2000. 584p. index. $79.95. ISBN 0-312-22947-X.

British politics presents continually fascinating developments and personalities and serves as a useful mirror to measure U.S. political developments and personalities against. *Twentieth-Century British Political Facts 1900–2000* is the latest edition of a long-standing reference source on British politics.

Following the obligatory introduction, the work provides detailed coverage of contemporary and historical British political events and personalities for the just-concluded twentieth century. Entries are arranged by broad categories, such as government ministries, political parties, Parliament, elections, civil service, royal commissions, social conditions, the economy, royalty, local government, international relations, armed forces, the press, broadcasting authorities, and relevant Internet resources.

Within these categories readers can find an enormous array of information. Examples of the kinds of information users can find include the Home Secretary under Prime Minister Stanley Baldwin's 1924–1929 conservative government; locations of annual Labour Party conferences since 1906; the dates, subjects, and results of critical twentieth-century House of Commons votes; monthly Gallup Poll results of political parties; enumeration of royal commission reports; housing and population statistics; parties controlling the local governments of major cities since 1945; major treaties signed by the United Kingdom; British ambassadors to major countries and international organizations; military leaders; and the editors and editorial philosophy of British newspapers.

Twentieth-Century British Political Facts is an essential reference source for anyone interested in British politics or political history. Its scope of coverage is staggering and will be useful in setting arguments on various British political subjects. Its list of Internet resources for government agencies, Parliament, political parties, newspapers, and television networks reflect the authors recognition of the Internet's growing importance in governmental debate, policymaking, and political discussion. Although this compilation does not contain analyses or data on current Members of Parliament, it belongs in the reference collection of any library desirous of having substantive British political science and British history collections. This volume is highly recommended. [R: Choice, Oct 2000, p. 308]—**Bert Chapman**

INTERNATIONAL RELATIONS

C, P

299.   Toropov, Brandon. **Encyclopedia of Cold War Politics.** New York, Facts on File, 2000. 242p. illus. index. $60.00. ISBN 0-8160-3574-1.

Few twentieth-century political events have had the enduring significance of the Cold War confrontation between the United States and the former Soviet Union. This confrontation influenced the domestic, foreign, and national security policies of these two countries as well as those of other countries to varying degrees.

Encyclopedia of Cold War Politics describes the individuals, concepts, and events shaping and defining the Cold War era and our views of this period at the beginning of a new century and millennium. Entries on these individuals, concepts, and events are arranged alphabetically, with most entries ranging in length from less than half a page to three pages. Entry topics include Alliance For Progress, Berlin Wall, James F. Byrnes, dentente, flexible response, hippies, iron curtain, the National Security Council, Reykjavik Summit, George Shultz, silent majority, Edward Teller, and the Yalta Conference. A selective bibliography of secondary sources and an index conclude the work.

This work's key attributes are the succinctly written entries and its ability to introduce high school students and undergraduate to key Cold War issues and personalities. Most entries are written in a nonideological or non-partisan manner, although the entry on Richard Allen (p. 3) should use "conservative" instead of "right wing" to describe his political views. Some entries cover personalities such as Bob Dylan, Jesse Jackson, and Huey Newton who were not policymakers directing governmental Cold War policy actions and should not be included in a reference work dealing explicitly with the Cold War. These criticisms aside, *Encyclopedia of Cold War Politics* is a relatively useful introduction to this era's important policies, personalities, and events. [R: BL, 1 Jan 01, pp. 1002-1004]—**Bert Chapman**

14 Psychology, Parapsychology, and Occultism

PSYCHOLOGY

Dictionaries and Encyclopedias

C, P

300.   Corsini, Raymond J. **Dictionary of Psychology.** Philadelphia, Taylor & Francis, 1999. 1156p. $124.95. ISBN 1-58391-028-X.

The author of *The Encyclopedia of Psychology* and *The Concise Encyclopedia of Psychology* (John Wiley, 1994 and 1996, respectively) has produced another outstanding reference work in this discipline. The preface states that the dictionary was developed from interviews with about 100 randomly selected psychologists who were asked what they wanted and did not want in a dictionary of psychology. Based on this, it includes more than three times the number of headwords, illustrations, biographies, and appendixes of any other dictionary of psychology in English. Its 30,000 entries include words and concepts from every area of psychology, including clinical, social, experimental, and physiological psychology. Commonly used, psychologically oriented phrases like "glass ceiling" and "worst scenario"; historical expressions like "sacred disease" for epilepsy; and some slang, foreign, and obsolete terms are included.

Its 10 appendixes comprise prefixes, suffixes, and affixes; DSM-IV categories; the Greek alphabet; medical prescription terms; systems of treatment; tests and measurements; symbols; leaning theory symbols; Rorschach descriptors; and mini-biographies of deceased persons important to the history of psychology. Headwords are presented in their natural order and definitions are short (averaging 31 words). Developed for psychologists and students of psychology and likely to become the standard scholarly resource, this dictionary's clear language, user-friendly organization, and unparalleled comprehensiveness will also serve a wider range of users in academic and large public libraries.—**Madeleine Nash**

Handbooks and Yearbooks

C, P

301.   **Mental Health Disorders Sourcebook.** 2d ed. Karen Bellenir, ed. Detroit, Omnigraphics, 2000. 605p. index. (Health Reference Series). $78.00. ISBN 0-7808-0240-3.

Using information on the subject of mental health and mental illness from a wide range of sources, including government agencies, professional organizations, and journals, the 2d edition of this reference tool is again written for the general reader. Primarily updating article information and URLs, it provides medical information about mental disorders and their treatments, specifically phrased in nontechnical terms, offering clear explanations to paraprofessionals, patients, and family members. Exploring both mental health and mental illness, the handbook provides information on early warning signs and symptoms of mental illness, identifying diagnostic tools, and even statistics about the incidence of mental illness. Composed of eight sections, each having its own chapters, such topics as anxiety disorders, depression, eating disorders, and bipolar disorders receive in-depth coverage. Beginning with an overview of the topic, the user finds definitions, organizations, and types of the disorder in every section. Along with specific disorders, the editor includes sections on treatment methods, both traditional and alternative, and medications currently in use and those in development. Of special note is the final section, titled "Additional Help and Information." It will be useful for anyone connected with those afflicted with mental illness. Names and addresses of organizations, a glossary of terms, services for veterans, and sources for additional reading are located in this section. A comprehensive, alphabetically arranged index can be found at the back of the book. This reference source is well organized and well written for its target audience of nonprofessionals investigating all aspects of mental disorders. It is suitable for public library collections and academic libraries with undergraduate programs in psychology.—**Marianne B. Eimer**

OCCULTISM

P

302.   Grimassi, Raven. **Encyclopedia of Wicca & Witchcraft.** St. Paul, Minn., Llewellyn, 2000. 470p. illus. index. $24.95pa. ISBN 1-56718-257-7.

This encyclopedia is an authoritative guide to the terms related to historical and present-day Wiccan religions. The author, a Craft Elder, and the publisher are well respected in the New Age tradition. The volume discusses the theology, history, rituals, verses, and influential practitioners of the Wiccan religions. The entries range in length from one or two paragraphs for common terms to several pages when describing sects among the religion (e.g., Dianic Wicca). Special features in the volume include the 140 traditional laws of witchcraft and the witches' alphabet. The four appendixes at the end of the volume provide words to classic Wiccan verses and telephone numbers, addresses, and e-mail and Web addresses (when available) for publications, organizations, shops, and mail order merchants of interest. An index concludes the volume.

Because of the renewed interest in Wiccan and New Age religions in today's society, this volume will be well received in many libraries. Medium-sized and large public libraries will especially benefit from its purchase.
—**Shannon Graff Hysell**

PARAPSYCHOLOGY

P

303.   Guiley, Rosemary Ellen. **Encyclopedia of Ghosts and Spirits.** 2d ed. New York, Facts on File, 2000. 430p. illus. index. $60.00. ISBN 0-8160-4085-0.

Guiley's 2d edition of the *Encyclopedia of Ghosts and Spirits* provides readers with an updated and improved reference work that details the history of paranormal activity. As in the last edition, published in 1992 by Facts on File (see ARBA 93, entry 810), the encyclopedia includes more than 500 entries on ghostly stories and legends, scientific investigations, spiritualism and mediumship, folklore, and noted personalities associated with the paranormal. Guiley has created a culturally balanced presentation by adding new entries on Japanese ghosts and folklore. In spite of these efforts, however, the author still seems to rely heavily upon British and, to a lesser extent, American ghost lore for her material.

The new edition contains dozens of new entries and photographs; new information about important myths; and updated entries on prominent people in the field, such as Hans Bender, Sir Simon Marsden, and Lorisa Rhine. The alphabetically arranged entries contain an abundance of *see* and *see also* references. The recommended reading lists provided at the end of most entries have also been updated. Guiley seems to have taken great care to discuss the subject matter in the most objective manner possible. In her presentation of these phenomena, she exhibits no obvious bias toward either skepticism or belief. This new edition is recommended for academic and public libraries.
—**Bronwyn Stewart**

15 Recreation and Sports

GENERAL WORKS

P
304. The ESPN Information Please Sports Almanac 2001. Gerry Brown and Michael Morrison, eds. New York, Hyperion, 2000. 959p. $12.99pa. ISBN 0-7868-8533-5.

Since it was first published as the *Information Please Sports Almanac* more than 10 years ago, this compact guide to sports statistics has become—especially since ESPN and Information Please joined forces 4 years ago—the quintessential sports information reference source. In most respects, little has changed since the 1st edition (see ARBA 94, entry 818 and ARBA 91, entry 800, for previous reviews). There is much to be said for that kind of continuity in the reporting of sports information because the comparison of facts and figures over an extended period of time is most often what sports fans are looking for and expect. This is one case in which the acquisition of the most current volume is always essential for libraries because, while much of the content remains the same year after year, each year a wealth of new information is added.

Once again, this almanac contains a quick summary review of the past year (1999–2000) that is followed by 23 sections on individual sports and other topics. Information about the major North American sports (baseball, college and professional football, college and professional basketball, and hockey) makes up almost one-half of the text. Lesser detail is provided for other sports (college sports, soccer, bowling, horse racing, tennis, golf, auto racing, boxing, and miscellaneous sports). There are also brief, but useful, sections devoted to such topics as halls of fame and awards, sports personalities, ballparks and arenas, business and international sports, and the 2000 Olympic games. The level of the writing in the introductory summaries and commentaries leaves much to be desired. It is, however, unsurpassed as a general source of information. Much of the information contained here, and more, may be found on the Internet, but not in such a single, readily available, and easy-to-use format. Even libraries with a minimal interest in sports should consider purchasing this inexpensive tool on an annual basis.—**Norman D. Stevens**

BASEBALL

Dictionaries and Encyclopedias

C, P
305. Baseball: The Biographical Encyclopedia. David Pietrusza, Matthew Silverman, and Michael Gershman, eds. Kingston, N.Y., Total Sports; distr., Emeryville, Calif., Publishers Group West, 2000. 1298p. illus. $49.95. ISBN 1-892129-34-5.

Public and academic libraries with *Total Baseball: The Official Encyclopedia of Major League Baseball* (see ARBA 2000, entry 712) in their collections now have a handsomely produced complementary volume to consider. The editorial team at Total Sports again has mined its huge database to produce a hefty book containing short biographical sketches of 2,000 individuals associated with baseball. The editors chose 1,500 subjects primarily on statistical criteria; the remaining 500 entries are more subjective in nature. The large number of biographies;

the thumbnail photograph included with each sketch; and the inclusion of nontraditional entries ranging from team executives, managers, umpires, lawyers, sportswriters, and announcers to the colorful characters who enjoyed only moments in the sun, make this eminently browsable volume distinctive.

Arranged alphabetically by popular name and written in lively, conversational style, the articles include nine essential career statistics for each player. Coverage begins with the National League (1876–) and includes the American Association (1882–1891), Union Association (1884), the Players' League (1890), the American League (1901–), and the Federal League (1914–1915), as well as selected Negro league players and managers for whom records are available. Readers ranging from young fans to seasoned sabermetricians will find the opinionated essays both accessible and provocative. Hall of Fame players, midget batters, flaky pitchers, and beloved broadcasters all find a place here, as do Ted Turner and Bart Giamatti. This work is far more comprehensive than *The Sporting News Selects Baseball's Greatest Players* (see ARBA 99, entry 719). The 400 biographies in the 6th edition of *Total Baseball* may be sufficient for many collections, but this popular encyclopedia now sets the standard in the history of this sport. [R: BL, 1 Oct 2000, p. 370; LJ, July 2000, p. 72]—**Julienne L. Wood**

Handbooks and Yearbooks

P
306.   James, Bill. **Bill James Presents ... STATS Major League Handbook 2001.** 12th ed. Morton Grove, Ill., STATS Publishing, 2000. 398p. $19.95pa. ISBN 1-884064-86-8.

P
307.   James, Bill. **Bill James Presents ... STATS Minor League Handbook 2001.** 10th ed. Morton Grove, Ill., STATS Publishing, 2000. 448p. $19.95pa. ISBN 1-884064-85-X.

Now in its 12th edition, *STATS Major League Handbook* continues to present baseball statistics in a straightforward and informative manner. The bulk of the book consists of career statistics for every major leaguer who played in 2000. Some of the statistical categories (e.g., times hit by pitches) in this section do not appear in other compilations. In addition, Bill James follows lists of leaders in 46 traditional statistical categories with his own tables in such areas as "cheap wins" and "isolated power." The technical definitions for these terms are included in the glossary. Another valuable section indicates manager tendencies in offense, defense, lineups, and pitching. Readers can tell, for instance, that Houston's Larry Dierker was more patient with his starting pitchers than all other National League managers. The remaining sections cover a variety of categories, such as fielding statistics, team statistics, and park data.

Devoted fans of losing teams may find some hope in the companion volume, *Stats Minor League Handbook*. This 10th edition includes the same detailed statistical tables, leader boards, and team statistics of previous editions. The unique "Major League Equivalencies" section, in which James estimates how a minor league hitter would have performed in the major leagues in the year 2000, is also retained. Finally, a special section on the 2000 Olympic baseball games offers Team USA composite statistics, box scores for the nine games that Team USA played, and statistics for minor league players who represented other countries. Both volumes are well-organized, contain statistics not easily found elsewhere, and are well worth the modest price.—**Ken Middleton**

BASKETBALL

P
308.   Bjarkman, Peter C. **The Biographical History of Basketball.** Lincolnwood, Ill., Masters Press, 2000. 590p. illus. index. $24.95pa. ISBN 1-57028-134-3.

Bjarkman's *The Biographical History of Basketball* is a cross between a standard biographical reference work and a book of lists. Highly opinionated, with lists that are a sure bet to start an argument in any bar, the book is nevertheless also a useful, if quirky, reference work.

The first two chapters present surveys of the evolution of the college and professional games, detailing changes in playing styles, rules, and the games' leading players and coaches. The next two chapters present lists of the games' most significant players and nonplayers. Again, the emphasis is on personal opinion. For example, among players Bjarkman includes Bob Kurland but not Jerry West, and among nonplayers he includes Ned Irish but not Abe Saperstein. The next three chapters, the heart of the volume, present brief biographical profiles of more than 500 players, coaches, administrators, and other people who have contributed to the development of the game. In the final chapter, in another foray into pure speculation, the author discusses whether Michael Jordan was or was not the greatest player in the history of the game. A handy timeline and a not very helpful bibliography conclude the book. The bibliography, for instance, does not list Bill Bradley's brilliant discussion of life in professional basketball, *Life on the Run*, or Chet Walker's sensitive autobiography, *Long Time Coming: A Black Athlete's Coming-of-Age in America*. But the bibliography does list 12 previously published or forthcoming basketball histories and basketball biographies by Peter C. Bjarkman. Quibbles aside, *The Biographical History of Basketball* should please students and fans of basketball.—**Randy Roberts**

CAMPING

P
309.   **National Forest Campground & Recreation Directory.** Whitefish, Mont., Coleman Company and Our Forests; distr., Guilford, Conn., Globe Pequot Press, 2000. 641p. illus. maps. $19.95pa. ISBN 0-7627-0787-9.

This well-organized and comprehensive directory lists 4,300 campgrounds that can be found in U.S. National Forests. Although some of these sites are well known, there are many that are less traveled and will therefore be less populated. The directory beings with a two-page map that locates 156 national forests in the United States and Puerto Rico, the majority of which are located in the western United States and the Rocky Mountain region. Next there is advice on finding the campgrounds listed, making reservations, and a list of campground rules. The directory is organized alphabetically by state first and then alphabetically by the campground name. Each state has a detailed map and a description of the national forests in the area. The campground descriptions include the name, elevation, whether or not it is handicap accessible, a three- to four-sentence description, directions on how to get there, the rate per night, how many sites are available, the dates it is open, and the maximum number of days a party can stay there. On the bottom of the page are symbols for additional information on whether or not the campground has hosts and reservable sites, and whether it is developed or rustic in nature. A final section lists Army Corps recreation lakes alphabetically by state, with information on where it is located, a short description, and directions on how to get there.

This guidebook provides a wealth of information for those who are interested in camping and mountaineering. It is recommended for public libraries.—**Shannon Graff Hysell**

FISHING

P
310.   Schultz, Ken. **Ken Schultz's Fishing Encyclopedia: Worldwide Angling Guide.** Foster City, Calif., IDG Books Worldwide, 2000. 1916p. illus. $60.00. ISBN 0-02-862057-7.

Schultz, fishing editor for *Field and Stream*, aims this unabridged dictionary-sized tome to update the late A. J. McClane's dated although extremely popular *McClane's New Standard Fishing Encyclopedia* (Gramercy Books, 1998). McClane's title, even at 1,156 pages, is just a little more than half the size of Schultz's 1,916-page book. Schultz covers species, geographic locations, methodologies, equipment, and angling philosophy. Articles on species and places comprise about two-thirds of the text.

For each sport or commercial species, it gives an illustration (generally in color), size and age, distribution, habitat, life history and behavior, food, angling tips, and Latin name and common names. Locations are by political unit, whether for country or for the United States and Canada, by state or province. Rivers are found under the geographic entity they flow through or abut. Thus, fishing the Mississippi River is covered under many different states. There is some duplication of data between articles on species and location because some species are so important in one locale.

Fishing methodologies review the different types of fishing, such as trolling or deep-sea. Under equipment there are articles on subjects such as boats (i.e., bass boats), tackle (with separate articles for fly or spinning reels), and lures. Schultz and his 125 worldwide contributors give unbiased coverage for commercial fishing yet follow a conservation ethic. Many of the articles are surprisingly long. Experienced anglers will find the articles in their areas familiar, but overall will learn many new aspects because the coverage is so broad. The writing style is clear and would be easily understood by junior high school students and up. The volume is very well illustrated and most species have a color line drawing that is often more informative than the mostly color photographs. Surprisingly, the illustrations for the spinning and casting reels could have been better done, and a page or two should have been devoted to illustrations of more popular flies.

There is no index, which will make users hunt for some topics if they do not have the correct name. There are *see* references within articles, but without either a cross-reference in the alphabetic list or an index, some information will only be found by guess, particularly among younger users. The volume is so large that it is uncomfortable to hold in the lap for reading, yet the articles are interesting, informative, and captivating enough to just sit and read. The price ($60) is low for a reference of this size and quality. This guide is very highly recommended for all sizes of public libraries, junior high and secondary school libraries, and almost a mandatory purchase where sport fishing is popular.—**Patrick J. Brunet**

FOOTBALL

P

311.   ***The Sporting News* Pro Football Register.** 2000 ed. Brendan Roberts and David Walton, eds. St. Louis, Mo., Sporting News Publishing, 2000. 523p. $15.95pa. ISBN 0-89204-636-8.

Published by Sporting News Publishing, the 2000 edition of the *Pro Football Register* is a must for every serious football fan. Its dedication to information and statistics is underscored by the fact that within its 523 pages there is not a single illustration or photograph. The objective of the book is to provide personal, high school, college, and professional data on every football player and head coach in the National Football League (NFL), as well as college statistics for all players selected in the 2000 NFL draft.

Although the book is filled with fine-print statistics, the information is well organized and easy to read. Most of the book consists of an alphabetic listing of veteran players—each includes single-game highs, number of games played in a season, and statistical averages. Defensive statistics include fumble recoveries, interceptions, and sacks. Offensive statistics include rushing and passing yardage and points scored. Kicking statistics include punting average and net average, kicks inside the 20, blocked kicks, and field goals completed. The last pages of the book (pp. 461–523) are devoted to personal and statistical profiles of the 2000 draft picks and the head coaches for each NFL team. Fairly priced at $15.95, this book provides every meaningful statistic and is an important resource for serious football fans, especially those who participate in fantasy football leagues.

—**Mark J. Crawford**

HOCKEY

P

312.   **STATS Hockey Handbook 2000–01.** Morton Grove, Ill., STATS Publishing, 2000. 567p. $19.95pa. ISBN 1-884064-83-3.

The *STATS Hockey Handbook 2000–01* is a compilation of statistics for every active NHL player and team from 1999 to 2000. This is purely a book of numbers with no attempt to intersperse text among the columns of figures—limiting its audience. While much of this information can be found through other sources, especially the NHL Web page, there are some figures listed that make this a singular record book. Each player's performance is evaluated by a number of unique factors, such as their effectiveness when appearing on national television with anywhere from zero to three or more days of rest, the number of hat tricks achieved in the course of the season, total power play and shorthand assists and points, a detailed breakdown by type of the number of penalties, and the players' numbers both against playoff and non-playoff teams broken down by period. Atypical team statistics include goals, assists, points, and penalties per period when the team is winning, losing, tied, or in a clutch game or blowout. Leader boards are incorporated, as is a ranking of players named game stars throughout the regular and postseason. There is also a listing of debuts, first goals, and first wins for newcomers to the NHL.

This record book does make some omissions. For example, there is no information on coaches or officials. Figures on shifts per game, as well as hits and takeaways per player are not included. Also, team statistics fail to mention fact-off wins or shots blocked in the course of the year. But while these expurgations are notable, they do not seriously undermine the book, which fulfills its purpose admirably.—**Philip G. Swan**

HUNTING

P

313.   Rue, Leonard Lee, III. **The Deer Hunter's Encyclopedia.** New York, Lyons Press, 2000. 283p. illus. index. $29.95. ISBN 1-58574-128-0.

The author of this volume is not only an avid hunter and photographer of deer but has spent much of his life studying deer in their natural habitat and collecting data pertaining to them. This, his fifth book on white-tailed deer, is laid out in question-and-answer format. The chapters provide information on hunting, deer antlers, deer behavior, anatomy, management, breeding, and miscellaneous deer facts. Each question is about a paragraph in length and each answer is generally one full page or more. Rue writes in a conversational style and offers often more information than the original question asked for. It is apparent he is passionate about the subject and knows it well. This volume can be used as a reference volume in public libraries but may be better suited for circulating collections where readers can take the book home and browse through its interesting dialog and beautiful photographs.—**Shannon Graff Hysell**

OLYMPICS

P

314.   Wallechinsky, David. **The Complete Book of the Summer Olympics: Sydney.** 2000 ed. Woodstock, N.Y., Overlook Press, 2000. 928p. illus. $23.95pa. ISBN 1-58567-046-4.

David Wallechinsky created the first *Complete Book of the Olympics* (see ARBA 85, entry 683) in 1984, and has brought out succeeding editions in every Olympic year since that time. The extensive contents continue to be a sport-by-sport, intriguing potpourri of Olympic Games facts, figures, charts, stories, anecdotes, and statistics, together with the readable, entertaining "Short History of the Modern Olympics," running to some dozen pages and making a nice introduction to the masses of detail that follow. Even though this large book presents massive amounts of data, something is missing. Now that the summer 2000 games in Sydney, Australia, have been completed, this book will be seen as incomplete, as it was published earlier in the last year (2000) as a companion to the summer games. But, as a reference book, it will still have value as the authoritative source for the modern games that have gone before (1896 in Athens, Greece, to 1996 in Atlanta, Georgia).

Almost anyone who enjoys sport and games will find much of interest here, especially if they appreciate the detail in evidence. Narrative writing is one of the author's strengths, as is the research on which it is based. The book contains a short statement of the rules for each event. The controversies leading up to the Sydney games have not been glossed over. In the "Issues" section of the prefatory matter, Wallechinsky discusses at some length corruption and expulsions, politics in the Olympics, amateurism, drugs, and gigantism (or the notion that the games have become too big, and present a serious problem for the organizers). *The Complete Book of the Summer Olympics* should make a fine addition to the sporting reference shelf of larger libraries, and librarians may rely on its accuracy, for it represents a feat of scholarship in itself.—**Randall Rafferty**

16 Sociology

GENERAL WORKS

C, P

315. **The Blackwell Dictionary of Sociology: A User's Guide to Sociological Language.** 2d ed. By Allan G. Johnson. Malden, Mass., Blackwell, 2000. 413p. index. $29.95pa. ISBN 0-631-21681-2.

Rather than trying to create a comprehensive work on the language of sociology, Johnson has instead focused the definitions in this dictionary on what he considers the classic conceptual core of sociology. To this he has added representative samplings from the diverse areas of study within sociology, important concepts from related disciplines, and a section of brief biographical entries. Entries are approximately 100 to 200 words in length, although definitions for terms such as *kinship*, *institution*, and *group* are longer. Most of the entries include suggested titles for further reading. The index includes concepts and examples used to explain these concepts.

The author has also chosen to write all of the entries himself, with the intention of giving the work continuity. The result is a dictionary that is clear and easy to read. Intended to serve as a guidebook, this dictionary is so well written that it could also be read cover to cover. Although the author states that the work is not comprehensive, it appears to include all of the terms found in other one-volume dictionaries of sociology. Additions to the 2d edition include 75 new entries, revisions, updates, and expanded cross-references. All public and college libraries should have a copy of this work in their reference sections. [R: Choice, Nov 2000, p. 512]—**January Adams**

AGING

P

316. **Eldercare: The Best Resources to Help You Help Your Aging Relatives.** Marty Richards, ed. Issaquah, Wash., Resource Pathways, 1999. 253p. index. $24.95pa. ISBN 1-892148-07-2.

There is a genuine need for a guide to resources on eldercare. Not only is this becoming an increasing concern for families in this country, but when searching for other directories on this topic there is almost nothing to be found. The editor who created this directory must have done a lot of research because many resources in many formats were found. The directory covers books, films, Internet and World Wide Web sites, videos, and software. The editor mentioned that the Internet and Websites were periodically checked for currency and to see if the access is still available. The coverage is impressive.

What makes this book so special is the work that went into the evaluations of the resources. The contributors are all professionals in the field and they used their experience to evaluate each entry in what is, to a large extent, a collection of reviews of the materials. Each resource is rated for its effectiveness. The descriptions are excellent.

Each page is a review, which includes a complete description of the document, a thorough evaluation, and information on how to get it. Along the outer edges of the pages is a column that contains how many stars it was given (one to four stars are assigned), ease of use, information about the authors, any bibliographic information needed, and Internet source information. The work is arranged in an easy-to-use format.

The book is organized into broad, general topics: general directories of caregiving, death and dying, employment and retirement, financial and legal matters, health and medical care, housing and living arrangements, and relationships with the family. At the end, it lists 13 resources separately because they exceeded the others in the superiority of their use and information. There is a small section on resources that address spiritual matters, and finally a list of helpful organizations that, by itself, is clearly worth the price of the book.

The book does not have an index in the usual sense. There would be no way that a person could index each and every resource without creating a document that is much larger than this one. So, for the most part, people need to be able to access information by way of the general categories. It would have been too difficult for someone to assign some general subject terms to each document so that a form of subject access could be established. For example, if a person wanted information on protecting an elderly person's life savings, he or she would have to read through the descriptions in the "Financial & Legal Matters" section to find the book *Avoiding the Medicaid Trap*. There is no other way to guess where that information is. This is the one disappointment about the book.

One hopes this book will be updated periodically and more brief indexing could be done to enhance its value. Not only people who are in need of this information should get the book, but libraries and offices serving eldercare clientele should also have it. [R: LJ, Jan 2000, p. 80]—**Lillian R. Mesner**

P
317.   Solomon, Lewis D. **Volunteer Opportunities for Seniors Away from Home.** Jefferson, N.C., McFarland, 2000. 130p. index. $28.50pa. ISBN 0-7864-0865-0.

As baby boomers begin to reach retirement age and the senior population continues to grow, there are becoming more and more opportunities designed around their lifestyles. This guidebook focuses specifically on the volunteer opportunities in the United States and abroad that are suited for seniors. As stated in the introduction, the information in this book makes it possible for seniors to combine "service with adventure."

The book begins with an introduction that explains the premise of the work. It then goes on to explain how to read the entries listed as well as how seniors may use their volunteer work away from home as a tax deduction. The bulk of the work is divided into two sections: "United States-Based Organizations" (62 opportunities) and "Foreign-Based Organizations" (68 opportunities). Each entry ranges about one page in length and provides contact information (e.g., address, telephone number, Website address, contact name), a short description of the organization, location of the work, requirements, accommodations, whether or not insurance is provided, job opportunities available for disabled persons, and information on the application process. The activities range from working with religious organizations and environmental groups to working with the homeless and helping disadvantaged children. An index to entry numbers concludes the volume.

This work is well thought out and provides a lot of pertinent information for seniors seeking volunteer opportunities. It is certain there are many organizations that were not included that may well have been, but this volume will be a good place to start. This volume is recommended for public libraries.—**Shannon Graff Hysell**

DEATH

P
318.   **Death and Dying Sourcebook.** Annemarie S. Muth, ed. Detroit, Omnigraphics, 2000. 641p. illus. index. (Health Reference Series). $78.00. ISBN 0-7808-0230-6.

This sourcebook aims to provide in a timely fashion information on the medical, legal, and ethical issues relating to death and dying specifically to the United States. As a librarian and as a Hospice caregiver, this reviewer found the data informative, useful, and comprehensive. Examples of topics covered include advice on selecting a health care facility, Medicare and Medicaid, patients' rights, advance directives, pain management, funeral costs, the grieving process, and much more.

The volume is divided into two main sections; these sections focus on broad areas. The eight parts include death and dying statistics, attitudes toward death, health care options for the terminally ill, end-of-life medical care, approaching death, final arrangements, bereavement, and additional help and information. The eight parts are then divided into chapters, which are devoted to single topics within a part. For example, within part 2 of "Attitudes toward Death and Dying," there are chapters pertaining to religious and cultural perspectives, gender differences in coping with life threatening diseases, and opposing the legalization of euthanasia and assisted suicide.

Part 8, "Additional Help and Information," includes a detailed glossary and a directory of resources. Resources include government agencies, professional associations, and Internet sites. In addition to the glossary and the resources, some chapters include additional readings. References to footnotes, tables, and illustrations are included in the index. Public libraries, medical libraries, and academic libraries will all find this sourcebook a useful edition to their collections.—**Earl Shumaker**

FAMILY, MARRIAGE, AND DIVORCE

P

319.　Adamec, Christine, and William L. Pierce. **The Encyclopedia of Adoption.** 2d ed. New York, Facts on File, 2000. 368p. index. $60.00. ISBN 0-8160-4041-9.

The 2d edition of *The Encyclopedia of Adoption* (see ARBA 93, entry 866 for a review of the 1st edition) has been extensively updated, rewritten, and slimmed down. The volume now contains 269 entries, down from the original 288 in the 1st edition; the appendixes, however, have been increased by one—covering foster care statistics until 1997—raising the total to 10. Some 20 new entries have been added, many of which cover the federal government's increasing role in adoption, intercountry adoption, foster care, and various other aspects of adoption (e.g., expenses, insurance, research studies, the Uniform Adoption Act, the National Council for Single Adoptive Parents). Approximately another 15 outdated or inappropriately worded entries, such as "criminal behavior in adopted adults" and "mixed families," have been dropped. Updated and rewritten entries include those on AIDS, fetal alcohol syndrome, and psychiatric problems of adopted persons. A few of the bibliographies, such as those for the birthfather entry, have been updated, and, in general, the writing is clearer and more succinct. This edition has been favorably redesigned—the font is larger, the spacing more generous, and the layout of the book more handsome than its predecessor. The improvements make the 2d edition of *The Encyclopedia of Adoption* an indispensable resource, and highly recommended for all libraries, groups, and individuals with an interest in adoption. [R: Choice, Jan 01, p. 881]—**E. Wayne Carp**

GAY AND LESBIAN STUDIES

C, P

320.　Kranz, Rachel, and Tim Cusick. **Gay Rights.** New York, Facts on File, 2000. 298p. index. (Library in a Book). $39.95. ISBN 0-8160-4235-7.

This comprehensive survey of the gay (which includes lesbian) rights movement in the United States and the issues involved, is divided into 2 parts of several chapters each. The first part is called "Overview of the Topic" and the second "Guide to Further Research." Most of the first part is contained in three narrative chapters. The first two of these chapters discuss the past and present status of many facets of the topic, including the nature of homosexuality; a history of gay rights; legal, employment, and family issues; laws involving gays; and important legal decisions. The third chapter covers, sketchily, the relationship between the gay rights movement and cultural institutions like schools, various religious denominations, and the mass media. There is a wealth of information in these chapters that reflects good scholarship and thorough research but, unfortunately, the information is poorly organized and difficult to retrieve (e.g., sodomy laws are treated in depth in two different places, some court cases are not indexed, there is no cross-referencing). Perhaps topical outlines preceding each chapter would help. The remainder of part 1 consists of a 12-page chronology of the landmark events in gay history ending in mid-2000, brief biographies of over 100 key people associated with gay rights (e.g., Barny Frank, Ellen Degeneres, Trent Lott), and a 5-page glossary of key terms and organizations. The second part is devoted to helping researchers. A short introductory chapter on types of reference sources and research tips is followed by an extensive 70-page bibliography of key book articles and Websites. Each entry contains an evaluative annotation of about three to five lines. The section on periodical articles is subdivided alphabetically by topic (e.g., adoption, housing rights, military).

In each area, the editors have made judicious, unbiased choices representing different points of view. Coverage ends with 1999. The last chapter is a list of pro- and anti-gay organizations with addresses and telephone numbers. There are three appendixes that supply excerpts from court decisions, government policy statements, and historical documents. They are followed by a useful subject index that perhaps should have been expanded (e.g., the section on organizations is not indexed). However, apart from the organizational difficulties mentioned above and minor indexing problems, this is an outstanding reference work notable particularly for its comprehensiveness. It is recommended for college, public, and some high school libraries.—**John T. Gillespie**

PHILANTHROPY

Directories

P

321.   **Operating Grants for Nonprofit Organizations 2000.** Phoenix, Ariz., Oryx Press, 2000. 273p. index. $29.95pa. ISBN 1-57356-396-X.

This volume is just one of the many excellent reference tools on grants produced by Oryx Press. Well organized and quite affordable, the directory provides pertinent information for those organizations seeking to increase their budgets through external funding. The major part of the directory includes profiles of grant opportunities, arranged alphabetically by state, then by the title of the grant. A typical entry includes the grant title; an accession number keyed to indexes; and directory and contact information for the organization that sponsors the grant, including telephone numbers and e-mail and Internet addresses. Separate indication of requirements and restrictions, a listing of areas of interest that are typically funded, and a listing of sample awards that have been made by the organization are also included.

Supplementing the main directory is a subject index, a sponsoring organizations index, and a geographic index. This latter index is meant to indicate which geographic areas are eligible for grants from organizations that might not be located in the same geographic area. All indexes are keyed to the accession numbers provided with each main entry.

Any fund-raiser involved with expanding budgets for nonprofit organizations will find this volume to be extremely useful, as it provides a starting point for identifying and communicating with a funding agency regarding particular grants. However, the scope of grants is limited to operational expenses only, which may not meet the needs of every organization. For its wealth of opportunity regarding educational support grants, this volume is highly recommended for educational and administrative libraries at all levels. [R: Choice, Jan 01, p. 874]

—**Edmund F. SantaVicca**

Handbooks and Yearbooks

P

322.   Grobman, Gary M. **The Nonprofit Handbook.** 2d ed. Harrisburg, Pa., Whit Hat Communications; distr., Chicago, Independent Publishers Group, 1999. 353p. index. $29.95pa. ISBN 0-9653653-2-8.

As a general introduction to the facets and processes of setting up and running a nonprofit organization, this volume is comprehensive in scope, functioning as a guide rather than a legal handbook. Each of the 30 chapters, with its own focus, presents a variety of information concerning the steps of incorporation, bylaws, setting up a board of directors, and strategic planning. Also included are chapters on ethics, tax-exempt status, insurance and liability, fiscal issues, personnel issues, fund-raising, lobbying, and political activity. The author also includes valuable basic information regarding the Internet with Websites that can be of value to nonprofits and the advantages of communicating and networking with other organizations. New to this edition are chapters on mergers, change management, quality, the Year 2000 problem, and a summary of significant developments affecting nonprofits that have occurred since the previous edition.

Of immense value is a separate state directory that presents a two-page profile outlining the basics of setting up a nonprofit organization. Each profile is divided into four sections: incorporation, lobbying, tax exemptions, and charitable solicitation. Directory and contact information is provided for each section. Supplementing the main text are sample bylaws, a bibliography, and an index.

Those considering starting up a nonprofit organization will benefit greatly from this work for its scope and treatment. Reference librarians in the academic and public library environments will also find it to be a handy guide capable of answering many inquiries.—**Edmund F. SantaVicca**

SEX STUDIES

C, P

323.   Westheimer, Ruth K. **Encyclopedia of Sex.** New York, Continuum Publishing, 2000. 319p. illus. index. $22.95pa. ISBN 0-8264-1240-8.

A revised and updated version of *Dr. Ruth's Encyclopedia of Sex* (see ARBA 95, entry 878), this work brings together a variety of medical experts and other experts who share their knowledge regarding various facets and concepts within the field of human sexuality. A list of the contributors and their credentials prefaces the volume. Alphabetically arranged, the entries range from about 100 to 1,500 words. Where appropriate, simple black-and-white illustrations or photographs accompany the text. Readers can also find a brief biography of individuals who have made historic contributions to the study of human sexuality.

As the publisher points out in a brief introduction, the work is written in a simple and readable language, aimed primarily at high school and college-level readers. Cross-references are used throughout to guide the reader to related entries. For those who might know a slang term, but not how to find it here, there is an authority file of sorts—a separate glossary of sexual slang that translates the "street" term to its official noun or verb. Also supplementing the main text are a glossary of short definitions (for terms used throughout the text), a four-page bibliography for further reading, and a full subject index that indicates cross-references and related articles.

For its straightforward treatment of the topics, its ease of use and understanding, and its affordability, this work is highly recommended for school, public, and academic libraries. Where budgets will allow, libraries should possibly purchase more than one copy, allowing for both reference and home use of the information.

—**Edmund F. SantaVicca**

SUBSTANCE ABUSE

C, P, S

324.   **Drug Abuse Sourcebook.** Karen Bellenir, ed. Detroit, Omnigraphics, 2000. 629p. index. (Health Reference Series). $78.00. ISBN 0-7808-0242-X.

According to a recent study by the Institute of Health Policy, substance abuse is the number one health problem in this country. Thus there is a need for good current information written in a nontechnical manner for the layperson. This book, like other books in the Health Reference Series, provides such readable information. The information is excerpted from U.S. government documents, nonprofit organizations, and periodicals. The book is organized into 7 broad parts and then subdivided into 69 brief chapters. Topics include drug use and abuse, the nature of addiction, descriptions of drugs, treatment issues, prevention issues, and additional help. This latter part includes a list of federal agencies, national drug enforcement agencies, state resources, and a resource guide for parents.

In addition, there is a short glossary of terms and a list of street terms. Some statistical information is also provided. Occasionally there is a bibliography for additional readings at the end of a chapter. Although the information can be found in other sources, this book provides a convenient compendium of general information at a reasonable price. Even though there is a plethora of books on drug abuse, this volume is recommended for school, public, and college libraries.—**Karen Y. Stabler**

17 Statistics, Demography, and Urban Studies

DEMOGRAPHY

General Works

P
325.   Keating, Raymond J., and Thomas N. Edmonds. **U.S. by the Numbers: Figuring What's Left, Right, and Wrong with America State by State.** Sterling, Va., International Publishers Marketing, 2000. 948p. $35.00pa. ISBN 1-892123-14-2.

At first glance, *U.S. by the Numbers* appears to be simply a compilation of statistics on the United States as a whole, as well as each of the 50 states and the District of Columbia. It is that, but it is also a lot more. Lively and perceptive commentaries breathe life into the numbers and make them relevant to the current political and socio-economic scene. Each entry contains data on politics, taxes, government expenditures, education, status of the economy, and the current business situation. Other series relate to quality of life; for example, there are statistics on crime, the environment, population, and lifestyle. The authors have included just enough data to understand and identify recent trends. Thus, the reader is not inundated with vast quantities of numbers that could mask the underlying significance of the data. However, a list of data sources is included for readers who require more detailed or additional data. Many of the statistical series are supplemented by small bar charts that provide convenient overviews of the numbers. Although the book is a reference volume, the data selected, along with the text provided by the authors, provide an authoritative yet entertaining perspective on life in the United States as well as in each state. It could also offer direction and insight for further study and analysis.—**William C. Struning**

STATISTICS

General Works

C, P
326.   **Statistical Yearbook 1996. Annuaire Statistique.** 43d ed. By the Department of Economic and Social Affairs Statistics Division. New York, United Nations, 1999. 885p. index. $125.00. ISBN 92-1-061180-2. ISSN 0082-8459. S/N E/F.98.SVII.1.

This edition of the *Statistical Yearbook* contains statistical series covering 1986–1995 or 1987–1996, using statistics available up to September 1998. As with previous editions, it continues to be updated by the *Monthly Bulletin of Statistics*, and is also available on CD-ROM. The statistics are extracted from both national and international sources with the aim of providing systematic and comparable information on a wide range of issues of concern both to the United Nations and to governments and people in general. The statistics are listed in 83 tables that cover 20 general topics divided into 4 broad categories: world and regional summaries, population and social statistics, economic issues, and international economic relations. The emphasis continues to be on economic data, with the section on population and social statistics being limited to seven tables. The number of tables presented continues to decrease with each edition—even from the 88 in the previous edition (see ARBA 98, entry 816). The tables are preceded by the usual introduction and explanatory notes and followed by four appendixes. Except for the index, everything is in both English and French. In its continuing attempt to provide data of contemporary interest, the one new table that was added to this edition gives statistics for the number of cinemas, their seating capacity, annual attendance, and box office receipts. Some tables were omitted in this edition, primarily due to lack of new data. This publication continues to be a basic reference tool for international and national statistics and should be found in any serious reference collection.—**Paul H. Thomas**

United States

C, P

327.   **Encyclopedia of the U.S. Census.** Margo J. Anderson, ed. Washington, D.C., Congressional Quarterly, 2000. 424p. illus. maps. index. $125.00. ISBN 1-56802-428-2.

The U.S. Census is required by the Constitution to be done every 10 years and is used to apportion House of Representatives' seats and electoral college votes. Therefore, the census is the foundation on which our democratic system is built.

The decennial census is the federal government's largest peacetime operation. Census 2000 required more than 860,000 temporary workers. Because of the magnitude of the task, the Census Bureau has been an early innovator in information processing. The 1890 census used punched cards and electrical counting machines that were designed by Herman Hollerith, a Census Bureau employee who later founded International Business Machines Corporation (IBM).

This volume uses 120 essays to explore the history, politics, and operations of census taking, from preparing, printing, and mailing the questionnaires to retrieving responses, protecting confidentiality, and using the data. Statistical procedures to adjust for omissions and erroneous enumerations are also outlined.

Although the original intent of the census was legislative apportionment, the value of expanded demographic and economic data was recognized early on. In addition to the household census, an economic census is done every five years focusing on American business establishments. Federal household surveys are also conducted between the major decennial censuses on specific socioeconomic issues.

Appendixes include a list of the superintendents and directors of the Census Bureau since 1850 and U.S. population summary numbers from 1790 to 2000. There is also information on congressional apportionment trends, descriptions of different congressional apportionment methods, statistics on each decennial census (number of enumerators and staff, pages in final printed reports, and cost), the questionnaire for the 2000 census, Internet references, and a glossary. This reference provides a fascinating look at the how and why of doing a census. [R: BL, 1 Jan 01, p. 1008]—**Adrienne Antink Bien**

C, P

328.   **State Rankings 2000: A Statistical View of the 50 United States.** 11th ed. Kathleen O'Leary Morgan and Scott Morgan, eds. Lawrence, Kans., Morgan Quitno Press, 2000. 569p. index. $52.95pa. ISBN 0-7401-0000-9. ISSN 1057-3623.

State Rankings is a reference book published and updated annually since 1990. This 11th edition contains 15 sections on topics ranging from transportation and taxes to housing and health. Except for the editorial commentary in "Which State is the Most Livable?," the rest of the rankings are in purely tabular format—presented alphabetically or in ranking order. There are more than 550 tables in the book.

This edition, according to the editors, put an emphasis on its user-friendliness and usability. For example, source information and footnotes are shown at the bottom of each page and national totals, rates, and percentages are displayed at the top of each table. Every other line is shaded in gray for easier reading, and a chapter thumb index is provided in addition to the back-of-the-book index.

Resources for the book are mostly obtained from government contracted agencies. However, a large percentage of data were compiled for the year 1998 or even 1997 in this 2000 edition of the book. A close look at the back-of-the-book index also reveals that the indexing seems inadequate. For instance, there are 12 locators under the entry for crime rates, all of which point to nothing else but what has been listed in the table of contents for the section labeled "Crime and Law Enforcement." It might be helpful to the reader if the index entry was further decomposed by crime types, such as murders and burglaries. Despite its weakness in getting the most recent source data and in index adequacy, it is still worthwhile for most libraries to have this new edition.

—**Heting Chu**

URBAN STUDIES

C, P

329.   Savageau, David, with Ralph D'Agostino. **Places Rated Almanac.** millennium ed. Foster City, Calif., IDG Books Worldwide, 2000. 684p. illus. maps. $24.95pa. ISBN 0-02-863447-0. ISSN 1526-517X.

The *Places Rated Almanac* takes 354 U.S. and Canadian metropolitan areas and ranks them according to living costs, transportation, job outlook, education, climate, crime, the arts, health care, and recreation. Using national statistics, this work gives each city points in each area, with 50 points being the average. Therefore, when a city scores 30 in an area, it means that 7 out of 10 other cities ranked higher. This new edition includes new metropolitan areas that have been declared since the 1997 edition.

Each chapter thoroughly explains how the statistics were gathered, lists each city in order from best to worst, and then breaks down that information for a better understanding of the results. For example, the "Cost of Living" chapter begins by explaining what factors influence the statistics, such as cost of housing, transportation, food, health care, recreation, state taxes, federal taxes, and other miscellaneous items. It then lists the metropolitan areas in order, with the best cost-of-living area being Clarksville-Hopkinsville, Tennessee-Kentucky, and the worst being New York. After that, all areas are listed alphabetically, and average income, housing costs, and other costs are listed individually. The ensuing chapters on transportation, job outlook, education, climate, the arts, health care, and recreation follow similar patterns. The final chapter, "Putting It All Together," shows how all the scores from each chapter on each city are averaged to get the final score, and therefore the final list of city rankings. This 2000 edition has Salt Lake City–Ogden, Utah; Washington, D.C.; Seattle-Bellevue, Washington; Denver, Colorado; and Tampa–St. Petersburg, Florida, rounding out the top five cities.

The three appendixes list the metropolitan areas by state, have a chart showing ethnic diversity in each metropolitan area, and list the publication's contacts within each area. This resource is valuable for its current statistical information on U.S. and Canadian cities as well as its unique way of interpreting that information for those looking to relocate. It will be a valuable addition to public and research libraries.—**Shannon Graff Hysell**

18 Women's Studies

ALMANACS

C, P
330.   Weatherford, Doris. **Women's Almanac 2000.** Phoenix, Ariz., Oryx Press, 2000. 370p. illus. index. $65.00pa. ISBN 1-57356-341-2. ISSN 1529-5311.

Women's Almanac 2000 uses an issue-oriented approach to deliver a variety of facts and figures on women. In the past, Weatherford has written on the history of women in the United States; her scholarship now incorporates histories and issues of women from around the world. The features that readers would expect in an almanac are present: statistics, chronologies, and organization listings. Yet, unlike more widely known almanacs, all of the information provided is about women and is issue focused.

Information is divided into two categories: U.S. women and world women. Biographical sketches cover politicians, writers, artists, and athletes. A unique feature of this almanac is its state-by-state histories of U.S. women. Weatherford acknowledges that more details could have been included, but effectively gives concise name, date, and place information pertaining to the historical condition of women. The introduction reminds the reader that additional information can be found by making use of the broad concept entries in the index. This is reinforced by the use of cross-references within biographical entries and chronologies. There is an appropriate list of Websites that is also issue and research focused.

The almanac creates expectations it does not always meet. For example, while the front cover design features a quote by Alice Walker, the book fails to include her biography. The introduction claims the inclusion in the timeline of all U.S. women featured on U.S. postage stamps, yet there is no entry for Marilyn Monroe. Furthermore, it cannot be determined if this is the inaugural almanac of an annual publication or a monograph.

Women's Almanac 2000 will prove useful to librarians answering general fact and figure questions about famous women and women's issues, both current and historical. Public and small academic libraries will benefit most by including this resource in their reference collections. [R: Choice, Dec 2000, p. 692]—**Courtney L. Holton**

BIBLIOGRAPHY

C, P
331.   Hardy, Lyda Mary. **Women in U.S. History: A Resource Guide.** Englewood, Colo., Libraries Unlimited, 2000. 344p. index. $45.00pa. ISBN 1-56308-769-3.

Women in U.S. History is primarily an annotated bibliography, but also discusses historiography, theory and methodology, and education in women's studies. Hardy, a school librarian, ties together the history and tools necessary for research in one volume.

The resources annotated focus on the writings and contributions of women chronologically, racially, and in "fields of endeavor" (p. xv). Aside from books (reference, general works, and biography), Hardy recommends video recordings, documentaries, and posters. As expected, Websites are also suggested with annotations. While not all of these sites provide static access to women's history research, Hardy indicates when that information is available, usually during Women's History Month in March. All annotations suggest an appropriate user level: middle school, high school, college, and adult.

The evolution of women's studies documentation and its integration into the curriculum is explained in the discussion portion of the guide. Hardy feels the ways in which women's history has been documented and researched has a direct impact on the writing of history and education today. These chapters map that progress, explaining and suggesting the strategy used for this research. At the end of these chapters, Hardy again includes a list of references.

Both an author/title and subject index are used. The appendix lists mailing addresses and telephone numbers for audiovisual producers. This is obviously to facilitate the rental or purchase of video recordings and documentaries. *Women in U.S. History* is recommended for all library collections, especially for the strength and accessibility of the bibliography.—**Courtney L. Holton**

DICTIONARIES AND ENCYCLOPEDIAS

C, P

332.   Cullen-DuPont, Kathryn. **Encyclopedia of Women's History in America.** 2d ed. New York, Facts on File, 2000. 418p. illus. index. $65.00. ISBN 0-8160-4100-8.

Cullen-DuPont's revised encyclopedia comes just four years after the 1st edition (see ARBA 97, entry 736). Major updates include death dates for women who have passed and expanded entries for major figures who continue to forge ahead, such as Janet Reno and Hillary Rodham Clinton.

One strength of the encyclopedia continues to be the full-text primary documents of significant legislation from women's organizations. Five documents have been added, including a list of women who have served as U.S. Congressional Representatives and U.S. Senators.

A list of additional reading at the end of each entry includes books, newspaper articles, and Websites. Books are listed simply by author's last name and book title—readers must discover the full citations in the bibliography. References to newspaper articles are incomplete, providing only the newspaper name and date and lacking page and column information. Improved citation format for the ease of readers should have been a priority in the 2d edition.

High school and public libraries will benefit from adding this updated edition. High school and public libraries not owning the 1st edition should consider it for serving general populations.—**Courtney L. Holton**

HANDBOOKS AND YEARBOOKS

C, P

333.   **Handbook of American Women's History.** 2d ed. Angela M. Howard and Frances M. Kavenik, eds. Thousand Oaks, Calif., Sage, 2000. 724p. illus. index. $99.95. ISBN 0-7619-1635-0.

The 1st edition of this work came out in 1990 (see ARBA 91, entry 929). This 2d edition is revised by the same principal editor and Frances Kavenik, an associate editor of the 1st edition, has become co-editor. The work contains 142 new entries and has 93 new contributors. There are 922 entries total, each from a long paragraph to a page or so in length, similar to the plan of the 1st edition. The purpose of the work is to introduce and give fundamental information necessary for a general understanding of the field of American women's history through summary definitions of crucial concepts, events, organizations, institutions, significant books and periodicals, and various historical persons. Each entry is completed with bibliographic references and is signed by the author. There has been some updating of the bibliographic references, including the mention of the very occasional Website. An unannotated page of references to basic general surveys and anthologies, basic reference works in women's history, and three collections of documents conclude the introduction to the 2d edition. The contributors are principally American professors in history, women's studies, sociology, English, and political science, with a smattering of entries by graduate students in these fields. Other article authors include knowledgeable lay persons, school teachers, librarians, research historians, and professional writers. As before, the work has a dictionary type arrangement, with one general index. The illustrations are practically all portraits of individuals. The editors do not claim comprehensiveness; the "*Handbook* . . . supplements . . . existing and newly developed reference and bibliographic sources."

The emphasis of this work is on the historical, yet there are many entries for contemporary persons (e.g., Sally Ride, Madeleine Albright, Maya Angelou) and topics (e.g., acquaintance/date rape, rape/sexual assault). There are some very general entries (Migration and Frontier Women, Politics, Progressive Legislation, and Religion) and some very specialized entries (Quilts, Ninety-Nines, Rochester Women's Anti-Slavery Societies, and Soap Operas). The same criticism of the index of the previous edition remains. Some of the entries, for instance, those of the National American Women's Suffrage Association, the NAACP, and Native American Women, have a great many page references to follow up in the text, with no way of knowing which entry on the said page to look at. Some sub-arranging of these long index entries would be helpful. Another thing that would improve the work is the inclusion of more illustrations of the topics. There is a picture of a lying-in chair and the Flint Auto Workers strike; there could be pictures of frontier life, musical instruments, magazines, marriage manual pages, schools, settlement houses, club meetings, monuments, and garment workers. More mention of Internet resources would be good as well. This is a very good resource for college students beginning term paper research; it is also useful for public library patrons. This reviewer intends to keep her copy for a desk reference. [R: BL, 15 Dec 2000, p. 845]

—**Agnes H. Widder**

Part III
HUMANITIES

19 Humanities in General

HUMANITIES IN GENERAL

C, P

334.   Blazek, Ron, and Elizabeth Aversa. **The Humanities: A Selective Guide to Information Sources.** 5th ed. Englewood, Colo., Libraries Unlimited, 2000. 603p. index. (Library and Information Science Text Series). $75.00; $60.00pa. ISBN 1-56308-601-8; 1-56308-602-6pa.

In its 5th edition, this guide continues to serve as an important source for librarians, scholars, and library science students and educators interested in humanities research. A. Robert Rogers wrote the 1st and 2d editions, published in 1974 (see ARBA 75, entry 174) and 1979 (see ARBA 81, entry 153). Blazek and Aversa updated the book with the 3d and 4th editions in 1988 (see ARBA 89, entry 817) and 1994 (see ARBA 95, entry 921).

The authors include philosophy, religion, the visual arts, the performing arts, and language and literature as fields of study within the humanities. The format is similar to previous editions, with descriptive chapters defining each field, its users, major collections, research centers, organizations, and the use of computers within the field. The bibliographic chapters for each field contain annotated entries of relevant print and electronic (online and CD-ROM) reference works. An asterisk next to an entry number indicates the electronic availability of a title. This work includes 1,374 numbered entries, 124 more than the 4th edition. Some titles from the previous edition have been deleted. Although the authors still include descriptions of classic titles, they emphasize sources published in the last 20 years.

The most substantial change in this edition is the selective reference to Websites in the annotations for numbered entries and in the chapters that define each field. The annotations in this edition also include more references to relevant titles not included as numbered entries. The references to these additional titles and selected Websites enhance the usefulness of this edition. [R: Choice, Dec 2000, p. 676; RUSQ, Winter 2000, pp. 194-195]
                                                                        —**Heather Martin**

20 Communication and Mass Media

AUTHORSHIP

General Works

P

335. **The Complete Guide to Literary Contests 2000.** William F. Fabio and James M. Plagianos, comps. Buffalo, N.Y., Prometheus Books, 2000. 658p. index. $23.95. ISBN 1-57392-770-8.

This guide covers nonfiction, fiction, poetry, and plays for published and unpublished authors; these are open contests, national in scope. About 450 contests are listed alphabetically, with cross-references by format category. Canadians and other foreigners are eligible for some prizes.

For each contest, there are data about submission criteria, entry forms and guidelines, rules, contact names, addresses, e-mail addresses, Websites for the contest, deadlines (given at the top), judging procedures, prize money, and some names of previous winners. Other material in the book includes a discussion of copyright issues, contacts (such as arts councils and granting agencies), and questions to ask literary agents. All the Canadian arts councils are listed except for the largest one (Ontario Arts Council) and that omission seems curious. The book, of course, is not "complete," but for the price asked, it is worthy of consideration by all budding writers. It is one way to get published. [R: LJ, 1 Feb 2000, p. 72]—**Dean Tudor**

P

336. Lockwood, Trevor, and Karen Scott. **A Writer's Guide to the Internet.** London, Allison & Busby; distr., Sterling, Va., International Publishers Marketing, 1999. 143p. index. $12.95pa. ISBN 0-7490-0444-4.

A Writer's Guide to the Internet is a small handbook designed specifically for authors with little experience on the Internet. The work discusses a wide range of topics, from simply defining terms relating to the Internet to creating a Website that will aid a writer's career. Other valuable information discussed herein includes how to use the Internet to market one's work, how to use the Internet to correspond with other writers, how to publish online and whom to contact, and the future of the Internet in publishing. The book concludes with a glossary of Internet terms and an index.

Writers unfamiliar with the Internet will gain plenty of valuable information from this guide. It serves mainly as an introduction, so those needing more information (which will be most) will need to look to other more technical computer guides for the answers to their questions. However, at only $12.95 this work is inexpensive enough for any public library to add to their collection.—**Shannon Graff Hysell**

C, P

337. **The Writer's Handbook 2001.** 65th ed. Sylvia K. Burack, ed. Waukesha, Wis., Writer/Kalmbach Publishing, 2000. 912p. index. $32.95. ISBN 0-87116-188-5.

Now in its 65th edition, *The Writer's Handbook* is designed for the budding and working freelance writer. The bulk of the book, and its greatest selling point, is the 104 short essays about writing, which were published in *The Writer* magazine. These are arranged under any of eight categories, from general tips on writing to special genres to editing, marketing, and finding an agent. Readers will be pleased by the quality of the essays, written by established authors, many critically acclaimed in the publishing world, such as Jane Hirshfield, Joan Lowery Nixon, Julia Alvarez, Peter Meinke, and Stephen King. Also included are six brief interviews with authors. The directory section of the book is well organized by publication type (primarily magazines and books) and subject area, and provides address, Website or e-mail address (if applicable), editor's name, content, submission guidelines, and pay rate. Writers' colonies, conferences, and organizations; state arts councils; and literary agents are also listed with contact and descriptive information.

The index features only publishers, so readers looking for a topic covered in the essays or for a particular author will have to scan the table of contents (although essay topics are usually obvious from their titles). It would also have been useful to include a byline for each contributor, or at the very least a short list of their publications, for readers who wish to pursue an author's work. After all, writes Maggie Murphy in "Are You Reading Enough?", "Reading inspires us, sparks new ideas, and teaches us by example how to write effectively" (p. 61).

No directory can ever be complete and up-to-date, so readers will also want to consult Writers Digest's *Writer's Market* (2000 ed.; see ARBA 2000, entry 818), Gale's *Publisher's Directory* (22d ed.; see ARBA 2001, entry 690), Dustbooks' *International Directory of Little Magazines & Small Presses* (36th ed.; see ARBA 2001, entry 687), and R. R. Bowker's *Literary Market Place* (see entry 291), all published annually. But thanks to its fine essays on the writing craft, *The Writer's Handbook* should find a place in both the reference and the circulating collection.—**Lori D. Kranz**

Style Manuals

C, P

338.   **The Oxford Dictionary for Writers and Editors.** 2d ed. R. M. Ritter, ed. New York, Oxford University Press, 2000. 404p. $24.95. ISBN 0-19-866239-4.

This 2d edition of *The Oxford Dictionary for Writers and Editors* is an updated revision of the 1981 volume (see ARBA 82, entry 1239, for a review of the 1st edition) that was itself the successor of the venerable *Authors and Printers Dictionary*. Its editor calls the volume the essential guide for anyone who works with words.

In addition to a 375-page alphabetic listing of words and letters that might puzzle writers and editors, appendixes include mathematical and logical symbols, proofreading marks, transliteration tables, and typographical marks such as diacritics and accents. Some of the word listings offer definitions, but most merely show how the word or abbreviation should be written. For example, the entries for *warship*, *warthog*, and *wartime* are all followed by "one word." While the next entry, *war-torn*, is followed by the word "hyphen."

American users should keep in mind that the British spellings used throughout make the volume a little less useful for the average user. This dictionary is basically a style manual that makes judgments about usage that might or might not agree with those of mainstream American editors. Although this volume makes for interesting browsing, it will be of value mostly for those who need information about British usage. [R: Choice, Jan 01, pp. 874-876]—**Kay O. Cornelius**

RADIO, TELEVISION, AUDIO, AND VIDEO

P, S

339.   **Bowker's Directory of Audiocassettes for Children 1999.** New Providence, N.J., R. R. Bowker, 1999. 400p. index. $55.00pa. ISBN 0-8352-4200-5.

In its 2d edition, this book remains the first and only existing directory of audiocassettes for children, listing more than 8,500 titles to books on audiocassette for ages K–12. With a growing demand for books on tape, this guide will prove highly useful to librarians and teachers, and even parents and young adults, in identifying and ordering titles either via the traditional way or directly from the publisher. Alphabetically listed, material is well organized into six indexes, including title, author, reader/performer, and subject. The final index lists the publishers and distributors. However, preceding all of these indexes is a "Special Index," which lists award-winning and notable books. The title index provides the full bibliographic entry for each title, including foreign language titles. It includes other useful information, such as audience, grade level, and a short description. Although the subject index does not include the description entry, it shows a diverse list of subjects that is impressive.

Although the reputation of R. R. Bowker implies sufficient validation, this directory is not without its shortcomings. Entries lack consistency. The sample entry for the audience lists "Juv," which one can guess stands for juvenile. After combing through hundreds of entries looking for "Juv," this reviewer realized that "(J)" was being used in place of "Juv." In addition, a list of acronyms and abbreviations is lacking and will make it difficult for the parent or young adult to use successfully. And notably missing are e-mail and Website addresses in the index for publishers and distributors. These shortcomings are not difficult to remedy and would greatly enhance the book's convenience. Despite the deficiencies noted, this volume is highly recommended for school and public libraries.—**Wilma L. Jones**

21 Decorative Arts

GENERAL WORKS

C, P

340. **Materials & Techniques in the Decorative Arts: An Illustrated Dictionary.** Lucy Trench, ed. Chicago, University of Chicago Press, 2000. 572p. illus. $60.00. ISBN 0-226-81200-6.

Trench has been a conservator at the Victoria and Albert Museum in London, editor of numerous publications for the National Gallery, and materials and techniques editor for the *Dictionary of Art* (see ARBA 98, entry 946). *Materials & Techniques in the Decorative Arts* includes more than 1,000 entries, 30 color plates, and 329 photographs and drawings. Coverage includes glass, ceramics, textiles, paper, plastics, leather, metal, stone, wood, paint, gemstones, lacquer, ivory, and shell. The emphasis of the dictionary is to explain the materials and techniques used in the decorative arts along with attempting to describe and illustrate the creative processes used in each medium. The work mainly covers crafts or what the author feels are "decorative" arts and not fine art objects.

Materials & Techniques in the Decorative Arts provides a source for better understanding the decorative arts and the materials used for the production of these objects. A number of dictionaries on decorative arts include materials and techniques, such as John Fleming's *The Penguin Dictionary of Decorative Arts* (Viking, 1989) and William Audsley's *Popular Dictionary of Architecture and the Allied Arts*, but the present work is the first one-volume guide that describes the raw materials of decorative arts and how they are used in making objects of art.

The volume is well illustrated and easy to use. The cross-references are well done and enhance the use of the dictionary. One would have preferred to have more color plates, but the black-and-white reproductions are clear and usually do the job. It is highly recommended for all academic and public libraries, and would make a great selection for most secondary school libraries. Also, because of the concise nature of the work it would be a good personal library selection for artists, curators, and critics. [R: BL, 1 Jan 01, p. 1012]—**Robert L. Wick**

COLLECTING

General Works

P

341. **Garage Sale & Flea Market Annual: Cashing in on Today's Lucrative Collectibles Market.** 8th ed. Paducah, Ky., Collector Books, 2000. 509p. illus. index. $19.95. ISBN 1-57432-167-6.

This collector's guide is over 500 pages of items readers are sure to find if they frequent garage sales or flea markets. It is very useful as a price guide for collectors or as a vehicle in a trip down memory lane, filled with many items of nostalgia and reminiscent charm. Everything from advertising collectibles, such as Bob's Big Boy 1956 menu and a Colonel Sanders bank, to watches, cookie jars, vases, and other knickknacks and personal treasures. A section covering personal interests is also included, featuring physical and Internet addresses of many companies that specialize in certain items. The introduction to this guide includes a section on how to hold a garage sale, become a successful bargain hunter, and evaluate holdings. It also offers some ideas on where to sell items to put them back into circulation. This attractive guidebook is easy on the eyes for hours of fun and research, but also offers the information in a helpful and easy-to-follow layout. All items include current market values, descriptions of item condition and sizes, colors, and so on. A must-have for anyone serious about turning items of the past into security and profits for the future.—**Michael Florman**

Toys

P, S

342.   Augustyniak, J. Michael. **Collector's Encyclopedia of Barbie Doll Exclusives and More: Identification & Values.** 2d ed. Paducah, Ky., Collector Books, 2000. 485p. illus. index. $24.95. ISBN 1-57432-134-X.

Since the first Barbie doll was created in 1959, these dolls have been collected by people all over the world. This guide provides beautiful color photos and current market values for collector dolls released from 1973 (the traditional cutoff year for "vintage" Barbie doll collectors) through the end of 1999 and the release of the Millennium Barbie. Entries include every department store special, Barbie doll exclusives, collector series, and fashions. This 2d edition features more than 500 additional dolls and 150 fashions not included in the 1st edition.

Collectors can find brief descriptions of store specials, such as the Sears 100th anniversary doll and J.C. Penney's Arizona Jeans Barbie, along with their current market value and stock numbers. Collector series featured include the Bob Mackie series, Happy Holidays Barbie dolls, and the Hollywood Legends series. The guide also includes entries for exclusive foreign-market Barbie dolls, dolls produced for Disney, every national Barbie doll Collector's Convention set from 1980 to the present, and many one-of-a-kind dolls auctioned by Mattel for charity.

Values listed in this book are for individual "never removed from box" (NRFB) dolls. Dolls that have been removed from their boxes for display and then replaced are "mint in box" (MIB) and are worth 25 to 50 percent less than NRFB dolls. Dolls without their boxes or that are damaged have even less value. The values in this book have been compiled and averaged from numerous dealer lists and catalogs, collector and dealer advertisements, Internet sales, and regional and national doll shows and conventions. The values are intended to be used only as a guide to Barbie doll sale prices. Prices may be higher or lower depending on what area of the country the doll is sold in.

This is an entertaining and informative guide for Barbie doll collectors. But as all collectors should know, the market values frequently change according to supply and demand. This guide, just as any other guide, will quickly become outdated. It is a good starting point to learn the history and variations in different releases, but market values will need to be further researched through other sources such as online auction sites.—**Cari Ringelheim**

FASHION AND COSTUME

P

343.   Miller, Anna M. **Illustrated Guide to Jewelry Appraising: Antique, Period, and Modern.** 2d ed. Woodstock, Vt., Gemstone Press, 1999. 194p. illus. index. $39.95. ISBN 0-943763-23-1.

Unlike many items of value, jewelry does not have a basic Blue Book listing prices. A jewelry appraiser must have experience and knowledge of the history behind the jewelry to make an accurate estimation. This volume is designed as an introduction for those new to jewelry appraisal or for those in the business looking for new methods for finding correct prices. The book begins with a short chapter defining the profession of jewelry appraisers. After this brief introduction the work is more practical, featuring chapters on appraisal concepts and principles (e.g., finding information, using price guides), making correct identification, estimating values of several different pieces of jewelry, how to correctly fill out an appraisal document, and valuing unfamiliar pieces of jewelry. There are many black-and-white photographs throughout these chapters that will help readers better understand the detailed text. The appendixes at the back of the volume include such information as new diamond cuts, a guide to gemstone handling, and a cubic zirconia stone conversion chart, among others. A glossary, bibliography, and index conclude the volume.

This work is a must-have for those in the jewelry and auction businesses. Public libraries that have patrons interested in the collecting and appraisal of modern and antique jewelry will benefit from its purchase.

—**Shannon Graff Hysell**

22 Fine Arts

GENERAL WORKS

Biography

C, P, S

344. **Encyclopedia of Artists.** William Vaughan, ed. New York, Oxford University Press, 2000. 6v. illus. index. $180.00/set. ISBN 0-19-521572-9.

This encyclopedia of artists from the Middle Ages to today is presented in six attractive, slim volumes. The set begins with an introduction to artists throughout this time period, explaining their cultural and societal influences. A timeline at the bottom of the introduction pages indicates the different art movements from 1100 to 2000. The first five volumes consist of biographies of more than 200 painters, sculptors, and printmakers. Each artist is given a two-page spread featuring an article about the life and work of the artist; a sidebar with information on the artist's full name, nationality, style, dates of birth and death (if applicable), key works, "things to look for," people they have been compared to, and terms to look for in the glossary that refer to their work; and one photograph of a famous piece of their art with a description. Each entry is well written and will lead researchers to similar artists. Volume 6 in the set provides 1-page definitions of the various art movements covered, a glossary, and an index.

This set is beautifully written and illustrated. It will not only provide reliable information for researchers but will also entertain the interested browser. It is most appropriate for high school, public, and undergraduate libraries.

—**Shannon Graff Hysell**

C, P

345. **The Yale Dictionary of Art and Artists.** By Erika Langmuir and Norbert Lynton. New Haven, Conn., Yale University Press, 2000. 753p. $30.00; $12.95pa. ISBN 0-300-08702-0; 0-300-06458-6pa.

In approximately 3,000 alphabetically arranged entries, salient aspects of the history of Western art from 1300 to the present are covered in this excellent single-volume work. About 90 percent of the entries are for individual painters, sculptors, and printmakers, with the remainder devoted to art terms, techniques, movements, concepts, and theories. There are no entries for architecture, museums, galleries, or specific art works, and only limited coverage on famous collectors and collections. Entries vary from a few lines, to three or four double-column pages depending on the importance of the subject (e.g., the longest articles are for terms like *abstract art* and artists like Pablo Picasso and Michelangelo). The biographical entries are concise and readable and, in addition to personal information, often give details on style, influences, the nature and historical importance of the subject's work, and a current assessment. In many cases specific landmark works are cited with their present gallery locations. The many *see* references direct the reader to variant spellings of artist's names or pseudonyms. There is also a copious use of asterisks within articles to indicate entries on related subjects. There are no bibliographies or lists for further reading.

Both of the editors are British (one a former administrator at the National Gallery in London, and the other a professor emeritus at the University of Sussex). This national bias is revealed in the outstanding coverage on post-war British artists (particularly contemporary figures) over the more limited entries on their American counterparts (e.g., no entries for Alice Neel or Lee Krasner are noted). This is a small reservation for what is otherwise a fine, easy-to-use work that will be particularly valuable in libraries for quick reference. Its closest counterpart is *The Oxford Dictionary of Art* (Oxford University Press, 1997), which contains roughly the same number of entries. It, too, is an excellent one-volume work but it is not as up-to-date as *The Yale Dictionary of Art and Artists*, nor has it as extensive coverage on art terms and movements. [R: Choice, Jan 01, p. 877]

—**John T. Gillespie**

Directories

C, P

346.   **Art Across America: A Comprehensive Guide to American Art Museums and Exhibition Galleries.** John J. Russell and Thomas S. Spencer, eds. Monkton, Md., Friar's Lantern, 2000. 898p. illus. maps. index. $29.95pa. ISBN 0-9667144-1-5.

Art Across America is an easy-to-use guide to U.S. art museums and nonprofit exhibition galleries. The types of galleries included are not only traditional museums but also college galleries that only present temporary exhibits, maritime museums, historic houses, ethnic museums, and corporate facilities supporting artwork. The entries are arranged alphabetically first by state, then by city, and then by organization name. A map precedes each state listing, which indicates how many exhibits are in that city. Entries provide address, telephone and fax number, and Internet address; the name of the director; admission cost; annual attendance; year established; parking instructions; hours the exhibits are open; information on facilities, activities, and publications; and a paragraph describing the facility and what type of artwork they typically cater to. Photographs throughout the volume will give readers an indication of what to expect from the exhibit they are reading about. The information provided is thorough and the descriptions are very well written. All information was provided by the facilities themselves, with the editors confirming details with follow-up telephone calls and checking Websites. This well-researched and equally well-written work will be a hit with all art lovers. It is highly recommended for public libraries of all sizes.—**Shannon Graff Hysell**

ARCHITECTURE

C, P

347.   Curl, James Stevens. **A Dictionary of Architecture.** New York, Oxford University Press, 1999. 833p. illus. (Oxford Paperback Reference). $16.95pa. ISBN 0-19-280017-5.

A concise reference work must provide a wide range of information in a minimum of space. This requires omissions deemed valid by the author or compiler. Given these restraints, Curl has produced a work of precise erudition with an appeal to both the general public and the more informed world of architectural specialists. The emphasis is on Western architecture, although notice is taken of Eastern influences and the globalization of current architectural design. Short biographies of architects and contributors to architectural thought appear alongside definitions of terms, styles, and movements, with references to the extensive bibliography where indicated. The scattered illustrations are helpful, but are all too few and, often, their small size obscures detail. The clutter created by the extensive use of asterisks interrupts the flow and distracts the reader. The section on art nouveau (57 lines) contains 31 asterisks, and terms such as *gothic* and *baroque* will obviously be consulted directly by any user of this work. Beyond these caveats, one must commend the author for his scholarship, impartiality, and lucidity. This is a valuable, reliable tool for amateur, student, and professional. [R: LJ, 15 Mar 99, p. 68]—**Paula Frosch**

GRAPHIC ARTS

C, P

348. Tresidder, Jack. **Symbols and Their Meanings.** London, Duncan Baird and Friedman/Fairfax Publishers; distr., New York, Sterling Publishing, 2000. 184p. illus. index. $24.95. ISBN 1-58663-046-6.

Symbols and Their Meanings provides a thematic approach to the study of symbols. This source is divided into eight subject areas, such as the animal world, the plant kingdom, and arts and artifacts. Within each section the author gives an overview of how symbols have been interpreted by different religions, regions, and cultures. This source is richly illustrated with color reproductions of paintings, sculptures, and architecture that add to the textual interpretation. Also included are a brief bibliography and an index.

There are many sources that provide analyses of symbols. Two of the more recent ones are *The Dictionary of Symbols in Art* and the *Illustrated Dictionary of Symbols in Eastern and Western Art* (see ARBA 96, entries 1030 and 1031). While this source is not as scholarly as other titles, it provides a good introduction and overview of the subject. The interdisciplinary approach is helpful and the illustrations are superior to other books on the same subject. It is recommended for general collections in both public and academic libraries.—**Monica Fusich**

23 Language and Linguistics

GENERAL WORKS

C, P

349. DeMiller, Anna L. **Linguistics: A Guide to Reference Literature.** 2d ed. Englewood, Colo., Libraries Unlimited, 2000. 396p. index. (Reference Sources in the Humanities Series). $57.50. ISBN 1-56308-619-0.

This book is an invaluable guide to bibliographies, indexes, abstracts, dictionaries, encyclopedias, and electronic databases in three areas. The 1st part on general linguistics contains such items as dictionaries, encyclopedias, Internet sites, and core periodicals. The 2d part on allied areas documents sources in anthropological linguistics, applied linguistics, mathematical and computational linguistics, psycholinguistics, semiotics, and sociolinguistics. The 3d part on languages contains subsections on general and multi-language sources, and nine language families plus artificial languages and Pidgin and Creole languages. This 2d edition (the 1st edition was published in 1991) is a greatly expanded edition, providing full coverage from 1957 to 1998, and also includes a few items from 1999 and Websites from 1999. Though the author necessarily had to be somewhat selective, the principles of selectivity are carefully spelled out in the introduction. The 1,039 annotations are clear and explicit. No research library should be without it. [R: Choice, Sept 2000, p. 92]—**Bethany K. Dumas**

C, P

350. Trask, R. L. **Dictionary of Historical and Comparative Linguistics.** Chicago, Fitzroy Dearborn, 2000. 403p. $75.00. ISBN 1-57958-218-4.

The series of terminological dictionaries covering various areas of linguistics keeps growing; this new member deals with diachronic aspects of the study of language. It needs to be stated at the beginning of this review that this dictionary is very good. It covers terminological repertories common not only in the study of Indo-European, Semitic, and other well-known and widely studied language families, but also those usual in studies of much less frequented areas, such as Basque and palaeo-Siberian. In addition, rare terms of general character are listed (*teknolalic words*, a synonym of the term *nursery words*, in German *Lallnamen*). Recent discoveries like that of Eblaitic are not omitted. Most welcome is the listing of all the hosts of classificatory terms established and created as late as the 1990s, and the listing of all the "laws" named for their discoverer, even of the somewhat shaky ones (e.g., Hjelmslev's Law).

Although all this guarantees a great wealth of information, the author also had the excellent idea to incorporate terms that do not belong to the terminological set mentioned in the title, but that can additionally be useful to the new practitioner. Sometimes these are old, traditional terms, frequent in Latin (e.g., *correptio iambica*, which is a shortening of words of a certain metric form). Advice on how to use such a term is added where needed. Some entries contain traditional jocose expressions, such as *lucus a non lucendo etymology*, which is said about an etymology weak in the semantic aspect. Also useful are terms and abbreviations from the field of textual criticism, such as *om. (omittit)*, telling the reader which manuscript lacks the expression marked. Finally, some general abbreviations and expressions used relatively frequently are welcome as well (e.g., *op. cit.* [*opus citatum*], *pace* [as in "*pace* Sturtevant, I still think there was only one laryngeal"], *passim*).

Still, a future edition should perhaps deal also with the names of languages in greater detail. For example, names like *Tubatulabal* quoted in the text (p. 79) deserve a gloss. Another candidate for inclusion is the set of terms that are not directly of historical character but occur in historical studies (e.g., *diathesis*).

Real omissions are few. This reviewer noticed that under *minority languages* Occitan is not mentioned as one of the minority languages of France. Sturtevant's highly useful differentiation of *laryngal* and *laryngeal* also deserves inclusion. This book will be most useful to every beginning and fairly progressed student of language. [R: LJ, 15 Sept 2000, p. 62; Choice, Jan 01, p. 878]—**L. Zgusta**

ENGLISH-LANGUAGE DICTIONARIES

General Usage

C, P, S

351.   **American Heritage Dictionary of the English Language.** 4th ed. Westminster, Md., Houghton Mifflin, 2000. 2074p. illus. maps. $60.00 (book); $24.95 (CD-ROM); $74.95 (book w/CD-ROM). ISBN 0-395-82517-2.

This newly revised, major American-language dictionary includes both print and CD-ROM versions that are basically intended to be used independently. The publication has well over 200,000 words and claims it contains 10,000 new words, which, although significantly fewer than the 16,000 added to the 3d edition, has brought such areas as computer terminology and business up to date. The book is bound to lie flat, although the middle margins are fairly small. The color illustrations are in the outside margins—many are new to this edition. The print is clear and pleasant to read. Words, terms, abbreviations, and biographical and geographic names are all interfiled. Some etymology is included. This 4th edition, like the 3d, includes lengthy essays, now revised, on the origins, history, and usage of American English.

The CD-ROM contains setup instructions and software for mounting the dictionary on a PC hard drive. If usage for more than one simultaneous user is desired, Houghton Mifflin provides a license for $10 per user. On the CD–ROM, Houghton Mifflin offers both the full and an expurgated version of the dictionary. The setup contains an option, mentioned no where else, to mount the dictionary with or without words labeled as "vulgar slang" that do appear in the print version.

The CD-ROM has fewer illustrations, incorporating only the drawings and not the color photographs of the print version. But the CD-ROM offers a somewhat different style of searching, with, in addition to the straight alphabetic browse, specific image, note, and word searches. Cross-references are also linked. A nice CD-ROM feature is the ability to enlarge the text size.

This is a solid, high-quality, American-language dictionary. The 4th edition does not disappoint, excepting the disconcerting provision of a censored version. [R: BL, 1 Jan 01, p. 994]—**Florence W. Jones**

C, P, S

352.   **Merriam-Webster's Collegiate Dictionary & Thesaurus.** deluxe audio ed. [CD-ROM]. Springfield, Mass., Merriam-Webster, 2000. Minimum system requirements (Windows version): Pentium-class processor. Double-speed CD-ROM drive. Windows 95/98, Windows 2000, or Windows NT. 4MB RAM. 60MB hard disk space. SVGA monitor (600x800). Mouse. Minimum system requirements (Macintosh version): PowerMac. Double-speed CD-ROM drive. OS 7.5 or higher. 4MB RAM. 60MB hard disk space. SVGA monitor. Mouse. $24.95. ISBN 0-87779-466-9.

Everyone seems to benefit from the technological advances being made with electronic dictionaries, and this CD-ROM product is a perfect example. Included are more than 215,000 definitions; more than 340,000 synonyms and related words; 1,000 color illustrations; and 25 tables, covering such topics as chemical elements, weights and measures, and so on. A typical entry includes the entry word, pronunciation, function label, etymology, date of origin, verbal illustration, and usage note. If an image or table is available, an icon at the end of the entry indicates it.

What makes this work stand out from the range of products available is that it allows the user 21 separate search options, whether performing a simple or an advanced search. Among these are the ability to find words that rhyme, a crossword function, a cryptogram function, the ability to jumble letters, location of homophones, words with common etymologies or language roots, the ability to search all quotes from one author, and a variety of other valuable access points. In addition to indicating pronunciation, the user can also access the spoken pronunciation for any entry.

The software provided allows the user to go online, and to connect to other Merriam-Webster resources on the World Wide Web. There are also capabilities of creating bookmarks, copying, pasting, editing, and so on. Given its scope, affordability, and ease of access, this product should readily be found in every reference collection. High school students and college freshmen and sophomores will find it quite useful.—**Edmund F. SantaVicca**

C, P
353.   **Random House Webster's College Dictionary.** New York, Random House, 2000. 1573p. illus. maps. $24.95. ISBN 0-375-42560-8.

Arranged in a strict letter-by-letter format, this latest revision provides all that can be expected from an abridged dictionary. Each entry in the dictionary presents spelling, along with alternatives, syllabication, pronunciation used in conversational speech (with alternatives), and part of speech. Entries also include meanings and definitions, with the most common usage listed first; historical, technical, or other usages of the term; date of first usage, including place of origin; and other related words that use the same root or stem. A suite of 26 introductory pages provides the user with sample pages and entries, instructions on how to use the dictionary, an overview of language evolution, and keys to abbreviations and pronunciation. Supplementing the whole is a ready-reference, hodgepodge of useful, yet oddly juxtaposed, guides and lists that include such things as signs and symbols, largest islands of the world, notable deserts, U.S. presidents, forms of address, and so on. A useful index to features is provided as the sole finding tool.

The dictionary includes over 207,000 definitions, many of them so new they are not yet found in competing products. Simple black-and-white line drawings and illustrations are scattered throughout, although not profusely. The work is also thumb-indexed for ease of use.

For libraries seeking a wide variety of dictionaries, this work will prove especially useful for its inclusion of recent terms and idioms. Purchase also allows for a free subscription to a dictionary newsletter and indication of related Websites that can enhance the user's search for semantic (or other) clarity. [R: BL, 15 Nov 99, pp. 653-654]
    —**Edmund F. SantaVicca**

P, S
354.   **World Book Dictionary.** millennium ed. Chicago, World Book, 2000. 2v. illus. $87.00/set. ISBN 0-7166-0297-0.

This is a new printing of a two-volume dictionary that first appeared in 1963 and last appeared in 1996. Although major updating has occurred since the 1st edition, there is no evidence of any, or at least any significant, updating since 1996. Indeed, this "millennium edition" fails to define Y2K.

The dictionary defines 225,000 words, terms, or abbreviations, arranged in a single alphabetical list. Since it is intended for use with the *World Book Encyclopedia*, it has no entries for biographical names or geographic entities. With nice clear print, the dictionary is easy to read. It includes well-done line drawings, an average of more than one per page.

This dictionary is intended for use by students from junior high school level through college undergraduate level, although some material is aimed as low as third grade. The introductory material, running to 124 pages, includes information on correct English usage, vocabulary, punctuation, spelling, grammar, English language history, and word construction in English. These sections are intended as instruction to students and help make the dictionary very useful.

This is a good solid dictionary of American English and pronunciation. The binding is apparently sturdy and should hold up to student use in a school library. It would also be good for home use. There is, however, no compelling reason to replace recent editions of the work.—**Florence W. Jones**

Idioms

C, P, S
355.   Spears, Richard A. **NTC's Dictionary of American Slang and Colloquial Expressions.** 3d ed. Lincolnwood, Ill., National Textbook, 2000. 560p. index. $100.00; $18.95pa. ISBN 0-8442-0461-7; 0-8442-0462-5pa.

Marking Spears's 1st revision of this work in 5 years (see ARBA 95, entry 1060, for review of previous edition), this edition, containing definitions to some 8,500 terms, contains several significant changes. Entries (words, phrases, and sentences) are now arranged alphabetically by letter rather than by word. Although each entry's headword remains in boldface type, the guideword atop each page of the dictionary is now set only in regular type. Also, the second edition's helpful keyword markers have been removed from the phrase-finder index.

Less noticeable alterations include the dropping of periods within acronyms and initialisms (e.g., FOB and AC-DC), the elimination of cross-referencing cues between entries in close proximity to each other, and the breaking out of nine sample numerical entries into a listing preceding the "A" entries. Also, within the guide of how to use this dictionary, Spears has regrettably removed more than 15 useful examples and has stricken 4 of the previous edition's 19 points of guidance.

As usual, the entries themselves—informal, colorful, and (in some instances) offensive expressions—have been drawn from such diverse sources as college life, street life, medicine, securities markets, the military, and the computer industry. Helpful caveats accompany entries whose use has been objected to regionally or historically, or whose original sense has evolved into self-parody. Regional, cultural, and ethnic contributions along with juvenile lingo and baby talk are represented. A number of entries evoke particular historical times or contexts. For the first time, Spears has included a sizable number of obscene terms among his entries. Not surprisingly, the author has set aside space in this edition's introduction to discuss and defend the presence of such language. Besides this expansion of entries that are sexual or scatological in their subject matter, a substantial number of entries carried forward from the 2d edition focus on drug abuse and states of intoxication. Several variants of included terms are unaccountably absent from this work. However, Spears does provide a sufficient number of variant spellings for entries.

On the other hand, cross-referencing between related entries is spotty. For instance, there are no *see* or *see also* notes between many entries. Some tightening up of entries is also needed. Essentially, there are several redundant entries. Although etymological information is scant in this work, Spears does provide insight into some entries' derivations. Also, it is unfortunate that the pages of this volume are so lightly peppered with pronunciation aids.

In summary, this volume is a serviceable and affordable reference work, though less comprehensive than its principal rivals—Green's *Cassell Dictionary of Slang* (Cassell, 1999) and Chapman's *Dictionary of American Slang* (HarperCollins, 1997). However, its value is enhanced when used in tandem with such companions as *NTC's American Idioms Dictionary* (National Textbook, 1993) and, to a lesser degree, *NTC's Dictionary of British Slang and Colloquial Expressions* (see ARBA 99, entry 908). [R: BL, July 2000, p. 2062; Choice, Sept 2000, p. 88]—**Jeffrey E. Long**

Thesauri

S

356.   McCutcheon, Marc. **The Facts on File Student's Thesaurus.** 2d ed. New York, Facts on File, 2000. 504p. $39.95. ISBN 0-8160-4058-3.

Addressed to junior and senior high school students "daunted" by adult thesauri (back cover), this student's thesaurus presents a clean, easy-to-read format. Entry works are in bold typefaced print and part of speech is given. Synonyms are separated by the sense or meaning. For example, under "domestic" (p. 127), three groupings of synonyms are given: "1. family, home, household, residential"; "2. tame, tamed, domesticated, trained, broken"; and "3. native, internal, homemade, endemic, indigenous." Sentences using the entry word are offered for each grouping. Antonyms, offered for about two-thirds of the terms, follow the same breakdown as synonyms, but no sentence examples are given.

The introduction defines a thesaurus as "a book that lists synonyms and antonyms" (p. v). While a dictionary does not support that definition, a few antonyms do appear in Roget's various thesauri and they do seem to add an important dimension to a thesaurus. The sentence illustrating each grouping of synonyms also makes the book user-friendly. A bonus is the word searches that occur about every five pages giving works that are not synonyms but are related to the selected entry word. For example, the word search under "dance" includes such items as "Cuban: rhumba, conga, mambo" (p. 101).

There are more entry words and more synonyms in the *Oxford Minireference Thesaurus* (1992) and in Roget's thesauri, but the clarity, the inclusion of antonyms, and the examples and word searches will help this book appeal to some adults as well as to middle and high school students. [R: BR, Sept/Oct 2000, pp. 76-78]

—**Betty Jo Buckingham**

Visual

P, S

357.   **Ultimate Visual Dictionary 2001.** New York, DK Publishing, 2000. 640p. illus. maps. index. $40.00. ISBN 0-7894-6111-0.

Although selective in its coverage as any book of this kind would have to be, there are visual answers in this book to many of the common questions that present themselves to readers every day. This is a new edition of the picture dictionary that was first published in hardback in 1994 as the *Dorling Kindersley Ultimate Visual Dictionary* (see ARBA 95, entry 52) and as a paperback in 1998 (see ARBA 99, entry 919). The content of the 2001 edition is identical to the 1994 edition with the exception of a 64-page addendum of new advances, processes, and devices that have emerged since 1994.

The original part of the book is arranged into 14 chapters covering such vast topics as the universe, the human body, sea and air, architecture, music, and everyday things. Illustrative of the information included is the section on baseball in the sports chapter. A brief description of the game is followed by color photographs of baseball equipment (the batter's helmet, the catcher's mask, a shoe, a bat, and a glove), a diagram of the baseball field, and the pitching sequence (windup, release, and follow-through). With such broad topic arrangement, a detailed index is the key to finding precise information. The new section in the 2001 edition contains topics such as the Hubble space telescope, genetic advances, body healing, the 2000 Olympics, digital photography, and the World Wide Web.

The *Ultimate Visual Dictionary* is ideal for school, public, and home libraries. Libraries owning the 1994 or 1998 editions may decide not to purchase the 2001 edition because the content is identical except for the 64-page addendum.—**Elaine F. Jurries**

NON-ENGLISH-LANGUAGE DICTIONARIES

French

P, S

358.   **Merriam-Webster's French-English Dictionary.** Springfield, Mass., Merriam-Webster, 2000. 804p. $19.95; $5.99pa. ISBN 0-87779-166-X; 0-87779-917-2pa.

This handy manual does not differ greatly from similar utilitarian publications, although it claims to include the terminology of today. Colloquialisms are not here, however, and the most recent meanings of "cookie" and "cool," for example, are ignored. The English section has an entry for a computer file, but that qualification lacks such a reference in "fichier." Some words are identified for familiar usage, but the less-polite (and -popular) vocabulary is absent. The initial 60 pages, however, offer a terse coverage of French grammar and conjugations. This will prove helpful for the new student of the language. Regional variants are also provided for those words unique to Canada, Belgium, or Switzerland, although idiosyncratic Parisianisms do not appear. Each word is provided with a guide to pronunciations by use of the International Phonetic Alphabet, making this publication superior to the much more attractively produced *Oxford Starter French Dictionary* (see ARBA 98, entry 1027).

—**Dominique-René de Lerma**

German

P, S

359.   **The Pocket Oxford-Duden German Dictionary.** 2d ed. M. Clark and O. Thyen, and the Dudenredaktion and the German Section of the Oxford University Press Dictionary Department, eds. New York, Oxford University Press, 2000. 938p. $11.95pa. ISBN 0-19-860280-4.

With 90,000 words and 115,000 translations, this new edition (see ARBA 99, entry 930, for review of the previous edition) has been enlarged and updated to reflect scientific and technological innovations as well as changes in politics, culture, and society. It includes such technological terms as *interface*, *World Wide Web*, *cellular phone*, *laptop*, and *hard drive*. It adheres to the spelling reforms in the German language ratified by the governments of Germany, Austria, and Switzerland in 1996. New to this edition are a calendar of holidays in German-speaking countries, an A to Z glossary of German culture, and a practical guide to letter writing. The German descriptions of American holidays present a surprising perceptibility; the definition of *Thanksgiving*, for example, emphasizes the prandial aspects of the holiday over the religious one. As one would expect with Oxford in the name, the usage is primarily British, although some accommodation has been made for U.S. alternates.

As far as translation dictionaries go, this new work joins the ranks of the *Langenscheidt's Pocket German Dictionary* (Langenscheidt, 1993) and *Collins Gem German Dictionary* (HarperCollins, 1999). It will adequately serve the student, traveler, and business professional for whom it is intended, and its price makes it attractive enough that libraries can buy a couple of circulating copies along with one in reference.—**Lawrence Olszewski**

Latin

P, S

360.   Stone, Jon R. **More Latin for the Illiterati: A Guide to Everyday Medical, Legal, and Religious Latin.** New York, Routledge, 1999. 208p. index. $16.99pa. ISBN 0-415-92211-9.

Stone has done a masterful job of rendering Latin phrases into palatable English. His Latin reference work is beautifully laid out and easy to access. The choice of entries introduces professional terms in style—neatly, succinctly, and gracefully. The front matter opens on a surprisingly droll preface commenting on the use of Latin in isolated and, at times, ill-chosen modern settings. Commentary on the medieval custom of *jus primae noctis* clarifies a troubling term that arises frequently in historical fiction and film.

Stone established his linguistic authority in two pages of references, which attest that he has researched thoroughly the sources of legal, liturgical, pharmaceutical, and medical terminology. His inclusion of whole and abbreviated forms, such as *uxor* and *ux.* increase the range of entries. He reduces the quandaries of Latinate pronunciation into three brief paragraphs, but chooses not to quibble over the shifts in sound that mark the passage of classical Latin into ecclesiastical Latin. Such a differentiation would have assisted many who puzzle over the era when Latin was metamorphosing into Italian and the other six or seven Romance languages. An accounting for changes from the hard *c* to a *ch* sound would have been especially valuable to the student transferring from a Catholic parochial environment to a public school or to the soloist or choral singer of Schubert's "Mass in G."

The arrangement of the text into separate lists answers the needs of the three target professions. Some of Stone's omissions (e.g., *q.l. [quantum libet]*) is particularly well chosen. Stone provides additional resources—a glimpse at the arcane Roman calendar, measures, primary colors, prepositions, ordinal and cardinal numbers, and Catholic liturgy—which precede a 26-page English-Latin index.

This work should find its way to the shelves of most serious students as well as reference librarians, teachers, journalists, editors, museum curators, and historians. Modestly priced, balanced, and scholarly, it is a reference treasure.—**Mary Ellen Snodgrass**

Russian

C, P

361.   **The Oxford Russian Dictionary.** 3d ed. Marcus Wheeler, Boris Unbegaun, and Paul Falla, eds. Revised by Della Thompson. New York, Oxford University Press, 2000. 1293p. $60.00. ISBN 0-19-860160-3.

Having encountered several sloppily put together dictionaries in recent years, it is great to report on one that is practically perfect. This edition, completely revised, features over 185,000 words and phrases and 290,000 translations, all aimed at providing a reliable resource for definitions in contemporary Russian and English. Because the dictionary originated in the United Kingdom, some of the English terms, such as *cash machine*, are provided. The coverage of contemporary terms is extensive, and it includes words such as *hyperinflation*, *multimedia*, *road rage*, *sound card*, *spacecraft*, and *proactive*. *Gay* exists in both meanings of the word. Some of the selected phrases are quaint, such as "he drove smash through the shop window," "the gas is escaping," "what kind of box do you want?" or "he kissed away her tears," but they are all translated correctly. The layout is attractive and the typeface (both in Cyrillic and Latin) is user-friendly (yes, *user-friendly* is also in the dictionary). This dictionary is a superior achievement.—**Koraljka Lockhart**

Spanish

P, S

362.   Raventós, Margaret H. **Spanish-English, English-Spanish Reference Dictionary.** Revised by David L. Gold. New York, Random House, 1999. 688p. $14.95pa. ISBN 2-8315-7125-1.

This new edition includes not just standard vocabulary entries but also stresses current usage, including useful items such as road and street signs. It also updates modern Spanish revisions to the language such as eliminating "ch" and "ll" as separate letters of the alphabet. Certain works are also identified as having regional or national usage. Subentries often follow a main entry to clarify usage in a phrase.

Extensive preliminary pages are devoted to Spanish and English pronunciation basics, usage of masculine and feminine forms, irregular Spanish verbs, and Spanish equivalents of "you." International Phonetic Alphabet (IPA) symbols are used throughout the text for both Spanish and English main entries. The dictionary consists of two parts: Spanish to English and English to Spanish. Following the main text are separate listings of Spanish irregular verbs; an explanation of English verb forms; and tables in both languages for numbers, days of the week, months, weights and measures, signs, and useful common phrases. Continuing a long tradition of excellence associated with the name Berlitz, this conveniently sized paperback should be handy for travelers and students. It is also recommended for school and public library collections.—**Louis G. Zelenka**

24 Literature

GENERAL WORKS

Biography

C, P, S

363. **World Authors 1990–1995.** Clifford Thompson, ed. Bronx, N.Y., H. W. Wilson, 1999. 863p. illus. $90.00. ISBN 0-8242-0940-0.

World Authors 1990–1995 is the latest volume in the Wilson Authors series. The format remains the same—alphabetically arranged biographical sketches, which are several pages in length and accompanied by a photograph of the author and short bibliographies of primary and secondary works. Most of the 317 authors came into prominence in the early 1990s, but a few older writers are included (e.g., Gregory Bateson). More than one-third of the authors contributed autobiographical sketches to their listings. There is little or no overlap in coverage with previous volumes.

Public, academic, and school libraries will want to add this volume of readable, accurate sketches to their collections, especially those libraries that cannot afford the Gale Contemporary Authors series. [R: Choice, Sept 2000, p. 94; BL, 1 Sept 2000, p. 181]—**Jonathan F. Husband**

Dictionaries and Encyclopedias

C, P

364. **Twentieth-Century Literary Movements Dictionary: A Compendium to more Than 500 Literary, Critical, and Theatrical Movements.** Helene Henderson and Jay P. Pederson, eds. Detroit, Omnigraphics, 2000. 1037p. index. $70.00. ISBN 1-55888-426-2.

The preface by Rene Wellek, distinguished Yale Professor Emeritus of comparative literature, sets the tone of this ambitious and well-designed reference book by discussing the principles that underlie the formation of movements in literary history. The book includes entries on more than 500 major and minor literary movements and schools associated with twentieth-century world literature. More than 80 nations and ethnic groups are represented within its pages, creating a volume that is truly international in scope. Also included are entries on hundreds of novelists, poets, dramatists, short story writers, theorists, essayists, genres, techniques, and terms identified with those movements.

The alphabetically arranged entries include the name of the movement, the country in which it originated, and the years of its greatest literary influence. A brief essay follows that covers the movement's philosophical and historical background, the writers, literary techniques, and literary works with which it is associated, and the way in which it influenced later movements and works. The length and depth of the essays vary depending upon the relative significance of the movement in literary history.

This volume includes a great deal of thoughtful and useful supplementary material. The editors have included separate indexes to countries and nationalities, authors, titles, and literary movements. Also included are four appendixes that provide a timeline of literary movements by date and by country, a list of journals cited, and an annotated list of useful Websites relating to various literary movements. Numerous *see* and *see also* references appear throughout the book. Readers attempting to locate the name of a foreign literary movement will find an entry under the foreign name cross-referenced to the English translation, under which the full entry always appears. This concise, neatly organized resource will make a valuable addition to academic and large public library collections. [R: LJ, 1 Feb 2000, p. 77; Choice, Mar 2000, p. 1268; BR, Jan/Feb 2000, p. 80; RUSQ, Sept 2000, p. 419]

—**Bronwyn Stewart**

CHILDREN'S AND YOUNG ADULT LITERATURE

Children's Literature

Bibliography

P, S

365.   **Adventuring with Books: A Booklist for Pre-K–Grade 6.** 12th ed. Kathryn Mitchell Pierce, ed. Urbana, Ill., National Council of Teachers of English, 1999. 605p. index. (NTCE Bibliography Series). $32.95pa.; $26.95pa. (NCTE members). ISBN 0-8141-0077-5. ISSN 1051-4740.

The 11 previous editions of this book have only made it better. The annotated bibliography of this edition covers books published from 1996 to 1998 for elementary children and is designed to help teachers, librarians, and parents find literature for children. The writing style and the range of topics for this edition are exceptional. Topics cover all aspects of a child's life, from the universe, world, family, and school to literature about cultures and gender issues.

Each topic is divided into primary and secondary reviews. Both types of reviews include all of the bibliographic information needed to order the book. Terms such as "sophisticated" and "adult mediation required" are used to describe a few books and a few titles designate reading level, but most are just listed as "picture book" or "chapter book." The primary reviews are different from other annotations because the reviewer includes children's reactions to the book and ideas for classroom use. Secondary reviews do not include as much detail as the primary annotations.

Each chapter starts with a well-written introduction to the topic and includes information on the criteria used to select books for the bibliography. Jane Yolen provides a wonderful foreword for the book about mage, image, and imagination.

For those who have used and loved this resource, they will find a familiar friend. For those who have not discovered this valuable bibliography, they will find a resource that not only lists books to use in the classroom but also provides ideas on how to effectively use those books.—**Suzanne Julian**

P, S

366.   **The Newbery and Caldecott Awards: A Guide to the Medal and Honor Books.** 2000 ed. Chicago, American Library Association, 2000. 167p. illus. index. $17.00pa.; $15.30pa. (ALA members). ISBN 0-8389-3500-1. ISSN 1070-4493.

This annotated bibliography of the winning and honor books for these two awards is framed by concise articles on the criteria and history of the two awards, a look at the life and art of Randolph Caldecott, and a definitive list of the media used in the Caldecott picture books. This list is an ongoing project, first published in 1988, to address the lack of archiving of the media used in creating these award-winning illustrations. Unlike the annotations that are in reverse chronological order, these listings begin with the first awards presented in 1938. These are followed by definitions of terms used in the illustration process.

Photographs of the authors and the covers of the books accompany the 2000 winning entries in the bibliographies themselves. The annotations are precise and informative without being overwhelming. An author and illustrator index and a title index complete this volume. This is a valuable resource for school and public libraries as well as teachers who may be looking for additional material to enrich their curriculum needs.—**Gail de Vos**

C, P, S
367.　Volz, Bridget Dealy, Cheryl Perkins Scheer, and Lynda Blackburn Welborn. **Junior Genreflecting: A Guide to Good Reads and Series Fiction for Children.** Englewood, Colo., Libraries Unlimited, 2000. 187p. index. (Genreflecting Advisory Series). $28.00. ISBN 1-56308-556-9.

Junior Genreflecting helps parents, teachers, and librarians recommend genre fiction to children in the third through eighth grades. The authors selected the best and most popular children's fiction published in the United States from 1990-1998. They used book review sources, best book lists, and recommendations from librarians, bookstores, and children to select their list of titles.

In addition to well-written book recommendations, the book contains information on how to encourage children to read. Recommendations for book and Internet resources add to the usefulness of the book. Scattered throughout the book are interesting tidbits on authors and titles. Each chapter ends with a section called "The Authors' All-Time Favorite. . . ." The table of contents and indexes for subject, title, and author provide good access to the material.

The genres cover adventure, animals, contemporary life, fantasy, science fiction, historical fiction, and mysteries. Each chapter contains an annotated list of titles and a list of paperback series titles. In addition to bibliographic information and an annotation, each title includes information on the awards the book has won and sequels to the title. Most of the entries in the book are for the third to sixth grade reading levels. A symbol is placed next to books for the sixth through eighth grade level readers.

The chapters do not list very many titles and sometimes the same author is listed multiple times for a series of books. For example, Patricia Wrede, author of the Enchanted Forest Chronicles, is listed three times for separate titles in this series. In a small section of 19 titles and with 3 other series being listed the same way, the number of recommended authors is not very large. To strengthen future editions of this book the authors may want to consider listing series titles once under the author and include more authors in each genre.

This book, by its very nature, is ambitious. Reading levels from the third to eighth grades vary greatly. While this book offers a wonderful selection of titles in these age ranges, the reading level designations are not helpful. For example, *The Watsons Go to Birmingham* is designated as a title for grades three to six. It would be a great book for a sixth grade student but a third grade student might struggle to read it. More precise definitions of reading levels would aid parents, teachers, and librarians in recommending books to children in a variety of reading stages.

Junior Genreflecting is on its way to becoming an important reference tool. The well-written entries, carefully chosen books, and interesting information scattered throughout the book make this a useful resource for adults who want to recommend enjoyable books to young children. [R: TL, Dec 2000, p. 45; SLJ, Nov 2000, p. 186]—**Suzanne Julian**

Biography

C, P, S
368.　**Eighth Book of Junior Authors and Illustrators.** 8th ed. Connie C. Rockman, ed. Bronx, N.Y., H. W. Wilson, 2000. 592p. illus. index. $75.00. ISBN 0-8242-0968-0.

Now in its 8th edition, and well over 70 years old, *Junior Authors and Illustrators* continues to be an essential reference tool for biographical information on the individuals who create literature for children and teenagers. Updated from the 1996 edition (see ARBA 97, entry 937), this volume contains 202 entries that cover fiction, picture books, poetry, and nonfiction. Each entry includes a personal essay, biographical information, a list of selected works, and often a list of suggested readings. The entries are enlivened with a photograph of the author or illustrator, jacket covers, and the signature of the subject. The personal essays make for very interesting reading and are sure to inspire potential writers.

The usefulness of the biographical information is about the same as the Contemporary Authors series from Gale in that it answers basic questions but is not sufficient for in-depth research. A listing of awards and honors granted to children's literature is included as well. Perhaps most useful of all in this edition is the cumulative index to the previous seven editions. Beneficial for the inside glimpse of an author's or illustrator's view on their work, inspiration, and life, this 8th edition will be of use in school and public libraries and in academic libraries that support education or library science curricula. [R: SLJ, Oct 2000, p. 199]—**Neal Wyatt**

C, P, S
369.   McElmeel, Sharron L. **100 Most Popular Picture Book Authors and Illustrators: Biographical Sketches and Bibliographies.** Englewood, Colo., Libraries Unlimited, 2000. 579p. illus. index. (Popular Authors Series). $49.00. ISBN 1-56308-647-6.

Teachers, librarians, and students will find this volume easy to read and very useful in identifying picture book titles and reading about their authors and illustrators. Over 100 persons are included due to the listings of husband-and-wife teams. Most of the books listed here are intended for the very youngest of readers, but they hold much utility for the older reader as well. The compilation of this volume is based upon a 1997 survey that attempted to identify the top 100 authors and illustrators of children's literature. There were more than 3,000 teacher and student responses. Top authors and illustrators included were identified by 90 percent to no less than 15 percent of survey respondents. The author has also written other useful volumes on popular children's authors, young adult authors, and nonfiction authors for children.

Entries are alphabetically arranged by the author's last name, and in some cases include a photograph. Each entry includes a birthplace, birth and death dates, an indication of the broad genre the author's work falls into, and books of note. There is also a section about the authors or illustrators that contains biographical information and background information on the books written or illustrated. Under the section on books of note is an introduction that provides additional information on the works created. A bibliography of works follows that usually groups the books under several categories like picture books, wordless books, early readers, journey books, books in a series, genre books, books written by the person, books illustrated by the person, and joint collaborations. Under a section of more information are references to other articles, books, and Websites that might be consulted for further information.

There is an appendix of photography credits, a genre or theme index, and a general index. The genre index is alphabetically arranged, with the author or illustrator listed alphabetically by the last name. Genres included are African American culture, community, family relationships, folklore, historical fiction, humor, poetry, and wordplay. The general index is an alphabetic list that includes all titles mentioned in the book and the authors' names. Page numbers are provided, and the ones that reflect the main entry for an author are in bold typeface. Books listed in the bibliographies of each section and genres are not included in this index. This work is highly recommended for school, public, and academic libraries, especially those with an early childhood education or children's literature program. [R: SLJ, Nov 2000, p. 94]—**Jan S. Squire**

Young Adult Literature

P, S
370.   **Best Books for Young Teen Readers: Grades 7 to 10.** John T. Gillespie, ed. New Providence, N.J., R. R. Bowker, 2000. 1066p. index. $65.00. ISBN 0-8352-4264-1.

Gillespie has compiled another excellent bibliography in R. R. Bowker's series of book selection tools to be used with young readers. Previous titles include *Best Books for Children* (6th ed.; see ARBA 2000, entry 948), *Best Books for Junior High Readers* (see ARBA 92, entry 1116), *Best Books for Senior High Readers* (see ARBA 92, entry 1117), and *Best Books for Young Adult Readers* (see ARBA 98, entry 1094).

The coverage in this volume is extensive. There are 11,147 individually numbered entries, with additional citations for related works listed within the annotations. Although the emphasis is on books appropriate for grades 7 to 10, the overall range covers materials for intermediate grades to senior high (roughly grades 5-12) as well as some adult works. Most of the titles included have had favorable reviews in at least two of four journals: *Booklist, Book Report, School Library Journal,* and *Voice of Youth Advocates.* The annotations contain references to these review sources.

Arrangement is by broad subject category, with annotations alphabetical by author under each category. Nearly 200 pages are devoted to fiction, which is subdivided by type. There is a detailed table of contents; a list of major subjects arranged alphabetically; and author, title, and subject/grade level indexes.

The emphasis is on recent new publications but older works, especially classics, are also included if there is a current edition. However, the original date of publication is not always cited. All titles included were in print as of December 1999.

This bibliography is highly recommended for collection building because of the wide range of inclusion; it is particularly useful for filling subject gaps. Because the annotations are brief and do not critique the works, users will often wish to combine its use with other review sources. [R: BR, Nov/Dec 2000, p. 75]

—**Patricia A. Eskoz**

C, P, S

371.   Carter, Betty, with Sally Estes and Linda Waddle. **Best Books for Young Adults.** 2d ed. Chicago, Young Adult Library Services Association/American Library Association, 2000. 229p. index. $35.00pa.; $31.50pa. (ALA members). ISBN 0-8389-3501-X.

This book is a product of the Young Adult Library Services Association (YALSA) and the Best Books for Young Adults Committee of the American Library Association (BBYA). It lists over 1,800 book titles that have been selected by BBYA since 1966. These titles are intended for classroom teachers, librarians, and parents who want to reach young adult or teenage readers.

In part 1 there are detailed chapters on how the titles were selected and trends in young adult publishing. There is also a very useful and practical chapter that contains topical lists of titles arranged in a format that is easy to copy and distribute. Among the topics covered are adventure, animals, family, fantasy, friendship, historical fiction, romance, sports, survival, war, westerns, and youths in trouble.

Part 2 consists of the book lists from 1966 through 1999. The 1st section lists titles alphabetically by author. The entries include the title, publication information, date, a brief description, whether the title is fiction or nonfiction, and an indication of which of the four publications the title is from. There were four publications based on four pre-conferences that the lists were culled from: "Still Alive: The Best of the Best, 1960–1974," "The Best of the Best Books, 1970–1983," "Nothin' But the Best: Best of the Best Books for Young Adults, 1966–1986," and "Here We Go Again: 2 Years of Best Books: Selections from 1967 to 1992." The next section has the book lists arranged by year, and the last section lists the best of the best by pre-conference.

An appendix lists the policies and procedures of the BBYA. This is followed by an index that includes names and titles listed in italics with the page numbers the titles appear on. This is a very helpful book and it is recommended for school, public, and academic libraries at colleges or universities that have a teacher education program or offer children's literature courses. [R: VOYA, Oct 2000, pp. 301-302]—**Jan S. Squire**

P, S

372.   **Writers for Young Adults, Supplement 1.** Ted Hipple, ed. Farmington Hills, Mich., Charles Scribner's Sons/Gale Group, 2000. 449p. illus. index. $80.00. ISBN 0-684-80618-5.

This is the 1st supplement to the original 3-volume set that covered 129 authors (see ARBA 98, entry 1104). As with the original, the primary intended audience is young adults at the middle, junior high and high school levels. In this volume there are 39 biographical and critical sketches on authors ranging from Jane Austen to Stephen King to Cynthia Rylant. The editors have included classic authors who are not thought of as writing specifically for young adults, but often are studied in school curriculums and read by young adults. Also included are authors who are on the edge, but highly popular with young adult readers, and authors who have won awards in young adult literature.

The highly readable and nicely formatted essays include biographical background information on the authors and a discussion of their works with some critical analysis. Entries are alphabetical by the author's last name and include a picture or drawing of the author. Notable works are addressed by title with a discussion of the story lines and characters following. This includes reflections and noted parallels on the author's life or the time period the work was written in. A nice feature is the sidebars on each page that serve as an area where definitions, notes, and other interesting facts are provided to supplement the text or explain a reference within the text. The sidebars also contain references to other works that might be of interest to the reader and information on how to contact the author. Each entry concludes with a selected bibliography of the author's works and works that have been written about the author.

There are two cumulative indexes. The category index lists titles alphabetically with the author in parentheses and corresponding volumes and pages. The general index is an alphabetical arrangement of authors, titles, series titles, and an embedded category index. What might have been very useful in the category index is a category for the award-winning titles such as Newbery winners.

This work is highly recommended for school and public libraries as an additional source for students to consult when researching young adult writers and their literature. [R: BR, May/June 2000, p. 76]—**Jan S. Squire**

DRAMA

C, P

373.   Bigsby, Christopher. **Contemporary American Playwrights.** New York, Cambridge University Press, 1999. 440p. index. $59.95; $22.95pa. ISBN 0-521-66108-0; 0-521-66807-7pa.

Bigsby attempts to address academe's neglect of American drama, particularly the works of contemporary playwrights. He writes that of post-World War II figures, only Edward Albee, Arthur Miller, Tennessee Williams, and August Wilson have received considerable attention, thus the need for more analysis of John Guare, Tina Howe, Tony Kushner, Emily Mann, Richard Nelson, Marsha Norman, David Rabe, Paula Vogel, Wendy Wasserstein, and Lanford Wilson. Only the latter has been the subject of a critical monograph. Choosing playwrights who deserve greater consideration or whose reputations are based on only a few plays or have been ignored, Bigsby, who co-edited *The Cambridge History of American Theatre, Volume 1: Beginnings to 1870* (see ARBA 99, entry 1247), examines each of their full-length plays within the context of their careers and the theater of their time. His goal is to emphasize the depth and quality of American dramatic writing.

Drawing extensively upon published interviews, Bigsby constructs each analysis around a similar formula. He begins with an overview of the playwright identifying the overall significance of the plays, their themes, and the critical consensus about the writer. He follows with a brief biography, focusing on the dramatist's first interest in the theater. The bulk of each chapter analyzes the works in chronological order. Some plays are treated briefly, with more in-depth analysis of the works Bigsby feels most significant. Details of productions and their receptions are included only when they help support his observations.

Bigsby's study helps fill the void in criticism of contemporary American drama and will be useful as introductions to the playwrights for high school students and college undergraduates. The book has negligible value, however, as a reference tool. It has footnote references to the works cited, but the only lists of titles by each dramatist appear in the index. It is unfortunate that each chapter does not include primary and secondary bibliographies and a list of the initial productions of each play.—**Michael Adams**

FICTION

General Works

C, P

374.   Jacob, Merle L., and Hope Apple. **To Be Continued: An Annotated Guide to Sequels.** 2d ed. Phoenix, Ariz., Oryx Press, 2000. 465p. index. $57.50. ISBN 1-57356-155-X.

Readers wanting to follow plots and characters from one of an author's novels to another will welcome this excellent guide to sequels that the authors define as novels that tell a continuing story or are united by a regional, philosophical, or social theme. For example, those who remember reading any one of Hervey Allen's enjoyable historical novels of the French and Indian War will find his three novels listed here. What they will also learn is that the trilogy was called *The Diminished Series*, a fact commonly unknown. Here, too, the World War II enthusiast will encounter a long listing of the sequel novelists, among them Herman Wouk, W. E. B. Griffin, Hans Kirst, and Theodore Plievier. And readers with a yen for Arthurian legends will find the listing and annotation of Persia Woolley's three Guinevere novels, as well as those of other sequel novelists (e.g., Mary Stewart, Marion Zimmer Bradley). Readers may be taken aback when looking for a well-known author, say Amanda Cross or Patricia Cornwell, and not finding a listing until remembering that mysteries, as a genre, have been excluded.

The work is alphabetically arranged by author, followed by the name of the series, the novels in the series, publication notes if necessary, an annotation of the novels, genre category, subject categories, and place and time categories. It should be noted that not all series have titles. Four very useful indexes are provided: title, genre, subjects and literary forms, and time and place. One unexpected genre, "Gentle Read," includes Christopher Morley, Richard Llewellyn, Elizabeth Goudge, and Paul Gallico. Reasonably priced, easily used, and attractively designed, this guide will be a worthwhile purchase for libraries with even modest fiction collections.

—**Charles R. Andrews**

C, P

375. Lesher, Linda Parent. **The Best Novels of the Nineties: A Reader's Guide.** Jefferson, N.C., McFarland, 1999. 482p. index. $39.95pa. ISBN 0-7864-0742-5.

The title of this book is dangerous. Anyone who dares to choose the "best" of anything (movies, buildings, books, etc.) is in for a battle. What the author has done is remarkable in its simplicity; she does not personally select the best books of the past decade, but offers readers commentary from other review sources ranging from *Wasafiri* to *Oprah Winfrey*, from *Library Journal* to *The Irish Times*, and from *Belles Lettres* to *The Lancet*. More than 100 well-recognized sources of book reviews in the English-speaking world are represented here. Lesher's personal touch is apparent in the division of the books into various subjects as well as in her well-written introductions to each section. From there, readers are offered the opinions of at least three review sources and an opportunity to get a good idea of what the book is about. Not all popular authors are covered in this book; no works by Stephen King or John Grisham are mentioned, and the period covered is a little short of a full decade, running from 1990 to just before the end of 1998. But Lesher offers potential readers a chance to sample the titles in a variety of subjects and themes—"readers' advisory service" at its best. Her commentaries are lively and well written and she selects reviews from a truly eclectic number of resources. There is a lot to enjoy in this book and it is highly recommended for all public libraries. [R: BL, Aug 2000, pp. 2194-2195; VOYA, Aug 2000, p. 219]—**Joseph L. Carlson**

C, P

376. **The Oxford Companion to Fairy Tales.** Jack Zipes, ed. New York, Oxford University Press, 2000. 601p. illus. $49.95. ISBN 0-19-860115-8.

Like other works in the Oxford Companion series, this volume provides thorough coverage and meticulous scholarship. Focusing on fairy tales from Europe and North America, the book contains more than 800 entries on specific tales, individual authors or illustrators, and many ancillary topics. For example, separate entries discuss use of folktale motifs by writers of mainstream adult literature (e.g., Margaret Atwood and Robert Coover), musical compositions inspired by fairy tales (e.g., work by Dvorak), treatment of fairy tales in popular culture (e.g., the British movie *Rapunzel Let Your Hair Down*), and even the use of folktales for propaganda purposes in former communist states. Substantial entries cover "Drama and Fairy Tales" and "Film and Fairy Tales," and shorter entries discuss individual plays and movies. The longest entries examine fairy tale traditions in specific regions (with the entry for France running 14 pages). Larger print and decorative borders give special emphasis to these essays, but their placement often interrupts shorter entries.

In the front matter, a scholarly introduction by Zipes explores the definition of a fairy tale. Major entries include short bibliographies within the text, and the back matter supplies comprehensive listings of fairy tale studies, collections, and specialized journals. An asterisk before a term or phrase within an entry provides an efficient cross-reference to another entry discussing that subject. Seventy black-and-white photographs and illustrations (many full page) add to the appeal of this very useful work. [R: Choice, Nov 2000, pp. 504-506; LJ, 1 Mar 2000, pp. 76-78]—**Albert Wilhelm**

Short Stories

C, P

377. **The Facts on File Companion to the American Short Story.** Abby H. P. Werlock and James P. Werlock, eds. New York, Facts on File, 2000. 542pv. index. $65.00. ISBN 0-8160-3164-9.

Arranged alphabetically, this sturdily bound work should find its way into the reference collection of most academic, public and high school libraries. Included here are author biographies and bibliographies; synopses and analyses of major short stories; summary descriptions of well-known characters; historical events that have influenced short story writers; notable awards for short fiction; and definitions of literary terms, themes and motifs. In addition, overview articles dealing with various cultural, literary schools or techniques are provided. Valuable cross-references enhance the entries.

Entries are for the most part terse and succinct, providing a capsule summary of the topic treated. Where appropriate, brief bibliographies are attached for further reading. Appendixes include winners of selected short story prizes (through 1998), such as the O. Henry Memorial Awards, Pushcart Prize, and so on. There is also a listing of short stories arranged by theme and topic such as "Americans in Asia," "Family Life," and "Marriage and Divorce," and a three-page selected general bibliography. A list of contributors followed by a full analytic index concludes the volume.

Breadth of treatment is impressive, as is the execution of this volume. Contributors tend to be college and university faculty specializing in literature. Careful editing and consistency of approach create a valuable reference tool that will be celebrated by librarians, students, faculty, and writers. This work is quite readable and highly recommended. [R: LJ, Jan 2000, pp. 82-84; VOYA, Aug 2000, p. 214; SLJ, Aug 2000, p. 136; BL, 1 Sept 2000, p. 178; BR, Nov/Dec 2000, p. 73]—**Edmund F. SantaVicca**

NATIONAL LITERATURE

American Literature

General Works

Bio-bibliography

C, P

378.   **African American Authors, 1745–1945: A Bio-Bibliographical Critical Sourcebook.** Emmanuel S. Nelson, ed. Westport, Conn., Greenwood Press, 2000. 525p. $99.50. ISBN 0-313-30910-8.

This work is a guide to the works of 78 African-American writers who flourished from 1745 to 1945. Well-known writers such as W. E. B. Du Bois and Richard Wright are covered, as well as less familiar authors such as Elizabeth Laura Adams and Zara Wright. Each article, 3 to 20 pages in length, contains sections on biography, major works and themes, critical receptions, and bibliographies of primary and secondary works. Authors of the articles are primarily academics, with some graduate students. *African American Authors* also contains an index and a selected bibliography of 35 books on African-American literature.

While the exclusion of Charlotte Forten and one or two others is questionable, no glaring omissions were found. The inclusion of Claude Brown (born 1937 and author of *Manchild in the Promised Land* in 1965) in a volume devoted to writers who did important work before 1946 is not explained. Entries are succinct, readable and accurate. The bibliographies are quite up to date, containing many works published in the 1990s. *African American Authors* contains entries not found in such reference works as the *Oxford Companion to African-American Literature* (see ARBA 98, entry 1129); *Selected Black American, African and Caribbean Writers* (2d ed.; see ARBA 86, entry 1134); or *African American Writers* (see ARBA 92, entry 1156). Two volumes in the Dictionary of Literary Biography series, *Afro-American Writers Before the Harlem Renaissance* and *Afro-American Writers from the Harlem Renaissance to 1940* (published by Gale), cover more authors and in greater detail but at three times the cost.

African American Authors, 1745–1945 is a very useful reference source. It should be acquired by all libraries, academic or public, where there is serious interest in American literature. [R: BL, 1 Dec 2000, p. 754; RUSQ, Fall 2000, pp. 80-81; C&RL News, June 2000, p. 527]—**Jonathan F. Husband**

Biography

C, P
379.   **African-American Writers: A Dictionary.** Shari Dorantes Hatch and Michael R. Strickland, eds. Santa Barbara, Calif., ABC-CLIO, 2000. 484p. illus. index. $75.00. ISBN 0-87436-959-2.

This book includes more than 530 biographical essays on African-American writers. These include very early writers like the poet Phyllis Wheatley, as well as many modern ones like James Baldwin. Most of these writers have established a literary reputation, which is broadly understood in this book to include, besides fiction, poetry, drama, historical writing, cultural and literary criticism, journalism, and political writing. A typical entry includes the author's birth and death dates, labels identifying major writing genres, brief biographical information related to the writing, some commentary about the meaning of the writing, and a brief list of references for further reading. There are also some entries for subjects such as spirituals, as well as publications like *Negro Digest*.

Especially useful—besides the author, title, and subject index—are an appendix by genre, such as biographies, nonfiction, and so on, and a chronology of all the writers in the book. There is also a chronology of firsts, such as the first published narrative written by a slave and a list of the abbreviations used in the references in the body of the dictionary.

Many general reference sources provide information about most of these writers, including especially the *Dictionary of Literary Biography* and *Contemporary Authors*. Other specialized reference books also cover selected African-American writers as a group, such as Valerie Smith's *African-American Writers* (see ARBA 92, entry 1156), but this new reference source will still be useful in addition to the many resources already published. [R: BL, 1 Oct 2000, p. 370; LJ, July 2000, p. 72; VOYA, Dec 2000, p. 373; BR, Jan/Feb 01, p. 74; Choice, Dec 2000, p. 676]—**David Isaacson**

C, P, S
380.   **American Ethnic Writers.** David Peck, ed. Hackensack, N.J., Salem Press, 2000. 2v. illus. index. (Magill's Choice). $95.00/set. ISBN 0-89356-157-6.

Secondary and higher education literature teachers and librarians everywhere will treasure this compilation of biography and criticism of authors for whom it is generally difficult to find much information. Each alphabetic entry provides enough information to get a student started on a research paper. The biographies are approximately one page in length. Each major work selected for inclusion receives a one-page critique.

Suggested readings at the end of the entries expand the resources available for research on each author. The citations listed have recent enough copyright dates to make them accessible either through acquisition or interlibrary loan. Each volume contains three indexes—author, title, and ethnic identity list.—**Lois Gilmer**

C, P, S
381.   Kort, Carol. **A to Z of American Women Writers: A Biographical Dictionary.** New York, Facts on File, 2000. 274p. illus. index. (Facts on File Library of American History Series). $40.00. ISBN 0-8160-3727-2.

Many of the 150 women profiled in this work have won prestigious awards and many have been relatively forgotten for hundreds of years. Criteria for inclusion are representation of a variety of literary genres, representation of the history of America, and accessibility of the works and bibliographic materials pertaining to them. All are American citizens and express themselves in English, even though many were born or lived in other countries.

Biographical entries range from Abigail Smith Adams, letter writer, to Zitkala Sa, short story writer and essayist. The entries include discussions of the writers' major works, varying from approximately one to three pages. All are followed by suggestions for further reading. Photographs are also included for some writers.

The book concludes with a bibliography of recommended sources on American women writers with entries by literary genre, region, subject matter, background, style, and year of birth. There is also a combined index of subject entries and illustration entries. This compact reference work fills a gap in American literary biography, providing hard-to-find information on increasingly popular writers. It is a must purchase for secondary school and academic libraries. It would also be a useful tool for public libraries. [R: VOYA, Oct 2000, p. 298; LJ, 15 Oct 99, p. 64; BR, Sept/Oct 2000, p. 62]—**Lois Gilmer**

British Literature

General Works

Bibliography

C, P

382.   **The Oxford Companion to English Literature.** 6th ed. Margaret Drabble, ed. New York, Oxford University Press, 2000. 1172p. $49.95. ISBN 0-19-866244-0.

The 6th edition of *The Oxford Companion to English Literature* is that rarest of creatures, a reference work that is brilliant in conception, magisterial in content, global in scope, and yet remarkably accessible and compulsively readable. It is a massive volume, containing more than 7,000 alphabetically arranged entries that survey the major writers, critics, periodicals, movements, and developments in English literature and related fields. Some 660 entries are new to this volume and the older entries have been rewritten and updated. New biographical entries profile writers as diverse as Kathy Acker, Nick Hornby, Carol Shields, and Stephen Zweig; and 16 new feature essays discuss such subjects as Anglo-Indian literature, black British literature, gay and lesbian literature, ghost stories, hypertext, and science fiction. The volume concludes with three appendixes—a monumental chronology of English literature from about 1000 C.E. to 1999, a list of the Poets Laureate, and a series of lists of the winners of the major literary awards.

For all that it is a superb achievement, *The Oxford Companion to English Literature* contains its share of lacunae. Why is the name J. S. LeFanu accorded a guide to pronunciation when such names as Ulrich Zwingli are not? Why does it date the first issue of *Weird Tales* as May 1923 rather than March? Why does the entry for Ezra Pound neglect to mention his association with *The Egoist*, whereas the entry for that magazine offers a cross-reference to Pound? Why does the entry for Arthur Machen fail to mention his birth name, and the entry for Rhoda Broughton fail to mention that she was niece to none other than J. S. LeFanu?

Such criticism is little more than nitpicking. Academic and public libraries alike will want the 6th edition of *The Oxford Companion to English Literature*. It is essential.—**Richard Bleiler**

African Literature

C, P

383.   Killam, Douglas, and Ruth Rowe. **The Companion to African Literatures.** Bloomington, Ind., Indiana University Press, 2000. 322p. maps. $49.95. ISBN 0-253-33633-3.

Billed as a comprehensive guide, Killam and Rowe's bio-bibliography dictionary provides a convenient, encompassing introduction to the major African literatures and African authors writing in English or in non-African languages available in English translation. Among those featured are well-known writers such as Nobel Prize winner Wole Soyinka and Chinua Achebe, and lesser-known writers such as Charity Waciuma of Kenya. In addition to author entries there are title entries for more prominent works. A selective list of topics discusses the major languages and literatures such as Gikuyu, Pidgin and Xhosa as well as Afrikaans, Francophone, and Lusophone literatures. Thematic entries include articles on Onitsha popular market literature, black consciousness, feminism and literature, writing systems in Africa, women in literature, apartheid, and oral tradition and folklore. The entries, contributed by more than 170 scholars and critics, are critical rather than descriptive, often comparing similarities among authors and works and citing other sources. Bibliographic references are identified within entries by year of publication, eliminating the need for an additional comprehensive bibliography. However, given the range of literatures, the suggestions for further reading are extremely minimal. The companion includes a useful country and author guide and two maps, one showing African nations with their dates of independence and the other identifying locations for the major languages treated in the entries. This valuable resource belongs in academic and public libraries, both those with major African Studies collections and those with limited resources given its broad scope. [R: C&RL News, April 2000, p. 323; Choice, Sept 2000, p. 90]—**Bernice Bergup**

Latin American Literature

C, P

384.   **Concise Encyclopedia of Latin American Literature.** Verity Smith, ed. Chicago, Fitzroy Dearborn, 2000. 678p. index. $75.00. ISBN 1-57958-252-4.

Compiled from a long list of renowned Latin American literature scholars, this volume is a useful reference tool for new users as well as experts. A condensation of the original *Encyclopedia of Latin American Literature and Culture* (see ARBA 97, entry 349), this edition has retained all the individual countries' literature surveys and all the thematic essays. The latter run the gamut, from general (African American literature, film, and the canon) to more specific topics (négritude, resistance literature, and metafiction). The rest of the alphabetically arranged entries include critical biographies and essays on specific works. This is the segment of the encyclopedia that, the editor of this volume states, has undergone a deliberate "guillotining." The reduced biographical essays, although limited to around 60, do not present a problem, since many writers are included in the country essays. There are also complete bibliographies for further reading suggestions.

However, some grouping choices are baffling. For example, Isabel Allende, whose merits are still debated by critics but who is recognized as an important Chilean writer, is grouped with Laura Esquivel, a less-prolific and recognized novelist, under the category of "best sellers." This could provide more misinformation than enlightenment. Nevertheless, the editor has been successful in concentrating a daunting amount of material into a concise and user-friendly, yet substantial, reference work.—**Stella T. Clark**

POETRY

C, P

385.   **World Poets.** Ron Padgett, ed. Farmington Hills, Mich., Charles Scribner's Sons/Gale Group, 2000. 3v. illus. index. $225.00/set. ISBN 0-684-80591-X.

This is an attractive set of 3 volumes with entries on 110 poets from classical to modern times from all continents except Australia. The entries are well planned: each entry has a photograph or portrait of the poet, a biography, a sample of the poetry, and a primary and secondary bibliography. The introduction indicates that the audience is conceived of as mainly high school students but also includes teachers. A leading consideration is which poets are studied in contemporary American high schools. But that is a consideration as much violated as observed—it is hard to imagine the difficult John Ashbery being taught in a high school, and a good many of the lesser-known poets in this collection are unknown even to trained college teachers.

The main weakness of the series is its wholesale deferral to contemporary political correctness. It is only secondarily concerned with literary merit, being chiefly concerned with trying to please various special interest or minority groups. Thus, there is no entry on Goethe or Schiller, none on Pushkin, and none on Victor Hugo, but there is a large contingent of gay and lesbian poets and a good number of African American and Native American poets. There is also only a moderate contingent of women poets.

There is a series of essays at the end of the third volume, some thematic (e.g., troubadours), some historical (e.g., Elizabethan poetry), and some technical (poetic forms and meter)—a mixed collection that points to incompletely resolved editorial principles. Some are so cursory that the reader is likely to remain as confused as informed. The series at its best is very useful, but users have to pick and choose more carefully than the editor did. [R: LJ, 15 Sept 2000, p. 62; BL, 15 Oct 2000, p. 486; VOYA, Dec 2000, p. 376]—**John B. Beston**

25 Music

GENERAL WORKS

Biography

C, P, S

386.   Slonimsky, Nicolas. **The Great Composers and Their Works.** Edited by Electra Yourke. New York, Schirmer Books/Gale Group, 2000. 2v. illus. index. $180.00/set. ISBN 0-02-864955-9.

Slonimsky is well known to every music librarian. He is the author/editor of numerous music reference works, such as *Baker's Biographical Dictionary of Musicians* (8th ed.; see ARBA 93, entry 1244). He also contributed articles, columns, and other short pieces to various journals throughout his life. His daughter, Electra Slonimsky Yourke, has taken it upon herself to gather and edit a portion of these writings. The result is *The Great Composers and Their Works*, a 2-volume study of selected popular works of 19 composers.

The volumes are divided chronologically, beginning with the baroque period and ending with modernism. Each chapter begins with a short biographical essay on the composer that includes a timeline. The following section of each composer entry concentrates on discussing and analyzing selected works, which are listed chronologically by date of composition within their genre (e.g., orchestral, chamber, vocal). These sections are also brief, as the number of works included ranges from 8 to 12 for each composer. Some pieces are accompanied by excerpts from original scores. A nice feature found throughout each essay is the highlighting of various musical terms, with definitions of each term given as marginal aids. There are black-and-white portraits of each composer at the beginning of each entry. Volume 2 includes a list of Websites as well as short bibliographies and discographers for each composer.

These slim volumes are too concise to do justice to the material covered. They have a textbook quality, and because of the style of writing, this reviewer would consider this work no better or worse than others of this nature. The audience for this book can range from high school students to undergraduate music majors. Nevertheless, it would make a decent addition to reference collections in school, college, and public libraries. [R: BL, 15 Oct 2000, p. 484]—**Richard Slapsys**

Dictionaries and Encyclopedias

C, P, S

387.   **The Harvard Concise Dictionary of Music and Musicians.** Don Michael Randel, ed. Cambridge, Mass., Harvard University Press, 1999. 757p. illus. $35.00. ISBN 0-674-0084-6.

Randel identifies this book as the successor to the 1978 *Harvard Concise Dictionary of Music*. However, the new work is much more substantial than the earlier pocket-size paperback one. Moreover, Randel cites two works as sources: *The New Harvard Dictionary of Music* (Harvard University Press, 1986) and *The Harvard Biographical Dictionary of Music* (see ARBA 97, entry 1024). Students of music history, theory, and performance;

amateur musicians; and those who simply listen to music and occasionally read about it are the intended audience for this work. The scope is primarily Western concert music, with some coverage of jazz and popular music, as well as some non-Western traditions. Illustrations of musical instruments, and in some cases musical notation, are provided, as are translations of terms in foreign languages. Cross-references are indicated by asterisks within the text, and some terms are explained within other entries rather than individually. Some entries are articles of several paragraphs, normally a characteristic of an encyclopedia rather than a dictionary, but in keeping with traditional lexicographical practice for music.

It is this traditionalism that both validates and bedevils the work. The rationale for providing yet another musical dictionary is questionable. Since the first source work is already 14 years old, the present one evidently did not arise from recent developments in the field. For example, the entry for "Multimedia" refers to "Mixed media," where one reads of combining live sound, movement, film, tape, and setting—a description that applied equally well 50 years ago. Also, some entries seem extremely obscure.

This criticism, however, is not merited by the work in hand so much as by the general publication practice of musical lexicography. Randel has produced no radical work here, but one that faithfully replicates the patterns of his forebears. That he might be expected to do otherwise may be considered unreasonable or even heretical in some quarters, considering the weight of musical traditionalism. Pleasant as this work is in itself, selectors of library reference materials may well already have adequate resources in their collection to cover most users' needs without adding this one. [R: LJ, Dec 99, p. 106]—**Ian Fairclough**

Directories

C, P

388.   **MusicHound World: The Essential Album Guide.** Adam McGovern, ed. Farmington Hills, Mich., Visible Ink Press/Gale, 2000. 1096p. illus. index. $26.95pa./with disc. ISBN 1-57859-039-6.

The writers of this book define world music as music that does not fit into the Anglo-Western pop universe. In this volume are reviews of more than 1,000 acts and 20,000 CDs from more than 85 countries. Entries in the main section are arranged alphabetically by the name of the individual artist or band. Each entry begins with biographical information and a discussion of the artist or band's sound and their stature and significance in music. Also included is the country where the artist is currently based. Each entry also provides a buyer's guide. "What to Buy" discusses the albums the compilers feel are essential purchases. "What to Buy Next," "What to Avoid," and "The Rest" include everything else that is available from the artist in question. "Worth Searching For" includes out-of-print items, bootlegs, guest appearances on other artists' albums, and so on. There are also sections entitled "Crucial Influences on This Act's Music" and "Acts That Have Been Influenced by This Artist or Group." Albums are rated if they were available for review before press time.

Other sections of the book include an alphabetical listing and discussion of compilation albums from around the world, a bibliography of books and magazines where one can read more about world music, and a listing of U.S. radio stations that feature world-music programming. There is also an index listing albums that achieved the highest rating from the *MusicHound World* writers, a country index that arranges the artists and groups covered in the main section according to the country where they were born (or where the bands were formed), a contributor's index with the names of the entries they wrote for this volume, and a series index to all the artists and groups included in the MusicHound series of books with the names of the books they appear in. A CD sampler of world music is also included.

The book features sidebars offering interesting information on subjects such as the bagpipe, Irish step dancing, polkas worldwide, and the talking drum. Black-and-white captioned photographs are interspersed throughout the text. Each entry is introduced with a boldfaced heading, while guide words at the top of each page facilitate access. The 1,096 pages make this a pretty hefty volume that music lovers will no doubt enjoy browsing for long periods of time. [R: LJ, 1 Feb 2000, p. 76]—**Dana McDougald**

INDIVIDUAL COMPOSERS
AND MUSICIANS

Biography

C, P

389. Studwell, William E. **They Also Wrote: Evaluative Essays on Lesser-Known Popular American Songwriters Prior to the Rock Era.** Lanham, Md., Scarecrow, 2000. 421p. index. $69.50. ISBN 0-8108-3789-7.

The search for lesser-known popular American songwriters of the nineteenth and twentieth centuries is a new and current topic in the area of music reference research. Warren Vache has recently published his extensive collection of less famous songwriters in *The Unsung Songwriters* (Scarecrow, 2000) and researchers also now have this title by Studwell. Both reference works are determined to dispel the myth that the majority of great and classic songs of the past hundred years or so were written by a handful of well-known composers, such as Irving Berlin, Cole Porter, or George Gershwin.

Unlike other standard reference works discussing songs and songwriters, such as *The Great Song Thesaurus* (2d ed.; see ARBA 90, entry 1279), Studwell has decided to organize the text by songwriter rather than song title. He profiles 344 American songwriters who were active from 1848 until 1955. Composers are collected into three distinct categories and arranged alphabetically by name. These categories are "Famous People Not Primarily Known for Their Songwriting," "Underappreciated Masters, Contributors, and Creators of Classics," and "Obscure Creators of Standards and Songs and Minor Songwriters of Note." Each entry is brief, some not more than a paragraph in length.

The entries are organized in three parts: brief biographical information on each songwriter, a discussion of their best-known songs, and a chronological list of lesser-known songs. The book concludes with a short bibliography, an index of people, and an index of titles. Some of the names mentioned in the first section of the contents will be familiar to people who know popular music and jazz, while the other two sections include names most likely familiar only to musicologists. Studwell should be commended for his effort to enlighten students, teachers, and others interested in this aspect of American popular music. His work is highly recommended for all music reference collections.—**Richard Slapsys**

Handbooks and Yearbooks

P, S

390. Opdyke, Steven. **The Printed Elvis: The Complete Guide to Books About the King.** Westport, Conn., Greenwood Press, 1999. 320p. index. (Music Reference Collection, no.75). $49.95. ISBN 0-313-30815-2.

Opdyke describes various types of books about Elvis Presley by his family, business associates, and fans, including reference works and guides to collectible items. He symbolically assigns each chapter the title of a song by Elvis Presley and then begins each with a narrative essay. Some annotations are more than one page in length and some are also anecdotal. Other times he has combined several books by the same author for annotations. Opdyke evaluates the quality of these books on Elvis. For example, he notes that Priscilla Presley's book is the cream of the crop for family members (p. 10). In many cases, Opdyke also gives the relationship of the writer to Elvis. For example, Joe Esposito was a manager, Sam Thompson was a bodyguard, Billy Smith was Elvis's cousin, and Red West was an original member of the group accompanying Elvis.

There are several photographs and illustrations, including one with President Nixon and another of the Elvis postage stamps. Opdyke concludes the book with a series of commentaries. He presents details that are not explained well in works about Presley's life, such as the reasons Elvis shot at a television with Robert Goulet on the screen. He then describes Elvis's phenomenal success, the use of the music of black Americans, and the relationship between Elvis and the Colonel (Tom Park). In the guide to collecting Elvis memorabilia, Opdyke tells what to look for and how to find it. He also includes two collector profiles and a chronological listing of books.

There are four indexes: authors; songs, films, and albums; books, magazines, and publications; and a general index. The index citations are by page number; this is quite sufficient given the length of bibliographic annotations. Most entries in the general index are straightforward, but the subdivisions under "Presley, Elvis" do not appear to have an alphabetical or classified order—these appear largely sequential. Annotations and listings of books are much more substantial than in John A. Whisler's *Elvis Presley: Reference Guide and Discography* (Scarecrow, 1981). [R: Choice, April 2000, p. 1436]—**Ralph Hartsock**

MUSICAL FORMS

Country Music

C, P

391.   **Country Music Annual 2000.** Charles K. Wolfe and James E. Akenson, eds. Lexington, Ky., University Press of Kentucky, 2000. 175p. illus. $20.00pa. ISBN 0-8131-0989-2.

This inaugural edition of the *Country Music Annual* contains a series of essays on various aspects of this culturally rich form of music. The editors define country music in a broad sense, both in subject matter and in analytical approach, and include articles that look at old-time music, western swing, honky-tonk, bluegrass, Cajun, country rock, and many other incarnations country music has taken. The contributors give a wide range of approaches to their essays—musical, historical, sociological, cultural, educational, and even medical.

The essays are scholarly studies on subjects such as country singers and religion, studio musicians, southern humor, and the structure of country songs. Each essay ends with bibliographic information and some contain illustrations and black-and-white photographs. The work ends with providing credential information about the contributors.

As the authors intended, this annual provides a publication platform for the music research community. But this is not a work for general country music fans. Instead, it is laid out for a very limited audience of music scholars. Some music libraries and universities with strong curriculums in music research may find this work useful.—**Cari Ringelheim**

Operatic

C, P

392.   Kuhn, Laura. **Baker's Dictionary of Opera.** New York, Macmillan Library Reference/Simon & Schuster Macmillan, 2000. 1047p. illus. $90.00. ISBN 0-02-865349-1.

Being a direct offshoot of *Baker's Dictionary of Music* (see ARBA 99, entry 1123), this effort contains the same type of information and detail found in the original, but with its emphasis being opera. It is noteworthy that Baker, for whom this dictionary is named, was the originator of this series but has been dead since 1934.

The actual dictionary portion of the book contains more than 900 pages and, according to the publisher, 1,000 entries. The entries, alphabetically arranged, include singers, conductors, and composers who were and are associated with opera from its beginnings in the sixteenth century to the present. In a decidedly anecdotal style, each entry contains standard biographical information plus details that pertain particularly to the man or woman's contribution to opera. Occasionally, the information becomes more personal—as in the instance of Leonard Warren dying on the stage of the Metropolitan Opera while performing in *La Forza del Destino*. Irregularly, some entries end with a bibliography or a list of works.

Following the dictionary portion, there is a series of appendixes for the remaining 120 pages. Of some interest is a timeline of famous operas that is followed by opera terms and opera synopses. This is an excellent work that gives a great deal of information for the relatively modest price.—**Phillip P. Powell**

Popular

C, P

393.   Cowden, Robert H. **Popular Singers of the Twentieth Century: A Bibliography of Biographical Materials.**
Westport, Conn., Greenwood Press, 1999. 497p. index. (Music Reference Collection, no.78). $85.00. ISBN 0-313-29333-3.

Cowden has developed a massive index to basic materials about 971 popular music performers of the past century. His criteria included those who sang on Broadway, in Hollywood films, in operettas, through recordings, and even in cabarets. The beginning list of artists was created only if a book or other substantial amount of material was written about the artists. The individual entries also have other performers noted in passing if references are made to them. Each entry has a brief two or three-line description with life dates and places.

The index includes 29 major reference sources (all coded), periodical articles (dated but with no page references), autobiographies and biographies, 346 collective titles, and "additional sources and cross-references" (p. 57), all published through early 1997. At the end, there is an all-in-one index to singers, authors, compilers, editors, and translators.

One major shortfall of this work is that there is no real information about the periodicals—just a title and a month or date. Also, not every performer has an article. Most have just a major reference source and a book. There is a lot of valuable information in periodical articles, so it would be beneficial if Cowden produced a second volume with just periodical articles, and more of them. Overall, the book is a good reference source. [R: Choice, Jan 2000, p. 896]—**Dean Tudor**

Sacred

C, P

394.   **Worship Music: A Concise Dictionary.** Edward Foley, ed. Collegeville, Minn., Liturgical Press, 2000.
332p. $45.00. ISBN 0-8146-5889-X.

True to its title, this dictionary is concise, focused on the religious aspects of music. In the composer and hymnist biographies the authors emphasize sacred music; thus, the article on Beethoven is short, while those on Isaac Watts or Johann Sebastian Bach are lengthy.

The scope is Judaic and Christian in a very ecumenical and comprehensive sense. The volume is excellent in coverage of Roman Catholic, eastern Orthodox, and Hebrew traditions in music. Entries for composers and theologians range from Boethius to Howard Hanson, and are arranged by the best-known form of the name (e.g., Ellington, Duke; Thomas Aquinas), with numerous cross-references. Articles include a bibliography of one to three major sources in English. Forms, styles, and events (such as motet, jazz, and Rosh Hashanah) are defined in a straightforward manner. Several specific compositions, settings, and collections have brief descriptions, such as B minor Mass (J. S. Bach), Stabat mater dolorosa, and Kentucky Harmony. Translations into English are given. Ensembles, such as Fisk Jubilee Singers and the Royal College of Organists, are included. Filing is letter by letter.

There are extensive cross-references because of the concise format. Operating from a bottom-up approach, there is one caveat—some references are not exact. There is no reference from Slavonic to Russian and Slavonic chant; Jewish music to classical music only refers one to the era dominated by Mozart; and there is no general article on music, linking or relating the various eras, such as baroque, classical, or romantic. There is also no article on twentieth-century movements or post-romanticism.

The layout is excellent, with the entries very readable in a compact format. Libraries from churches and synagogues to academic music libraries will find this volume quite useful.—**Ralph Hartsock**

26 Mythology, Folklore, and Popular Culture

FOLKLORE

C, P

395.   **Brewer's Dictionary of Phrase & Fable.** 16th ed. Revised by Adrian Room. New York, HarperCollins, 1999. 1298p. illus. $50.00. ISBN 0-06-019653-X.

Adrian Room, the editor of *Brewer's Dictionary of Phrase & Fable*, is a Fellow of the Royal Geographical Society and a member of the English Place-Name Society and the American Name Society. He has authored over 50 reference books. Cassell, in the United Kingdom, publishes new reference works under the name Brewer. Ebenezer Cobham Brewer, a nineteenth-century British compiler of reference books, first published *Brewer's Dictionary of Phrase & Fable* in 1870.

The newest edition includes recent expressions, names of historical and fictional characters, famous nicknames, and examples of phrases that include the cited word. This dictionary contains old and new words and phrases not found in other resources on ancient, classical history of Britain and Ireland. It also has world mythology, religion, and British customs and beliefs. This reference work is prolific with regard to Shakespeare's works. The editor includes cross-references, with *see* and main entries. Words and names in small capital letters in definitions have entries of their own. American phrases are included and noted as such, but are less numerous. It refers to many terms of American rock and roll. Some American versions of words could have been included but were not.

The book is fascinating, humorous, and engrossing. This reference book is highly recommended for any library with students or patrons wanting to know more about British culture, history, and literature, plus other esoteric items of trivia or consequence. [R: BL, 15 Oct 2000, p. 480; LJ, July 2000, p. 72]—**Peggy D. Odom**

C, P

396.   **Myths and Legends.** New York, Macmillan Library Reference/Simon & Schuster Macmillan, 2000. 436p. illus. index. (Macmillan Profiles). $75.00. ISBN 0-02-865376-9.

Part of Macmillan's Profiles series, *Myths and Legends* is an impressively ambitious and assured reference work that will become one of the indispensable books on myth and legend to supplement middle and high school curricula. This work features over 140 articles representing different historical periods and cultures that depict gods, goddesses, monsters, heroes, supernatural beings, and legendary people and places from ancient times through the twentieth century. Myths and legends are presented as natural, dynamic stories created by people of every society. Entries cover Baba Yaga, a witch and ogress who is the ancient goddess of death and regeneration of Slavic mythology with roots in the pre-Indo-European matrilineal pantheon. Also from Greek mythology emerged a race of giants with one eye in the middle of their forehead called Cyclopes, as well as a mythic race of female warriors, the Amazons, who are mentioned by Homer in his famous epics, the *Iliad* and the *Odyssey*. American folk hero Paul Bunyan, a giant lumberjack of tall tales, is an example of an occupational folk hero. The tall tale flourished in the U.S. and is characteristic of the popular psychology that resulted from the rapid expansion of the developing country in the nineteenth century.

This volume also features mythological characters from ancient Egypt, Mesopotamia, and Rome. Aztec, Inca, and native North American myths are alongside important myths from Asian and African cultures. Also covered are Germanic, Irish, and Scandinavian cultures. The choice of material is eclectic, based on relevance to the history and social studies curricula of American schools, and represents a broad cultural, geographic, and chronological range. Brief definitions of important terms in the main text can be found in the margins. At the end of the book is a glossary that provides the reader with a broader list of definitions. Appearing in shaded boxes throughout the volume are sidebars that relate to and amplify topics. Additionally, in the margins are pull quotes highlighting essential facts. For further research on mythological and legendary figures there is an extensive list of suggested reading, from books and articles to Websites. Finally, a thorough index provides thousands of additional points of entry into the work. *Myths and Legends* will reward anyone interested in this compelling topic and is appropriate in public libraries and colleges. [R: BL, 1 May 2000, p. 1688; SLJ, May 2000, p. 90]

—**Magda Zelinská-Ferl**

C, P

397.   Simpson, Jacqueline, and Steve Roud. **A Dictionary of English Folklore.** New York, Oxford University Press, 2000. 411p. $32.95. ISBN 0-19-210019-X.

This attractive English folklore dictionary is both interesting and informative. While "folklore" is broadly defined and the tooth fairy discussed along with dragons, barrows, and standing stones, "English" is narrowed to exclude Scotland, Wales, the Isle of Man, and the Channel Islands. The customs of the many ethnic groups in England have been omitted as too fluid and complex. The belief that most folklore traces back to pre-Christian practices is viewed with skepticism.

Entries include such places as Stonehenge, Glastonbury, and Cadbury Castle; mythical forms like mermaids, fairies, and vampires (but only white witches); customs such as mumming, maypole dancing, and well-dressing along with games like hopscotch, and prisoners' base; folklorists (e.g., Peter and Iona Opie, the Grimm brothers, and William Hone) and societies devoted to folklore and folk songs; and purely mythical figures (e.g., Puck, Merlin, and Old Mother Hubbard) or historical figures surrounded by folklore (e.g., Guy Fawkes, St. Swithin, King Arthur). Sources are frequently listed at the end of the entry and copious cross-references also appear, but more would be helpful; for example, Chalk figures as well as Hill figures or Troy Towns separate from Mazes could be found here.

The extensive bibliography of almost 300 works alone will make this volume valuable as a resource for folklorists. There has been a need for such a modern study of the folklore of England, which this study admirably fills. Entertainingly written, it should appeal to a wide readership. [R: LJ, 15 Sept 2000, pp. 60-62; BL, 15 Dec 2000, p. 841]—**Charlotte Lindgren**

MYTHOLOGY

P

398.   Dubios, Pierre. **The Great Encyclopedia of Faeries.** Illustrated by Claudine Sabatier and Roland Sabatier. New York, Simon & Schuster, 1999. 183p. illus. $25.00. ISBN 0-684-86957-8.

This richly illustrated encyclopedia provides an entertaining and informative look into the faery kingdom. Dubios presents dozens of entries on the most powerful and enchanting denizens of this magical world. He provides readers with authoritative information detailing the customs, habitat, and activities of various mystical creatures including the Valkyries of Valhalla, the Babouchka of Russia, Banshees, Dryads, Bogey Beasts, and Sirens.

The encyclopedia opens with several essays that discuss the origin, history, and mythology of faeries. Entries are divided under six chapters: "Maidens of Clouds and of Time," "The Faeries of the Hearth," "The Golden Queens of the Middle World," "The Faeries of Rivers and the Sea," "The Maidens of the Green Kingdom," and "The Ethereal Ones of Infinite Dreams." A bibliography is also included. Judging by the advanced vocabulary and some of the more mature illustrations, this work is recommended for older audiences. It is not recommended for children.—**Cari Ringelheim**

POPULAR CULTURE

Dictionaries and Encyclopedias

P, S

399.   Gulevich, Tanya. **Encyclopedia of Christmas.** Illustrated by Mary Ann Stavros-Lanning. Detroit, Omnigraphics, 2000. 729p. illus. index. $48.00. ISBN 0-7808-0387-6.

The *Encyclopedia of Christmas* is Omnigraphics' prized contribution to the world of reference tools. It is the most thoroughly researched example of the publisher's volumes covering holidays and fills a gap in the literature. Highly readable entries chronicle all aspects of Christmas, both historical and modern, in over 20 countries, regions, and cultures. This is an outstanding background source for all ages and levels because it presents complex traditions, complete with attendant vocabulary, in easily digested summaries.

The 186 entries, arranged alphabetically by topic, range from 100 to 2,000 words in length. Longer entries are subdivided into sections such as legends, origins, history, and so on. Although the book is not comprehensive, the coverage is surprisingly multicultural. Standout articles include "Kwanzaa," "Commercialism," "Gifts," and those on Christmas in individual countries. Bold text identifies references to other entries. Most entries conclude with references for further information and relevant Web addresses.

Appealing black-and-white illustrations drawn by Mary Ann Stavros-Lanning adorn the book, but a few color illustrations would improve the publication significantly. Appendixes include a comprehensive bibliography and lists of groups and Websites relating to Christmas. The index covers the important concepts and other details embedded within entries, including countries, customs, symbols, characters, foods, and ethnic groups. As a superb handbook to holiday traditions in the United States and internationally, the *Encyclopedia of Christmas* is highly recommended for all types of libraries and is essential for K-12 and public libraries. [R: C&RL News, Mar 2000, p. 229; RUSQ, Sept 2000, pp. 408-409]—**Anne C. Moore**

P, S

400.   Thompson, Sue Ellen. **Holiday Symbols.** 2d ed. Detroit, Omnigraphics, 2000. 694p. index. $58.00. ISBN 0-7808-0423-6.

Thompson's 1st edition was a splendid start, and a much-needed, quick-reference source for all libraries worldwide. The 1st edition covers thousands of international holidays and celebrations and, most importantly, links the symbols with each celebration. Obviously answering to an inundation of requests to be included, Thompson's 2d edition has added several hundred entries. A simple check of the index shows at least 10 added pages, which translates into multiple actual additions. Librarians will be pleased.

There is one small cavil. It is very American. For example, of the 2d edition entries, Thompson includes annual events, many of them promotional in nature, such as the Kentucky Derby, the Indianapolis 500, and the "I Have a Dream" speech. Do these events truly count as holiday symbols? What is missing are so many non-American celebrations such as Victoria Day, St. David's Day, Dominion Day, the Eisteddfodd, the Bonhomme Carnival, and Caribanna. Indeed, Thompson must rely on readers to send that information in. Then the 3d edition will be a truly international research tool.

Otherwise, the eclectic nature of the entries is quite charming. Thompson has done her research well. This is a good reference source for anyone searching the not-so-usual sources of celebration throughout the world. However, the next edition should not call itself *Holiday Symbols*, as this work's scope is evidently much more than events, celebrations, and their symbols. [R: SLJ, Nov 2000, p. 97; BR, Jan/Feb 01, pp. 79-80]—**Gail Benjafield**

Handbooks and Yearbooks

C, P, S

401.   Trawicky, Bernard. **Anniversaries and Holidays.** 5th ed. Chicago, American Library Association, 2000. 311p. index. $68.00. ISBN 0-8389-0695-8.

This latest edition of the American Library Association's *Anniversaries and Holidays* is an easy-to-use and reliable guide to finding information on celebrations throughout the United States and abroad. The 5th edition provides listings on 3,500 celebrations, 33 percent more than what was presented in the 4th edition. The book is divided into three sections: "Calendar of Fixed Days," "On Calendars," and "Resources Related to Anniversaries and Holidays." The "Calendar of Fixed Days" lists civil holidays, holy holidays, and anniversaries for important dates in history. The second section on calendars will help readers become familiar with the Gregorian, Christian Liturgical, Jewish, Islamic, and Chinese calendars. This resource will be a valuable edition to any public, school, or academic library needing ready-reference information on holidays and anniversaries.

—**Shannon Graff Hysell**

27 Performing Arts

GENERAL WORKS

Dictionaries and Encyclopedias

C, P, S

402. Moore, Frank Ledlie, and Mary Varchaver. **Dictionary of the Performing Arts.** Chicago, Contemporary Books, 1999. 565p. $50.00; $24.95pa. ISBN 0-8092-3009-7; 0-8092-3010-0pa.

This dictionary encompasses terms from all of the performing arts, focusing on the vocabulary used by people who perform and work on or around the stage. The dictionary is intended to make understandable the specialized vocabularies between disciplines in the performing arts. More than 6,700 terms are defined by Moore, a professional composer and author of *Crowell's Handbook of World Opera* (Greenwood Press, 1972), and Varchaver, a professional pianist, writer, and editor.

The disciplines included are as diverse as puppetry, circus, carnival, acoustics, recording, stagecraft, makeup, and vaudeville. Television, motion pictures, and the recording industry are included when definitions in these areas are useful within the scope of stage performance. Differences in meaning between disciplines in the arts are made clear. For example, the term "mask" has six different definitions in the disciplines of acting, costume, lighting, makeup, stagecraft, and theater. Slang and jargon are included, as well as terms that are no longer in common use, but illuminate the definitions of works in current usage. Moore and Varchaver demonstrate their passion for the arts, and for this dictionary, by returning to the original Aristotle's *Poetics* and consulting scholars to ensure precision of definitions in Greek drama for modern users.

Definitions are in simple alphabetic arrangement and are meticulously crafted with numerous cross-references, *see* references, and examples. The authors are attentive to variant spellings and indicate the derivation and pronunciation of terms that originate in foreign languages. The appendix, an alphabetic listing of people mentioned in the text, is disappointing in that it includes only birth and death dates, country of origin, and discipline. Appendix entries do not allow the user to refer back to the definition where the person was originally mentioned and serve only to highlight this work's Western focus.

Overall, the authors succeed in their goal to make this book practical and useful for the performer, technician, student, writer, and researcher. It is highly recommended for all academic, public, and secondary school libraries. [R: LJ, Jan 2000, p. 86]—**Arlene McFarlin Weismantel**

DANCE

C, P, S

403. **The Oxford Dictionary of Dance.** By Debra Craine and Judith Mackrell. New York, Oxford University Press, 2000. 527p. $39.95. ISBN 0-19-860106-9.

In this dictionary more than 2,500 entries focus mainly, and at great length, on ballets and dances, dancers, choreographers, teachers, designers, and organizations. Technical terms are also explained. Selected subjects range from ice dancing to rock ballets, and include country entries and ballet subjects such as Dracula ballets. Composer entries are concerned with dance works composed or used for dance. Yet the dancers' entries often cause wonderment as to why some names appear and others are omitted. All of the big names are here, but few of the new young principal dancers of New York's major companies, no matter how dazzling (such as Angel Corella), are included.

Care is taken to clarify confusing issues. The entry under "Ballet Russe" exists solely to explain how these two words have been used by a number of ballet companies in both Europe and America as part of their company's official name. Each individual company using these words gets its own entry in its proper alphabetical spot. The proportion of space allotted the entries has been accomplished with great skill. When a short, terse entry is sufficient that is what it gets, but some of the biographies of dance's greats are detailed and long enough to grace a multivolume work. Best of all, the entries are written with grace and style.—**George Louis Mayer**

FILM, TELEVISION, AND VIDEO

Dictionaries and Encyclopedias

C, P

404.   Netzley, Patricia D. **Encyclopedia of Movie Special Effects.** Phoenix, Ariz., Oryx Press, 2000. 291p. illus. index. $65.00. ISBN 1-57356-167-3.

Special effects, very loosely defined as "trick photography" employed to create illusory impressions, have been a staple of motion pictures almost since the beginning of the medium. Pioneer French filmmaker George Melies was routinely using stop motion, fast motion, and exposure techniques since the late nineteenth century (*Cinderella*, 1899). While the techniques utilized by special effects technicians have obviously become more sophisticated over time, the goal remains the same: create a visual effect that can "fool" the audience. Netzley's encyclopedia is a clear, concise, well-illustrated, and useful guide to all aspects of special effects (visual, mechanical, and makeup) in motion pictures. Information targeted toward the lay reader is provided in an A-to-Z format in 366 entries that cover terms (postproduction), techniques (compositing), equipment (telemetry device), films, and individuals. Every movie awarded an Oscar for special effects is discussed (*The Thief of Baghdad*, 1940; *Star Wars*, 1977; and so on), as are films that introduced significant advances in the medium (*Wonder Man*, 1945; *Lost in Space*, 1998). Entries for special effects wizards like Willis O'Brien (*King Kong*, 1933), Ray Harryhausen (*Jason and the Argonauts*, 1963), and makeup artist Rick Baker (*Men in Black*, 1997) are particularly useful. Special effects houses like Industrial Light & Magic are discussed in expanded entries. Appendixes include a list of Academy Award winners and nominees for special effects (1939–1998), special effects magazines, and special effects houses. The encyclopedia also includes topical and general indexes as well as a select bibliography. Well researched and highly readable, this reference work is recommended for academic and public libraries with film studies collections. [R: LJ, 1 Mar 2000, p. 76; BR, May/June 2000, p. 80]—**David K. Frasier**

C, P

405.   Singleton, Ralph S., and James A. Conrad. **Filmmaker's Dictionary.** 2d ed. Edited by Janna Wong Healy. Hollywood, Calif., Lone Eagle, 2000. 358p. $22.95. ISBN 1-58065-022-8.

This is a surefire hit for every public and academic library. With his seminal 1st edition of this work, author Singleton established himself as the authority on terms, phrases, and jargon of the motion picture industry. This knowledge was gleaned from several years spent working as a movie and television producer, along with working with such luminaries as Sidney Lumet, Martin Scorsese, and William Friedkin. Conrad brings academic expertise to the work. Together they have produced a valuable, authoritative look at the often confusing terminology used in filmmaking. More than 5,000 words and phrases are examined, most in paragraphs ranging from 30 to 75 words. Mingled in with the obvious expressions are such in-house words as *moo print*, *inkie*, and *insqueeze*. Occasionally, snippets of history are thrown in: Buffalo Bill Cody and Wild Bill Hickok were Pony Express riders, the Oscar award is made out of pure britannia, and African American cowboy Bill Picket introduced steer wrestling to modern rodeos. The lack of an introduction, which would have explained the scope of the work, and the absence of a bibliography are two minor quibbles with an otherwise exceptional reference item. Similar titles include Ira Konigsberg's *The Complete Film Dictionary* (see ARBA 98, entry 1285) and Desi Bognar's *International Dictionary of Broadcasting and Film* (1999). The ever-changing movie and television industries make this contemporary work a popular and welcome addition to all libraries. [R: Choice, Jan 01, p. 878]—**Joseph L. Carlson**

Filmography

C, P

406.   McCarty, Clifford. **Film Composers in America: A Filmography, 1911–1970.** 2d ed. New York, Oxford University Press, 2000. 534p. index. $75.00. ISBN 0-19-511473-6.

McCarty, editor of *Film Music I* (Garland, 1989), identifies over 1,500 composers who have written musical scores for more than 20,000 U.S. feature films, cartoons, shorts, documentaries, trailers, and avant-garde works through 1970. McCarty only includes original or background scores composed expressly for a particular film. Source music, preexistent music, and individual songs are excluded. The chief purpose of this volume is to establish the authorship of film scores—composer's biographies and score particulars are also excluded.

Entries are alphabetically arranged by composer, with film titles listed chronologically within each entry. A supplementary list of names not found in the book's main section and an index to film titles conclude the work and improve its usefulness. Patrons should be aware, however, that the information provided here is minimal. For example, readers can get a chronological list of all of Carl Stalling's scores for hundreds of cartoons, but McCarty provides no further detail (length of score, key, exact release dates, and so on). Some biographical information on the more obscure composers would also have been helpful.

Despite its limitations, McCarty's work is an essential resource for anyone interested in the history of film music. It supplements his earlier, much smaller edition of the same title (Da Capo, 1972) and serves as an excellent companion to Film Score Monthly (http://www.filmscoremonthly.com/) and James Limbacher's Keeping Score Series, 1972–1997 (Scarecrow, 1981–1998). It is recommended for all film and music collections. [R: Choice, Oct 2000, pp. 302-303]—**Anthony J. Adam**

Videography

C, P

407.   **VideoHound's Golden Movie Retriever 2000.** Martin Connors and Jim Craddock, eds. Farmington Hills, Mich., Visible Ink Press/Gale, 2000. 1700p. index. $21.95pa. ISBN 1-57859-042-6. ISSN 1095-371X.

Containing about 1,000 more capsule movie reviews than the previous year's edition (to bring this volume's number to about 24,000), this annual directory is multiply indexed by director, cinematographer, award, composer, and so forth. Gale's directory exclusively lists movies that are available on videocassette (in the U.S. or elsewhere, up to about October 1999). Users should also be aware that the release dates that appear in this work's "Videos A-Z" section actually designate the year of each film's theatrical, film festival, or television premiere, rather than the year of its release onto video. Newly reviewed movies include such disparate works as *Notting Hill*, *True Crime*, *Guinevere*, *The Mummy*, *Election*, and *An Ideal Husband*.

Movie videos released during the closing months of 1999 often appear in truncated entries containing cast names and plot synopses, but lacking genre classifications and critical assessments. The index to foreign films has been eliminated from this year's edition. The editors suggest that filmgoers who are interested in foreign works should consult a Gale companion volume that, sadly, covers only about one-quarter as many titles as the previous index. The cast index has added several hundred new names. Added as well are some actors' nicknames ("Robert 'Tex' Allen"). To their credit, the editors have dropped very few entries. However, animal actors continue to be omitted from this index. The "Kibbles and Series" index has also witnessed a substantial number of modifications, with the infusion of about a dozen new entries and the deletion of some 20 others. Unfortunately, more than 40 terms from the category index of the previous edition have been dropped.

Although generally reliable, the videographies in this section should not be regarded as comprehensive. Despite some shortcomings, this annual remains the most wide-ranging, versatile, and affordable film directory that money can buy. [R: LJ, Dec 99, p. 112]—**Jeffrey E. Long**

THEATER

C, P

408.   Willis, John. **Theatre World, Volume 53: 1996–1997 Season.** New York, Applause Theater Book Publishers, 1999. 288p. illus. index. $25.95pa. ISBN 1-55783-344-3.

Volume 53 of *Theatre World* covers the 1996–1997 season of Broadway, Off-Broadway, touring companies, and professional regional companies. Entries contain complete cast listings, replacements, producers, directors, authors, composers, opening and closing dates, song titles, an overview of reviews, and much more. The text is enhanced by over 1,000 black-and-white photographs, both live shots and stills. There is also a section of black-and-white photographs of the 1997 Theatre World Award recipients along with a list of previous winners and photographs from the 1997 award presentation. Lists of Pulitzer Prize, New York Drama Critics Circle Award, and Tony Award winning productions are also provided. Brief biographical entries are provided for many cast members from the 1996–1997 season. Obituaries are also provided for performers who passed away between June 1, 1996 and May 31, 1997. An index concludes the work.—**Cari Ringelheim**

28 Philosophy and Religion

PHILOSOPHY

Dictionaries and Encyclopedias

C, P

409. **Concise Routledge Encyclopedia of Philosophy.** New York, Routledge, 2000. 1030p. index. $40.00. ISBN 0-415-22364-4.

The *Concise Routledge Encyclopedia of Philosophy* properly presents itself as "a complete introduction to world philosophy." It is a condensation of the 10-volume *Routledge Encyclopedia of Philosophy* (1998), and it is comprised of entries that often are the introductory matter from the more extended, technical entries of the full *Routledge Encyclopedia*. There are over 2,000 entries in the *Concise Routledge Encyclopedia*. They cover the major areas of philosophy (e.g., ethics, metaphysics, epistemology), time periods and schools of thought periods (e.g., medieval philosophy, stoic philosophy), national and ethnic topics (e.g., Chinese philosophy, Yoruba epistemology), definitions, and biographies (including biographies of living philosophers). No entry is more than six two-column pages long, and most are less than two columns. Particularly useful are the annotated lists of further readings that accompany each entry. The entries are authoritative, straightforward, and well written. There is a good one-page introduction, a list of contributors (which, unfortunately, are listed alphabetically by entry and not by contributor name), and an excellent index. Owners of the full *Routledge Encyclopedia* will obtain no new information by purchasing the *Concise Routledge Encyclopedia*, but, since it provides such good non-technical introductions, definitions, and descriptions, it is valuable for anyone not willing or able to handle the technical content of the full encyclopedia. Owners of the *Encyclopedia of Philosophy* (Macmillan) and its supplements should purchase the full *Routledge Encyclopedia of Philosophy* if possible. It is more up-to-date and includes topics of current interest (artificial intelligence, Bell's Theorem, environmental ethics, private language argument). If a library cannot afford the full *Routledge Encyclopedia*, it should purchase the *Concise Routledge Encyclopedia*.

This is a superb reference work. It must be numbered among the three best one-volume guides to philosophy in the English language. The other two are the *Oxford Companion to Philosophy* (see ARBA 97, entry1166) and the *Cambridge Dictionary of Philosophy* (see ARBA 2000, entry 1212). It is difficult to decide among them. All are well written, reliable, and provide serious coverage of contemporary issues and non-European philosophy in addition to more traditional topics. The *Cambridge Dictionary* does not include an index, and thus it is the least useful of the three. The *Oxford Companion* stands out because it includes illustrations and because some of the most prominent names in late twentieth-century Anglo-American philosophy are among its contributors (Davidson, Dummett, Dworkin, Searle, and Quine, among others). Nonetheless, the lucid prose and annotated lists of further readings of the *Concise Routledge Encyclopedia* make it the best choice for general readers, including high school and undergraduate students. All libraries should seriously consider buying the *Concise Routledge Encyclopedia*, even those who own the full version. [R: BL, 1 Oct 2000, pp. 372-374]—**Richard H. Swain**

RELIGION

General Works

Atlases

C, P

410.   **The Routledge Historical Atlas of Religion in America.** By Bret E. Carroll. New York, Routledge, 2000. 144p. illus. maps. index. (Routledge Atlases of American History). $17.95pa. ISBN 0-415-92137-6.

This historical atlas provides an introductory overview of religion in the United States. The author explains in the introduction that by mapping such themes as migration, immigration, geographic expansion, and regional concentration, researchers can trace how certain religions and religious communities formed and expanded (or died out) and how they contributed to and shaped U.S. history. The book begins with the indigenous American religions of native culture. These include northern hunting religions and agricultural religions. The book then jumps forward to the European settlers' contributions to religious society, from Spanish Catholic colonization to Russian Orthodoxy. The bulk of the book deals with the English colonies' impact on America with their widespread Protestant beliefs. With the use of maps, the author is able to visually show the growth of Baptist and Methodist beliefs and the rise and fall of the Quaker religion. Parts 5 and 6 explore religion's place in modern America by focusing on the growth of Catholicism; the development of American Judaism; and expansion of Islam, Hinduism, and Buddhism. Part 6, titled "Religions of the Modern Age," explores the futures of the fundamentalist movement, urban African American religions, and Unification and Scientology. A chronology and a list of further reading conclude the volume.

This interesting approach to exploring religion's impact on U.S. history will be useful in the religion and history collections of academic libraries. By visually defining the role immigration has played on religious U.S. history, researchers will be better able to understand the cultural impact of living in such a diverse society.

—**Shannon Graff Hysell**

Dictionaries and Encyclopedias

P, S

411.   Melton, J. Gordon. **American Religions: An Illustrated History.** Santa Barbara, Calif., ABC-CLIO, 2000. 316p. illus. maps. index. $99.00. ISBN 1-57607-222-3.

True to its title, this illustrated history includes a wealth of prints, photographs, maps, and document excerpts that focus on highlights of America's religious movements and traditions. As a complement to the text, they add an element of humanness and personality that make the subject much more accessible, enhancing the reader's understanding of social and philosophical changes at various points in time.

With a nod to the pre-historic studies of America's belief systems by several scientific branches, Melton devotes the first tenth of the book to indigenous religious practices, drawing on the observations of post-Colombian explorers and colonists. This sets the stage for a comprehensive review of the waxing and waning of America's faiths.

The titles of various religious doctrinal texts serve as chapter subheadings, giving a flavor of authenticity, and occasional unfamiliarity, to spur the reader toward perusing further. Following the path of Spanish pioneers, the founding of the American Republic, and the effects of urbanization up to the contemporary scene, Melton charts the development of denominationalism, pluralism, modernism, and religion in the increasingly secular world. A controversial author on the topic of what may be referred to as "cults," Melton presents relatively unbiased descriptions of various sects that have appeared in America or migrated to our shores, and whose tenets gained in popularity.

The bibliography includes a useful listing of recently published general titles (including two others by Melton), and more extensive listings for each of the chapter topics. An additional resource, especially for those visually inclined, are the illustration credits. The index mostly covers names of individuals, movements, publications, and organizations. This title is recommended for high school level and beyond, and would make a good addition to a public library, community college, or undergraduate college collection.—**Druet Cameron Klugh**

Handbooks and Yearbooks

C, P

412.   **Yearbook of American and Canadian Churches 2000.** Eileen W. Lindner, ed. Nashville, Tenn., Abingdon Press, 2000. 408p. maps. index. $35.00pa. ISBN 0-687-09094-6. ISSN 0195-9034.

First published in 1916 as the *Federal Council Yearbook*, this well-known yearbook has been published annually since 1951 and has provided directory and statistical information about U.S. and Canadian churches. The theme of the 2000 volume is "Religious Pluralism in the New Millennium." Two essays address this theme and are accompanied by a "Directory of Selected Faith Traditions in America." The remainder of the volume consists of a directory section and a statistical section. Within the directory section are separate listings for the United States and Canada for religious bodies, national cooperative organizations, theological seminaries and Bible colleges, religious periodicals, archives, ecumenical bodies, research centers, and Websites for various religious bodies. The statistical section provides membership and financial information for U.S. and Canadian churches and trends in seminary enrollment. There are separate indexes for organizations and individuals. This volume could have benefited from one more vigorous proofreading. An excellent source of up-to-date information on North American Christianity, this book belongs in any reference collection with at least a moderate interest in religion.

—**Ronald H. Fritze**

Bible Studies

Dictionaries and Encyclopedias

C, P

413.   **Dictionary of New Testament Background.** Craig A. Evans and Stanley E. Porter, eds. Downers Grove, Ill., InterVarsity Press, 2000. 1328p. index. $39.99. ISBN 0-8308-1780-8.

In 1992 InterVarsity Press began a publishing project that, when completed, would include *Dictionary of Jesus and the Gospels* (see ARBA 93, entry 1428), *Dictionary of Paul and His Letters* (see ARBA 95, entry 1450), *Dictionary of the Later New Testament and Its Developments* (see ARBA 99, entry 1274), and this final volume on the background of the New Testament and earliest Christianity. Whereas the first three dictionaries focus on specific subsets of the New Testament literature, this one provides illumination on the entire corpus (and, of course, related subjects). It comprises more than 300 articles, including a few that were brought over and updated from the previous volumes, on the Jewish and Greco-Roman world into which Christianity was born and in which the New Testament documents were written. Among the wide range of topics treated are geography and archaeology ("Archaeology of the Land of Israel," "Judea," "Rome"), historical figures and events ("Destruction of Jerusalem," "Jewish Wars with Rome," "Roman Governors of Palestine"), political institutions and movements ("Hasmoneans," "Herodian Dynasty," "Revolutionary Movements, Jewish"), religion ("Creeds and Hymns," "Festivals and Holy Days: Jewish," "Mysteries"), and culture and society ("Honor and Shame," "Social Values and Structures," "Women in Greco-Roman World and Judaism"). There is also extensive treatment of Jewish literature of the second-temple period, including the Dead Sea Scrolls. In fact, its coverage of the Dead Sea Scrolls surpasses that of the recent, and otherwise thorough, *Eerdmans Dictionary of the Bible* (see entry 414). The articles are current and well written, and are on a level appropriate for scholars, students, and informed lay readers.

In addition to being the largest group of contributors to any of these volumes (152), this is also the most theologically diverse. Alongside such well-known evangelical scholars as D. A. Carson, Peter H. Davids, Scot McKnight, and Edwin M. Yamauchi are several outstanding non-evangelicals, such as Lester L. Grabbe, Jerome Murphy-O'Connor, Carol A. Newsom, Eugene Ulrich, and James C. VanderKam. All were chosen for their expertise in their fields rather than to impose a uniform point of view on the volume. The *Dictionary of New Testament Background* is up-to-date, informed, and balanced. It should be part of all biblical and religious studies collections in academic and public libraries.—**Craig W. Beard**

C, P

414.   **Eerdmans Dictionary of the Bible.** David Noel Freedman, Allen C. Myers, and Astrid B. Beck, eds. Grand Rapids, Mich., William B. Eerdmans, 2000. 1425p. illus. maps. $45.00. ISBN 0-8028-2400-5.

As the *Anchor Bible Dictionary* (ABD; see ARBA 2000, entry 1244) differs from other multivolume Bible dictionaries and encyclopedias, so does *Eerdmans Dictionary of the Bible* (EDB) differ from its peers among 1-volume dictionaries. This is not surprising, given that Freedman (a professor of Hebrew biblical studies at the University of California, San Diego) is the driving force behind both. Also, like the ABD, this is a new work rather than an updating of an earlier one (although the publisher's original intention was to revise and update the 1987 *Eerdmans Bible Dictionary* [see ARBA 89, entry 1317]), providing users with the results of cutting-edge biblical scholarship.

The EDB comprises approximately 5,000 entries written by an international and interconfessional team of some 600 scholars, many of whom are acknowledged experts in their respective fields. The articles deal with all matters that bear directly or indirectly on interpreting and understanding the Bible. Every book of the Bible (including the Old Testament apocryphal/deuterocanonical books) and all the persons, places, and significant terms mentioned in them (based on the New Revised Standard Version) receive entries. In addition, related subjects, such as biblical theology, cultural and historical background, geography, Near Eastern archaeology, textual and literary studies, and noncanonical writings (including the Old Testament Pseudepigrapha, New Testament Apocrypha, and Dead Sea Scrolls), are treated.

The large number of articles equates to more specific access points than in comparable works, such as the *New Bible Dictionary* (3d ed.; see ARBA 98, entry 1373). Yet it is odd that EDB does not have individual entries for most of the well-known Dead Sea Scrolls texts, among them the Copper Scroll, Miqtsat Ma'asei ha-Torah, and Rule of the Community.

One of Freedman's goals was to provide a balanced presentation of subjects, especially where there are substantially differing viewpoints. Through the diversity of the team of contributors, an overall balance is achieved for the volume. However, within some of the articles it is lacking, as can be seen in "Conquest: Biblical Narrative," which exhibits an extremely negative view of the historicity of the narrative material in the Old Testament. Primarily because of this, balanced reference collections should place EDB alongside the dictionary mentioned above on their shelves. [R: LJ, Jan 01, p. 86]—**Craig W. Beard**

C, P

415.   **The NIV Theological Dictionary of New Testament Words: An Abridgment of New International Dictionary of New Testament Theology.** Verlyn Verbrugge, ed. Grand Rapids, Mich., Zondervan Publishing/HarperCollins, 2000. 1544p. index. (Zondervan Interpreting the Bible Series). $49.99. ISBN 0-310-21650-8.

This is an excellent reference volume for scholars, preachers, and serious lay people interested in New Testament theology. It is a wisely abridged version of the *New International Dictionary of New Testament Theology* (Zondervan, 2000) edited by Colin Brown, itself a translation of *Theologisches Begriffslexikon zum Neuen Testament* edited by Lothar Coenen, Erich Beyreuther, and Hans Bietenhard. A wise abridgement because it has omitted items like many archaic roots of words that are not particularly illuminating and bibliographies and essays that have become outdated. Some up-to-date material has been added.

Two indexes are very helpful in locating appropriate entries. The first is a listing of scriptural passages indicating where there are relevant entries. The second is an index of subjects in English that makes it easy for persons who do not know Greek to find the articles on Greek words. The dictionary itself considers Greek works in Greek alphabetical order, although it helpfully transliterates all Greek words.

The articles are well written and bring in discussion of cognate words. Articles on the more important words (like "Resurrection," "Saviour," "Christ," "Sin," and "Holy") run about five or six pages. "God" is treated in 11 pages and "Son" is a surprising 20 pages. References are made to other helpful entries. All words are number coded to the Goodrick-Kohlenberger numbering system and an appendix equates these numbers with Strong's numbering.—**Robert T. Anderson**

Christianity

Almanacs

C, P

416.   **Our Sunday Visitor's Catholic Almanac, 2001.** Matthew Bunson, ed. Huntington, Ind., Our Sunday Visitor, 2000. 608p. $28.95; $23.95pa. ISBN 0-87973-907-X; 0-87973-906-1pa.

One of the most used references relating to the Catholic religion, this edition of the almanac follows the pattern set by its many predecessors. It includes information on just about anything readers could ask about Catholicism, both historically and in the modern world. It includes sections on doctrine; saints; the papacy; education; the Church in other countries; and its relationship with other religions, such as Islam, Hinduism, and Buddhism. Similar to other almanacs, it presents mostly factual material. It tends to offer more detailed explanations of the facts, however, even though it does not purport to present both sides of such controversial topics as the morality of abortion and homosexuality.

The arrangement is a familiar one for this type of reference work: a topical list of contents followed by a detailed index at the beginning of the book. Most of the main part of the almanac is straight text with a few statistical tables and charts. Some of the most useful sections for recent material are in the beginning under "Year in Review," "News in Depth," and "Special Reports." Another useful section is the glossary, but unfortunately it is buried within the other text and not easily found without going to the index or list of contents where it is found, for some strange reason, between "Blessed Virgin Mary" and "Church Calendar."

The 24-page index is quite adequate for most reference questions, but the fact that there are no subheadings makes it difficult to find some information. Under "Catholic Schools," for example, there are 35 pages of references. If readers wanted information on textbook aid for religious schools, there is no clue as to which of the 35 pages would lead to such information. Likewise, in seeking the name of the first Mexican female saint, readers would have to go through many pages under "Mexico" or the related topic of "Canonization." Aside from these limitations, this almanac remains the most valuable work for ready-reference facts related to Catholic beliefs and practices.—**Lucille Whalen**

Dictionaries and Encyclopedias

C, P

417.   **Oxford Companion to Christian Thought.** Adrian Hastings, Alistair Mason, and Hugh Pyper, eds. New York, Oxford University Press, 2000. 777p. index. $55.00. ISBN 0-19-860024-0.

Planned and written over a period of eight years, this is a truly grand book. It is imposing in its scope, its depth, and in the quality of its contents. Here is a rich resource for scholars who want to better visualize how their own personal research fits into the context of the whole panorama of Christian thought. It is equally appropriate for laypersons exploring ideas in a study group or spiritual searchers of any faith who are eager to understand concepts and ideas heard but never explained.

The mission or objective of the book, crucial to its best use, is presented in the fine introduction by Hastings. He reminds the reader that "thought" is not "fact," and, while the articles may be described as authoritative, they are also expressions of the individual author's personal scholarship and convictions. The contributors, 260 scholars from all over the world, include Catholics, Protestants, Orthodox, and "agnostics of various sorts," and, at most points, the editors "have deliberately attempted to balance one writer with another so that a diversity of viewpoints could be reflected without forcing each contributor to maintain an absolute balance" (p. ix).

Entry headings include biblical subjects, theological and philosophical subjects, persons who have had an outstanding influence on Christian thought, places that carry uncommonly strong symbolic power, and the list goes on. The choice of subjects treated is diverse and exciting. Hastings writes: "While it would be impossible to cover the wider sea of thought at all adequately, we have put a toe bravely in here and there, not only with considerable general articles on science, music, art, poetry, and novels, but with particular studies of Shakespeare, Dante, Bach, and Milton, among other figures" (p. xi).

The organization and indexing of the book is meticulous and reader-friendly, traits readers have come to expect from Oxford University Press. Articles are arranged in the traditional encyclopedic manner, in alphabetic order by entry title. Within articles, cross-references to other articles are indicated by means of asterisks. Numerous asterisks may have a somewhat jarring effect on the reader, but the usefulness of the cross-references is certainly great enough to justify them. Almost all of the articles end with a list of books to guide the reader in further exploration.

Preceding the articles are three lists: Contributors, Entries, and Abbreviations. The list of contributors includes each person's professional position, the name of the institution in which he or she teaches or works, and the headings of the encyclopedia article(s) contributed. The alphabetic list of entry headings serves as a quick-search table of contents. The list of abbreviations used in the book is delightfully short, a relief from the multitudinous abbreviations and acronyms present in many reference books. There is a name index in the back of the book for people who are discussed within articles but who do not have their own entries. Each of the names is followed by the titles of entries in which that person is discussed. This book is recommended without reservation for public and academic libraries, and for any individuals, groups, or institutions interested in "humanity's long march across the centuries in search of the meaning of things" (p. xiii).—**Dorothy Jones**

Part IV
SCIENCE
AND
TECHNOLOGY

29 Science and Technology in General

BIOGRAPHY

C, P, S

418.   **Concise Dictionary of Scientific Biography.** 2d ed. Farmington Hills, Mich., Charles Scribner's Sons/Gale Group, 2000. 1097p. illus. index. $125.00. ISBN 0-684-80631-2.

This is a book based on the multivolume *Dictionary of Scientific Biography* (see ARBA 91, entries 1461 and 1462; and ARBA 81, entry 1372). The original biography was first published in 1981 and covers scientists who died prior to that year. This concise biography is complete through the second supplement to the 18-volume set. This concise version of the biography is a single book just over 1,000 pages with 2 indexes. One index lists scientists by field of study making it very easy to locate information on any given scientist and their areas of study.

The biographies are short, one to only a few paragraphs, giving a general understanding of the importance of the scientist's achievements and contributions. This book would be useful as a quick introduction and as a starting point for further study. The set covers only the most famous of scientists so it lacks in completeness of coverage. Yet, it does cover scientists that most people will ask questions about.

This dictionary is a valuable purchase for any library because it gives a short explanation and biography of scientists and their gifts to society. Although buyers may prefer to own the full set, this is a very cost-efficient alternative.—**James W. Oliver**

DICTIONARIES AND ENCYCLOPEDIAS

C, P

419.   **Chambers Dictionary of Science and Technology.** Peter M. B. Walker, ed. New York, Larousse Kingfisher Chambers, 1999. 1325p. illus. $50.00. ISBN 0-550-14110-3.

This is a thick dictionary, as one would expect given the blizzard of new words and new meanings for old words that accompany today's technological society. Its size is thickened by the author's commendable practice of inserting encyclopedic articles for topics deemed worthy, such as creep and deformation, polymers, mitochondrion, and the Internet. Words whose meanings depend on context receive separate listings. Thus, there are three entries for *crest*. The definitions themselves are written clearly in simple terms. The appendixes include computing acronyms and a glossary of nuclear terms. [R: Choice, April 2000, p. 1438]—**Robert B. McKee**

C, P

420.   **The Cutting Edge: An Encyclopedia of Advanced Technologies.** New York, Oxford University Press, 2000. 360p. illus. index. $75.00. ISBN 0-19-512899-0.

This useful book makes information on advanced technology accessible to high school and college students (especially in science, technology, and society programs) and the general public. Technologies treated in this work are in current general use while technologies used in research or new technologies now under development are not covered. Roughly grouped into general areas, the book includes 7 articles on aerospace, 27 on biomedicine, 10 on chemistry and materials, 26 on computers and communication, 8 on energy, 4 on transport, 15 on visual imaging and sound, and 5 others. Each of the 102 articles has sections on scientific and technical description; historical development; uses, effects, and limitations; and issues and debate. Each article is accompanied by a generous further reading list including books, articles, and Websites. Articles are 4–5 pages (4,000–5,000 words) long. Given the short articles, the technical descriptions are sometimes too brief for full understanding of the mechanisms, but the excellent further reading list will guide the user to more detailed sources. There is also a substantial index. This book was produced by 13 contributors, mainly science writers and editors, with a 6-member advisory board of mainly consultants and academics.

The articles are generally clear and accurate, although the article on digital libraries largely ignores the difference between free and paid digital library collections. Library Websites restrict access because they pay dearly to license use of many digital collections, and the amount paid depends on breadth of allowed access. Although aimed at general readers, many terms are used but not explained (i.e., download, Java, platform, SSL) or are explained independently and to varying extents in different articles (i.e., ascii). The book needs a glossary, or the index should highlight pages where terms are explained. An introductory chapter on PCs and current computer technology would clarify the articles and allow tighter and deeper technical description sections, but there is no article on personal computers. A supplementary Website (http://www.cuttingedge.oup.com) is being planned. This book is highly recommended for most public and academic libraries. [R: Choice, Nov 2000, p. 509; BL, 1 Dec 2000, pp. 746-748]—**Frederic F. Burchsted**

P, S

421. **Scholastic Science Dictionary.** By Melvin Berger. Illustrated by Hannah Bonner. New York, Scholastic, 2000. 224p. illus. index. $19.95. ISBN 0-590-31321-5.

School children today are bombarded with a myriad of technical and scientific terms that extend beyond their vocabularies. Recognizing this, the author states that he has compiled this dictionary in order to provide a quick, easy way for young children to familiarize themselves with the vocabulary, ideas, objects, and people of science. In order to contain the immensity of "science" into one manageable dictionary, the author focused the scope of the dictionary to those areas that he felt would have most relevance to a school child's daily exposure. Entries were culled from basic elementary school science curricula, current scientific journals, magazines, newspapers, and the author's own 40 years of experience writing children's science books.

There are more than 2,400 entries covering the major branches of science. In addition to scientific terminology, there are entries for many diseases, drugs, treatments, and medical specializations. More than 140 biographies of important scientists representing a diversity of backgrounds are also included. All of these entries are intermingled in alphabetic order. True to its intention to be an elementary school level tool, the definitions are written in very basic language, and most are kept to a couple sentences in length. All entries include pronunciations—etymologies are given sparingly. The work is carefully formatted, utilizing cross-references, guide words, and bold text within definitions to indicate words defined elsewhere in the dictionary.

A very valuable feature is the "How to Use This Dictionary" guide. These two pages provide a thorough diagram of all that a dictionary offers, a valuable lesson in itself. The dictionary is generously illustrated with engaging renderings that avoid looking like cartoons, and that incorporate a variety of ethnic and gender representations. An "Index of Picture Labels" covers words that are not entry words. The dictionary concludes with a two-page guide of resources that lists museums, science competitions, and Websites, but it is too superficial to be of much use. Yet, this is a minor flaw in an otherwise useful and appealing work. It is highly recommended for school and public libraries.—**Diane Donham**

P, S

422. **Science & Technology Encyclopedia.** Chicago, University of Chicago Press, 2000. 572p. illus. $22.50pa. ISBN 0-226-74267-9.

Comprehensive (and small) scientific encyclopedias are usually not worth the effort to construct or consult. They are often not comprehensive enough for consistent use, and their broad scope typically means that many articles are outdated or misleading. This small, comprehensive encyclopedia, however, is an exception. It is well done, from the number of entries (more than 6,500) to the excellent illustrations (over 250) to the quality and accuracy of the writing. Anyone with a job that crosses disciplinary boundaries in the sciences, such as an editor, librarian, historian, or philosopher of science, will find this book useful, as will any science student.

The key to the success of this encyclopedia is its tight editing. It has more than 20,000 cross-references within the articles, and many articles are approached from more than one discipline. The concept of "solution," for example, is given a typical definition from chemistry, but it is also defined for geology. The publisher is also judicious in the selection of technical concepts covered, often using topics that convey scientific principles as well as engineering.

Another innovation is the addition of more than 850 biographies of scientists, engineers, and inventors, including many alive today. This book will be one of the first sources a student or professional consults for scientific biographical information because it is so easy to use.

What the technical differences are between dictionaries and encyclopedias is a bit mysterious. This book is probably called an encyclopedia because of its numerous illustrations and full prose without etymology or pronunciation. Nevertheless, it is a "concise" encyclopedia that resembles a dictionary with its relatively short articles. It will not replace a full encyclopedia of many volumes. Instead, it nicely fills the niche of a first reference for terms in science and technology.—**Mark A. Wilson**

HANDBOOKS AND YEARBOOKS

P, S

423.   **Science Year 2000: The World Book Annual Science Supplement.** Chicago, World Book, 1999. 352p. illus. index. $29.00. ISBN 0-7166-0550-3. ISSN 0080-7621.

Science Year, a supplement to the *World Book Encyclopedia*, has been published annually since 1965. This latest volume includes the editors' choices of the major science news stories of 1998, in-depth reports on significant topics, a special section looking forward to the year 2000, and an update of 28 articles reporting on important developments in science and technology from 1998 and 1999. There are also five articles on science and technology applied to the consumer, a supplement of new or revised articles from the 1999 *World Book Encyclopedia*, and a cumulative index for the 1998–2000 editions of *Science Year*. A quaint feature retained from earlier editions is a set of cross-reference tabs to paste in the *World Book Encyclopedia* as links from that work to this supplement.

The work is produced under a distinguished editorial board. Authors are either experienced researchers in the fields on which they report or well-known writers of popular scientific works. Some, such as James Trefil and Jay Pasachoff, are both. Not surprisingly, the articles are both accurate and entertaining. The entire book is profusely illustrated in color with well-selected images and is very attractively produced.

Pre-college students and the general public will find much of interest in this book. Unfortunately, the absence of references makes it much less useful for beginning college students.—**Robert Michaelson**

30 Agricultural Sciences

GENERAL WORKS

P, S
424.   Hoag, Dana L. **Agricultural Crisis in America: A Reference Handbook.** Santa Barbara, Calif., ABC-CLIO, 1999. 270p. index. (Contemporary World Issues). $45.00. ISBN 0-87436-737-9.

The author cites seven areas he sees as agricultural crises—the survival of farms and ranches, modern technological changes in agriculture, a growing world to feed, safe drinking water and food, environmental concerns in agricultural management, urbanization, and conflicts with city "outsiders" moving into the country. These and many other related issues are discussed in an easy-to-read yet informative text.

This reference source gives a nice selection of background information on this topic, including a chronology of the history of agriculture in the United States, with biographical sketches of some of the more important agriculture figures. The author also presents statistics and other facts illustrating the seven crises. A selective list of agriculture organizations accompanies a chapter with an annotated list of books that further discuss aspects of the agricultural crises. Useful Internet sites are provided for information on associations, magazines, software, government agencies, and agricultural policies. A glossary of terms used in the text and an index complete the book.

This resource will be valuable to high school and college students researching a paper on agricultural problems in the United States. It gives all the necessary ingredients of a good paper, plus it gives references for other sources. It belongs to the quality Contemporary World Issues series, which has similar books on issues such as wilderness preservation and legalized gambling. In addition to clear and readable historical background information, there is hard-to-find statistical information provided in tables and graphs for easy reading and use. This handbook is recommended for high school, public, and undergraduate academic library collections. [R: LJ, Dec 99, p. 108]—**Diane B. Moore**

FOOD SCIENCES AND TECHNOLOGY

C, P
425.   **The Oxford Companion to the Wines of North America.** Bruce Cass and Jancis Robinson, eds. New York, Oxford University Press, 2000. 301p. illus. maps. index. $45.00. ISBN 0-19-860114-X.

This is another major must-buy reference book in the world of wine. Both editors are accomplished wine writers and educators—Cass is American, while Robinson is British. The latter is also editor of the well-known *Oxford Companion to Wine* (OCW; see ARBA 96, entry 1528). This current book repeats some of the material but adds much more, and updates it all rather nicely.

There are 550 alphabetically arranged entries concerning terms, vintners, varietals, viticulture, and places (such as the VQA or AVA name designations). Each entry is followed by appropriate cross-references within the book or in the larger OCW, an occasional bibliography, and Web URLs. Entries are either long or short, depending on what they have to say, and sprawl over three closely typeset columns on each page. Additionally, there are 24 color plates, appendixes about matching food and wine in long tabular format, 17 black-and-white line maps, and statistics. There are also 15 introductory essays (written by most of the 21 writers and academics who contributed to the volume) covering consumer trends, distribution systems, auctions, microbiology, varietals, organic wine, and the wine media critics

Significant contributors include Dan Berger (former wine critic of the *L.A. Times*), Patrick Fegan (educator in Chicago), and Linda Bramble (educator in Canada who is responsible for much of the Canadian material). The issue of the Internet is not really addressed, although Websites are noted. Distribution and auctions of wines are all being changed by new media such as the Internet. Even consumer-driven information is now easily available on the Web from various magazine sites and wine association and business sites. Also, the OCW itself is available on two different sites for free.

Despite some minor carping (lack of material covering the Internet, some typographical errors, no overall bibliography, and lousy line maps), this companion work does what it promises to do. It provides a range of updated, well-informed material designed to cover just about everybody's basic needs for data about North American wines and is highly recommended.—**Dean Tudor**

VETERINARY SCIENCE

P

426.   Pinney, Chris C. **The Illustrated Veterinary Guide.** 2d ed. New York, McGraw-Hill, 2000. 934p. illus. index. $29.95pa. ISBN 0-07-135186-8.

A quick-thinking pet owner can render first aid for many conditions, including lacerated paws and eye irritants. This guide shows the way. Striking a superb balance between breadth and depth for cats, dogs, and exotic pets (such as chinchillas, pot-bellied pigs, and hermit crabs), the guide presents useful and interesting information in graceful, comfortable prose. The three variables in the pet equation are prudent selection, affectionate and firm training, appropriate and loving care, and timely response to illness or injury. Each one of these variables gets good coverage. There is even a nod to holistic pet care. Whether the question is how to determine the sex a cockatoo (males generally have black eyes) or what the downside of an automatic pet feeder for dogs is (predisposes them to obesity), the rich diversity in the pages make it likely for a reader to find an answer. For example, forget using cedar chips that so nicely filled a dog bed as burrowing material for a prairie dog. To the rodent, the cedar is a respiratory irritant. Separate indexes for general, bird, cat, and dog entries are useful, as is the thoughtfully subdivided table of contents.—**Diane M. Calabrese**

31 Biological Sciences

BIOLOGY

P, S
427.   **A Dictionary of Biology.** 4th ed. New York, Oxford University Press, 2000. 641p. (Oxford Paperback Reference). $14.95pa. ISBN 0-19-280102-3.

A Concise Dictionary of Biology was first published in 1985 with subsequent paperback editions in 1990, 1996, and this newly titled 2000 edition. The work stands as a spin-off of over 4,000 biology, biochemistry, and related terms from geology, physics, chemistry, medicine, and paleoanthropology selected from an Oxford University Press work called the *Concise Science Dictionary* (2d ed.; see ARBA 92, entry 1455). Two companion volumes, *A Concise Dictionary of Chemistry* (see ARBA 92, entry 1725) and *A Dictionary of Physics* (see entry 472), were also pulled from the original science dictionary.

Each new edition of the dictionary has added terms from fields interrelated to biology, such as genetics and genetic engineering, molecular biology, and immunology. The 4th edition notes an additional 400 terms as well as new brief biographical entries (e.g., Jenner and Pavlov). Also new to this edition are several chronologies tracing the history of key areas in biology and a few two-page feature articles on selected topics.

Entries vary in length from a single line to several dozen, about 10 words to several hundred, depending on the complexity of the term defined. Asterisks and cross-references continue to mark words in a definition that are included elsewhere in the dictionary—or terms not used. Rudimentary line drawings are located near some terms, and four appendixes give such data as SI units, simplified animal and plant kingdom classifications, and a geological timeline. English spelling is used, and the pulp-like paper does not provide a good contrast to the printing. Robert Hine's 3d edition of *The Facts on File Dictionary of Biology* (see ARBA 2000, entry 1322) is far more readable in its design and printing. This latter title does not include as many terms or, in some instances, as complete of definitions. Thus, science collections should have both as current, basic reference dictionaries in the field. [R: Choice, Jan 01, pp. 879-880]—**Laurel Grotzinger**

BOTANY

General Works

Handbooks and Yearbooks

P
428.   Harper, Pamela J. **Time-Tested Plants: Thirty Years in a Four-Season Garden.** Portland, Oreg., Timber Press, 2000. 351p. illus. maps. index. $39.95. ISBN 0-88192-486-5.

Harper has been gardening for 30 years in the same 2-acre garden near a sheltered tidal creek off Virginia's Chesapeake Bay. She has established a garden containing not only many endemic plants, but also exotics from several continents. Her purpose in writing this book is to share her experiences in establishing and cultivating the same garden for three decades through the weather extremes typical of an east coast continental climate.

Harper's book is organized into four main sections dealing with spring, summer, combined autumn and winter, and the transition to spring. Within each section, the book is broken down into plant types or structures, such as bulbs, trees, shrubs, vines, foliage, grasses and ferns, annuals, winter berries, and winter flowers. The book is written in the first person and treats each plant in nontechnical terms, describing where in the garden it is grown, why it was selected, how it is cultivated and propagated, what its special needs are, and what unique problems it has. Plants are referred to with their scientific names, but common names are offered when known. The book is beautifully illustrated with all but two of the photographs taken in the author's garden. The two exceptions were obtained from a neighbor's garden as the author deemed them better specimens.

This book should be of interest to gardeners anywhere, even though it is written entirely about one two-acre garden. The author is well aware of the importance of hardiness zones to successful gardening, and stresses that her garden is in zone 7. But even gardeners beyond zone 7 will enjoy reading the first-hand account of the trials and tribulations of a fellow devotee. The book is well written and is recommended to all plant lovers.
—**Michael G. Messina**

P
429.   Taylor, Patrick. **The 500 Best Garden Plants.** repr. ed. Portland, Oreg., Timber Press, 2000. 320p. illus. index. $19.95pa. ISBN 0-88192-257-9.

First published in 1993, this reprint is a handy source for the novice gardener. A typical nursery offers a bewildering variety of plant choices, and without guidance it is easy to make mistakes—going for new or flashy cultivars without regard to space or site considerations. The author has chosen these 500 plants not just for their flowers but also for their foliage, bark, berries, and buds. These selections are mostly older varieties that have stood the test of time.

The book is divided into five sections covering bulbs, herbaceous perennials, shrubs, climbers and wall plants, and trees. Annuals are not included, but this is not a serious omission since the temporary nature of annual plantings makes them one area in which the gardener can experiment at will. Within each of the book's sections, plants are listed alphabetically by genus. A color photograph depicts a typical member of the genus, and each entry discusses the place of origin, availability, space and soil requirements, advice on where and how each plant is best used in the garden, means of propagation, and the hardiness zones for each. Appendixes include a list of plants useful for particular sites, a bibliography of the best books on different plant types, and maps of the hardiness zones for both Europe and the United States.

The limitations of this type of book are obvious, given the fact that the author gardens in southern England and views gardening from that perspective. His book leaves out the native plants and wildflowers that make gardening in diverse areas of the world interesting. Still, for the beginner, this could be a valuable introduction to some of the dependable plants around which a garden can be built.—**Carol L. Noll**

Trees and Shrubs

P
430.   Benvie, Sam. **The Encyclopedia of North American Trees.** Willowdale, Ont., Firefly Books, 2000. 304p. illus. index. $35.00. ISBN 1-55209-408-1.

Trees dominate much of the North American continent; even the deserts and prairies are dotted with the occasional tree. They are important sources of food and shelter for native wildlife and although much of the old-growth forest that once seemed limitless is now gone, forests are still one of our most important natural resources, both for their lumber and paper products and their recreational uses. This encyclopedia is a comprehensive guide to the individual species of trees that make up these forests, desert oases and suburban parks. Only trees that are native to North America are included (no gingko or eucalyptus).

Trees are listed in alphabetical order by genus. Genera with four or more members feature an introductory section sketching out their worldwide distribution, characteristics, and economic importance. Each of the 278 species is pictured in a full-color photograph, then described in clear, readable prose, emphasizing the tree's distinctive characteristics such as fall color, fruits, preferred soil and habitat, and importance in the ecosystem.

The encyclopedia also includes a glossary, a tree-hardiness and climate-zone map of the United States and Canada, a bibliography with tree-related Internet sites, and an index of common tree names. While this is not a field guide, this book makes a valuable companion since it gives much more information than the simple description and range map found in most tree guides. It will be of most interest to landscapers and gardeners, opening their eyes to the great variety of trees native to the North American continent. [R: BL, 1 Oct 2000, pp. 376-377; LJ, 1 April 2000, p. 88; Choice, Nov 2000, p. 508]—**Carol L. Noll**

ZOOLOGY

General Works

S

431.   **Dorling Kindersley Animal Encyclopedia.** New York, DK Publishing, 2000. 376p. illus. index. $29.95. ISBN 0-7894-6499-3.

Once again, Dorling Kindersley has published a captivating book on animals for children. The volume is divided into two main sections. The "Animal Life" section covers 19 topics on animal classification, anatomy, behavior, habitats, adaptation, migration, and conservation issues. Animal classification is not only explained in understandable terms but is illustrated with pictures of the Manx species of cat belonging to each group from the genus through the animal kingdom. The user can easily visualize how groups narrow from the kingdom down to the species.

The main section is the alphabetic arrangement of information for more than 2,000 animal species. Animal group pages on amphibians, birds, fish, mammals, and reptiles are also included. Each entry covers from one to three pages. Each photograph has a caption that is the main source of information. Annotations and labels provide extra details. Fact boxes provide essential data, such as family name, habitat, distribution, food, number of young or eggs, life span, and size. At-a-glance scale indicators compare the animal to a human hand or an average adult human male. The "Find Out More" boxes refer the user to pages of related topics.

The photography is outstanding. It includes close-up shots of animals, animals in their natural habitat, and detailed artwork. Through time-lapse photographs the reader can view each sequence in the movement of a kangaroo hopping and a dolphin and penguins moving through water. The number and quality of the photographs is the strongest feature of the book. Many of the photographs of the animals in their natural habitat are full page.

The "How to Use This Book" section introduces the book with clear explanations of how the entries are arranged. A glossary and index are also provided. The encyclopedia is fully cross-referenced. This volume is reasonably priced and suitable for home, school, or public library use.—**Elaine Ezell**

P, S

432.   **World Book's Animals of the World Series.** Chicago, World Book, 2000. 10v. illus. maps. index. $139.00/set. ISBN 0-7166-1200-3.

World Book's Animals of the World Series is a 10-volume set designed to appeal to young students' curiosity about the animal kingdom. Each volume focuses on a group of animals with something in common, such as marsupials, pennipeds, birds of prey, and wild dogs. Information is given about the various groups in an easy-to-follow and eye-catching format. Numerous color photographs and illustrations will capture the attention of young readers. The question-and-answer format promotes critical thinking by presenting similarities and differences among members of the animal groups. Each volume begins with animals that are most familiar to children—such as ants, kangaroos, owls, and wolves—and then advances to less-familiar members of the featured groups (e.g., lantern sharks, capuchins, bandicoots). Each book concludes with a volume-specific glossary and index.

Specifically geared toward children in grades one through four, this set will be ideal for elementary school libraries and children's reference collections in public libraries. Many children will enjoy learning about their favorite animal and other animals related to it. This reference set is highly recommended for teachers, librarians, and parents who want to introduce the fascinating world of the animal kingdom to young learners.

—**Cari Ringelheim**

Birds

P, S

433.   **Field Guide to the Birds of North America.** 3d ed. Washington, D.C., National Geographic Society, 1999. 480p. illus. maps. index. $21.95pa. ISBN 0-7922-7451-2.

This book provides basic information on more than 900 species of birds that live in North America (north of Mexico). This latest edition of the guide has incorporated a wealth of new information and is the most comprehensive "pocket-sized" book describing the birds that occur on the continent. The guide is designed for those with some background knowledge about birds. Without that knowledge, it may be difficult to use.

Previous editions were well received in the birding and scientific communities, with a few criticisms focusing on minor technical errors, inaccurate range maps, or poor illustrations. Since the last edition was published in 1987, recent advances in knowledge have led to a number of taxonomic changes and to an improved understanding of distribution.

This edition was designed to address these issues and does so admirably. Every species account and range map has been revised to reflect the most current knowledge available. More than 30 plates have been added and others have been revised to depict 80 new species, or add new diagnostic features or plumages. In identification guides, the plates are key to the success of the book. In this edition the new artwork is superb, successfully depicting subtle variations in color and posture that are important in distinguishing species difficult to identify. As the guide assembles a variety of information from diverse sources, it will serve a useful role as a standard reference on the identification, distribution, and habitats of North American birds.—**David J. Argo**

Mammals

C, P

434.   **The Smithsonian Book of North American Mammals.** Don E. Wilson and Sue Ruff, eds. Washington, D.C., Smithsonian Institution Press, 1999. 750p. illus. maps. index. $75.00. ISBN 1-56098-845-2.

The editors successfully coordinated the efforts of 229 mammalogists to produce this comprehensive account of the biology of mammals that live in the United States and Canada, with distribution maps dipping into Mexico to show complete range for mammals indigenous to the Southwest. The work presents a mighty effort sponsored by the Directors of the American Society of Mammalogists (ASM). An important objective of ASM membership and the editors was to produce a reference guide to complement two standard guides located in most large library reference collections. These titles are E. R. Hall's *The Mammals of North America* (see ARBA 82, entry 1494) and Don E. Wilson and DeeAnn M. Reeder's *Mammal Species of the World: A Taxonomic and Geographic Reference* (2d ed.; see ARBA 94, entry 1743).

This important new subject guide contains information for approximately 415 species (arranged phylogenetically under 10 orders and 40 families), each written by a zoologist affiliated with academic or government programs. Entries provide information on an animal's habits, habitat, life cycle, diet, survival skills, and reproduction. Ready-reference information given in all entries includes size, identification details, common name(s), scientific name, recent synonyms, subspecies, population status, maps, and photographs. All entries are signed and end with citations to scientific literature. If completed, these bibliographic citations include "Mammalian Species" accounts, an important series published by the ASM. All but a few illustrations are in color and show the whole animal, face-on views as a rule.

The appendix includes a list of food plants mentioned in articles (their scientific names are given to help users identify more information on them), and the expected listings of common names and scientific names for all mammals discussed in the text. There is a glossary and a complete bibliography of papers or books cited in the discussions.

A preface provides users with a good survey of geographical exploration and discovery in the United States, primarily those organized by our enterprising federal government. Unfortunately, Canadian efforts are not discussed and there are few if any citations to scientific research conducted in Canada. However, Canadian scientists are among the contributors. It is churlish perhaps to point out a fault that far too many general users in the United States will have with this guide to mammals: the metric system is used throughout.

This important guide to mammals living north of Mexico is an essential purchase for all libraries. It complements the standard works cited above and helps serious users to locate the best scientific literature available today. [R: LJ, 15 Nov 99, p. 62]—**Milton Crouch**

32 Engineering

GENERAL WORKS

C, P

435. Lord, Charles R. **Guide to Information Sources in Engineering.** Englewood, Colo., Libraries Unlimited, 2000. 345p. index. (Reference Sources in Science and Technology Series). $75.00. ISBN 1-56308-699-9.

Lord, a current campus librarian at the University of Washington, Tacoma, and former engineering librarian at the Seattle campus, has compiled a resource list of 1,639 items designed to facilitate the search for current, reliable information for engineers and engineering information providers. He acknowledges the challenge inherent in finding resources that can be updated to add value to the engineer's primary activity of solving design problems. Even with increasing numbers of integrated information databases, engineering information itself is fragmented and expensive. This coherent guide addresses the challenge well.

The bibliography contains relatively current information. Most items were published between 1996 and 1999. Lord includes the dates he accessed URLs; the majority of which were late 1999 or early 2000. The book contains 12 chapters, an appendix of publishers, and a 45-page index. The first chapter lays the groundwork by defining the difference between scientists and engineers and their approach to the research world. General reference sources are listed in chapter 2, followed by chapters with sections devoted to 14 different engineering specialties—from general to nuclear. Grey literature is covered in chapter 5, and Internet resources in chapter 8. In chapter 9, Lord explains the great reliance engineers have on regulations, standards, and specifications to provide technical definitions and guidelines for their designs.

Each entry in the book has full bibliographic information, including the ISBN and the price. Annotations vary in length from one sentence to long paragraphs. Most listed items are in English, but several dictionaries in the general reference section have foreign-language entries. The index is very extensive, but Internet sources are not included, nor is there a separate index devoted to them.

There are several good guides to information resources in science and technology, including H. Robert Malinowsky's *Reference Sources in Science, Engineering, Medicine, and Agriculture* (see ARBA 95, entry 482) and C. D. Hurt's *Information Sources in Science and Technology* (3d ed.; see ARBA 2000, entry 1273). However, Lord's book is the most comprehensive new resource for librarians, faculty, engineers, and students needing information specific to engineering disciplines. This work is recommended for academic, public, and high school libraries. [R: Choice, Jan 01, p. 880]—**Laura J. Bender**

CIVIL ENGINEERING

C, P

436. **Dictionary of Architecture & Construction.** 3d ed. Cyril M. Harris, ed. New York, McGraw-Hill, 2000. 1028p. illus. $69.95. ISBN 0-07-135178-7.

For 25 years the editor of the *Dictionary of Architecture & Construction*, Cyril Harris, has strived to create a reference that is useful to the professionals in the building trades. The new 3d edition continues to build on the success of the earlier editions, providing 24,500 terms and abbreviations and 2,200 drawings and diagrams. The entries are brief and clearly written, averaging approximately 20 words in length. No etymology is provided.

Cross-references are indicated by presenting a word or phrase in bold typeface within the definition. Harris acknowledges that many definitions come from such tools as the *AIA Glossary of Construction Terms* and various publications of the American National Standards Institute and the American Society of Testing and Materials. Both the technical specialist and the interested layperson will enjoy using the dictionary. It is an exceptionally practical and comprehensive tool and a good value for most academic and public libraries.—**John M. Robson**

ELECTRIC ENGINEERING
AND ELECTRONICS

C, P

437.   Graf, Rudolf F. **Modern Dictionary of Electronics.** 7th ed. Woburn, Mass., Newnes/Butterworth-Heinemann, 1999. 869p. illus. $59.95pa. ISBN 0-7506-9866-7.

Now in its 7th edition (the 1st edition was published in 1961), Graf's dictionary has become a standard for the discipline. Approximately 25,000 terms are included, which cover this rapidly developing area of technology. Significant terms from earlier time periods that have fallen from contemporary need or use have been retained for historical value. The definitions are terse but have great clarity, are free of unneeded technical jargon, and are sufficient for those knowledgeable about the field. In instances of multiple meanings, users are given in a numerical order, not one of primary and secondary usages. Illustrations, mainly diagrams and tables, are good if relatively few in number. Appendixes include the Greek alphabet, schematic symbols, and SI system of units. This is a good desk reference and a basic title for most libraries to own.—**John M. Robson**

33 Health Sciences

GENERAL WORKS

Bibliography

C, P

438. **Consumer Health Information Source Book.** 6th ed. Alan M. Rees, ed. Phoenix, Ariz., Oryx Press, 2000. 323p. index. $59.50pa. ISBN 1-57356-123-1.

Rees's *Consumer Health Information Source Book* is now available in its 6th edition, a testament to its usefulness as a resource and Rees's authority on consumer health resources and librarianship. This work, written by Rees and other consumer health information professionals, is dedicated to empowering health consumers through their use of information, but it is also a bible to librarians developing collections and providing reference assistance. Rees, along with health consumers, has embraced the World Wide Web as an information resource and performs a valuable service in this edition by directing consumers toward reliable, quality consumer health information on the Web. Because readers are not likely to read this work from cover to cover, the topic of Web health information quality is addressed in several different chapters. This is an effective strategy, since readers are exposed to this issue at appropriate points in the text.

Although a myriad of health information is now available via the Internet, many consumers still prefer information from newsletters, pamphlets, books, and other printed resources. Chapters provide a mix of advice for information seekers, essays on consumer health trends, topical subject guides, and select lists of recommended resources with evaluative and descriptive reviews. A "best of" list includes recommended and highly recommended resources listed in other chapters, for those who want to identify the most essential resources quickly. Rees reviews books and pamphlets in English on over 50 medical subjects, and recommends pamphlets in Spanish on nearly as many topics. An entire chapter is devoted to alternative and complementary healing resources. One chapter is devoted to clearinghouses, information centers, hotlines, and toll-free telephone numbers. Indexes provide access to entries by author, title, and subject. This thoughtful and thorough work is an essential purchase for any library that provides assistance to health care consumers.—**Lynne M. Fox**

Dictionaries and Encyclopedias

P

439. **Encyclopedia of Complementary Health Practice.** Carolyn Chambers Clark, ed. New York, Springer Publishing, 1999. 635p. index. $59.95pa. ISBN 0-8261-1239-0.

Millions of dollars are spent each year on alternative/complementary health care in the United States, yet no general reference has been available to assist the health care consumer or practitioner in better understanding these options. This encyclopedia begins to fill that void. The editors, the majority of whom are nurses, have compiled an extensive amount of reliable information about this topic, and presented it in an easy-to-use format. The book is composed of four major sections. The first gives a theoretical introduction to health, healing, and complementary therapies. Part 2 provides encyclopedic entries on approximately 100 medical conditions and their suggested alternative therapies. A particular strength in this section is that only alternative practices based on research are included. A 3d section discusses "substances," and a 4th section provides a brief explanation of more than 100 complementary health care practices. A variety of practices are included, some requiring a trained practitioner, whereas others can be practiced autonomously. The reference concludes with an extensive list of bibliographic references, a directory of organizations associated with the various practices, and a subject index. The book does what it intends to do—provide an encyclopedia-type overview of a comprehensive list of alternative/complementary health practices. It is a welcome addition to the health care literature. The *Encyclopedia of Complementary Health Practice* is highly recommended for public libraries and libraries serving health care practitioners and students. [R: Choice, Jan 2000, pp. 904-905]—**Mary Ann Thompson**

P, S

440. **Webster's New Explorer Medical Dictionary.** Darien, Conn., Federal Street Press, 1999. 764p. $8.98. ISBN 1-892859-07-6.

Webster's New Explorer Medical Dictionary is a product of Merriam-Webster's Federal Street Press. Created in 1998, Federal Street Press produces value, popularly priced, reference books. The intention of this work is to provide an affordable medical dictionary for the average consumer and, at the listed price, this book fulfills that intent.

The dictionary has over 35,000 entries, including frequently prescribed drugs and medical abbreviations commonly used in medicine but little known by laypersons. The dictionary begins with 27 pages of helpful explanatory notes, including information on cross-references, eponyms, pronunciation, abbreviations, and illustrations of usage. Additional information in some entries includes brief biographical notes, chemical symbols, and even a table of chemical elements.

This dictionary is affordable enough to be accessible to both health-conscious consumers and students—especially students in health-related educational programs. This medical dictionary is highly recommended for the above groups and for high schools, public libraries, and any consumer health collection. [R: LJ, 1 Nov 99, p. 75; Choice, Feb 2000, p. 1083]—**Lynn M. McMain**

Handbooks and Yearbooks

P, S

441. Alford, Raye Lynn. **Genetics & Your Health: A Guide for the 21st Century Family.** Medford, N.J., Medford Press/Plexus Publishing, 1999. 267p. index. $29.95; $19.95pa. ISBN 0-9666748-2-0; 0-9666748-1-2pa.

The goal of this book is to explain genetics and its current and future applications to personal health in a language that is accessible to the average reader. The book is written by a highly qualified genetic scientist. Short chapters with illustrations discuss basic and more complex topics such as patterns of human inheritance and ethical, legal, and social implications. Individual chapters explain cloning and the Human Genome Project, and a well-balanced discussion of the promises and pitfalls of gene therapy is also included.

For the reader seeking specific disease information or professional help, the various genetic professionals are clearly explained. A directory of organizations and Internet sites, a chart of the most common genetic diseases, and a glossary are also included. A bibliographic listing of additional reading is probably at too advanced a level for the average person, but a listing of children's books on genetics is a unique addition.

Although written for the lay public, a high school or better reading level is required to understand the content. The book does make a contribution to the dissemination of rather complex health information and would be appropriate for public libraries or health libraries serving the public.—**Mary Ann Thompson**

P

442. **The Merck Manual of Diagnosis and Therapy.** 17th ed. Mark H. Beers and Robert Berkow, eds. West Point, Pa., Merck Research Laboratories/Merck, 1999. 2833p. index. $35.00. ISBN 0-911910-10-7. ISSN 0076-6526.

This is the centennial edition of *The Merck Manual*, one of the oldest and most widely used general medical textbooks in the world. The objective of this work is to provide clinical information to physicians, medical students, interns, residents, nurses, pharmacists, and other health care professionals in a concise, complete, and accurate manner. The manual covers all aspects of general internal medicine as well as pediatrics, psychiatry, obstetrics, gynecology, dermatology, pharmacology, ophthalmology, and otolaryngology.

The centennial edition is the product of a seven-year effort to update or completely rewrite every section and includes a brief review of medical practice as reflected in *The Merck Manual* during the past 100 years. A number of topics new to this edition include hand disorders, prion diseases, death and dying, probabilities in clinical medicine, multiple chemical sensitivity, chronic fatigue syndrome, rehabilitation, smoking cessation, and drug therapy in the elderly.

The table of contents includes listings not only for the topical sections but also for editorial board members, consultants, additional reviewers, contributors, abbreviations and symbols, and the index. Thumb tabs with abbreviations and section numbers mark the sections and index. Each section begins with its own table of contents, listing chapters and subchapters. The work is thoroughly indexed, including tables and figures, with careful cross-referencing, and boldface page numbers signify major discussions of a topic within the index. Drugs are referred to by their generic name throughout the text, but a chapter is devoted to listing the trade names of commonly used drugs.

With its tissue-thin pages, *The Merck Manual* is light and easily portable. Its broad coverage, careful editing, concise style, ease of use, and affordability will ensure its continued status as one of the most widely used medical textbooks in the world among both health professionals and the sophisticated layperson. *The Merck Manual* is essential for all general and health-related reference collections.—**Arlene McFarlin Weismantel**

MEDICINE

General Works

P, S

443.   Gilbert, Patricia. **Dictionary of Syndromes and Inherited Disorders.** 3d ed. Chicago, Fitzroy Dearborn, 2000. 373p. index. $45.00. ISBN 1-57958-226-5.

The number of syndromes in child health care is rapidly increasing and few doctors, social workers, school counselors, and parents are able to recognize the early onset of these conditions. This reference work is intended for the broad audience of health care providers, educators, and families who are forced to confront the complexity of this wide range of childhood health syndromes.

The compiler uses two criteria for selecting the 100 syndromes included in this volume: the syndrome must produce long-term or lifelong physical or mental problems, and there must be assistance available to deal with these conditions. The type of information provided for each syndrome includes alternative names, incidences, history, causation, characteristics, management implications, and future goals. There is also contact information for self-help groups that are valuable to parents trying to handle their children's health problems.

This 3d edition includes 20 additional syndromes as well as an expanded glossary. Thorough indexing directs the reader to both specific disease conditions and general health categories. These updates, along with the self-help group material, make this reference guide considerably more useful for the general public than standard syndrome dictionaries that contain briefer and much more technical coverage. [R: BL, 15 Oct 2000, p. 478; Choice, Sept 2000, p. 95]—**Jonathon Erlen**

Alternative Medicine

P

444.   **The Complete Illustrated Encyclopedia of Alternative Healing Therapies.** C. Norman Shealy, ed. Boston, Element Books, 1999. 383p. illus. index. $29.95pa. ISBN 1-86204-662-X.

There are many encyclopedias and dictionaries on alternative medicine and healing on the market, and their large and small differences can make selecting one difficult. This is a beautifully designed, well-organized, and objective work aimed at the general reader. Its editor is the founder of the American Holistic Medical Association and a well-known American surgeon and chronic pain specialist. The book presents 54 therapies that aim to enhance self-healing and their applications to a variety of illnesses, and is the companion volume to *The Illustrated Encyclopedia of Healing Remedies* (see ARBA 99, entry 1462). It is organized into four parts: "Energy Therapies" (acupuncture, shiatsu, yoga, and therapeutic touch); "Physical Therapies" (osteopathy, therapeutic massage, and relaxation techniques); "Mind and Spirit Therapies" (music, art, and light therapies); and "Common Ailments" (anxiety, back problems, pneumonia, and diabetes). Entries are comprehensive, well written, and meaningfully illustrated, and therapy and ailment entries are cross-referenced. Therapy descriptions include history, philosophy, precautions, what to expect from a treatment, and how the therapy is viewed by conventional medicine. Entries on ailments include description, symptoms, conventional medical treatment, and cautions. A reference area at the back of the book contains a full glossary, but recommendations for further reading and address and contact information are limited. In general, this is an outstanding guide for new and more experienced readers in this field and is appropriate for all libraries.—**Madeleine Nash**

Pediatrics

P, S

445.   Coleman, Jeanine G. **The Early Intervention Dictionary: A Multidisciplinary Guide to Terminology.** 2d ed. Bethesda, Md., Woodbine House, 1999. 410p. $17.95pa. ISBN 1-890627-05-4.

The 2d edition of this revised and updated dictionary reflects the ever-changing and expanding role of the early intervention field in identifying and treating infant and early childhood special needs. Hundreds of medical, therapeutic, and educational terms are defined that have been commonly used in current literature, reports, and discussions. The aim has been to foster understanding and collaboration among families of young children with developmental delays and disabilities, and those professionals providing services for them. This collaboration could then enhance the development of effective and comprehensive programs for children with special needs.

Entries, ranging in length from one line to one paragraph, are prefaced by a pronunciation guide, and define terms as they apply to early intervention or child care and development. Cross-references add to the volume's usefulness. Appendixes have charts and tables providing health and nutritional information.

Early intervention is the best recourse in helping children with specific problems, and the dictionary part of the publisher's "Special-Needs Collection" supplies a common foundation for these efforts. Future editions could include other terms used in describing age-appropriate behavior, such as "separation anxiety" and "permanence," and would be welcome references. [R: Choice, Jan 2000, p. 908]—**Anita Zutis**

Specific Diseases and Conditions

AIDS

C, P

446.   Huber, Jeffery T., and Mary L. Gillaspy. **Encyclopedic Dictionary of AIDS-related Terminology.** Binghamton, N.Y., Haworth Press, 2000. 246p. $59.95; $24.95pa. ISBN 0-7890-0714-2; 0-7890-1207-3pa.

Clear and concise definitions aimed at the general reader are the highlight of this reference tool. Arranged alphabetically, the volume presents a variety of terms related to AIDS and to disciplines or areas that have some relevance to the topic. Here the user can find legal, social, psychological, and religious terms, as well as those that pertain to medicine, care giving, insurance, pharmacology, and other areas. Whether reading an article or book, using the Internet, or writing a research paper, users can avail themselves of this dictionary as a handy thesaurus for synonyms, usage for standard abbreviations, and understanding the interrelationships of various concepts. Discipline-specific and popular terms are interfiled and cross-referenced for ease of use and understanding. Slang and colloquial idioms are also included.

A separate appendix provides directory and contact information to more than 70 governmental agencies and entities in the United States. In addition to name, address, and telephone number, listings include URLs, fax numbers, and contact information for specialized services. Although the price may keep this title from being in every academic or public library, it should receive strong consideration for purchase for those collections where interest and research in AIDS is significant.—**Edmund F. SantaVicca**

Cancer

C, P

447.   Altman, Roberta, and Michael J. Sarg. **The Cancer Dictionary.** rev. ed. New York, Facts on File, 2000. 387p. illus. index. $40.00. ISBN 0-8160-3953-4.

Co-authored by a former cancer patient and an oncologist, this dictionary provides concise and understandable information for the layperson on more than 2,500 types of cancers. Entries note causes, incidence, symptoms, diagnosis, states, and treatment. Diagnostic tests, surgical procedures, anticancer drugs, radiation and biological therapies, side effects, risk factors, carcinogens, prevention, and support services and organizations are also covered. Extensive cross-referencing is used to lead the reader to the word that is most common and most well known.

Although arranged alphabetically, an index is also included to aid the reader. An additional subject index groups dictionary entries under broad general headings. National associations, support organizations, and cancer research and treatment centers are listed in the appendixes.

While many people use the Internet to search for the very latest information and treatment options, this dictionary can still provide assistance in sorting through the many intimidating terms and procedures associated with cancer. Public libraries will find it a useful addition to their consumer health sections. [R: LJ, Jan 2000, p. 78; BR, Sept/Oct 2000, p. 66]—**Vicki J. Killion**

PHARMACY AND PHARMACEUTICAL SCIENCES

Dictionaries and Encyclopedias

P

448.   Graedon, Joe, and Teresa Graedon. **The People's Pharmacy Guide to Home and Herbal Remedies.** New York, St. Martin's Press, 1999. 428p. index. $27.95. ISBN 0-312-20779-4.

The goal of *The People's Pharmacy Guide to Home and Herbal Remedies* is to educate consumers on the available herbal supplements, how they affect the human body, and who should and should not be taking them. The authors stress that because the Federal Drug Administration does not monitor herbal supplements, they are often not used correctly or can be taken in doses that are dangerous to consumers. The book begins with the authors' favorite home remedies, many of which will be new to readers. It then discusses dangerous herb-drug reactions that commonly occur. After a short introduction and explanation of how to use the book, the authors discuss healing herbs and home remedies. These are listed in alphabetic order and include everything from relief from allergies to soothing bug bites to treating varicose veins. Throughout this section are well-written anecdotes from the authors and sidebars of questions and answers. After this section there is a 16-page section of references listed.

The second half of the book focuses specifically on herbal supplements and remedies. Each herbal therapy has a description of the active ingredients, its uses, the adequate dose, special precautions, adverse effects, and possible interactions. This section contains information that will be new to many readers and that may prevent future medical complications. The book concludes with a list of Websites containing additional herbal supplement information and a subject index, with topics that are treated in depth printed in bold typeface.

This book is intended for the general public and will therefore be most beneficial for public libraries. Medical libraries with patrons outside of the medical profession may also want to purchase it; however, those catering to medical professionals will benefit more from a resource such as *Natural Medicines Comprehensive Database* (see ARBA 2000, entry 1450), which is a more scholarly choice. [R: LJ, Dec 99, pp. 104-106]

—**Shannon Graff Hysell**

Directories

P

449.   Snow, Bonnie. **Drug Information: A Guide to Current Resources.** 2d ed. Chicago, Medical Library Association and Lanham, Md., Scarecrow, 1999. 752p. index. $70.00; $46.00pa. ISBN 0-8108-3320-4; 0-8108-3321-2pa.

This 2d edition is arranged so it can be used either as a textbook for a class or as a reference tool for librarians. The book is described as being a "problem solver" and not just a list of useful tools or Internet sites. The 16 chapters cover where to find information on everything from nomenclature, laws and regulations, searching protocols, evaluating sources, specific areas of drug information such as side effects or patient information, business and statistical data for drugs, market research areas, and regulatory sources. Print, CD-ROM, and online sources are covered. Appendix A covers the core drug collection for a hospital library and also lists a separate collection for public libraries. Appendix B covers online sources listed by subject category. The other appendixes cover full-text online newsletters, professional and trade associations, practicum exercises, and abbreviations. The book also includes a glossary and an extensive index. Due to the wealth of information, this is a tool any librarian should have. It is a must for hospital libraries and pharmaceutical libraries.—**Betsy J. Kraus**

34 High Technology

COMPUTING

C, P

450.   **Encyclopedia of Computer Science.** 4th ed. Anthony Ralston, Edwin D. Reilly, and David Hemmendinger, eds. New York, Grove's Dictionaries, 2000. 2034p. illus. index. $150.00. ISBN 1-56159-248-X.

The 4th edition of this 1-volume encyclopedia that began in 1976 is intended as a general reference work for the highly technical field of computer science. It features 623 articles written by more than 450 contributors. There are more than 100 new articles in this edition, and the editors estimate that roughly 40 percent of the text is essentially new—factoring in the articles that have been rewritten or updated.

Each entry begins with a short definition of the topic and proceeds to a more in-depth examination. Entries direct the reader to related articles with *see also* references and feature bibliographies and lists of relevant Websites. A classification scheme for the article subjects is listed in the front of the book to provide readers with an overview of the scope of the entries. The text is enlivened frequently with figures, tables, diagrams, illustrations, and photographs. There is even a 16-page color insert. The appendixes include a list of abbreviations and acronyms, a list of computer journals, a five-language glossary, and a timeline of significant milestones. Both name and subject indexes are included as well.

The range of articles seems as thorough as it could be in a single-volume encyclopedia. Some topics may be questionable, such as spelling checkers, but largely they are exactly what users would want to find in this sort of work. The contents are current with such entries as "e-commerce" and the "Electronic Frontier Foundation."

The editors have adopted a policy of no new biographies of living people, but current figures such as Bill Gates and Jerry Yang are given subentries under the entry for entrepreneurs. While the text can be very complex in covering complicated matters, it is generally very readable. This encyclopedia covers a popular and essential field well and is highly recommended for all academic and large public libraries. [R: BL, 1 Dec 2000, p. 748; LJ, Jan 01, p. 86]—**John Maxymuk**

C, P

451.   Lopez, Victor D. **Free and Low Cost Software for the PC.** Jefferson, N.C., McFarland, 2000. 206p. illus. index. $32.00pa. ISBN 0-7864-0847-2.

Following a brief but informative introduction, this book describes and evaluates about 75 of the author's favorite freeware, shareware, and demo programs. The evaluations are organized into "Utility Programs," "Personal Productivity," "Educational Programs," "Internet Tools," and "Games." Each evaluation consists of a two- to three-page description telling where to get the program, registration and cost details, and how it works, and possible problems of installing or using it. Screen shots give the reader the "look and feel" of each program, and each is rated in terms of utility, ease of use, ease of learning, documentation, and an overall evaluation. The evaluations and descriptions are well written and helpful. The selections are reasonably up-to-date, although evaluations like this become rapidly dated. The programs were evaluated on Wintel machines running Windows 95 or Windows 98. Nothing is said about how well, or whether, the programs will run on Windows ME or Windows 2000.

There are thousands of junky shareware/freeware programs that are not worth the time to download, and the author is to be commended for compiling evaluative reviews of some of the better ones. His intent is to provide a broad cross section of software that will appeal to a wide audience. He wisely chooses not to include programs of limited use, those with restrictive use conditions, cumbersome registration reminders, or unreasonably brief evaluation periods. He also skipped those that are nothing more than "free" commercials for expensive software. There is a bit of irony in the fact that this slim paperback book describing 75 free and low-cost programs itself costs $32.—**A. Neil Yerkey**

INTERNET

C, P

452.   Hock, Randolph. **The Extreme Searcher's Guide to Web Search Engines: A Handbook for the Serious Searcher.** Medford, N.J., Information Today, 1999. 212p. index. $24.95pa. ISBN 0-910965-26-9.

There is probably no Internet tool used with more frequency and with less effectiveness than a Web search engine. Hock's objectives are to provide readers with an operational understanding and a comparative evaluation of the major commercial search services so that they can utilize the full retrieval potential of these powerful tools. Do not be misled by the term "extreme searcher" in the title. With its straightforward explanations, high quality screen shots, and many useful searching tips, this guide by an expert in the field is appropriate for anyone wishing to search the Web more efficiently.

Hock covers eight leading search engines in depth: Alta Vista, Excite, HotBot, Infoseek, Lycos, Northern Light, Yahoo!, and WebCrawler. He explains the mechanics of their indexing programs and retrieval algorithms; presents the range of search options available in their basic and advanced search modes; and highlights their strengths, weaknesses, and unique features.

It comes as no surprise that since this book's publication all the search engines described have undergone at least cosmetic if not substantive changes, and important new search engines have appeared. Hock has met the challenge of keeping the book current by developing an excellent companion Website that references specific chapters and pages of the book.

Affordable as it is illuminating, *The Extreme Searcher's Guide to Web Search Engines* is recommended for circulating and reference collections. For large libraries it would not be too extravagant to have a copy in each collection.—**Cindy Lee Stokes**

C, P

453.   Horton, Sarah. **Web Teaching Guide: A Practical Approach to Creating Course Web Sites.** New Haven, Conn., Yale University Press, 2000. 242p. illus. index. $35.00; $15.95pa. ISBN 0-300-08726-8; 0-300-08727-6pa.

The World Wide Web hit higher education so quickly that many college professors were introduced to it only recently by keen and enthusiastic students. Except for those in a few institutions with unusual foresight, most faculty members found themselves trying to adapt to the quickly changing Internet culture by simply mimicking what seemed useful and hitting or missing with other ideas. There were no comprehensive resources for learning how to incorporate the Web into teaching. This book at last fills that crucial niche by providing detailed and timely instruction on designing academic Websites. Because the Web is becoming as important as textbooks to higher education, this book should be in every college and university library where teaching is taken seriously.

This book covers the entire process of developing Websites for college courses, from why a Website can be a critical part of the course curriculum to actually getting the students to use it. The approach of the author is highly academic, starting with the initial planning, which emphasizes adapting current resources when possible. Content development is covered next, in detail and with practical discussions of where Web materials are most easily obtained and how copyright laws work in cyberspace. Actually creating the site is the subject of the longest chapter because it includes even the smallest details about site design, and the use of images, animation, and video. Another chapter follows on the effective use of Websites in courses. A quick look at current course Web pages cluttering the Internet demonstrates the author's primary point that just placing a syllabus online does not even come close to exploiting the value of this medium. Students must have a reason to return to a Website frequently, which means giving them unique information and opportunities for interaction. The last chapter provides tools for the inevitable (and tedious) "assessment" many of us will have to complete on their new Websites to formally demonstrate their value. This book is highly recommended for all teaching faculty.—**Mark A. Wilson**

C, P

454.   Trinkle, Dennis A., and Scott A. Merriman. **History Highway 2000: A Guide to Internet Resources.** 2d ed. Armonk, N.Y., M. E. Sharpe, 2000. 600p. index. $79.95; $29.95pa. ISBN 0-7656-0477-9; 0-7656-0478-7pa.

The premise of this book is twofold: to provide a short yet succinct history of the Internet and an annotated bibliography of Internet sites for academic and amateur historians of all time periods. Chapter 1 details the history of the Internet, uses of the Internet, hardware and software to get on the Internet, and netiquette and copyright. E-mail, Usenet groups, listservs, telnet, and FTP are all described. Chapter 2 is the heart of the book, dividing history into time periods from ancient to modern, national histories, world and European history, and U.S. history. A number of special topics follow, such as women's history, Jewish Holocaust studies, military history, and psychohistory, to name a few. Discussion groups, newsgroups, electronic journals, libraries, and other resources for historians conclude the bibliography.

In order to maintain currency the editors have established a Website at http://www.theaahc.org/historyhighway/hh2000.htm to record address changes and list new sites of interest. The annotated bibliography is organized for easy use, and is compiled by numerous historians who are recognized experts and authorities in their fields. The short primer on the Internet is of relatively little use, as most of this information is readily available over the Internet or already known by experienced Internet users. Overall, this book is an important resource for academic historians and amateur history buffs.—**Bradford Lee Eden**

TELECOMMUNICATIONS

Bibliography

C, P

455.   Sterling, Christopher H., and George Shiers. **History of Telecommunications Technology: An Annotated Bibliography.** Lanham, Md., Scarecrow, 2000. 333p. index. $65.00. ISBN 0-8108-3781-1.

In this work, Sterling has updated George Shiers's *Bibliography of the History of Electronics* (Scarecrow, 1972). This bibliography is a standard classed bibliography, written by an individual who understands the essential elements of classical bibliography. The work has some 2,500 annotated entries on telecommunications, primarily in the United Kingdom and the United States. The annotated classed areas are: general reference works, serial publications, general surveys, institutional and company histories, biographies of inventors and scientists, telegraph, telephone, electromagnetic waves, radio, electroacoustics and recording, electron tubes, solid-state devices, television, newer media, transmission, and telecommunications history on the Internet.

Most, but not all, of the categories in the 1972 work have been retained. New or expanded topics covered are museums and archives; chronologies; historical statistics; atlases; foreign and international telecom systems; military telecommunications; naval and maritime commerce; and collecting vintage telegraphy, telephone, radio, and television equipment. The annotations are accurate and relevant and follow a numbering scheme of chapter number and alphabetical order. Some numbers are listed with the annotation "not used." The reader is left to guess as to the fate of these missing annotations. There is an author name index and a title index to works cited.

This bibliography deserves to be in most libraries. It provides a handy reference for general and specialized patrons wanting more information on the history of the telecommunications industry. For example, if readers want to know what the standard history of Western Electric is, this volume will tell them.—**Ralph Lee Scott**

Dictionaries and Encyclopedias

C, P

456.   **McGraw-Hill Illustrated Telecom Dictionary.** 2d ed. By Jade Clayton. New York, McGraw-Hill, 2000. 750p. illus. index. $29.95pa. (w/CD-ROM). ISBN 0-07-136037-9.

The *McGraw-Hill Illustrated Telecom Dictionary* aspires to be a comprehensive dictionary of the technical terminology of the telecommunications sector, broadly defined to include a wide range of datacom terms as well as traditional telecom activities. It comes close to meeting this target, close enough to make it a must-buy volume for libraries that seek to offer comprehensive reference collections.

The scope of coverage is wide, ranging from basic electrical terminology (e.g., volts, ohms, amperes) through traditional telecommunications technical terms (e.g., 110 block, PBX, party line) and common and advanced data communications terminology (e.g., Ethernet, MAC address, SYN). It also covers Internet terminology such as TCP/IP, the Web, other standard services, and routing protocols.

For the most part the definitions themselves are good, written both clearly and with informative content. The more extensive entries, such as the one for "TCP/IP," are complete enough to serve as a useful reference for the absent-minded professional who needs a momentary refresher on a detail, while remaining clear enough to help educate the novice.

Organization of the book is good, a must in an alphabetic work. The author and editor never take the easy way out, almost always making the organizational decision that makes it easy for the readers. A separate section for terms that begin with numbers makes them easy to find. When a term is commonly used both as an acronym and spelled out (for example, "DHCP" and "Dynamic Host Configuration Protocol"), the definition is repeated in both places, instead of using a cross-reference that makes the reader do extra work. Small touches like these are a mark of real professionalism in the editing stage of a comprehensive reference.

The book has a companion CD-ROM that also does well. Instead of imposing yet another custom interface and installation program on users, McGraw-Hill provides an electronic copy of the book that is accessed through Acrobat Reader. Choosing a standard application, one in common use, makes it easy for the reader to simply pop the CD-ROM in any handy Windows or Mac computer, a convenience especially valuable in library settings. The CD-ROM includes excerpts from other McGraw-Hill books, conveniently cross-referenced to the dictionary to provide greater depth in selected areas.

But the book is not without its flaws. Wireless technologies generally seem to get skimpy coverage and, on rare occasions, the definitions themselves become incomprehensible. There is also an editing slip every so often. For example, the last line of the entry for "Ethernet" is "The following is a list of Ethernet protocols and the type of wiring used for each"—but no list follows. On balance, however, the flaws are minor and the strengths are impressive. This is the too-rare combination of an excellent reference book supplemented by an equally excellent CD-ROM.

—**Ray Olszewski**

C, P

457.   Muller, Nathan J. **Desktop Encyclopedia of Telecommunications.** 2d ed. New York, McGraw-Hill, 2000. 1113p. illus. index. $49.95pa. ISBN 0-07-135893-5.

This desktop encyclopedia is a source of information about telecommunications on several levels. Its primary function is "to provide non-technical professionals with the essential knowledge required to succeed in the dynamic, fast growing telecommunications industry" (p. xxxvii). Coverage of the many elements of the telecommunications world is thorough, up-to-date, and well written. The several hundred entries arranged in alphabetic order range from advanced intelligent networks to the World Wide Web. Each entry defines the topic; places it in its technical, social, or other appropriate context; provides a summary of its current status; and indicates potential areas of development. Most articles are from one to three pages in length and many include useful diagrams. Additional related entries within the encyclopedia are cited.

An element unusual in scientific and technical tools is that threads of the history of telecommunications (e.g., the development of the telephone, history of satellite transmission) can be followed. Social, legal, and management threads emerge as well, and the reader can see how a particular technology has had its effect on these areas. The reader can also see how one technology builds upon another and how technology is changing the world.

In addition to the extensive table of contents an index is provided, as is a list of acronyms. It is a rare technical encyclopedia that provides quality technical information while at the same time placing it in the context of the larger issues of our information society. [R: Choice, Dec 2000, p. 686]—**Ann E. Prentice**

P, S

458.   Muller, Nathan J. **Desktop Encyclopedia of Voice and Data Networking.** New York, McGraw-Hill, 2000. 757p. illus. index. $49.95. ISBN 0-07-134711-9.

Muller's encyclopedia covers both the circuit-switched and packet-switched environments, including information at the voice data, wireline-wireless, and business communications levels. In fact, like most encyclopedias aimed at a specific area, this one also includes information on basic computer topics such as firewalls, computer fraud, multimedia documents, printer management, and performance baselining. This is the third in a series of desktop encyclopedias—*Desktop Encyclopedia of the Internet* and *Desktop Encyclopedia of Telecommunications* (see ARBA 99, entry 1493).

    With this encyclopedia it is important to use the index; almost every topic is covered somewhere in the text. For example, the definition of "caching" is found embedded in the "proxy servers" entry and information on hubs can be found in a number of articles including one specifically on hubs. The articles are easy to understand. This will be a good tool for any library serving a general population, including public and high school libraries. There is no reference list. Engineering, computer science, and telecommunications collections would find this competent but simplistic.—**Susan B. Ardis**

35 Physical Sciences and Mathematics

PHYSICAL SCIENCES

General Works

C, P
459. Stern, David. **Guide to Information Sources in the Physical Sciences.** Englewood, Colo., Libraries Unlimited, 2000. 227p. index. (Reference Sources in Science and Technology Series). $65.00. ISBN 1-56308-751-0.

This book is a good overview of the major trends and information resources in physics. Although not as comprehensive as Shaw's *Information Sources in Physics* (see ARBA 95, entry 1737), Stern's guide serves as an excellent resource for librarians and scientists relatively new to the field. There are chapters devoted to the usual types of resources, such as abstracting and indexing databases, bibliographic sources, books, journals, and other nonbibliographic databases and paper resources. Stern also includes chapters on bibliographic management tools, document delivery, and copyright. Each chapter includes brief annotated entries and short descriptions of the general characteristics of the resource. There is a strong emphasis on electronic resources available on the Internet and Stern has carefully chosen sites that every science librarian should know. Stern concludes his book with two chapters on the future and the past. His chapter on future developments and trends touches on such topics as smart agents, full-text data files, and knowledge databases, and includes a few examples of these technologies. The final chapter is an annotated list of important works in the development of physics from 1600 to 1900.

Stern's guide is an excellent resource for librarians and scientists unfamiliar with the major information sources of physics. Although it highlights just the major resources, it serves well as an update to the more comprehensive work by Shaw, particularly in the area of electronic resources. As expected, there is not an in-depth discussion about any one topic, but there are a few references to guide the reader to more information. Overall, this is a highly recommended source for academic and special libraries. [R: BL, 1 Dec 2000, pp. 750-752; Choice, Dec 2000, p. 686]—**Teresa U. Berry**

Chemistry

Dictionaries and Encyclopedias

C, P, S
460. **World of Chemistry.** Robyn V. Young and Suzanne Sessine, eds. Farmington Hills, Mich., Gale, 2000. 1360p. illus. index. $99.00. ISBN 0-7876-3650-9.

This is a substantial one-volume reference book for the general reader on the various aspects of chemistry including basic concepts, techniques, and important types of compounds, as well as entries on their discoverers. The arrangement is alphabetical and there are plenty of cross-references, *see* also references at the ends of the articles, and a lengthy index. There are also a 29-page historical chronology and a list of consulted resources at the end of the book.

The present edition, though, could use a number of improvements. The cross-references are erratic—from too detailed (the entry on "ethyne" says that it is virtually insoluble in water, with "water" cross-referenced) to inexcusably missing (the entry on aerosols mentions and misspells chlorofluorocarbons as a source of ozone layer depletion without cross-referencing the "chlorofluorocarbon" entry). The index is extensive and generally good, but with odd lapses (under "second law of thermodynamics" it does not cite the entry on entropy). The entries lack references for further information, and it is difficult to find references on a specific topic in the list of consulted resources. Chemists regard their science as best understood in the three-dimensional structures of molecules, so it is odd to find so few chemical formulas even in two dimensions; apart from the entry on "stereochemistry" hardly any molecules are pictured in three dimensions. There are minor, but annoying, errors (the entry on Onsager claims that Feynman's superfluid helium work was done at Princeton). More disturbingly, in striving for nontechnical language and avoidance of equations, some of the entries are confusing or even misleading.

Public and high school libraries may find this a useful source, especially for biographical entries, although a revised edition could much improve it. Colleges and universities are generally better off with the more scholarly *Macmillan Encyclopedia of Chemistry* (see ARBA 98, entry 1601). [R: BL, July 2000, p. 2063; Choice, Oct 2000, p. 307; RUSQ, Fall 2000, p. 89]—**Robert Michaelson**

Handbooks and Yearbooks

P, S
461.   **The Facts on File Chemistry Handbook.** By the Diagram Group. New York, Facts on File, 2000. 223p. illus. index. $29.95. ISBN 0-8160-4080-X.

The Facts on File Chemistry Handbook is a handy ready-reference of basic facts and terms. It contains four sections: a glossary of terms, which includes more than 1,400 entries; biographies of more than 300 scientists who contributed in the area of chemistry; a chronology of approximately 9,000 years of events in the history of chemistry; and essential charts and tables. There is also a comprehensive index.

The glossary includes labeled diagrams to help clarify the meanings of many of the entries. Many of the biographies are accompanied by line drawings of the people featured. There are also drawings and diagrams with many of the entries in the chronology to illustrate inventions and discoveries.

If one needs formulas, tables, and values, *Lange's Handbook of Chemistry* (15th ed.; see ARBA 2000, entry 1490) may serve better, with well over 1,000 pages of material compared to 7 pages of essential charts and tables here. For definitions, Facts on File's *Dictionary of Chemistry* (3d ed.; see ARBA 2000, entry 1479) contains more than 3,000 terms compared to the 1,400 here and would be a good companion to *The Facts on File Chemistry Handbook*. Still, when considering cost and intended use (high school), this is a practical guide that will serve the needs of most beginning chemistry students. [R: SLJ, Nov 2000, p. 90]—**Dana McDougald**

Earth and Planetary Sciences

General Works

P, S
462.   Goldstein, Natalie. **Earth Almanac: An Annual Geophysical Review of the State of the Planet.** Phoenix, Ariz., Oryx Press, 2000. 387p. illus. maps. index. $65.00pa. ISBN 1-57356-230-0.

This 1st edition of this annual almanac reviews the major geophysical events that occurred in 1998 and provides an overview of the state of the planet. Goldstein, a freelance environmental science writer, has compiled a useful compendium of facts and data derived from reliable scientific, academic, and government sources. The almanac is divided into four major sections: atmosphere, oceans, land, and fresh water. Each section reviews the basic geophysical processes and cycles, the significant events of 1998, and current research and issues. Topics include global warming, fisheries, El Niño, volcanoes, deforestation, and urbanization. Goldstein includes more than 300 tables, graphs, and charts with mostly pre-1998 information. Some data lack any kind of date, making it difficult for the user to put them in perspective, but she always gives a Website address for the organization generating the data. The appendixes provide brief information about selected treaties and laws; however, the selected international and national scientific programs are rather slim. It is puzzling to see the omission of some obvious agencies, such as the U.S. Geological Survey. A glossary, earth facts, conversion formulas, a geologic timeline, and a good index are also included. There are some typographical errors, but overall this almanac is a nice resource for finding quick, factual information. [R: LJ, July 2000, p. 78; BR, Sept/Oct 2000, p. 78]—**Teresa U. Berry**

Astronomy and Space Sciences

C, P

463.   Angelo, Joseph A., Jr. **Encyclopedia of Space Exploration.** New York, Facts on File, 2000. 305p. illus. index. $50.00. ISBN 0-8160-3942-9.

This excellent encyclopedia actually offers more than its title promises. It not only covers space exploration, it is a good first reference to space itself and the science behind space technology, observations, and ideas. "Hubble's Law," for example, precedes the "Hubble Space Telescope," and there are clear definitions and descriptions of concepts like the Big Bang Theory, relativity, extrasolar planets, and even global change on Earth. Nevertheless, space exploration and the language describing it is the primary focus of this volume. All the major space missions of the past are included, and a good number of future projects as well. Rockets, satellites, space stations, and space suits are typical items among the more than 350 entries. There are numerous black-and-white photographs and line drawings, along with a central section of color plates. The text is highly readable.

Another bonus of this book is the inclusion of several entries concerning extraterrestrial life. The Drake Equation, which attempts to estimate the number of intelligent civilizations in the galaxy, is especially well explained, as are even more esoteric ideas, such as Dyson Spheres and "detailed cosmic reversibility." Some of these items add a touch of whimsy and wonder to what could otherwise be a dreary account of space probes and rocket motors. Like the best encyclopedias, this book encourages readers to randomly explore its pages.

Students from high school on up will find this book useful, as will teachers, journalists, librarians, and others who have a need for a quick, easy, and comprehensive description of terms used in astronomy and space exploration. The *Encyclopedia of Space Exploration* is highly recommended.—**Mark A. Wilson**

C, P

464.   **The Facts on File Dictionary of Astronomy.** 4th ed. Valerie Illingworth and John O. E. Clark, eds. New York, Checkmark Books/Facts on File, 2000. 490p. $50.00; $19.95pa. ISBN 0-8160-4283-7; 0-8160-4284-5pa.

First published in 1979, this standard work now appears in a 4th edition, its first updating in six years. The format is little changed and much of the content is the same. However, the book includes newer discoveries in the realm of astronomy, revised data, information on international activity, and the latest solar system data—in particular, newly found planetary satellites. Definitions range from a single sentence to several paragraphs and in a few cases a page or more. Cross-references are one of this dictionary's strong points—they appear both as separate entries and as capitalized words within the definitions themselves.

Most useful for upper-level high school students and beginning undergraduates, the book will also be helpful for nonspecialists needing a quick definition. Entries are broad ranging and include names of stars and other interplanetary objects, famous telescopes and observatories, units of measure, space missions and spacecraft, planetary features, terms from physics, instrumentation, and more. It also includes black-and-white line drawings and several appendixes of tables of numerical data, lists of constellations, and famous astronomers. Appropriate for quick reference, this volume is recommended for high school, junior college, and college libraries.
—**Robert A. Seal**

P, S

465.   Lee, Wayne. **To Rise from Earth: An Easy-to-Understand Guide to Spaceflight.** 2d ed. New York, Checkmark Books/Facts on File, 2000. 317p. illus. maps. index. $65.00. ISBN 0-8160-4091-5.

Written in terms that laypersons can understand, *To Rise from Earth* discusses the history of spaceflight, examines the various equipment used in the field (e.g., satellites, rockets, shuttles), explores the planets of the solar system, and looks at the future of space travel. The first several chapters discuss the use of satellites and rockets in space. Without talking in technical jargon or using complicated mathematical equations, this work explains how these different vehicles maneuver in space and how they project images back to the Earth. The following chapters discuss such topics as the landing of the first humans on the surface of the moon, how the space shuttle works, and the 1986 tragedy of the space shuttle Challenger. Throughout these chapters photographs of the pioneering astronauts are shown with descriptions of their careers. The final two chapters discuss space travel to other planets throughout the solar system. The planets, the sun, and comets are discussed in detail, and each is accompanied by beautiful photographs and illustrations. The book concludes with an index.

Although this work contains much reference material, it may be better suited for circulating collections due to its well-written text and excellent photography. If chosen for the reference collection, *To Rise from Earth* would be well suited for high school, undergraduate, and larger public libraries. [R: BR, Nov/Dec 2000, p. 77]

—**Shannon Graff Hysell**

C, P

466.   Zimmerman, Robert. **The Chronological Encyclopedia of Discoveries in Space.** Phoenix, Ariz., Oryx Press, 2000. 410p. illus. index. $55.00. ISBN 1-57356-196-7.

Beginning with the launch of Sputnik on October 4, 1957, and ending with the launch of Galaxy 11 on December 22, 1999, this intriguing reference tool chronicles the major and minor events and discoveries that have resulted from the exploration of space. Over 1,000 entries, arranged chronologically, discuss every manned mission, scientific probe, communications satellite project, military mission, and private commercial project instigated by any nation during this time period. Every entry includes a date and launch time, the name of the spacecraft, and the name of the nations involved. This information is followed by a brief (200–300 words) summary and findings of the event. If several spacecraft were launched together, they are all indicated; if a spacecraft has more than one name, that is also indicated; and if satellites were separately deployed from a spacecraft, they are listed as well. Although there are some exclusions, they are few.

More than 250 photographs, illustrations and drawings enhance the summaries and discussions. A section of color plates covers the time period 1966–1997. Cross-references are included for easy charting of related projects and launches. Separate appendixes provide an alphabetical list of satellites cross-referenced to date, a listing of missions (both chronological and alphabetical) by research subject, and a listing of nations that have participated in space exploration with indication of relevant satellites and launches. The encyclopedia is supplemented by a glossary, a bibliography and a comprehensive index to provide quick access to needed information. Comprehensive and seemingly exhaustive, this work will prove an asset to any science reference collection. [R: Choice, Sept 2000, p. 100; BL, 1 Sept 2000, pp. 173-175; BR, Nov/Dec 2000, p. 78; RUSQ, Fall 2000, pp. 81-82; C&RL News, June 2000, p. 528]—**Edmund F. SantaVicca**

Climatology and Meteorology

P

467.   Engelbert, Phillis. **The Complete Weather Resource, Volume 4: Recent Developments in World Weather.** Farmington Hills, Mich., Gale, 2000. 179p. illus. index. $42.00. ISBN 0-7876-4834-5. ISSN 1528-2791.

This is the last of a series of four books on weather and climate; the first three cover basic atmospheric processes, weather phenomena, and forecasting and climate history. Entitled *The Complete Weather Resource*, it describes specific results and numerical data, including the latest on El Niño, La Niña, and other weather extremes of the last few years. After an extensive and current glossary, it brings the reader up-to-date on these subjects and on human influences on climate and climate change, including global warming. This is an excellent second text for a course on meteorology, with the first book being any of a number of excellent general texts on introductory meteorology, perhaps including earlier volumes of this series. Topics include the Kyoto Convention of 1997, which the U.S. Congress refuses to ratify or even raise for discussion, and earlier international meetings at Rio de Janeiro and Montreal, as well as the ways in which global warming has been substantiated. This volume is recommended as a text; a general reference; and an account for the general reader of the current status of global warming, acid rain, and ozone depletion. [R: BR, Jan/Feb 01, p. 80]—**Arthur R. Upgren**

Oceanography

C, P

468.   Svarney, Thomas E., and Patricia Barnes-Svarney. **The Handy Ocean Answer Book.** Farmington Hills, Mich., Visible Ink Press/Gale, 2000. 570p. illus. maps. index. $19.95pa. ISBN 1-57859-063-9.

     The world's oceans are clearly going to be the environmental focus of the twenty-first century. Global warming will flood crowded coastlines as sea ice and glaciers melt and oceanic currents shift, dramatically changing terrestrial climates. The general public knows little about the oceans, except for fading memories of Jacques Cousteau and the sunken *Titanic*, yet they control our ecological destiny. Every library should be well stocked with the latest books on the oceans, and this book could be one of them.

     The "answer book" format is awkward, but since there are so many of them, it must have its appeal. By writing a long series of questions and answers, authors do not have to make the many intellectual connections necessary in standard prose. It reads a bit like an old church catechism, but has less direction. The questions are usually straightforward and mundane ("What is a V-shaped valley?"), and often forced ("How do Florida's specialty license plates help protect dolphins?"). Nevertheless, by reading through a chapter one, will learn much one would not have thought to ask. This book is not a substitute for a good oceanography text, especially because it almost entirely lacks interpretive diagrams, but with its thorough index it can serve as a quick reference guide.

     The material in this book is mostly accurate and timely, except for a strange statement that the dolphin and human genomes are "basically the same." It starts with a review of physical oceanography, including good sections on ancient oceans, plate tectonics, and the dynamics of water. The "Life of the Oceans" section is also thorough and fairly well illustrated, with numerous black-and-white and color photographs. The book ends with an extensive treatment of humans and the oceans, including good discussions of oceanography and lists of agencies that work with the sea. The book costs surprisingly little, and so is well worth the investment for libraries with science sections.—**Mark A. Wilson**

Paleontology

P, S

469.   Glut, Donald F. **Dinosaurs: The Encyclopedia, Supplement 1.** Jefferson, N.C., McFarland, 2000. 442p. illus. index. $60.00. ISBN 0-7864-0591-0.

     The original 1997 book by this author, *Dinosaurs: The Encyclopedia*, quickly became a reference legend among amateur and professional paleontologists because it is lavishly illustrated, cleverly written, and extraordinarily comprehensive. As would be expected in such a fertile field as dinosaur paleontology, there have been many significant discoveries and new ideas in the past three years. In order to keep the original encyclopedia the most useful single reference in vertebrate paleontology, this superb supplementary volume is necessary.

     This supplement could stand on its own as a reference for modern concepts and evidence of dinosaur paleobiology and evolution. It begins with an overview of the most significant finds since 1996, including new dinosaur physiology. Two especially good sections cover the highly debated endothermic hypothesis and the continuing battles over the relationship between dinosaurs and birds. The various competing positions are fairly well and thoroughly referenced. The bulk of the book is an update on dinosaur systematics and genera, with many useful black-and-white drawings and photographs. The scope of this work is phenomenal—no relevant dinosaur article appears to have escaped this author. In some ways there are too many citations, especially on controversial topics like the Cretaceous extinctions, because numerous abstracts from professional meetings are discussed. These abstracts are important indicators of ongoing scientific debates, but until the work they represent is published in peer-reviewed journals, they should be rare in a reference work. This may be inevitable in a book that seeks to be as updated as possible at publication. There is an extensive bibliography emphasizing works since 1996, a glossary, and a thorough index.

     This book is recommended for all libraries with the original *Dinosaurs: The Encyclopedia*. For those without the classic reference book, now is an excellent time to buy it and this supplement. [R: C&RLNews, Feb 2000, p. 136]—**Mark A. Wilson**

S

470.   Svarney, Thomas E., and Patricia Barnes-Svarney. **The Handy Dinosaur Answer Book.** Farmington Hills, Mich., Visible Ink Press/Gale, 2000. 493p. illus. index. $19.95pa. ISBN 1-57859-072-8.

This is one of a series of books written by two scientists, one a science writer, aimed at informing young adults about an important area of science. Simply and accurately written, it presents material in an easy-to-use and readable format.

The question-and-answer format works well as it breaks topics into discrete items, each represented by a question and its answer. While the focus is on dinosaurs, the context is the broader fields of geology and natural history. The authors begin with a description of the solar system and the formation of the Earth and other planets, then move to a discussion of geologic time and the formation of fossils. At that point they focus on the evolution of dinosaurs and their presence during the Triassic, Jurassic, and Cretaceous periods. They discuss the geologic events during these periods, and the rise and fall and extinction of dinosaurs. Additional chapters focus on what can be learned from dinosaur bones, dinosaur anatomy, and about dinosaur behavior such as what they ate, how fast they moved, and if they were intelligent.

A valuable set of lists is included: dinosaur finds in the U.S. and internationally, whom to contact if one wishes to go on a dig, locations of museums with dinosaur exhibits, publications with addresses and Websites, an annotated list of videos, an annotated list of films with dinosaurs as part of the story line, Internet sites, a bibliography, and so on. These lists would benefit from some reorganization to put like materials together such as combining the listing of state museums with those of national museums and outdoor sites. Putting all bibliographic lists together and all video lists together would also make use simpler. The title promises handy answers and it delivers them.

—**Ann E. Prentice**

Volcanology

C, P

471.   **Encyclopedia of Volcanoes.** Haraldur Sigurdsson and others, eds. San Diego, Calif., Academic Press, 2000. 1417p. illus. maps. index. $99.95. ISBN 0-12-643140-X.

Like dinosaurs, volcanoes are an aspect of earth science that attract strong interest. However, the curious non-volcanologist quickly finds out that "volcano literature" is dominated by its two end points—popularizations and technical journal articles. This book fills a niche to the technical side of the middle ground, but is a magnificent introduction to the subject that could be read by scientist and nonscientist alike.

It is not an encyclopedia in the sense of a long alphabetic list of terms with brief definitions, but rather a collection of 83 essays written and reviewed by a variety of experts in the field. The breadth of the book is exemplary. The bulk of the chapters treat the physics and chemistry of magma, and the geologic features involved in its expression on the Earth's surface. While 5 chapters treat volcanism elsewhere in the solar system, 28 chapters focus on the role of volcanoes in human life, from their threat to civilization to their ecological impact and their role in art, literature, and horticulture. Those wishing for further data will find each chapter ends with a bibliography leading to the technical literature. Nonspecialists will appreciate the glossary of important terms that introduce each chapter.

The book is extensively illustrated with both color and black-and-white photographs, a range of line drawings, and tables. The writing is generally clear and accessible to those with serious interest in the subject. While unusual in its presentation, this is an outstanding reference book belonging in public and research libraries alike. [R: LJ, 1 April 2000, pp. 90-93]—**Bruce H. Tiffney**

Physics

C, P, S

472.   **A Dictionary of Physics.** 4th ed. Alan Isaacs, ed. New York, Oxford University Press, 2000. 546p. illus. (Oxford Paperback Reference). $14.95pa. ISBN 0-19-280103-1.

Now in its 4th edition, this handy guide is an excellent place to seek a brief definition of a physical term or concept. Arranged alphabetically, not topically, it has extensive cross-references to lead the researcher to related terms. Although most of the more than 3,500 entries are concise, consisting of just a few sentences, there are selected "feature articles," which provide more detail and run several pages long. These are on such topics as relativity, group theory, and elementary particles. Another useful feature of this dictionary are the chronologies of key areas or discoveries, including cosmology, atomic theory, and microscopy. Most appropriate for academic libraries, this latest edition now includes brief biographical sketches of key physicists. The book also has black-and-white illustrations and several appendixes, with information on physical constants, units of measure, and conversion factors. [R: Choice, Dec 2000, p. 685]—**Robert A. Seal**

P, S

473.   **The Facts on File Physics Handbook.** By the Diagram Group. New York, Facts on File, 2000. 223p. illus. index. $29.95. ISBN 0-8160-4082-6.

The Facts on File handbooks in the sciences are useful for quick, simply worded information. This one is no exception. It contains a glossary (the largest section), biographies of famous physicists throughout history, a chronology of significant discoveries that have occurred over the past 9,000 years, and various charts and tables.

The glossary is the primary area of the handbook, giving simple definitions to 1,400 words. It is arranged by the term, with a header and footer that shows the alphabetic range of the words on the page. Many diagrams accompany the words to give a clearer explanation. As a result, the handbook can be useful for upper elementary, middle school, and up.

The biographies are very short, one sentence to a short paragraph in length, but give a level of importance to the scientist. The chronology, from 6000 B.C.E. to 1993 C.E., covers major events. The charts and tables are for various units, such as physical quantities, SI units, and electrical circuit symbols, among others. [R: SLJ, Nov 2000, p. 90]—**James W. Oliver**

MATHEMATICS

P, S

474.   Kornegay, Chris. **Math Dictionary with Solutions: A Math Review.** 2d ed. Thousand Oaks, Calif., Sage, 1999. 570p. index. $39.95; $19.95pa. ISBN 0-7619-1784-5; 0-7619-1785-3pa.

This math "dictionary" is different from other dictionaries. Rather than just providing definitions for terms or tables of values, this book also provides solutions to a variety of standard problems and discusses a variety of topics with sample solutions. This rather unusual combination makes for a valuable resource for math students. The book is arranged alphabetically, with four appendixes, natural logarithmic and common logarithmic tables, trigonometric functions and a table of conversions, and an index.

The articles are written to the level appropriate for the topic, from elementary fractions to high school-level geometry or calculus. Explanations are clearly written, with examples and illustrations. Every operation or calculation is shown. There are extensive cross-references, directing the reader to the correct expression or topic. Terms used in articles, which are defined elsewhere in the book, are shown in bold typeface for easy look-up and reinforcement of the discussion.

The coverage of the book is extensive, including arithmetic, geometry, algebra, calculus, and more. It will be useful for students from middle school and beyond. This would be an excellent review source for students preparing for standardized tests. This reference tool is appropriate and highly recommended for school, public, and academic libraries.—**Margaret F. Dominy**

C, P

475.   **Mathematical Sciences Professional Directory 2000.** Providence, R.I., American Mathematical Society, 2000. 227p. index. $50.00pa. ISBN 0-8212-2043-5. ISSN 0737-4356.

It can be argued that most, if not all, of the information in this directory could be found on the Web, but the value added by the American Mathematical Society (AMS) in this work is all of the bits and pieces collected together in one place. This directory is not a membership listing. It is a medley of data of interest to mathematicians and students alike. The directory contains seven sections on the AMS, other professional organizations, government agencies, reciprocity societies, addresses of individuals, academic institutions (sorted by state), and nonacademic organizations. There is also an index of colleges and universities sorted alphabetically by name.

In the sections concerning the AMS and other professional organizations, users will find lists of officers, staff, and various committees along with information on publications, services, and other activities. The mathematician or student seeking information on the structure and scope of activities of mathematics-related organizations would find these sections useful and convenient. The section on government agencies provides information specifically geared to funding in the mathematics fields. This is probably the most useful section. This information tends to be elusive even on the government's Websites. Reciprocity societies are professional mathematical societies outside the United States.

The list of academic institutions contains colleges (including community colleges) and universities that have math departments. Minimal contact information is provided, including the school's address, telephone number, and name of the math department head. This would be appropriate for high school students browsing for prospective college programs. The section on nonacademic organizations is a list of companies, corporations, and labs that have either mathematics groups or some related research and development interest. The contact information is minimal. Wherever possible, e-mail addresses and Websites are included. This directory is definitely worthwhile having in print and is recommended for academic and public libraries.—**Margaret F. Dominy**

36 Resource Sciences

ENVIRONMENTAL SCIENCE

Bibliography

P, S
476. Nordquist, Joan, comp. **Global Warming: A Bibliography.** Santa Cruz, Calif., Reference and Research Services, 1999. 64p. (Contemporary Social Issues: A Bibliographic Series, no.55). $20.00pa. ISBN 1-892068-08-7.

This useful bibliography on global warming (number 55 in the Contemporary Social Issues series) provides a selective list of books, journal articles, pamphlets, and government documents. Other environment related bibliographies in this series are *Toxic Waste* (1988), *Environmental Issues in the Third World* (see ARBA 92, entry 1771), and *Environmental Racism and the Environmental Justice Movement* (see ARBA 97, entry 513). Divided into 9 sections covering environmental, economic, and social concerns of global warming, this bibliography provides quick access to over 600 entries, arranged alphabetically by author and title. Valuable Internet sites of organizations and additional resources are also listed.

It would take students and researchers hours to find the information listed in this compact ready-reference source. Reasonably priced, this 64-page paperback represents a variety of current social and political views from small presses, alternative presses, feminist presses, government agencies, and so on. Vance Bibliographies has also published similar works on climatic change, global warming, and the greenhouse effect. These bibliographies are excellent ways to help high school and college students get started on research and prove that sources such as these are far more effective than getting lost in the vastness of the Internet. This work is recommended for high school, public, and academic libraries.—**Diane J. Turner**

Dictionaries and Encyclopedias

C, P
477. Mongillo, John, and Linda Zierdt-Warshaw. **Encyclopedia of Environmental Science.** Phoenix, Ariz., Oryx Press, 2000. 450p. illus. maps. index. $95.00. ISBN 1-57356-147-9.

This one-volume encyclopedia is similar yet more up-to-date than other environmental reference works, such as *The Encyclopedia of the Environment* (see ARBA 95, entry 1765) and the *Green Encyclopedia* (see ARBA 94, entry 1996). The authors spent several years researching a wide variety of print and electronic sources as well as public, private, and international organizations to provide the reader with a better understanding of the global environment. More than 1,000 entries provide an insightful glimpse into the ever-expanding list of issues related to the planet we inhabit. Topics covered include acid rain, ecofeminism, an ecological pyramid, Aldo Leopold, a time capsule of major famines of the world, endangered species listed by state, and many more interesting entries about the environment that will provide the user with an excellent background for further research.

Some of the features that enhance this useful, multidisciplinary A to Z reference source are an easy-to-read format, an environmental timeline, over 200 illustrations, a list of 400 related Websites, a general bibliography, and useful appendixes. Although not as comprehensive as the three-volume set of the *Encyclopedia of Environmental Issues* (see ARBA 2001, entry 1548), this source does provide unique entries and photographs that will complement the three-volume set. The reasonable price, the multidisciplinary approach, and the easy-to-understand format will make this an excellent addition to reference collections in high school, public, and academic libraries.

—**Diane J. Turner**

37 Transportation

AIR

P
478.   **Airlife's Commercial Aircraft and Airliners.** By Rod Simpson. Shrewsbury, England, Airlife Publishing; distr., Stillwater, Minn., Voyageur Press, 1999. 256p. illus. index. $29.95pa. ISBN 1-84037-073-4.

P
479.   **The Vital Guide to Commercial Aircraft and Airliners.** 2d ed. Robert Hewson, ed. Shrewsbury, England, Airlife Publishing; distr., Stillwater, Minn., Voyageur Press, 2000. 119p. illus. index. $14.95. ISBN 1-84037-064-5.

Although at first glance both of these books appear to describe jet and propeller-driven commercial aircraft produced since World War II, including military versions where relevant, they are different in scope. *The Vital Guide to Commercial Aircraft and Airliners* is now in its 2d edition, and covers "current" aircraft, which means currently being flown rather than currently being manufactured. The arrangement is alphabetic by manufacturer and model, making it convenient to zero in on a specific airplane assuming the manufacturer is known. Each page presents two attractive color photographs for each model, shown in service at different airlines. The text provides a quick history of the series and the specific models produced. A specifications box notes engine types, dimensions, weights, and performance guidelines (speed and range). The index basically duplicates the order of the contents and some cross-references for models, but is not as comprehensive as *Airlife's Commercial Aircraft and Airliners.*

Airlife's Commercial Aircraft and Airliners is also arranged by aircraft manufacturer but its presentation is more of a text-based survey of all the models produced by the company, not just those in service today. A table of each specific model follows the history, showing the various models and types, the number built, and specific details of each that made the model unique. The text is more in depth than in *The Vital Guide*, covering the historical development of each company's offerings since 1946. The index is more important here, since the text presentation does not make quick reference easy and there are more models to cover. The color photographs are not as numerous as in the other book, but the photographs are indexed too. A separate chart lists each airplane model and how many were built in each year from 1946 through 1996.

Both works will inform and be enjoyed by aircraft enthusiasts. *The Vital Guide* is better for quick reference and good color photographs. *Airlife's Aircraft* offers more detailed text and has greater coverage of aircraft models no longer flown or produced. Both are inexpensive and together form a pair that is recommended for any library where there is an interest. [R: Choice, Oct 2000, pp. 306-307]—**Gary R. Cocozzoli**

GROUND

C, P

480.   Heraud, Daniel. **Road Report 2000: The Motorist's Bible.** Willowdale, Ont., Firefly Books, 2000. 397p. index. $24.95pa. ISBN 1-55209-436-7.

The first of the series that the reviewer has seen, this generously and colorfully laid-out volume is impressive. At the beginning there is an index by "category," and at the end, another by make and model, along with U.S. and Canadian base prices. In between are sections on use of the book, abbreviations, glossary, new technology, and auto shows (four in the United States and two in Europe), with many beautiful photographs of real and concept cars, and the body of the work. Here are hundreds of models, arranged in the aforementioned categories, from "minicars" to luxury, sports, minivans, SUVs, and trucks. Each entry has a catchword or phrase at the top of the first page (e.g., "Solid" [Oldsmobile Alero], "Lack of Style" [Cadillac Catera], "Messiah" [Jaguar S-Type]), five good color photographs, and fairly detailed descriptions and pros and cons in a dozen or so categories. At the end of each section is a comparative test chart, which summarizes many of the technical aspects of the cars in that section. Based on checks of several cars familiar to the reviewer, the entries are generally good. There is a great deal of information here in an attractive format and for a reasonable price, even if bought annually. This work is recommended for all but the smallest public libraries and many academic libraries.—**Walter C. Allen**

Author/Title Index

Reference is to entry number.

Subject Index

Reference is to entry number.